William Kirby

Elementary text-book of entomology

William Kirby

Elementary text-book of entomology

ISBN/EAN: 9783337276096

Printed in Europe, USA, Canada, Australia, Japan

Cover: Foto ©Andreas Hilbeck / pixelio.de

More available books at **www.hansebooks.com**

ELEMENTARY TEXT-BOOK

OF

ENTOMOLOGY·

BY

W. F. KIRBY

ASSISTANT IN ZOOLOGICAL DEPARTMENT, BRITISH MUSEUM (NATURAL HISTORY),
SOUTH KENSINGTON
AND CO-SECRETARY TO THE ENTOMOLOGICAL SOCIETY OF LONDON

With 87 Plates containing over 650 Figures

LONDON
W. SWAN SONNENSCHEIN AND CO.
PATERNOSTER SQUARE
1885

TABLE OF CONTENTS.

ORDER COLEOPTERA.

ORDER DIPTERA.

INTRODUCTION.

In classifying the various objects around us, we divide them primarily into three great divisions, which are known as the Animal, Vegetable, and Mineral Kingdoms. These are again divided into smaller groups; and one of the principal sections of the Animal Kingdom is the sub-kingdom *Annulosa*, or *Articulata*, so called from the animals included in it having bodies composed of a number of joints or segments. Four classes are included in the sub-kingdom *Annulosa: Arachnida*, including Spiders, Scorpions, and Mites; *Crustacea*, including Crabs, Lobsters, Shrimps, Woodlice, etc.; *Myriopoda*, or Centipedes; and *Insecta*, or Insects. It is unnecessary to characterise the three first classes in detail, but a few words will suffice to point out the chief characters by which they differ from each other and from insects. The *Arachnida* are destitute of the long jointed organs called antennæ, so conspicuous in the other classes. They increase in size without undergoing any great changes of form. They are provided with eight legs, and their body is composed of two principal parts only—the cephalothorax and the abdomen. The *Crustacea* are provided with two pairs of antennæ, and a variable but moderate number of legs. Their bodies are covered with hard shelly armour, and are not divided into two or three well-defined sections, as in the Insects and *Arachnida*, and they frequently pass through a very complicated metamorphosis. The *Myriopoda* have long worm-like bodies, one pair of antennæ, and do not undergo a regular metamorphosis, but as they grow the number of segments of their bodies continues to increase, and each segment being provided with a pair of legs, the number of their legs also continues to increase until they have reached their full growth.

Insects differ from all the other groups in many important characters. They are provided with one pair of antennæ, six legs only in the perfect state, their body is divided into head, thorax, and abdomen, and they pass through four stages of existence, called respectively egg, larva, pupa, and imago. These changes

A

are often very sharply separated from each other, involving an entire change of form, although, in the case of insects with incomplete metamorphoses, the earlier stages pass gradually into the later without involving so total a change as to resemble the production of a new animal. In the larva state insects are sometimes provided with from ten to twenty-two legs, but instead of this number increasing, as in the *Myriopoda*, the number in the perfect state, as already mentioned, is invariably six. In the perfect state, too, insects, with rare exceptions in one or both sexes, always acquire one or two pairs of wings, a character which does not appear in any representative of the other three classes.

Insects are frequently very highly gifted by Nature, much more so, in fact, than the so-called higher animals. They are provided with two large eyes, one on each side of the head, composed of facets varying in number from sixteen to many thousands, according to the species. In addition to these, many insects are provided with one, two, or three visual organs, called simple eyes, ocelli, or stemmata, placed in the crown of the head. Nor is this all, for the compound eyes of certain water-beetles are actually divided horizontally, so that, when swimming on the surface of the water, they have literally two eyes to look upwards, and two to look downwards. Many observations have been placed on record, which show plainly that insects can discriminate between colours, and some recent experiments of Sir J. Lubbock on ants appear to indicate that they are able to perceive the ultra-violet rays of the solar spectrum, which are perfectly invisible to our eyes.

Of the other senses of insects it is difficult to speak positively. Their nervous system is composed of a double chain of ganglia, and it is therefore probable that their perceptions are less exclusively located in the brain than our own. Their hard integuments protect them from liability to casual injuries from trifling causes, and therefore we might be led to infer, *a priori*, that the sense of pain would be of but little use to them. And this actually appears to be the case, for they frequently appear to be just as lively and comfortable after the severest injuries as before. It is scarcely doubtful that they do not feel pain in anything like the same degree as a vertebrate animal.

But, with this exception, there is every reason to believe that insects possess the same senses as vertebrate animals in the highest perfection. Among the most important organs possessed by insects are the antennæ, two organs which project in front of the head, and which have been variously conjectured to be organs of hearing, touch, and smell. Their structure differs so much in different insects that it is highly probable that they may serve one purpose in one insect and another in another. They are composed of a very variable number of joints—from two or three to thirty or forty,—and they may be so short as scarcely to project in front of the head, or they may be several times as long as the whole body. They differ very much in shape and structure also, and are called filiform, serrated, pectinated, clavate, ramose, lamellated, bifurcate, etc., accordingly. Not unfrequently some of the terminal joints are much thickened, sometimes into a very distinct knob. Sometimes the joints are very distinctly separated, and at other times the antennæ are covered with down or bristles, so that the separation between the joints is hardly visible. The basal joint is called the scape, and it is often much longer than the other joints, occasionally measuring half the length of the antennæ, or even more.

In addition to the antennæ, insects are provided with one or two pairs of small jointed organs called labial and maxillary palpi. These form part of the mouth organs, and are probably organs of taste, and perhaps also of touch. Many insects are provided with large mandibles, while others, which live entirely on liquid food, are furnished with a long proboscis instead. In some insects both mandibles and a proboscis are developed.

The head is regarded by Professor Huxley as morphologically consisting of six segments (or somites), of which, however, the existence of only four can be demonstrated. The three following segments form the thorax, which is sharply separated in the perfect insect from both the head and the abdomen. The three segments of the thorax are called prothorax, metathorax, and mesothorax above, and prosternum, mesosternum, and metasternum beneath. The upper portion of the thorax is frequently called the pronotum.

The three pairs of legs are attached to the three segments of the thorax respectively. The legs are composed of five parts : the coxæ, or hips, the trochanters (a small joint between the coxæ and the femora), the femora, or thighs, the tibiæ, or shanks, and the tarsi, or feet. The tarsi are composed of five joints, but are liable to numerous modifications, and one or two joints are frequently undeveloped. The last joint of the tarsi usually terminates in a double claw. In leaping insects, the coxæ and femora are sometimes very largely developed. The legs may be

simple, or hairy, bristly, or spiny. The commonest appendage of
all is perhaps one or two spines at the end of the tibiæ. In leaping
insects the coxæ and femora are sometimes greatly thickened.

The wings are attached to the sides of the meso- and metathorax. They are usually formed of a transparent membrane,
traversed by branching tubes called nervures, and may be either
naked, or clothed with hair or scales. The base of the fore wings
is usually protected above by small plates called tegulæ, not
unlike epaulets in appearance. At the back of the mesothorax is
another plate called the scutellum. In many insects it is small and
inconspicuous, but in others it is large and conspicuous. It
attains its maximum of development in the *Pentatomidæ*, belonging to the Order *Hemiptera*, in some of which it is so large as to
cover the whole abdomen, and the wings are folded beneath it
when at rest.

The limbs of insects are worked by powerful muscles, not
attached to a comparatively weak and jointed internal skeleton,
like our own, but to the tough and often rigid or horny outer
covering of their bodies, which is often termed an external
skeleton. The strength and activity of many insects are so great
as to be truly gigantic in comparison with that of the Vertebrata,
allowing for difference in size. It has been said that if an
elephant were as strong as a stag-beetle, it could tear up rocks and
level mountains; a race-horse with the speed of a fly could fly
round the world like lightning; and a man with the activity of a
frog-hopper could leap through the air for half a mile, or with
the voice of a cicada could make himself heard all over the
world.

The last portion of the body of an insect is the abdomen,
which usually consists of from nine to eleven segments, and contains part of the organs of digestion and respiration, and those of
reproduction. Of the internal anatomy of insects our space will
not permit us to say much. The nervous system, to which we have
already alluded, lies along the ventral surface of the body, instead
of the dorsal surface, as in Vertebrata. Along the back extends an
organ called the great dorsal vessel, which fulfils the functions of
a heart. Insects breathe by means of openings along the side of
the body. These openings are called spiracles, and are placed one
on each side of several segments of the body; but their number
varies in different insects. They open into branching air-vessels
called tracheæ.

The abdomen is frequently terminated by various appendages connected with the reproduction of the species. The most conspicuous of these is generally the ovipositor of the female, which is very various in form, and is sometimes of great length, and not unfrequently bifid or trifid. In the order *Hymenoptera* it is frequently modified into a sting.

As a rule, there are two sexes in insects. In some cases the males and females resemble each other closely, but they frequently differ so much that they are liable to be placed in different genera until their relationship is clearly ascertained. Among the social insects (ants, wasps, bees, and termites) the bulk of the community consists of sterile females, called workers, or neuters, of which there are frequently more than one class, which perform all the work of the nest. Among other insects, two forms of males, or two forms of females, are often met with, a phenomenon known as sexual dimorphism. At other times, both sexes will exhibit a similar phenomenon, the species occurring normally in two well-marked forms. When these appear at different times of the year it is called seasonal dimorphism. Apart from this, local or accidental variations from the type of a species are of very common occurrence.

When insects are found paired, the presumption is that they belong to the same species; but this is not invariably the case. Instances have even been recorded in which a butterfly has been found paired with a moth; and although such a union would be almost certainly sterile, yet hybrids are not unfrequently produced by the crossing of allied species. Hermaphroditism is a phenomenon of occasional occurrence among insects, and when, as sometimes happens, the sexes of an insect differ considerably, the effect is very striking. Thus, in hybrids of the Common Blue Butterfly (*Polyommatus Icarus*), one pair of wings may be blue, and the other quite brown, with a border of orange spots. I have mentioned this here, because there appears to be good reason for believing that hybridity has a direct tendency to produce hermaphroditism, though of course it is not the sole cause.

In the majority of cases, union of the sexes is necessary for the continuance of the species; but parthenogenesis, or the laying of fertile eggs by an unfertilised female, is common in several groups, and is the rule in others. The males of such insects are frequently unknown, and in some cases appear to be actually non-existent. Among the *Cynipidæ* and *Aphidæ*, sexual and seasonal dimorphism

appears to have reached its furthest stage, winged and apterous
forms, and sexual and sexless (or possibly perfect hermaphrodite?)
forms, succeeding each other alternately.

Among the curious phenomena presented to us by insect life,
those connected with protective resemblance, and above all,
mimicry, are not the least remarkable. Many insects present a
striking resemblance to other natural objects, as leaves, sticks,
seeds, lichen, bird-droppings, etc., and thus escape the notice of
their enemies.   Others resemble various insects which either
enjoy an immunity from the attacks of certain enemies, or are furnished with means of defence.   Thus a beetle may resemble
an ant, or a moth may resemble a wasp, or a butterfly (or
perhaps only its female) may resemble a butterfly of a different
family which is protected from birds by an unpleasant smell and
taste ; and in extreme cases this resemblance is so close that the
two insects can hardly be distinguished from one another, except
by structural characters, although there may be no real affinity
between them.

Insects are usually abundant in proportion to the exuberance
of the vegetation, but the richer the native fauna of any country,
the poorer will it become when that is destroyed. Hence it
happens that cultivated districts in the tropics often disappoint the
collector very much ; while a dense tropical forest, with its dim
shade cast by the crowns of the trees a hundred feet above, is
anything but rich in insects, though they will swarm in a new
clearing, or in other favourable localities.   In temperate climates
the insects which have maintained their ground as inhabitants of
the country are tolerably equally distributed over it in suitable
localities ; but even here the draining of marshes and felling of
forests speedily exterminates species which inhabit such localities.

Although insects reach their maximum of size and brilliancy
in tropical countries, yet it does not follow that size and brilliancy
distinguish all tropical productions.   Whole families consist
chiefly of small and dingy species, and the number of large and
conspicuous species in the tropics is below rather than above the
average of those of temperate climates ; and although, on the
other hand, some families consisting almost exclusively of large
and brilliant insects are confined to the tropics, yet the tropical
representatives of insects found in temperate climates are frequently
inferior to the latter, both in size and colour.   Variety of vegetation is more necessary to insect life than great heat ; and many

more species of insects inhabit the Alpine countries of Central
Europe than are met with in Spain or Italy.

When we consider that every species of plant nourishes several
different kinds of insects (and in some cases hundreds), and that
apart from the number that derive their sustenance, directly or
indirectly, from the higher animals, insects prey on each other to
a great extent—insect parasites attacking other insects in all stages
of their existence, many parasites even preying on other parasites;
when we consider all this, we need not be surprised that insects
should be exceedingly numerous. About 12,000 species of insects
are known to inhabit England; and the adjacent parts of the
Continent support a considerably larger number. The total
number of insects known to inhabit the world is estimated at
present at 222,000; but this must be very far indeed below the
real number in existence, for several thousand species of insects
are described as new every year. Nor let any one imagine that
our British Fauna is by any means exhausted. It is true that the
British *Coleoptera* and *Lepidoptera* have been so far investigated
that a man must work very hard before he can hope to add a
new British species to either Order; but any entomologist who
cares to take up one of the less-studied groups of any of the other
Orders, may rely on adding a considerable number of new species
to the British Fauna, a certain proportion of which will be new
to science. Even among our commonest insects the habits and
structure of any one species would furnish any person with a
taste for such pursuits with sufficient employment for a lifetime.
The collector's province may be exhausted in a few years; but
the observer's, never.

The importance of the study of entomology is now so fully
recognised that although we have no "State Entomologist," which
is an American institution rendered necessary by the immense
damage frequently caused to crops by insects in the United States,
yet the Foreign Office not unfrequently applies to the Entomological
Society of London for information and advice on the invasion of a
swarm of locusts, or the reputed appearance of the *Phylloxera* of
the vine in a British colony. The Society then appoints a com-
mittee of specialists to investigate the matter, and in due time
reports upon it to the Government.

Crustacea are the only annulose animals which appear on our
own tables; but insects furnish important supplies of food in
many countries. The Romans regarded their Cossus, which was

probably the larva of a large wood-feeding beetle (possibly the
Stag-Beetle, or perhaps the larva of *Oryctes Nasicornis*, or of some
Longicorn) as a great delicacy, and that of the Palm Weevil is
still highly prized in the West Indies. The Australians make
"bugong" cakes of a species of moth (*Agrotis Spini*), and the
inhabitants of Southern Africa make "konga" cake of gnats and
other small insects. Locusts are likewise eaten all over Africa,
and when properly prepared are, as I am informed by Mr. Cowan,
the well-known missionary to Madagascar, very good eating—much
better than some travellers have reported, or than Mr. Riley, the
State Entomologist of Missouri, found the destructive Rocky
Mountain Locust. Mr. Cowan was inclined to think that when
locusts proved distasteful, it was due either to defective cooking
or preparation, or to the locusts themselves not being sufficiently
fresh; but while allowing for this, I am also inclined to believe
that there may really be a great difference in flavour between
different species of locusts, or even between the same species at
different times, according to its food. The inhabitants of Mexico
and Central America make great use of the eggs of some of the
large water-boatflies (*Hydrometridæ*) which abound in their rivers;
and many savages share with our "poor relations," the monkeys,
their taste for a still more objectionable insect delicacy.

Insects are exposed to the attacks of numerous enemies,—many
of the smaller vertebrate animals, more especially birds, feeding
entirely or in a large measure upon them. They are likewise
exposed to the attacks of other insects, many large families of
insects feeding almost entirely on others. Almost every family of
the great Order *Hymenoptera* (if we except the *Apidæ*, or bees) is
either carnivorous or parasitic, or provisions its nest with other
insects. The *Diptera*, too, many of which are most annoying to
the higher animals, and often destroy them when they attack
them as parasites, are likewise destructive to other insects, for
some groups prey upon insects, and others infest them as parasites.
Many families of the *Coleoptera*, *Orthoptera*, *Neuroptera*, and
Hemiptera are likewise more or less carnivorous; the *Lepidoptera*
being the only Order which confines its attacks almost exclusively
to the vegetable kingdom. Insects are likewise destroyed by
spiders, parasitic worms, and various species of mould or fungi.

Insects act as general scavengers, attacking decaying vegetable
or animal matter at once, and speedily clearing it away by their
numbers. They likewise check the inordinate growth of vegeta-

tion, and form a very considerable factor indeed in the great system of checks and counterchecks by which existing Nature is upheld, and room for constant change and progress is secured without disturbing a general equilibrium of forces. That our crops should sometimes suffer largely from their attacks is not surprising; and although insects are less numerous and destructive in England than in many other countries, yet the perusal of a work like Miss Ormerod's *Manual of Injurious Insects* is quite sufficient to make it plain to even the most unentomological reader that British crops are exposed to the attacks of a great number of enemies, which the farmer would do well not to under-estimate from their minuteness, but which he cannot combat successfully without some technical knowledge of insects and their habits.

A farmer or gardener who is ignorant of entomology is exposed to great disadvantages. If his crops suffer, he is not unlikely to mistake a harmless insect for the real depredator, or even to destroy the beneficial insects which keep the others in check, under the idea that they are the real authors of the mischief; or again, by his own neglect to seize the fitting moment for destroying the enemy, he may expose himself to very severe losses, which might have been averted, or at least greatly lessened, by a little timely precaution. A striking illustration of this occurred a few years ago in South Russia, where a small species of cockchafer (*Anisoplia Austriaca*, Herbst.) has lately been very destructive. A vast swarm were blown into the sea, and washed up on the beach in heaps in a half-torpid state, so that they might easily have been collected and destroyed in large quantities. But they were allowed to remain till they had recovered from their bath and dried their wings, when they flew inland to breed, and to carry ruin and desolation throughout the district.

Insects have many ways of defending themselves against their numerous enemies. Those which are distasteful to birds are frequently very conspicuous in their colours, and are often sluggish, and weak flyers. Their uneatable character, however, being apparent, they are easily recognised and passed over; and, as already mentioned, edible species which sufficiently resemble them share in their immunity. Other insects have different means of concealing themselves, or of escaping observation; while many are able to defend themselves with their jaws or stings, which are formidable even to the largest animals. Many insects discharge an offensive fluid when alarmed or seized, and some even

emit a volatile and very corrosive fluid, which explodes and volatilises as soon as it comes in contact with the air. Almost all
insects possess the power of producing sounds, and some are
phosphorescent; but these powers appear to be exerted rather to
attract their mates than for defensive purposes.

At first sight, the enormous number of insects in existence
would appear to render it a hopeless task to attempt to learn anything about them. The larger animals are comparatively few in
number, and when we speak of an elephant, a horse, a lion, a dog,
etc., it is sufficiently intelligible for most practical purposes; but
how can we make ourselves understood when we wish to speak of
some particular insect among the thousands that inhabit any given
country? This can only be effected by an arbitrary system of
classification; and the want of this placed almost insuperable
difficulties in the way of those who would have studied natural
history; for it made any satisfactory and permanent register of
acquired knowledge almost impossible. At length, however, in
the course of the last century, and partly guided by the tentative efforts of earlier naturalists, Linné, after various experiments,
devised the binomial nomenclature, and applied it, so far as his
knowledge extended, to the whole system of nature. Every
animal and plant has now two names, a generic and a specific
name, by which it is always spoken of, and which distinguishes it
from any other species. The specific name is frequently a Latin
adjective, and the generic name is generally of Greek derivation.
Every assemblage of individuals which appears sufficiently distinct
from its nearest relatives is called a species; and those species
which have a distinct general resemblance are said to belong to
the same genus. Genera again are assorted into sub-families,
families, tribes, and orders; and thus it becomes possible to discriminate between the immense numbers of the insect race. Those
specimens of a species which agree best with its characters are
called typical, while those which present casual or local variations
are called aberrations, varieties, or local forms; and of course many
entomologists differ in their estimate of species and varieties; but
this does not affect the general principle. To avoid confusion, no
two species of one genus are allowed to bear the same name; and
no generic name is allowed to be used twice in zoology. The
name used by the first describer of a species is always retained,
and if the same species has accidentally received two names, the
name of later date is called a synonym, and drops out of use.

For convenience of reference, and still further to lessen the chance of confusion, the name of the describer of a species is generally appended to the specific name, whenever the latter is quoted. Some have argued that if a later writer moves a species into a different genus from that in which the original describer placed it, the name of the more recent author should be appended to it, instead of that of the original describer; but this practice is most mischievous and misleading, and has not even a shade of practical utility to recommend it.

Having thus explained the general principles of Zoological Nomenclature, we will now proceed to discuss the Classification of Insects. Linné in the two last editions of his *Systema Naturæ*,[1] published in 1758 and 1767, divided all the insects known to him into seven great Orders, which he called *Coleoptera, Hemiptera, Lepidoptera, Neuroptera, Hymenoptera, Diptera*, and *Aptera*. These Orders were established on the number and consistency of the wings, and are all recognised nearly in the Linnean sense at the present day, with the exception of *Hemiptera* and *Aptera*. The *Aptera* included the Classes *Arachnida, Crustacea*, and *Myriopoda*; the Lice, Fleas, and Springtails; and *Termes*, the winged forms of which were unknown to Linné. The Linnean Order *Hemiptera* was composed of at least two distinct Orders; and Olivier subsequently divided it into *Hemiptera* and *Orthoptera*. Soon after the time of Linné, his eminent pupil Fabricius prepared a new classification of insects founded on the structure of the mouth, and he re-named all the Linnean Orders, even when they coincided with his own. His nomenclature speedily fell into disuse, and the only Orders which he proposed, which it is necessary to remember, are the *Odonata* (Dragon-flies) and *Ryngota* (Hemiptera).

Several modifications were proposed by Leach, Latreille, and other authors; and the arrangement of Orders adopted by Westwood, in his *Introduction to the Modern Classification of Insects*, published in 1839, but still a classical work, is as follows :—

Orders.	Representatives.
Coleoptera.	Beetles.
Euplexoptera.	Earwigs.
Orthoptera.	Crickets, etc.
Thysanoptera.	" Black Fly."

[1] These are called the 10th and 12th editions; but the so-called 11th edition, published in 1760, is a mere reprint of the 10th.

Orders.	Representatives.
Neuroptera.	Dragon-flies, etc.
Trichoptera.	Caddis flies.
Hymenoptera.	Bees, wasps, ants, etc.
Strepsiptera.	Bee parasites.
Lepidoptera.	Butterflies and moths.
Homoptera.	Froghoppers.
Heteroptera.	Bugs.
Aphaniptera.	Fleas.
Diptera.	Flies.

Westwood rejects the Lice and Springtails from his work, not regarding them as true insects. The principal names or synonyms not mentioned above, which have been proposed for Orders of insects, are as follows, Westwood's (or English) equivalents being added :—

Dermaptera.	Orthoptera.
Dermaptera.	Euplexoptera.
Dictyoptera.	Cockroaches.
Thysanura.	Springtails.
Collembola.	
Parasita.	Lice.
Anoplura.	Lice.
Mallophaga.	Bird lice.
Homaloptera.	Forest flies.
Siphonaptera.	Aphaniptera.
Rhipiptera.	Strepsiptera.
Achreioptera.	Beaver parasites.
Pseudo-Neuroptera.	Neuroptera, etc.

Of late years the tendency has been to again reduce the Orders to seven,—viz. *Coleoptera* (including *Strepsiptera*), *Orthoptera* (including *Euplexoptera* and *Dictyoptera*), *Neuroptera* (including *Trichoptera, Thysanura, Collembola, Mallophaga,* and *Thysanoptera*), *Hymenoptera, Lepidoptera, Hemiptera,* or *Rhynchota* (including the sub-orders *Hemiptera-Heteroptera* and *Hemiptera-Homoptera,* and the *Anoplura*), and *Diptera* (including *Aphaniptera,* and possibly *Achreioptera*), and this arrangement will be followed in the present work. The first four Orders, which possess jaws in the perfect state, are sometimes called *Insecta Mandibulata,* and the remainder, which are provided with a sucking proboscis, are called *Insecta*

Haustellata. But different authors are not agreed as to the sequence in which they place the Orders of Insects.

Of all the principal Orders, the Order *Neuroptera* is in the most unsatisfactory state, including a great number of very discordant groups, which differ extremely in the structure of their mouths and in the character of their metamorphoses. It has even been proposed to unite the bulk of the *Neuroptera* with the *Orthoptera*, under the improper title of *Pseudo-Neuroptera*, leaving only a very few (scarcely typical) groups to represent the *Neuroptera*. But the *Neuroptera* which most resemble the *Orthoptera*, differ from them so widely in the structure of their wings that even Linné did not place them in the same Order; and it would be a mistake to do so at the present day.

No system can, however, be regarded as *perfect*. Organic Nature is now believed to have grown up into the form in which we see it from infinitesimal beginnings, by the effect of gradual changes acting and reacting on each other in the course of countless ages. We have consequently nothing before us to classify but the extreme ends of the branches of a vast tree, of the rest of which we are scarcely able to catch even the slightest glimpse. Consequently, while every group and every species is more or less related to others, a book-arrangement can only be linear, and while it expresses a certain amount of affinity between the groups and species placed in juxtaposition, it likewise tends to conceal the fact that equally important affinities frequently exist between other species or groups, which may chance to be widely separated in our necessarily artificial arrangements.

Of fossil insects but little need here be said. Comparatively few species have yet been described, for the correct identification of the fragmentary remains of insects which are sometimes met with (occasionally in considerable abundance) presents difficulties which are almost insuperable to the best entomologists, who are not always agreed respecting even the Order to which an insect belongs; while in other cases, fragments originally supposed to belong to insects have ultimately proved to be of vegetable origin. Sometimes, however, fossil insects are met with in such good preservation that but little difficulty exists in determining their approximate affinities. The oldest known fossil insects appear to belong to the Orders *Orthoptera* and *Neuroptera*, and some of the latter were of gigantic size compared to their nearest living allies. Even such fragile insects as butterflies are occasionally met with in good preservation, the best known example of which was found at Aix, in Provence, many years ago. It is considered to belong to the sub-family *Satyrinæ*, and is called *Neorinopis Sepulta*, Boisd.

Our Introduction may be brought to a fitting conclusion by a table exhibiting the approximate round numbers of insects known to inhabit the British Isles and the world.

Orders.				Britain.	World.
Coleoptera,	.	.	.	3,000	93,000
Orthoptera,	.	.	.	60	7,000
Neuroptera,	.	.	.	640	4,000
Hymenoptera,		.	.	3,000	31,000
Lepidoptera,	.	.	.	2,000	45,000
Hemiptera,	.	.	.	900	17,000
Diptera,	.	.	.	3,000	25,000
				12,600	222,000

ORDER COLEOPTERA.

MANDIBULATE insects; wings, four; the first pair (or elytra) horny or leathery, covering the membranous hind wings when closed, and meeting down the back in a straight suture; larva, with six legs, or apodous; pupa, inactive.

The *Coleoptera*, or Beetles, form an exceedingly numerous and compact order, and the insects of which it is composed have usually so strong a family likeness that they are seldom likely to be mistaken for those of any other order. They have been more assiduously studied than any other insects, and consequently, out of the 222,000 insects known at present, nearly 100,000 are beetles. In this country about 3000 species are known to occur, amounting to one-fourth of our native insects. It is, however, probable that the actual number of species of beetles existing will be found to be less than those of the *Hymenoptera* and *Diptera*, when these Orders have been collected and studied with equal assiduity.

Beetles and their larvæ feed on a great variety of substances, both animal and vegetable; a few abnormal forms are parasitic on bees and wasps, but this is quite exceptional. Some are carnivorous, feeding on other insects; others feed on dung, carrion, and other animal products; and others again live on the roots, leaves, etc., of living plants,—some feeding in long galleries which they excavate in the solid wood of trees.

Beetles and their larvæ frequently live in concealment, but many species live quite exposed, and are found on flowers and bushes, or running on the ground in the heat of the day.

Generally speaking, the wings are ample, but occasionally the wings are absent. In this case, the elytra may either be moveable, soldered together, or completely absent. In some families, the elytra are shorter than the abdomen, more or less of the extremity of which is left exposed. However, in these insects the wings are generally ample, being folded under the short elytra.

The pupæ of beetles are necromorphous, or mummy-like, the pupa-skin closely enveloping the different organs of the future beetle, which are often enclosed in separate coverings, and very clearly defined. In the case of beetles which assume the pupa state in a cell of agglutinated earth, the beetle is often fully developed and remains inactive for a considerable time before quitting its cell.

The German and American coleopterists often recognise no divisions higher than genera in this extensive Order, except families, of which seventy-four are enumerated in Gemminger and Von Harold's great *Catalogus Coleopterorum;* but English and French writers employ a more complicated system of classification. In the present work, the families will be brought together under the main groups, and all those of special interest will be noticed; but the more minute subdivisions between families and genera will not always be alluded to. The arrangement of the above-mentioned catalogue is generally followed.

SECTION I.—ADEPHAGA.

Tarsi generally five-jointed; six palpi (four maxillary, *i.e.* two to each maxilla), and two labial; antennæ filiform; habits carnivorous.

This section includes two groups, the *Geodephaga* and *Hydradephaga*, comprising the bulk of the carnivorous beetles. But it must be remembered that there is no rule without an exception, especially in natural history; and thus we find species among the *Adephaga* which have fewer than five joints to the tarsi; and others which are wholly or partially herbivorous.

SUB-SECTION I.—*Geodephaga.*

Autennæ and legs long and slender; mandibles not concealed by the upper lip; eyes large and prominent; body oblong, convex.

The *Geodephaga*, or Carnivorous Ground Beetles, are a very extensive group, and, with few exceptions, may be regarded as beneficial insects, as they generally feed on other insects, which would otherwise multiply to a far more injurious extent than at present. They are very similar in shape to some of the *Heteromera* from which their filiform antennæ and five-jointed tarsi will at once distinguish them.

FAMILY I.—*Cicindelidæ.*

Maxillæ terminating in a moveable hook; head large, broader than the thorax; eyes very large and prominent; mandibles large, sharply pointed, and armed with several large teeth.

The typical genus of this family is *Cicindela*, Linn., which includes the Tiger Beetles. Four species occur in England, the commonest of which is the Green Tiger Beetle (*Cicindela Campestris*, Linn.), which is common in sandy places. It is of a bright green colour (coppery beneath), with white markings. It runs very fast, and, if disturbed, takes to its wings, and darts away with great rapidity, but soon settles again. Its larva makes a burrow in the sand, where it lies in wait for insects in the manner of an ant-lion. The beetle is about half an inch in length. *Cicindela* is a very extensive genus, but none of the species are much more than twice the size of our own, and all strongly resemble each other. They are generally green or brown, with white or yellow spots and markings, and one or two of the North American species are white.

The largest species of this family belong to the South African genus *Mantichora*, Fabr. They are about two inches in length, and their large size and great scissors-like jaws give them a most formidable appearance. They are of a black colour, and run with great speed over the sand, or hide themselves under stones.

Tetracha, Hope, is a genus closely allied to *Cicindela*, but more uniform in colour. Most of the species are American, but a few are Australian. *T. Carolina*, Linn., is a common North American species, and is green, with the apex of the elytra broadly bordered on the sides with white.

At Caripé, on the Amazons, Mr. H. W. Bates met with two species of *Tetracha* which are nocturnal in their habits, hiding by day in burrows several inches in depth, and issuing forth at night, when they run over the sand with extraordinary rapidity, doubling if an attempt is made to seize them. One species is similar to the sand in colour, while the other is of a brilliant copper colour, but defends itself when alarmed by emitting a powerful and offensive odour. But the great majority of the *Cicindelidæ* collected by Mr. Bates on the Amazons belonged to the genus *Odontocheila*, which includes slender, long-legged species, generally of a bronzed colour, with white spots on the elytra. They much resemble the true *Cicindelæ*, but are entirely arboreal in their habits.[1]

The genus *Collyris*, Fabr., and its allies are nearly confined to the East Indies. They are of a beautiful blue or green colour, and

[1] Bates, *Naturalist on the Amazons*, vol. i. pp. 207, 208, 323, and 324.

differ from the more typical forms of the *Cicindelidæ* by their
more elongated form, and especially by their long narrow neck.

FAMILY II.—*Carabidæ*.

Maxillæ terminating in an unarticulated point; head generally
narrower than the thorax; eyes not remarkably prominent; mandibles strong, and hooked at the tip, but with no prominent
teeth.

This family is much more extensive and varied than the last,
and, instead of being represented by one genus and four species in
Britain, includes a very large proportion of our native species,
many being of considerable interest and importance. Although
none of the species are strictly aquatic, yet many of them frequent
very marshy localities close to the water, and several are even
found habitually on the sea-beach at low-water, and must be able
to sustain a long-continued immersion without injury.

The species of *Elaphrus*, Fabr., are of a greenish coppery colour,
with rows of large, deeply-impressed, bluish punctures. They
frequent marshy localities. *Nebria*, Latr., includes several black or
tawny species, some of which frequent mountainous districts, while
others are met with in woods, under bark, and *Nebria Complanata*,
Linn., which is common in South France, abounds on the sea-shore,
and is sometimes found congregated in vast numbers under planks
washed up by the sea.

Carabus, Linn., the typical genus of this family, is of great
extent, and includes the largest and most conspicuous of our
British *Geodephaga*, several of which exceed an inch in length.
They are long oval insects, and are of a black or bronzy colour, or
more or less metallic. Some of the species are smooth, and others
are strongly punctured, or ridged. Several of our commonest black
species, such as *Carabus Catenulatus*, Scop., and *Violaceus*, Linn.,
are smooth, and are narrowly bordered with purple or violet. One
of our most beautiful species is *Carabus Nitens*, Fabr., which is
green, splendidly glossed with coppery red; it is about half an inch
in length, and is somewhat local. *Carabus Auratus*, Linn., which is
about an inch long, is scarcely met with in England except as a
casual importation, but is abundant in many parts of the Continent.
It is of a bright green colour, much less strongly glossed with
copper than *C. Nitens*, and is called the Gold Beetle in Germany,
where it is common in gardens, and along roads and foot-paths.
The *Carabi* are very predaceous insects, and generally come out at

night, though they may frequently be seen in the day-time, or at dusk, especially in spring. They are apterous, but the elytra are not soldered together.

The largest of the European *Carabidæ* belong to the genus *Procerus*, Dej., which much resemble *Carabi* in shape, but are double the size, sometimes measuring two inches in length. They are black and strongly punctured, and are peculiar to South-Eastern Europe and Western Asia.

Damaster, Koll, is a genus remarkable for its peculiar shape, which will be seen in our figure. It only includes a very few black species, closely resembling each other, and all peculiar to different islands in Japan.

Calosoma, Web., is a widely-distributed genus, including several very beautiful species. The thorax is transverse, much narrower than the abdomen, and more or less convex; the wings are well developed. The commonest species, *C. Inquisitor*, Fabr., is about half an inch long, of a dull coppery green, with three rows of golden-green punctures on each elytron. *C. Sycophanta*, Fabr., which is much larger, is a great rarity in England, though common on the Continent; it is of a splendid golden green, and is generally met with on oaks, where it feeds on the destructive Processionary Caterpillars (*Cnethocampa Processionea*, Linn.) and other insects.

Casnonia, Latr., is a tropical genus found in marshy places, which is remarkable for its very long slender thorax. The species are black and rugose, sometimes with pale yellowish spots.

The genus *Brachinus*, Web., includes several reddish beetles, with bluish or greenish elytra. They are about a quarter of an inch in length, and are found under stones. Many species of *Geodephaga* and other beetles will attempt to defend themselves by discharging a disagreeable acrid fluid when handled, but the *Brachini* possess a much more curious method of defence. If they are alarmed, they discharge a slightly acid fluid, which instantly volatilises into smoke, with a slight explosion ; and this manœuvre they can repeat several times.

The genus *Agra*, Fabr., includes a great number of slender species, peculiar to tropical America, which are entirely arboreal in their habits, like many other *Coleoptera* which inhabit the same countries. *A. Variolosa*, Klug, is bronzy-brown.

One of the most remarkable genera of the *Geodephaga* is *Mormolyce*, Hagenb., which has extraordinary dilated elytra, and scarcely resembles a beetle at all. The few known species are all dark-brown insects, and are very much alike; they are confined to the Malayan Peninsula and the adjacent islands, the type, *M. Phyllodes*, Hagenb., being from Java. The transformations are not specially remarkable, but the fully developed beetle, which is about two inches long, much resembles a fiddle, both in shape and colour, and is actually called "the Fiddler" by the European inhabitants of the countries where it occurs.

Anthia, Web., is a genus of large and handsome beetles inhabiting the tropics of the Old World. *A. Orientalis*, Hope, which is common in India, is a black species, about an inch and a quarter in length, with two large white spots on the thorax, and four on the elytra.

Scarites, Fabr., includes a number of species remarkable for the great size of their head and thorax, which are closely united, but sharply separated from the abdomen; their great mandibles; and their strongly-dentated front tibiæ. They are common in the warmer parts of the earth, where they burrow in loose soil, but are not met with in Northern Europe. Some of the species are diurnal, but the greater number only seek for prey at night. The nearest ally to this genus which we possess in England is a small dark-brown or reddish-brown species, with red legs and antennæ (*Clivina Fossor*, Linn.), which is met with in sandy places near water, under stones, or at the roots of trees, etc.

Panagæus, Latr., is a pretty genus containing black species marked with red or yellow; *Panagæus Crux-major*, Linn., which is about an eighth of an inch in length, is not uncommon in England.

A great number of small and moderate-sized *Carabidæ*, generally of a more or less oval form, and black, bronzy, or green in colour, often with red legs, are met with in England. The most important genera are perhaps *Chlænius*, Bon.; *Anisodactylus*, Dej.; *Bradycellus*, Erichs.; *Ophonus*, Steph.; *Harpalus*, Latr.; *Stenolophus*, Dej.; *Pœcilus*, Bon.; *Argutor*, Dej.; *Pterostichus, Calathus, Platynus, Abax*, and *Amara*, Bon., etc. Many species may be found running on paths by day, especially in spring. Although the smaller *Carabidæ*, like the larger, are carnivorous as a rule, yet many species of *Harpalus*, etc., will sometimes indulge in a vegetable diet; and *Zabrus Gibbus*, Linn., is a highly destructive insect. It is of a shining black or pitchy black colour, and the antennæ and legs are pitchy brown. It is of a cylindrical form, winged, and with shorter antennæ than most of its allies, and measures about half an inch in length. Both the larva and the beetle feed on corn, and sometimes commit great ravages, but the beetle will devour its companions, if pressed by hunger, and is therefore not exclusively herbivorous.

Several of the small species of *Carabidæ* placed towards the end of the family are interesting in their habits. *Bembidium,* Latr., is a very extensive genus of minute *Carabidæ*, very few of which reach the length of a quarter of an inch, while many are only half that size. They are generally of a black or bronzy colour, with yellowish spots and markings. They are very active in their movements, and although not exactly aquatic, are always found in marshy places, under stones, or running among sand, mud, and refuse, in the immediate neighbourhood of water. A few species, however, are found in mountainous districts, or under bark. They generally appear in spring; and, in fact, most of the *Carabidæ* are more numerous in spring and early summer than later in the year.

The genus *Aëpus,* Leach, only includes three very small apterous yellowish beetles, two of which are found on the shores of England, France, and Denmark, and the third in Madeira. They are met with only at low-water mark, and as they are covered by the tide for several hours every day, they may fairly be regarded as true marine insects. They are sometimes accompanied by *Aëpophilus Bonnairei,* Sign., a small insect much resembling them in appearance and habits, but which belongs to the order *Hemiptera.*

The last genera of the *Carabidæ* which we shall notice are— *Anophthalmus,* Schmidt, and *Aphænops,* Bonv. They are small reddish or brownish eyeless beetles, which are found under stones in the great caves of South-Eastern Europe and North America, which, as is well known, possess a very peculiar fauna of their own.

SUB-SECTION II.—*Hydradephaga.*

Antennæ slender; long or short; mandibles concealed by the upper lip; eyes not remarkably prominent; body broad and often flattened; legs formed for swimming.

The *Hydradephaga* are entirely carnivorous, and are almost wholly aquatic insects, but, as their wings are well developed, many of the species leave the water at night, and fly to great distances. They are divided into two families—the *Dytiscidæ* and the *Gyrinidæ.*

FAMILY I.—*Dytiscidæ.*

Antennæ filiform, rather long; palpi short; eyes not divided; front pair of legs not longer than the hinder pairs, which are fringed with hairs.

Haliplus Fulvus, Fabr., is a reddish beetle about an eighth of an inch long, with dusky streaks on the elytra. The species of *Haliplus,* Latr., and *Cnemidotus,* Ill., are found in stagnant water, and differ from the other *Dytiscidæ* in the antennæ being only ten-jointed, instead of eleven-jointed.

The most extensive genus of the *Dytiscidæ* is *Hydroporus,* Clairv., which includes a great variety of small species, found in all parts of the world, but especially numerous in Europe. They are generally black, reddish, or yellowish, and more or less convex. In this and some allied genera the front tarsi of the males are only four-jointed.

Colymbetes, Clairv., includes larger species, measuring half an inch or more in length. One of the commonest species is *C. Fuscus,* Linn., a brown oval beetle, with the sides of the collar and of the elytra tawny. In this and several allied genera the front tarsi are dilated in the males.

The genus *Agabus,* Leach, includes a considerable number of species about a quarter of an inch long, some of which are remarkable for the antennæ being dilated and serrated at the extremity in the males. The type of the genus is *A. Serricornis,* Payk.

Hyphydrus Ovatus, Linn., a species rather less than a quarter of an inch long, is remarkable for its shape, being much shorter and broader than most of its allies, and very convex; it is of a reddish-brown colour, and is found in stagnant water.

The largest species of the *Dytiscidæ* belong to the genus *Dytiscus,* Linn., and measure from an inch to an inch and a half in length. The tarsi of the males are dilated, and the elytra of the females are strongly furrowed. They are of an olive brown or dull greenish colour, with yellowish borders to the thorax and elytra. They are broad insects, hardly convex; and *D. Latissimus,* Linn., one of the largest, but by no means one of the commonest species, is nearly as broad as it is long. The larvæ of these insects are sometimes called "Fresh-water Shrimps." Both the beetles and their larvæ are very voracious, and the former will even attack and devour small fish. They are more often found in standing water than in streams.

Cybister Rœselii, Fabr., much resembles a *Dytiscus* in size and colour, but is less flattened.

The genus *Hydaticus*, Leach, is one of the prettiest of this family. The species are oval, rather flattened, and about half an inch long. They are generally black, with reddish or yellowish markings, or yellowish with black markings, and are far less numerous in Europe than in the warmer parts of the world. The elytra of the females are not furrowed.

The foreign species of *Dytiscidæ* hardly surpass our own in size or beauty.

FAMILY II.—*Gyrinidæ*.

Antennæ very short ; front legs very long, and rather slender ; hind legs very short and broad; eyes completely divided by the margin of the head.

The *Gyrinidæ*, or Whirligig Beetles, are among the easiest recognised of any family of *Coleoptera*. They may be seen on any fine day in summer spinning in circles on the surface of the water, sometimes remaining motionless for a moment, and then either diving or darting off suddenly, or recommencing their erratic dance as before. The European species of *Gyrinus*, Geoffr., are small, oval, bluish-black beetles, about a quarter of an inch long. Like most water-beetles they are very smooth and shining. Some foreign species, belonging to the genera *Enhydrus*, Cast., and *Dineutes*, Macl., are nearly half an inch long, and of a violet-blue colour.

The eyes of the *Gyrinidæ* are perhaps their most remarkable peculiarity, for they are divided in such a manner that the insect has really four eyes, two situated above and two below, so that it can see what is passing above in the air, and below in the water, at the same time. An arrangement very similar to this is met with in the genus *Tetraops*, in the *Longicornia*.

SECTION II.—PALPICORNIA.

Tarsi generally five-jointed ; palpi four, maxillary palpi very long, sometimes longer than the antennæ ; antennæ short, clavate ; habits partly herbivorous, at least in the perfect state.

FAMILY I.—*Hydrophilidæ*.

Body oval; first joint of the tarsi short, never longer than the other joints ; habits aquatic.

The long palpi and short clubbed antennæ will at once distinguish the beetles of this family from the *Dytiscidæ*. Their larvæ feed on other insects, but the beetles are much less voracious than the *Dytiscidæ*, and feed to a greater or less extent on vegetable matter.

One of our largest water-beetles is *Hydrophilus Piceus*, Linn., which is more than an inch and a half in length, though narrower and more convex than the species of *Dytiscus*. It is sometimes called the Great Water Beetle, and sometimes the Harmless Water Beetle. *Hydrous Caraboïdes*, Linn., is a much smaller insect, not measuring quite three-quarters of an inch in length; but it is shorter and broader in proportion than *Hydrophilus*. Both these species are black and shining, and are found in stagnant water.

The remaining species of this family are of small size (measuring a quarter of an inch in length and under), and are of little special interest. They are found in stagnant water, among the roots of plants, or else in damp marshy places, close to water. *Hydræna Riparia*, Kug, measures less than one-twelfth of an inch in length. It is brown, with reddish legs and antennæ, and strongly punctured. It is found among water-plants, or under stones by the side of small streams. Its palpi are of extraordinary length,—more than twice as long as the antennæ.

FAMILY II.—*Sphæridiidæ*.

Shape oval or nearly round ; first joint of the tarsi longer than the other joints ; thorax narrowed in front.

A few of the species of this family live in running water, but the greater part are met with in damp places, in dung, or in fungi. The family is not very extensive; and the species are of small size. They are generally of a black colour, more or less marked with red.

One of our largest and prettiest European representatives of the group is *Sphæridium Scarabæoides*, Fabr. It measures a quarter of an inch in length, and is black, with a blood-red spot at the base of the elytra, and a large yellow spot towards the extremity of each. It is met with in fresh cow-dung.

SECTION III.—Brachelytra.

Tarsi variable; palpi four; antennæ short; elytra generally very short, with a straight suture ; wings ample, folded beneath elytra.

FAMILY I.—*Staphylinidæ*.

Antennæ slender, the apical joints rarely thickened; tarsi generally five-jointed; elytra usually much shorter than half the abdomen, which is freely moveable.

The *Staphylinidæ*, or Rove Beetles, are an extensive family, of small or moderate-sized species, which are very numerous in Europe, and doubtless in most other parts of the world, though they have been much less assiduously collected abroad than the larger and more attractive groups of beetles. They feed on decaying vegetable and animal matter, and the smaller species are found among moss, dung, or fungi, under bark, etc., and several inhabit ants' nests.

Aleochara Fuscipes, Fabr., measures about a quarter of an inch in length, and is black, with brown or blackish elytra, and reddish-brown legs. It is a carrion feeder, and most of the species of *Aleochara*, Grav., a large genus which is well represented in most parts of the world, feed either on dung or carrion.

Several genera allied to *Aleochara*, such as *Dinarda*, Mannerh., and *Myrmedonia*, Er., are found chiefly, if not exclusively, in ants' nests. The species are brown or black, measuring a quarter of an inch in length, or under; and are not unlike the ants among whom they live, apparently on friendly terms enough, though some writers have conjectured that they feed upon the ants.

Oxypoda Opaca, Grav., a black insect, about an eighth of an inch in length, may serve to represent the smaller species allied to *Aleochara*, which are extremely numerous; *Oxypoda* and *Homalota*, Mannerh., being two of the largest genera. They are very small beetles, generally of a black, brown, or yellowish colour, and are chiefly found in damp places, among decaying vegetable matter; and some species of *Oxypoda* are met with in ants' nests. One small black beetle allied to these (*Diglossa Mersa*, Hal.) is found between tide-marks, like the species of *Aëpus*.

Leaving the *Aleocharinæ* we pass on to a less extensive group, the *Tachyporinæ*, in which the abdomen is longer and more pointed. The species are generally met with in dung, or among dead leaves or other vegetable refuse. *Tachinus Subterraneus*, Linn., is a shining black insect, with a reddish spot on each shoulder, and brown legs; it is about a quarter of an inch in length.

The largest species of this family belong to the typical sub-family *Staphylininæ*. One of the largest and commonest is the Devil's

Coach Horse (*Ocypus Olens*, Linn.), a black insect about an inch long, with the antennæ tipped with reddish. It is often seen running on paths, etc., and, if alarmed, turns up its head and tail. It is armed with powerful jaws, and is capable of inflicting a severe bite. The species of *Staphylinus*, Linn., are rather smaller, and are black, with red elytra. One or two genera are more or less covered with downy hair, which is most remarkable in *Emus Hirtus*, Linn., a black insect, with downy yellow hair, which some authors have compared to a *Bombus*, and others to a *Bombylius*. It measures about three-quarters of an inch in length, and though common in some parts of the Continent, is considered a great rarity in England, though I have lately seen a specimen which was taken in Cornwall.

Velleius Dilatatus, Fabr., is a black insect, about three-quarters of an inch in length, with reddish-brown antennæ. It is rarely common, although gregarious, and is generally found in hornets' nests, but is sometimes met with in hollow trees, where no hornets are present. Its larva somewhat resembles that of the hornet.

Pæderus Caligatus, Er., may be taken as typical of the *Pæderinæ*. It is rather a pretty insect, and measures about a quarter of an inch in length. It is black, with blue elytra, and the collar and first four segments of the abdomen are red ; the base of the antennæ and the legs are also reddish.

Stenus, Fabr. (typical of the sub-family *Steninæ*), includes a number of small species, which are found in marshy places.

Stenus Oculatus, Grav., a species widely distributed in Europe and North Africa, is black, with a leaden lustre, and the legs and antennæ are brownish yellow.

Oxyporus Rufus, Linn., figured as a representative of the *Oxytelinæ*, is a black species, about one-third of an inch long. The collar, the elytra, the four first segments of the abdomen, a spot on each shoulder, and the greater part of the legs, are red. The beetles and their larvæ are found in fungi.

Homalium Rivulare, Payk., belonging to the *Homaliinæ*, is about one-eighth of an inch long, and is black, with brown elytra and yellowish legs. The species of *Homalium* differ in their habits from any *Staphylinidæ* that we have yet mentioned, being found on grass or among flowering plants or bushes, and sometimes under bark.

The *Piestinæ* are a sub-family of rather large species, most of which are exotic; they are remarkable for their long projecting jaws, and are generally found under the bark of dead trees. *Leptochirus Javanicus*, Cast., is black, often with reddish thorax and legs, and measures about half an inch in length.

FAMILY II.—*Pselaphidæ*.

Antennæ short and thick; elytra nearly half the length of the abdomen; tarsi generally three-jointed; abdomen not freely moveable.

This family is not extensive, and the species are not of large size; but they differ considerably in structure, especially in that of the antennæ. *Chennium Bituberculatum*, Latr., is about one-eighth of an inch long, and of a reddish chestnut colour; it is found in various parts of Southern and Western Europe in the nests of *Myrmica Cæspitum*; its antennæ are clothed with long bristles; in *Faronus Lafertei*, Aubé, a chestnut-coloured insect, less than one-twelfth of an inch in length, and a great rarity in France, the antennæ are quite naked. In the typical genus *Pselaphus*, Herbst, the last joint of the antennæ is of considerable size, but this character perhaps reaches its maximum in the genus *Trimium*, Aubé. *T. Brevicorne*, Erichs., is a shining reddish-brown beetle, with yellowish legs, and measuring less than the twelfth of an inch in length; it is found in vegetable refuse. The genus *Claviger* includes a few reddish- or yellowish- brown species, not more than one-tenth or one-twelfth of an inch in length. Their heads are long and narrow, their eyes are absent, and their wings rudimentary. They are found in the nests of *Formica Flava*, or under stones in the immediate neighbourhood.

We have still to notice two very singular foreign genera of this family. *Metopias Curculionoides*, Gory, is a red, velvety-looking species from Cayenne, which is the type of a small South American genus. The head is furnished with a broad transverse projection, on which the very long and bristly antennæ, with a very long basal joint, are placed, and the legs are also covered with bristles. It is one of the largest of the *Pselaphidæ*, measuring one-eighth of an inch in length.

Articerus, Dalm., an Australian genus, much resembles *Claviger* in shape, but has prominent eyes, and the antennæ are composed of a single joint only. The typical species, *A. Armatus*, Dalm., is of a rusty red colour, and was found in gum copal.

Although the short elytra lead authors to include the *Pselaphidæ*

in the *Brachelytra*, yet they might almost as well be included
in the *Necrophaga*, being closely allied to the *Scydmænidæ*.   It
has often been remarked that our systems are only approxima-
tions to a natural arrangement at best, for we not only find it
difficult to lay down characters which shall hold good without
being liable to many exceptions, but even if we find such
characters, they are always more or less arbitrary, and frequently
result in our systems widely separating groups that are in reality
more or less closely allied.

SECTION IV.—NECROPHAGA.

Tarsi generally five-jointed; antennæ of moderate length, generally clavate; elytra generally covering the abdomen.

The *Necrophaga* or *Clavicornia* are an extensive and varied
group, including, besides the families which strictly belong to it,
several of somewhat doubtful position.   A great number feed on
decaying animal matter, others are found in dung or among
vegetable refuse, and several species inhabit ants' nests.

Some of the smaller families of this group will be left un-
noticed here.

FAMILY I.—*Paussidæ*.

Body depressed, oblong, antennæ either two-jointed, the second
joint being triangular or ovoid, or with from six to ten much
enlarged joints; palpi large, conical; elytra truncated at the tip;
tarsi short, four-jointed.

This is a very remarkable family of beetles, and its position
has been much debated by entomologists, several of whom have
referred it to the *Carabidæ*, while others have considered it to be
nearer allied to the *Xylophaga*.   The species are of small size, and
almost exclusively exotic, only one or two having been observed
in South Europe.   They inhabit ants' nests, where they probably fulfil the functions of artillerists, for when disturbed they
discharge a volatile detonating fluid like *Brachinus*, and although
less in quantity, it is so highly corrosive that its stains take many
days to disappear from the hands.

The extraordinary antennæ render the *Paussidæ* unmistakeable;
and in some species, such as *Homopterus Brasiliensis*, Westw., a
reddish-fulvous insect a quarter of an inch long, the legs are
remarkably dilated as well.   Two other species of the family are

here figured : *Paussus Armatus*, Westw., from Senegal, which is of a reddish-brown colour ; and *Platyrhopalus Mellyi*, Westw., a dark chestnut-coloured species from Malabar. These measure rather less than one-third of an inch in length.

FAMILY II.—*Scydmænidæ.*

Tarsi five-jointed ; antennæ as long as the head and thorax, clavate; maxillary palpi very long, four-jointed.

A small family of very minute species, which are met with under stones or bark, or in ants' nests. *Cephennium Thoracicum*, Müll., is about one-fifteenth of an inch in length, and is of a shining pitchy-black colour, with reddish legs and antennæ; it is not a common species.

FAMILY III.—*Silphidæ.*

Tarsi five-jointed; antennæ ten- or eleven- jointed, the last four or five forming a club; head and body more or less depressed, the former frequently narrowed behind into a neck.

This family includes both large and small species, the former being the largest of the *Necrophaga.* The genus *Necrophorus*, Fabr., includes the burying beetles. These are rather long black beetles, from half an inch to an inch long, generally more or less banded with red or orange, and often adorned with yellow hairs on the sides or under-surface of the body. The tip of the abdomen generally extends beyond the elytra. They generally hunt in pairs, sometimes more than one pair together; and if they find a dead bird or mouse, they hollow the earth below, and drag and stamp it till it is sunk below the level of the soil, when they cover it over, burying the females with it, when they lay their eggs in the carcass, and then make their way up to the surface.

Silpha, Linn., includes smaller and rounder species, not exceeding half an inch in length. They are generally of a black colour, often with raised ridges on the elytra; but in *S. Thoracica*, Linn., the thorax is reddish, and in *S. Quadripunctata*, Linn., the elytra are yellowish, with two black spots on each side. *S. Peltata*, Catesby, is a conspicuous North American species, with the head and thorax of a reddish-yellow (the latter with a large black spot in the middle), and black elytra. The species of *Silpha* are often to be seen running on paths, etc., in the day-time, and are almost omnivorous, feeding on dung, carrion, insects, and vegetable matter almost indiscriminately.

The smaller genera of the family, such as *Choleva*, Latr., and *Colon*, Herbst, include very active insects, not averaging more than one-sixth of an inch in length, and generally of dull colours; they feed on decaying animal and vegetable matter.

FAMILY IV.—*Trichopterygidæ*.

Tarsi three-jointed; antennæ eleven-jointed, clothed with long hairs, the three last joints thickened.

These small dark-coloured beetles are the smallest of all the *Coleoptera*, and many do not exceed one-twentieth or one-thirtieth of an inch in length. They are found in decaying vegetable matter, under bark, in ants' nests, etc.

FAMILY V.—*Histeridæ*.

Tarsi five-jointed; mandibles prominent; antennæ short, ending in a large three-jointed club; body square or oblong-quadrate, flattened or convex, very hard and polished; elytra truncated; legs contractile; front legs dentated or spined on the outside.

The *Histeridæ* are small black beetles, which play the part of general scavengers, feeding on dung, carrion, and decaying animal and vegetable matter generally. Several species are adorned with bright red spots or markings, and a few are metallic. They may often be seen running on paths in the day-time, like other beetles of similar habits, but some of the smaller species are met with under bark, and in ants' nests.

In general the *Histeridæ* are short and broad, and a few figures will give a sufficiently good idea of the appearance of the whole. Most of the species are black and shining. In *Hololepta Fossularis*, Say, the mandibles are unusually prominent; it is found under bark in the United States. *Platysoma Coarctatum*, Lec., is another North American species of a more elongated form than is usual in this family. The typical genus *Hister*, Linn., is of considerable extent, and is fairly well represented in all parts of the world. *Hister Bimaculatus*, Linn., a common European species about one-fifth of an inch in length, is black and shining, with reddish legs and antennæ, and six raised stripes on each elytron. At the outer angle at the tip of each is a rather large reddish-yellow spot

FAMILY VI.—*Nitidulidæ*.

Tarsi five-jointed, the first three generally enlarged, the fourth minute; body compact, oval; elytra sometimes covering the whole abdomen, and sometimes rather shorter; antennæ with a three-jointed club.

The *Nitidulidæ* are small vegetable-feeding beetles, which are generally found on flowers or flowering bushes, or else under bark; a few species, however, feed on dung. They are all of small size, the largest only reaching a quarter of an inch in length, and the majority are much smaller. They are much more varied in their colours than the *Histeridæ*.

The genus *Cercus*, Latr., is often remarkable for the structure of the antennæ; the first or two first joints are very large in the male, and the following ones small, but gradually increasing in size to the tip. *C. Pedicularius*, Linn., is a pale reddish beetle, about one-twelfth of an inch in length, which is not uncommon on flowers. *Carpophilus Hemipterus*, Linn., is a rather larger insect, which occurs under bark; it is of a dull black or brown colour, with yellowish-red legs and antennæ, and the elytra either wholly brownish-yellow or (more commonly) of the ground colour, with a broad yellow transverse band near the tip, and a yellow spot on each shoulder. In both these species the elytra are truncated.

Some species of this family are very prettily spotted; thus *Epuræa Decemguttata*, Fabr., which measures about one-sixth of an inch in length, is brown, with yellow spots; the legs are also yellow. *Nitidula Bipustulata*, Fabr., another well-known European species about the same size, is dark-brown, or black, with red legs, a red border to the collar, and a large red spot on each elytron. *Meligethes*, Steph., is one of the largest genera of this family, though the greater number of the species are European; *M. Rufipes*, Gyll., which measures about one-eighth of an inch in length, is dull black, with reddish legs and antennæ.

The genus *Rhizophagus*, Herbst, is very unlike the rest of the family, being long and narrow, almost of the shape of an *Elater*.

FAMILY VII.—*Trogositidæ*.

Tarsi five-jointed, not dilated, the first joint minute.

The insects of this family are closely allied to the *Nitidulidæ*, but are larger, and are generally met with under bark. They differ considerably in shape. *Thymalus Limbatus*, Fabr., is about a quarter of an inch in length, and is nearly round. It is of a dark bronzy colour, with a rather broad red rim extending round both the thorax and elytra. The typical genus *Trogosita*, Oliv., is about twice as long as broad; *T. Mauritanica*, Linn., the only

European species, is shining pitchy brown, with rather prominent mandibles, and measures about half an inch in length. The genus *Nemozoma*, Latr., differs considerably from the rest of the family in shape ; *Nemozoma Elongatum*, Linn., the typical European species, is very long and narrow. It is black, with reddish-yellow legs and antennæ, and measures about one-fifth of an inch in length. This beetle and its larva live in the galleries of wood-boring beetles, and devour their larvæ.

FAMILY VIII.—*Colydiidæ.*

Tarsi four-jointed ; front and middle coxæ globular ; hind coxæ transverse.

Includes a number of small species, most of which are found under bark, or among rotten wood and other decaying vegetable substances. The European species of the typical genus *Colydium*, Fabr., are rather long and narrow beetles, about a quarter of an inch in length, and are black, with reddish legs and antennæ.

FAMILY IX.—*Cucujidæ.*

Tarsi four-jointed ; antennæ long, hardly clubbed ; body long, parallel, and flattened.

A family of small extent, but more interesting than the last. Most of the species are exotic, and the majority of those whose habits are known live under bark, though some are found in ants' nests.

Passandra Brasiliensis, Chevr., is of a pitchy-black colour, and nearly an inch long. It somewhat resembles a *Scarites* in appearance, but is flatter, and its four-jointed tarsi would immediately distinguish it. The species of the typical genus *Cucujus*, Fabr., are bright scarlet insects about half an inch long ; about six or eight species are known, which are met with in Europe, North America, and the East Indies. Most of the *Cucujidæ*, however, are of a shining black colour.

FAMILY X.—*Cryptophagidæ.*

Tarsi five-jointed (hind tarsi four-jointed in the females of same species) ; antennæ with a well-marked club ; first segment of the abdomen very large.

The beetles of this family are all of small size, and are generally found among decaying vegetable matter, in fungi, under bark, among dead leaves, etc. *Cryptophagus Lycoperdi*, Herbst, a reddish-brown beetle, about one-eighth of an inch in length. is common in fungi, and may be regarded as a typical representative of the family; it is of an oval form, with the hinder part of the prothorax as broad as the abdomen. In the genus *Paramecosoma*, Curt., the thorax is convex. *Epistemus*, Erichs., includes a number of very small beetles which do not exceed one-twentieth or one-thirtieth of an inch in length. They are of a black colour, more or less varied with red or yellow. One of the most extensive genera of this family (*Atomaria*, Steph.) has received its name from the extreme minuteness of most of the species included in it.

Family XI.—*Lathridiidæ*.

Tarsi three-jointed (front tarsi occasionally four-jointed); front coxæ globular; antennæ clubbed; head and thorax generally narrower than the abdomen.

Includes small species found among decaying vegetable matter, under bark, or in ants' nests. The species differ considerably in shape. *Lathridius Exilis*, Mannerh., is a yellowish insect, with brown elytra; it measures about one-twenty-fifth of an inch in length. *Dasycerus Sulcatus*, Brongn., is a brown insect, much broader, and nearly twice the size of the last.

Family XII.—*Mycetophagidæ*.

Tarsi four-jointed (front tarsi in the males generally three-jointed); front coxæ globular, hind coxæ cylindrical; antennæ gradually thickened, or with two or three larger apical joints.

The beetles of this family are all small, and live in fungi. *Diplocœlus Fagi*, Chevr., is a somewhat aberrant species, included by Redtenbacher with the *Cryptophagidæ ;* it is a reddish-brown insect, about one-eighth of an inch long, and is met with under bark. *Mycetophagus Quadriguttatus*, Müll., is a more typical representative of this family. It is of a pitchy-brown or reddish-brown colour, and of the size of the last species, but is a much broader insect, and has a yellow spot on each shoulder, and another on each elytron, beyond the middle.

Family XIII.—*Thorictidæ*.

Tarsi five-jointed; coxæ transverse; antennæ short, thickened into a cylindrical club; scutellum very broad; elytra entirely covering the abdomen.

The few species of this family appear to be almost confined

to the Mediterranean district. One of the commonest species is *Thorictus Grandicollis*, Germ., a chestnut-brown beetle about one-twenty-fifth of an inch in length, which is met with in South Europe and Algeria. Of its habits nothing is known.

FAMILY XIV.—*Dermestidæ*.

Tarsi five-jointed; front coxæ conical, hind coxæ cylindrical; antennæ clubbed; one ocellus only present; larvæ bristly.

Though not a very extensive family, the *Dermestidæ* are well known by their destructive propensities. The majority of the species feed on dead animal matter, at least in the larva state, but many of the beetles frequent flowers. Many are very destructive to hides, furs, collections of birds and insects, etc. The Bacon Beetle (*Dermestes Lardarius*, Linn.) is about a quarter of an inch long, and is black, with a broad brownish-grey band on the elytra, marked with three black spots on each side. A brood of its larvæ will soon hollow out a ham, leaving nothing but the skin. *Attagenus Pellio*, Linn., is a blackish insect, rather smaller than the last, with reddish-brown legs and antennæ, which is destructive to furs. Its larva has a curious bushy tail. *Anthrenus Musæorum*, Linn., is equally destructive, but much smaller, not exceeding one-twelfth of an inch in length; it is brown, with the base of the antennæ and the tibiæ and tarsi reddish; the elytra are marked with three waved yellowish-grey bands.

FAMILY XV.—*Byrrhidæ*.

Tarsi five-jointed; all the coxæ transverse; antennæ gradually thickened, or with several of the terminal joints large; body round or oval; antennæ and legs generally contractile.

Most of the species of this family are found in grassy places, under stones. *Byrrhus Pilula*, Linn., is not an uncommon brown species; it measures about one-third of an inch in length.

FAMILY XVI.—*Parnidæ*.

Tarsi five-jointed; claws and terminal joint very large; antennæ filiform, or gradually thickened, sometimes very short; body more or less completely clothed with water-proof hair; habits semi-aquatic.

These are beetles of sluggish habits, generally found in or close to water, under stones, and among the stems of water-plants. *Potamophilus Acuminatus*, Germ., a dark-brown insect, rather more

than a quarter of an inch long, and clothed with silvery hairs on
the under surface, may be taken as an example of the family.
Elmis Æneus, Müll., is a bronzy-black species, about one-twelfth of
an inch in length, with reddish antennæ.

FAMILY XVII.—*Heteroceridæ*.

Tarsi four-jointed; front tibiæ enlarged, spiny, and serrated;
antennæ short, the two first joints large and triangular; body
oval, clothed with fine silky pubescence.

The species of this family are semi-aquatic, and live gregariously
in the mud by the side of ponds. *Heterocerus Marginatus*, Fabr., is
a brown species, about one-twelfth of an inch in length.

SECTION V.—LAMELLICORNIA.

Antennæ short, nine- or ten- jointed, and terminated by a large
abrupt three-jointed lamellated or pectinated club; tarsi five-
jointed, outside of front tarsi always serrated; habits herbivorous.

Many large and handsome beetles, both British and foreign,
belong to this section, which includes the Stag Beetles, Chafers, etc.

FAMILY I.—*Lucanidæ*.

Antennæ angulated, ten-jointed, with a large pectinate club;
mandibles (except in the genus *Passalus* and its allies) very large,
especially in the males.

This family includes the Stag Beetles, the type of which is
Lucanus Cervus, Linn. It is a blackish insect, with brown wing-
cases, and the males vary very much both in size and in the
development of their mandibles. The beetles measure from one to
more than two inches in length, and the large specimens exceed
any other British beetle in size. In the female the mandibles are
always small. The Stag Beetle may often be found in woods,
resting on or near the roots of trees. The larva is a large fleshy
grub, which feeds on the wood of trees; and some writers think
that this was the Cossus, which the Romans regarded as a delicacy,
and used to fatten with flour. The Roman Cossus may, however,
have been the larva of *Oryctes Nasicornis*. It is almost certain that
it was a large wood-feeding beetle, and not the larva of the Goat Moth
(*Xyleutes Cossus*), although Linné applied the name to the latter. The
beetle feeds on the sap of trees, etc., and is said to saw off the ends

of twigs with its jaws by whirling itself round and round upon the wing.

Many of the foreign *Lucanidæ* allied to *Lucanus Cervus* are black or brown; but in others, as in *Odontolabis Cuvera*, Hope, the sides of the elytra are broadly bordered with yellowish tawny. Other exotic species are of bright colours, and sometimes of extraordinary shapes. One of the most beautiful is *Chiasognathus Grantii*, Steph., a golden-green beetle found in Chili. *Lamprima*, Latr., is a genus of moderate-sized Australian species, generally of a metallic green or bronzy colour, with short projecting parallel mandibles. *Pholidotus*, Macl., includes two South American species with large diverging mandibles. *Dorcus*, Macl., is remarkable for the enormous size of the head and thorax; most of the species are black, and have a general resemblance to *Lucanus*. *D. Titanus*, Boisd., is a native of Java and the Philippines.

Passalus, Fabr., and its allies form a very distinct section of the *Lucanidæ*, with long and rather flattened bodies, and without large and prominent mandibles. They are generally of a black or brown colour, and are all very similar in general appearance; they measure from half an inch to two inches in length. All the species are extra-European, and by far the greater number are natives of the East Indies or South and Central America; *Paxillus Pentaphyllus*, Beauv., is a North American species.

FAMILY II.—*Scarabæidæ*.

Antennæ eight- to ten- jointed, not angulated, and terminated by a large lamellated club, generally composed of three plates; mandibles seldom much developed. This extensive group is divided into several sub-families, the most important of which it will be desirable to treat separately.

SUB-FAMILY I.—*Scarabæinæ*.

Antennæ eight- or nine- jointed; club three-jointed; clypeus covering the mouth, and projecting more or less above the eyes; middle coxæ widely separated.

The true *Scarabæinæ* are large or middle-sized beetles, easily recognised by the broad flat rim of the head, which is often serrated or horny. The typical genus *Scarabæus*, Linn., which includes the Egyptian Sacred Beetle (*Scarabæus Sacer*, Linn.), contains many black species, found in South Europe, Africa, and the East Indies. The beetles of this family feed on dung, and are often seen rolling balls of it along the ground, which they afterwards bury as a nidus for their progeny. *S. Sacer* is found all round the Mediterranean; and several allied species are found in the deserts, where they are said to contribute in no small degree to the gradual improvement of the soil by the zeal with which they bury every particle of camel's dung as soon as it is dropped. *S. Sacer* is black, oval, with a broad, flat, dentated head, and is nearly an inch long. Its nearest ally among our British species is *Copris Lunaris*, Linn., a black species, about three-quarters of an inch in length, with a broad flat head, armed with a long horn in the middle in the male. Some of the exotic species are of great size and singular shapes. *Heliocopris Gigas*, Linn., is a very large, black, heavy-looking beetle, found in all parts of Africa and the East Indies, with two horns on the top of the head in the male, projections at the front angles of the thorax, and a very thick projection directed forwards from the middle of its upper portion, which is slightly bidentate at the tip. Some exotic genera of this sub-family are of brighter colours than its European and North African representatives. In the South American genus *Phanæus*, Macl., the beetles are varied with green or purple, and furnished with a horn on the head about half an inch long. These beetles are very thick and heavy-looking, and are nearly an inch long, with strongly striated elytra.

SUB-FAMILY II.—*Aphodiinæ.*

Antennæ nine-jointed; club composed of three lamellæ; clypeus covering the mouth; scutellum distinct; middle coxæ near together.

The *Aphodiinæ* are small dung-beetles, resembling cockchafers in miniature, which may often be seen flying about over dusty roads. They are black, reddish, or yellowish, highly polished, and oval, and rarely exceed a quarter of an inch in length. *Ægialia Arenaria*, Fabr., is a blackish insect with undeveloped wings, often met with on sandhills near the sea.

SUB-FAMILY III.—*Orphninæ.*

Antennæ ten-jointed; club large, three-jointed; clypeus not covering the mouth; middle coxæ approximate, oblique.

A small group, confined, in Europe, to the south. The largest species is *Hybalus Dorcas*, Fabr., a black beetle, one-third of an inch in length.

Sub-Family IV.—*Geotrupinæ*.

Antennæ twelve-jointed; club three-jointed; legs strong, formed for digging; scutellum of moderate size; elytra covering the tip of the abdomen.

The species of the typical genus, *Geotrupes*, Latr., are black beetles, often measuring more than half an inch in length, which are commonly seen crawling on paths by day, and which fly in a heavy, blundering manner on summer evenings. They are generally of a purple colour beneath, and are often much infested with mites. The head and thorax are unarmed; but in the closely allied *Typhæus Vulgaris*, Leach, the male has a short horn on the top of the head, and three horns in front of the thorax, projecting forwards.

Sub-Family V.—*Troginæ*.

Antennæ nine- or ten- jointed; club three-jointed; abdomen composed of only five segments; eyes not divided by the rim of the head.

The species of *Trox*, Fabr., are dull black beetles about one-third of an inch in length, with striated elytra. When disturbed, they simulate death. They feed on dried animal remains, such as bones and hoofs, and prefer a sandy soil.

Sub-Family VI.—*Glaphyrinæ*.

Antennæ nine- or ten- jointed; club three-jointed; abdomen composed of six segments; scutellum moderately large; all the feet armed with two claws of equal size; elytra slightly divergent at the extremity.

A family of limited extent, most numerous in the Mediterranean district, and unrepresented in Northern Europe. They are moderate-sized insects, with rather soft integuments, more or less pubescent, and generally of a uniform colour. They live on flowers in spring, and are sometimes very abundant. *Glaphyrus Serratulæ*, Fabr., an Algerian species, may be regarded as typical. It is about half an inch long, and brilliant golden-green above; the under surface is more golden, and the legs are coppery.

Sub-Family VII.—*Melolonthinæ*.

Antennæ seven- to ten- jointed; club composed of three or more joints; abdomen with the tip pointed, not covered by the elytra.

This extensive group includes the Cockchafers, which are among the most destructive of insects in all their stages. The larvæ are whitish grubs, which live, doubled up, under ground, where they feed upon the roots of plants, and the beetles feed on plants in the open air. The Common Cockchafer (*Melolontha Vulgaris*, Linn.) is about an inch long, and is a reddish-brown insect, dusted with white in the male, and the under surface is banded with black and white. The thorax is black, with a slight greenish shade. The larva takes three years to arrive at maturity. *Rhizotrogus Solstitialis*, Linn., is a more local insect, but equally abundant where it occurs; it is of a lighter brown, about half an inch long, and the scutellum and under surface are very hairy. Both these insects feed on leaves, and fly round trees in swarms in the evening.

Most of the European species are blackish or brownish; one of the best known is *Polyphylla Fullo*, Linn., a local insect on the Continent, which has been reputed British. Its larva feeds on the roots of grass in sandy places, and the perfect insect feeds on the leaves of fir and other trees. The beetle, which measures nearly an inch and a quarter in length, is shining black or brown, with the thorax and elytra varied with white. Some of the smaller species of the genus *Hoplia*, Ill., which measure about one-third of an inch in length, are very pretty, being of a pale silvery blue or greenish colour.

Many of the foreign species much resemble the European, though sometimes considerably surpassing them in size. They are often marked with a whitish spot near the tip of each of the elytra, as in *Lepidiota Bimacolata*, Saund., a common East Indian species.

Sub-Family VIII.—*Euchirinæ.*

Antennæ ten-jointed; club three-jointed; front tibiæ of the males very long, and clothed with hair on the inside.

This group includes but two genera : *Euchirus*, Kirb., which inhabits the East Indies, and *Propomacrus*, Newm., from Turkey and Asia Minor. *Propomacrus Bimucronatus*, Pall., is a pitchy-black species, with dark-brown elytra, and the whole thorax is clothed with reddish-yellow silky hair. This insect measures nearly an inch and a half in length. *Euchirus Macleayi*, Hope, from Assam, is of a bronzy-green colour, with reddish spots, and measures two inches in length.

SUB-FAMILY IX.—*Rutelinæ.*

Antennæ nine- or ten- jointed, with a compact three-jointed club; front tibiæ narrow, with two or three teeth; scutellum variously developed.

The species of this family much resemble the *Melolonthinæ*, but are often more brightly coloured. Some are very destructive, such as the June Bug (*Phyllopertha Horticola*, Linn.), which sometimes swarms on various plants. It is rather less than half an inch long, and the elytra are of a yellowish brown; the head and thorax are of a brassy green or bluish green. A closely-allied species (*Anisoplia Austriaca*, Herbst) has committed fearful ravages within the last few years in Southern Russia. It is rather larger than the last species, and is black, with the elytra either entirely reddish or yellowish brown, or bordered with black, or wholly black. The prettiest European species of this sub-family is *Anomala Vitis*, Fabr., which is wholly green; it is rather more than half an inch in length.

Phyllopertha Viridis, Fabr., is one of the commonest beetles in China; it is wholly of a bright leaf green above, and coppery on the under surface; it is about three-quarters of an inch long. *Cotalpa Lanigera*, Linn., is a handsome North American species about an inch in length. It is of a bright yellow colour above, and pale green, clothed with long white hair, on the under surface.

One of the largest beetles of this family is *Heterosternus Buprestoides*, Dup. It is a native of Mexico, and is of a rich brown colour. The hind legs are unusually large, the femora being considerably thickened, and somewhat resemble those of a locust when seen sideways.

SUB-FAMILY X.—*Dynastinæ.*

Antennæ eight- to eleven- jointed; club oval, three-jointed; head and thorax nearly always more or less horned, especially in the males; elytra covering the tip of the abdomen.

This sub-family includes many of the largest and most strangely-shaped of the *Lamellicornia;* but, with few exceptions, the species all inhabit warm climates, and although a few are met with in South Europe, we have no representative of the group in Britain. The larvæ feed on the wood of trees, like those of the *Lucanidæ* and *Longicornia.*

Among the smaller beetles of this group, we may mention the

genus *Hexodon*, Oliv., which includes black species, much rounder
and broader than the more typical representatives of this sub-
family. Another genus comprising species of comparatively small
size is *Cyclocephala*, Latr. These beetles are all American, and
are generally of a reddish-brown or black colour.

The Rhinoceros Beetle (*Oryctes Rhinoceros*, Linn.) is a black
beetle, two inches in length, with a long recurved horn on the
upper part of the head, and a bidentate projection from the front
of the thorax. *O. Nasicornis*, Linn., is a smaller chestnut-brown
beetle, found in South Europe, which exhibits a similar structure.
The great cephalic and thoracic appendages of the *Dynastinæ* are
more developed in some individuals of the same species than in
others, and are always more or less rudimentary in the females.

The genus *Dynastes*, Kirb., includes the largest species, such as
D. Hercules, Linn., from the West Indies, and *D. Neptunus*,
Quens., from Colombia. They are black, and the elytra in the
former are olive-grey. There is an enormous projection from the
thorax, bending downwards, and almost meeting another long projection from the head, which curves upwards. These species,
with the appendages of the males, are nearly six inches long.
Some genera of this group have a long horn from the head, often
bidentate at the extremity, and others have a long or short projection from the thorax, either slender or thick, and this too is
generally more or less bifurcate; while in others there is a large
horn on the head, and instead of a central horn on the thorax,
there is one projecting forward from each of the front angles.
Most of the *Dynastinæ* are either black or brown.

SUB-FAMILY XI.—*Cetoniinæ*.

Head rather broad and flattened; antennæ ten-jointed, with a
compact three-jointed club; head rarely with conspicuous appendages; elytra not quite covering the abdomen.

This sub-family, which includes the Goliath Beetles and Rose
Chafers, comprises a large number of brilliantly-coloured species,
most of which are active on the wing, and are found on flowers in
the day-time. The larvæ feed on roots, or on rotten wood. Some
Goliath Beetles (the giants of the group, and among the bulkiest
of the *Coleoptera*) have black and white or red elytra, and the
thorax is longitudinally striped with black and white. The head
is white, and furnished with a short vertical horn on each side,
and with two larger projections at the extremity. The larger

species of *Goliathus*, Lam., measure upwards of four inches in length, and two in breadth. They are exclusively found in tropical Africa. Many smaller species allied to *Goliathus* inhabit the same country. The genus *Ceratorrhina*, Westw., includes green species, frequently spotted with white, several of which have short projections on the head, the most remarkable of which is perhaps *C. Harrisii*, Westw., a native of Guinea. *Heterorrhina*, Westw., is a genus allied to the last, which is represented by numerous species, both in Africa and in the East Indies. *Rhomborrhina*, Hope, is another East Indian genus. *R. Roylii*, Hope, which is found in Cashmere, is greenish black, with luteous spots on the elytra.

Our common English Rose Chafer (*Cetonia Aurata*, Linn.) is a beautiful metallic-green beetle, with white markings on the elytra, and brassy beneath. It is rather more than half an inch in length, and of a slightly oval shape. It is often found nestling in roses, whence its name, but it is just as fond of thistle, elder, and other flowers. This insect is said to be a specific against hydrophobia. *Oxythyrea Stictica*, Linn., a rather smaller insect, which is rare in England, is of a bronzy black, spotted with white. Among foreign species, *Cetonia Marginata*, Drury, a West African beetle, rather more than an inch long, is remarkable for its colour, being of a velvety black, with a broad orange border extending around the whole insect. *Clinteria Hilaris*, Burm., is a handsome black East Indian beetle, with yellow spots. *Inca Clathratus*, Oliv., is a large black white-speckled beetle, with white or pale yellow lines on the head and thorax, and three stout teeth on the outside of the front tibiæ. It is found in tropical America, and is remarkable for two long thick diverging prominences on the head.

Trichius, Fabr., the last genus which we propose to mention, is very downy, and the elytra are much wider than the thorax. *T. Fasciatus*, Fabr., is black, with reddish-yellow markings on the elytra; it is found on thistles, etc., like the species of *Cetonia*.

SECTION VI.—STERNOXI.

Tarsi five-jointed; antennæ very rarely clubbed, but generally pectinated or serrated; prosternum oval, dilated in front, and frequently produced into a point behind; body hard, generally long and narrow; elytra covering the abdomen; exclusively vegetable feeders.

FAMILY I.—*Buprestidæ.*

Hinder projection of the prosternum not fitting into a cavity in front of the mesosternum; hinder angles of the thorax obtuse or rectangular, never produced into spines; antennæ short, filiform, or serrated; eyes oval; body not fitted for leaping; larvæ wood-feeders.

The *Buprestidæ* are not remarkable for their peculiar forms or gigantic size, but for the brilliancy of their colours. They are poorly represented by a few small and insignificant species in Northern Europe, but are very numerous in tropical climates. They are quite harmless, and Linné has incorrectly applied the classical name of *Buprestis* to them, as that designated an insect which destroyed cattle if they swallowed it. This may possibly have been a species of *Mylabris.*

The genus *Sternocera*, Esch., includes large species peculiar to the East Indies and Africa; the thorax is deeply punctured. *S. Castanea*, Oliv., from West Africa, is black, with reddish depressed spots on the thorax, and chestnut-brown elytra.

Julodis, Esch., is remarkable for being covered with short tufts of bristles; the species are found in all parts of Africa and Western Asia; there are also a few in the extreme south of Europe, and in India. *J. Cirrosa*, Schönh., from the Cape, is black, with yellow tufts.

Some of the largest species of the *Buprestidæ* belong to the genus *Catoxantha*, Sol. *C. Bicolor*, Fabr., is of a brassy green, with a reddish spot on each elytron; in other species, as in *C. Opulenta*, Gory, this mark is white. *Chrysochroa*, Sol., is another very beautiful East Indian genus; all the species are of large size, and of a brilliant green; in some, as in *C. Ocellata*, Fabr., there is a large white spot surrounded with blackish on each elytron; in others, as in *C. Vittata*, Fabr., the beautiful green elytra are each traversed by a longitudinal stripe of fiery red.

Euchroma Gigantea, Linn., is a common Brazilian species about two inches in length; it is of a dull green, with reddish reflections. A figure of its enormous larva is here appended (796).

But the *Buprestidæ* are not all of brilliant colours; the species of *Capnodis*, Esch., a genus almost confined to South Europe and Western Asia, are of a dull black, and rugose; they measure about an inch in length.

The typical genus *Buprestis*, Linn., is most numerously represented in the Mediterranean district and in North America. *B. Octoguttata*, Linn., a South European species, is steel blue, with yellow spots.

Stigmodera, Esch., is a very large Australian genus, including a number of pretty species of small or moderate size, generally black, more or less varied or spotted with red.

Agrilus is another very extensive genus, which has representatives in all parts of the world. The species are about a quarter of an inch in length, and of a blue, green, or brown colour; one or two are found in England. The smallest of the *Buprestidæ* belong to the genus *Trachys*, Fabr., which is well represented in Europe, the East Indies, etc. The European species are black or brassy, and several do not exceed one-twelfth of an inch in length. The allied Brazilian genus *Brachys*, Sol., is of a more oval form than most of the family.

FAMILY II.—*Trixagidæ*.

Body cylindrical, not fitted for leaping; eyes round; antennæ inserted at the lower border of the eyes, filiform or clubbed, and received into cavities of the thorax.

The typical genus of this small family is *Trixagus*, Kug. (*Throscus*, Latr.), represented in Europe by a few brown or reddish species of very small size (the largest not exceeding the eighth of an inch in length), which are found among dead leaves, etc. Most of the species belonging to other genera are American.

FAMILY III.—*Eucnemidæ*.

Body cylindrical, not fitted for leaping; eyes round; antennæ received into cavities of the thorax, and generally pectinated; inserted on the upper part of the head; larvæ feeding on rotten wood.

Most of the *Eucnemidæ* are insects of small size and dull colours, and are generally found on flowers; few of the European species exceed one-third of an inch in length. The typical species is *Eucnemis Capucinus*, Linn., a black cylindrical species, with brown legs, and nearly a quarter of an inch long. Two foreign species may be noticed—*Fornax Madagascariensis*, Cast., a dark-brown beetle from Madagascar; and *Pterotarsus Tuberculatus*, Dalm., from Brazil, which is red, with black markings.

FAMILY IV.—*Elateridæ.*

Structure adapted for leaping; body more or less oval; projection behind the prosternum fitting into a cavity of the mesosternum; hinder angles of the thorax often produced into spines; eyes oval; antennæ generally serrated or pectinated; larvæ feeding either on the roots of plants or on rotten wood.

This important family includes the well-known Click Beetles, so called from their power of leaping up with a slight noise. Their larvæ are but too well known to farmers and gardeners as wire-worms, being long, slender, and exceedingly tough. To this family also belong the Fire-flies of the Tropics. Although less brilliant than the *Buprestidæ,* many of the *Elateridæ* are of considerable size and variegated colours, and they are far more numerous in cold climates than the former family.

The European species may easily be recognised by their peculiar shape; they are generally from a quarter to half an inch in length, and of uniform colours : black, bronzy, brown, greenish, or red. They frequent flowers, and several species are always abundant in corn-fields, their larvæ feeding on the roots of the corn. *Alaus Oculatus,* Linn., is a common North American species, about an inch and a half in length; it is black, with two white rings on the thorax, and longitudinal white lines on the elytra. *Chalcolepidius,* Esch., a genus confined to America, is remarkable for the great breadth of the hinder part of the thorax and the base of the elytra. *C. Eschscholtzii,* Chevr., is of a dull green colour, lined with black, and bordered with dull orange. *Semiotus,* Esch., another American genus, is long, slender, and pointed behind; the species are rather more than an inch in length, and of a reddish-brown colour. Nearly all the largest and handsomest species of this family are American; the luminous species belong to the genus *Pyrophorus,* Ill. One of the commonest West Indian and South American fire-flies is *P. Noctilucus,* Linn., which is dark brown, with two dull yellow spots at the back of the thorax. The two spots of light which it emits at the juncture of the thorax and abdomen, and which it can withdraw at pleasure, resemble a small flame of fire of a slightly greenish shade. Live fire-flies have been exhibited in London on several occasions lately.

SECTION VII.—MALACODERMATA.

Tarsi generally five-jointed; body more or less soft; prosternum not dilated or prolonged in front, and very rarely prolonged into a point behind; antennæ generally serrated or pectinated, and not received into thoracic cavities; abdomen with six or seven segments; habits generally more or less carnivorous.

FAMILY I.—*Cebrionidæ.*

Antennæ eleven-jointed, inserted near the eyes; pectinated or serrated, and longer than the head and thorax; prosternum produced behind, nearly as in the *Elateridæ.*

A small group, which is more numerously represented in the Mediterranean region than elsewhere. The species figured (*Cebrio Fuscus*, Fabr.) is a native of the Cape. The European species are found on plants in the neighbourhood of water, and the males are said sometimes to appear in swarms after a thunderstorm. *Cebrio Gigas*, Fabr., a well-known South European insect, is reddish-brown, and about an inch long.

FAMILY II.—*Rhipidoceridæ.*

Antennæ with eleven or more joints, inserted in front of and below the eyes, pectinated or flabellated in the males; prosternum not pointed behind; a large tuft of hairs between the claws of the tarsi.

A small family, entirely exotic, though one species (*Callirhipis Blanchei*, Chevr.) is found in Syria. *Rhipidocera Cyanea*, Cast., is a Brazilian species.

FAMILY III.—*Dascillidæ.*

Antennæ eleven-jointed, filiform or branched; prosternum hardly pointed behind; claws of the tarsi simple; elytra covering the abdomen; shape oblong or oval.

These beetles are met with on flowers, and their larvæ are also plant-feeders; some feed on water-plants, and others under bark. The most typical European species of this family is *Dascillus Cervinus*, Linn., which is pitchy black, often with yellowish-brown elytra, legs, and antennæ. It is clothed with very fine greyish hair, and is about half an inch in length. It is found on the flowers of Umbelliferæ in mountainous districts. Among the foreign species

may be noticed *Ptilodactyla Serricollis*, Say, a chestnut-brown North
American species, remarkable for its very long ramose antennæ.

FAMILY IV.—*Telephoridæ*.

Body soft, flattened; head not contracted behind, sometimes
visible, and sometimes entirely concealed by the thorax; antennæ
and mandibles various in structure; palpi thickest at the extremity,
the maxillary palpi generally longer than the labial; elytra soft,
sometimes obsolete in the female; habits carnivorous.

SUB-FAMILY I.—*Lycinæ*.

Head not concealed by the thorax; eyes small; antennæ close
together at the base; abdominal segments not phosphorescent.

The *Lycinæ* are an almost exclusively exotic group. The elytra
are often much widened behind, and they are generally black,
varied with red or yellow. The curious *Lycus Latissimus*, Linn., is
found at the Cape of Good Hope. Among the few European
species we may mention *Lygistopterus Sanguineus*, Linn., a red
flower-frequenting species with a black head. The other
European species of this family belong to the genus *Dictyoptera*,
Latr. They are all of a bright red colour, and measure from one-
fourth to one-third of an inch in length.

SUB-FAMILY II.—*Lampyrinæ*.

Head more or less concealed by the thorax; antennæ close
together at the base; eyes of the male very large; elytra often
wanting in the female; segments of the abdomen often phosphorescent.

To this sub-family belong the Glow-worms of the south of
England and the Fire-flies of the continent of Europe. In the
common glow-worm, the male, which is but slightly luminous, is a
long, narrow, greyish-brown insect, nearly half an inch in length; the
female, which is generally found resting on grass in the evening,
is entirely wingless; the larvæ are said to feed on snails. The male
is hardly luminous, but the males of the nearly-allied but rather
smaller *L. Splendidula*, Linn., may be seen in the evening in most
parts of the Continent floating about like little sparks. Those of
Luciola Italica, Linn., a dark brown species about a quarter of an inch
long, with a reddish thorax, and reddish-yellow legs, are common
everywhere south of the Alps, and shine with a brighter light,
and are much more active on the wing, than the northern species.

The foreign *Lampyrinæ* much resemble the European species, though some far surpass them in size : they are usually of a black or yellow colour. *Lucernula Savignyi*, Kirb., is a large Brazilian species.

Sub-Family III.—*Telephorinæ*.

Body flattened ; head not contracted behind, nor covered by the thorax; eyes rather large ; antennæ separated at the base; segments of the abdomen seldom or never phosphorescent.

The genus *Telephorus*, Schäff., and its allies include the long and narrow beetles, generally of a black or yellow colour, and with soft elytra, which are common in leaves and flowers in summer, and feed voraciously on other insects. As an example we may mention *T. Abdominalis*, Fabr., which is black in the male, with bluish elytra, and the mouth and abdomen reddish yellow, while the female has the front of the head, the collar, prothorax, and front femora also of a reddish-yellow colour. One of the commonest species is *T. Livida*, Linn., which is reddish yellow, with ochre-yellow elytra, and the eyes and pectus black.   This is of the same size as the last species ; but others, as *Malthinus Biguttatus*, Linn., are smaller and more slender, with longer antennæ. The species referred to is pitchy black, with the base of the antennæ, the front femora, and the tips of the elytra yellow ; it is about an eighth of an inch in length.

Sub-Family IV.—*Drilinæ*.

Antennæ dentated or flabellated, inserted in front of the eyes ; female apterous ; habits carnivorous.

The commonest species of this small family is *Drilus Flavescens*, Linn., which much resembles a glow-worm, but is only half the size, and not luminous. The male is black, with yellowish elytra. The larva feeds on snails, and forms its pupa in the shells.

Sub-Family V.—*Malachiinæ*.

Antennæ eleven-jointed (occasionally ten-jointed), filiform, serrated, or pectinated ; palpi short, filiform ; body long and narrow, head only overlapped by the prothorax at the base.

The species of this family are found in flowers in the day-time. They are not so rapacious as the *Telephoridæ*, for although they feed on small insects, yet they also feed on plants. Several of the European species are of a black colour, often with a red or

yellow band at the base and tip of the elytra ; or the thorax may
be of one of these colours. *Malachius Insignis,* Buq., is an Algerian
species of a green colour, tipped with yellow in the male. *Chalcas,*
Dej., is a South American genus remarkable for its very broad
oval shape, which resembles that of some of the *Lycinæ,* and
differs much from any European species of *Malachiidæ.* The
species frequent potato and other solanaceous plants. *C. Tra-
beatus,* Fairm., is black, with a large red blotch on each side at the
base of the elytra, and another at the tip.

FAMILY V.—*Cleridæ.*

Body cylindrical, narrowed in front ; antennæ rather short,
gradually thickened, the last three joints forming a club ; head not
contracted behind ; abdomen soft, covered by the elytra ; tarsi
variable ; habits carnivorous.

A rather extensive family. Many of the species which it
includes are of bright colours, but they are often sluggish insects.
Clerus Formicarius, Linn., is an insect which slightly resembles an
ant in shape and general appearance, whence its name. It is
about one-third of an inch long, and is red, with the head, the
front of the collar, the femora and tibiæ, and the elytra, black.
The elytra are red at the base, beyond which is a slender angulated
whitish band, and there is another towards the tip. *Trichodes,*
Herbst, includes several larger species, with four-jointed tarsi. They
are half an inch long, and of a red colour, banded with steel blue,
and extremely pubescent. The larvæ have been met with in the
nests of various species of bees, but their economy is not yet
clearly understood. Among the more interesting foreign species
of this family we may mention *Evenus Filiformis,* Cast., from
Madagascar, which is reddish brown, with yellow elytra, marked
with a transverse black spot in the middle ; and *Pelonium Trifas-
ciatum,* Cast., from Brazil, which is black, also with yellow elytra,
but marked with three black stripes.

SECTION VIII.—TEREDILIA.

Tarsi generally five-jointed ; body hard ; prosternum neither
dilated in front nor produced into a point behind ; antennæ generally filiform ; abdomen nearly always composed of five segments.

This section, though not very extensive, includes several
insects which are exceedingly injurious, and which we have now
to consider. Most of the larvæ are wood-borers.

D

FAMILY I.—*Lymexylonidæ.*

Tarsi five-jointed; body long and slender; head contracted behind; mandibles dentated.

The most important species of this small family is *Lymexylon Navale*, Linn. The male is black, with the basal half of the elytra along the suture, and the abdomen and legs yellow; the female is yellowish, with the head and the border and tips of the elytra black. It measures from a quarter to half an inch in length. This insect feeds on oak, and though fortunately rare in England, has sometimes committed great ravages among the timber intended for shipbuilding in several parts of the Continent.

FAMILY II.—*Ptinidæ.*

Body oval or cylindrical, with the ends rounded off; head not contracted behind, partly covered by the prothorax; antennæ filiform and tapering, or pectinated, sometimes terminating in three large apical segments; tarsi generally five-jointed.

These are small beetles, some of which feed on wood, while others are met with in houses, not only attacking wood, but also dried animal products, such as leather, wool, preserved objects of natural history, etc. A few of the more interesting species may here be mentioned.

Ptinus Fur, Linn., is a small beetle about an eighth of an inch in length. It varies from red to pitchy brown, with red legs and antennæ, and the elytra are marked with two more or less distinct transverse stripes of white hairs. *Anobium Domesticum*, Fourcr., is an insect not exceeding one-sixth of an inch in length. It is of a pitchy-brown colour, and feeds on old wood. It is often common in the woodwork and furniture of old houses, and is popularly known as the Death-Watch, from its habit of producing a slight ticking noise by striking its head against the wood as a call to its mate. The name of *A. Tessellatum*, Fabr., has frequently been applied to this insect, but *A. Tessellatum* is a brown species, measuring about a quarter of an inch in length, and although it likewise feeds on old wood, it is seldom or never found in houses.

FAMILY III.—*Bostrychidæ.*

Body cylindrical; head generally covered by the prothorax; antennæ nine- to eleven- jointed, inserted at the front edge of the eyes, and the three last joints forming a club; tarsi generally five-jointed, the first small, and the second and third large; abdomen with five segments, the first very large.

A small family of wood-feeding beetles, which, like many other wood-feeding insects, vary considerably in size within the same species. Thus, *Bostrichus Capucinus*, Linn., varies from less than a quarter of an inch to more than half an inch in length. It is black, with the very coarsely punctured elytra and the abdomen red. The genus *Psoa*, Herbst, is remarkable for the ramose antennæ of the male. *P. Blanchardii*, Luc., is an Algerian species, about half an inch long; it is of a shining black colour, with a red dot on each side of the thorax; there are also reddish bands on the elytra near the suture, and the segments of the abdomen are bordered with red below. The tarsi are apparently only four-jointed.

FAMILY IV.—*Cioidæ*.

Body cylindrical; head short, covered by the prothorax, and retractile; antennæ eight- to eleven- jointed, inserted at the front edge of the eyes, and terminated by a three- (or two-) jointed club; legs short, tarsi four- (rarely five-) jointed, the first small, but distinct, and the last long; abdomen with five segments, the last longest.

These are small beetles, of a brown or reddish-brown colour, which are usually found in fungi, sometimes in great abundance. *Orophius Mandibularis*, Gyll., is of a chestnut colour, and varies from one-fifteenth to one-tenth of an inch in length. It frequents fungi growing on trees. *Cis Boleti*, Linn., is a much commoner species about the same size, which varies from black to yellowish brown.

SECTION IX.—HETEROMERA.

Body more or less oval, sometimes nearly round; four front tarsi five-jointed, hind tarsi four-jointed; antennæ moniliform, or bead-like.

The *Heteromera* are an extensive group, and many of the species much resemble *Carabidæ* in shape and general appearance, but they may always be easily distinguished by the peculiar structure of the legs and antennæ.

FAMILY I.—*Trictenotomidæ.*

Aspect of the *Prionidæ:* eyes transverse, slightly emarginate; antennæ of moderate length, filiform, the three apical joints serrated on the inside; mandibles large, broad, and dentated.

This family only includes a few large species from the East Indies, which resemble *Prionidæ* and *Lucanidæ* rather than any other *Heteromera.* The type is *Trictenotoma Childreni*, Gray, from No thern India. It is more than two inches in length, and is covered with a yellowish-grey down; the antennæ, mandibles, legs, and two raised spots on the mesothorax, are black.

FAMILY II.—*Tenebrionidæ.*

Head not narrowed behind; antennæ moniliform, of nearly equal thickness throughout, or slightly enlarged towards the tip, inserted on the sides of the head, third joint longest; wings frequently absent, and elytra often soldered together; middle and hind legs near together; claws simple.

The beetles contained in this family are generally heavy-looking, with broad elytra, and are of a black or grey colour. They are of moderate size, and are frequently strongly ridged and punctured. The abdomen is often more or less pointed. Many of the species prefer sandy places, and although the family is more or less numerously represented in all parts of the world, the species are particularly numerous in Africa. A few only of the larger and more typical genera can here be mentioned. *Adesmia*, Fisch., is remarkable for its long slender legs. *A. Candidipennis*, Brême, is found on the Congo. *Zopherus*, Cast., is an American genus with sh rt, thick antennæ, and rugose elytra. *Acis*, Herbst, is a genus which includes a number of comparatively small species from South Europe and North Africa. *A. Goryi*, Sol., is found in the latter locality. *Blaps*, Fabr., is one of the most typical genera of this family; the species are all very similar, and are abundant in the Old World. Two species are common in Britain, where they are known as Cellar Beetles. They are black wingless insects, with the abdomen pointed, and are found in dark places. *Pimelia*, Fabr., is another large genus, very numerously represented on the coasts of the Mediterranean, but not British; it is of a much rounder form than *Blaps*. *P. Punctata*, Sol., is a Spanish insect. *Moluris*, Latr., includes a few handsome shining black species of considerable size from the Cape of Good Hope. The genus

Sepidium, Fabr., is remarkable for the elytra being studded all
over with short blunt spines; *S. Tomentosum*, Erichs., is a native
of Algeria. *Hopatrum*, Fabr., and its allies are small oblong
winged beetles. *H. Elongatum*, Guér., is an East Indian species.

Several small species, of more varied colours than *Blaps* and
its allies, are met with among fungi or under bark. One of the
commonest of these is *Diaperis Boleti*, Linn., an oval insect about a
quarter of an inch long, with short thick antennæ. It is shining
black, with a broad dentated yellow band at the base of the elytra,
a narrower one beyond the middle, and the tips yellow.

One of the most remarkable genera of the *Heteromera* is
Cossyphus, Oliv. The whole insect is very flat, and the thorax and
elytra are expanded into a broad rim, covering even the head.
Several species are found in South Europe, Africa, and the East
Indies. *C. Depressus*, Fabr., an East Indian insect, is of a yellowish
brown, and about half an inch long. Some species are said to
hide under stones and clods, concealing themselves with a covering
of earth, so that they cannot be seen until they move.

Tenebrio Molitor, Linn., which may be regarded as the type of the
Tenebrionidæ, is a winged dark-brown beetle about half an inch long,
with striated elytra. It is common in houses, especially in bakehouses, where its reddish-yellow larva feeds on flour, etc. This
larva is called the Meal-worm, and is much used to feed caged birds.

The species of *Helops*, Fabr., are shining black or brown beetles,
about half an inch long, which much resemble the *Carabidæ* in
shape. This genus has representatives in all parts of the world,
but the species are most numerous in the Mediterranean district;
a few, however, inhabit Northern Europe.

Strongylium, Kirb., is an extensive genus, rather longer and more
slender than any of the foregoing, and with long and slender legs
and antennæ. It has representatives in most parts of the world,
but by far the greater number of known species are American.
S. Rufipes, Kirb., is blue, with two yellow bands on the elytra, one
at the base, and one across the middle; the legs and antennæ are
reddish.

In the species of *Cistela*, Geoffr., the antennæ are often more or
less serrated. Some are shining black insects, with reddish legs,
and measure about a quarter of an inch in length. *C. Serrata*,
Chevr., an Hungarian insect, and *Cteniopus Sulphureus*, Linn., not an
uncommon European species, are yellow. The species of *Cistela* and
its allies frequent flowers, and their larvæ feed on rotten wood.

FAMILY III.—*Nilionidæ*.

Head contracted behind; antennæ eleven-jointed, moniliform; apical joint ovoid; thorax short and broad; elytra broad, convex, and covering the body.

These are yellowish beetles of moderate size, which resemble large *Coccinellidæ* in appearance. They feed on *Boleti* growing on the trunks of trees, and simulate death when disturbed. They are almost exclusively confined to tropical America.

This and the following families of *Heteromera* are distinguished from the *Tenebrionidæ* by the head being contracted behind, a character which it will be unnecessary to notice further.

FAMILY IV.—*Pythidæ*.

Antennæ eleven-jointed, filiform, generally thickened towards the tips; claws simple; head triangular, or produced into a beak, and overlapped by the thorax as far as the eyes.

Another small family, the species of which are usually met with under the bark of dead trees. *Pytho Depressus*, Linn., is rather scarce everywhere, though found in most parts of Europe. It is about half an inch long, and is of a shining black colour, with red antennæ and legs; the elytra are blue or reddish, sometimes with blue tips; and in specimens with reddish elytra the thorax also is sometimes of the same colour.

FAMILY V.—*Melandryidæ*.

Antennæ filiform, ten- or eleven- jointed, and generally somewhat thickened at the tips; claws simple; thorax generally rounded at the sides; maxillary palpi very large, and serrated on the inside.

The *Melandryidæ* generally live on rotten wood or on tree fungi. It will suffice to mention one or two representative species. *Serropalpus Striatus*, Fabr., is rather long and narrow, and is found in most parts of Europe. It is brown, and about half an inch long; it feeds on pine and fir. *Eustrophus Dermestoides*, Fabr., on the other hand, another common brown species which is found in the wood of the oak and beech, is of a short oval form, and about a quarter of an inch long. The species of *Melandrya*, Fabr., are black or dark blue, and about twice as long as broad.

FAMILY VI.—*Lagriidæ.*

Antennæ eleven-jointed, filiform, with short joints; claws simple; head round; body rather long; thorax cylindrical, narrower than the head and elytra; elytra widened towards the tip.

The type of this family is *Lagria Hirta*, Linn., a black hairy insect, about half an inch long, with rather soft yellowish-brown elytra; it is not uncommon on flowers.

FAMILY VII.—*Anthicidæ.*

Antennæ filiform, twelve-jointed, more or less thickened at the tips; claws simple; head broader than the thorax, which is strongly convex, heart-shaped, and narrowed behind, and is generally furnished with a horn in front; elytra convex, cylindrical, broader than the thorax.

The *Anthicidæ* are more numerous than the *Lagriidæ*, and are represented in Europe by several genera, which are of a black, red, or yellow colour, and are met with in meadows, or under bark. *Anthicus Affinis*, Laf., from South Europe, is of a brown colour, with a pale band on the elytra, and about one-tenth of an inch long.

FAMILY VIII.—*Pyrochroidæ.*

Antennæ eleven-jointed, serrated or pectinated; claws simple; body long, compressed; thorax narrower than the head, almost round, but rather broader than long; elytra wider behind.

The genus *Pyrochroa*, Geoffr., typical of this small group, includes several European species of a bright red colour, and measuring from a quarter to three-quarters of an inch in length. The larvæ live under dead bark, and the beetles are met with either there or resting on the trunks of trees.

FAMILY IX.—*Mordellidæ.*

Antennæ eleven-jointed, filiform, slightly thickened towards the tip, or serrated on the inside; claws simple or toothed; thorax narrowed in front, but as broad as the elytra behind; elytra narrowed behind, and not extending to the tip of the abdomen.

These are small active beetles, found on flowers or among rotten wood. They possess the power of leaping. The European species are generally of a black colour. *Mordella Picta*, Chevr.,

from Cayenne, is black, with pale yellow transverse markings.
Anaspis Frontalis, Linn., which represents another section of the
family, is a common European species about one-eighth of an inch
in length. It is black, with the front of the head, the base of the
antennæ, and the front legs, yellow or brown.

FAMILY X.—*Rhipidophoridæ.*

Antennæ eleven-jointed, pectinated, or in the females serrated;
filiform only in perfectly apterous females; thorax as wide as the
elytra at their base; elytra sometimes shorter than the body;
habits parasitic.

One of the best-known species is *Metœcus Paradoxus*, Linn. It
is about one-third of an inch in length, and is black, with yellow
elytra in the male; the sides of the thorax and the abdomen are
red. The larva lives parasitically in the nest of the common wasp.
In the genus *Rhipidophorus*, Bon., the elytra are as short as in the
Staphylinidæ, but the large wings are not covered by them. *R.
Subdipterus*, Bon., a South European species, is shining black,
with grey hair; the antennæ are reddish in the male, the elytra
are ochre-yellow; the hind wings transparent, with a brown spot
in the middle; and the abdomen and legs are reddish, the former
being tipped with black in the female. *R. Fasciatus*, Say, from the
Southern United States, is black, with yellowish elytra.

FAMILY XI.— *Stylopidæ.*

Elytra very short; hind wings very broad, and folded longitudinally; tarsi with from two to four joints; eyes large; antennæ
bifurcate or ramose; metathorax very large; female apterous;
habits parasitic.

This peculiar family includes only a few species, which were
formerly included in a separate Order (*Strepsiptera*) but are now
regarded as *Coleoptera*. They are small black insects, not more
than a quarter of an inch long. They are parasitic on various
species of wasps and bees, a situation which the female never quits,
though the head of the female, or of the male pupa, may frequently
be seen protruding from between the segments of the abdomen of
the host. The commonest species in England is *Stylops Melitta*,
Kirb., which infests various species of *Andrena*. The males are
rarely observed on the wing, owing to their small size and the
rapidity of their movements.

FAMILY XII.—*Cantharidæ.*

Antennæ nine- to eleven- jointed, filiform, slightly thickened at
the tips; claws bifid; elytra soft, long, and narrow, or else much
shorter than the abdomen; larvæ often parasitic.

The present family, though not very extensive, is one of the
most interesting of the *Heteromera.* The first genus included in
it is *Meloë,* Linn., which includes the well-known Oil Beetles.
These are bluish-black beetles, measuring from half an inch to an
inch and a quarter in length. They have very short, soft elytra,
and no wings, and the abdomen is large, soft, and bloated.
They are sluggish insects, found among grass and low plants in
spring. Their transformations are very remarkable, and resemble those of *Sitaris.* The eggs are laid on or in the ground,
and when the young larvæ hatch, they spread over the plants
in the neighbourhood, and attach themselves to the bodies of
the insects which visit them. Those which are sufficiently
fortunate to be carried into a hive in this Sindbadlike fashion
begin by devouring the egg which they find in one of the cells.
Then they change into a second form of larva, and feed on the
pollen intended for the larva of the bee, and continue their
changes. But the life-history of *Sitaris Muralis,* Forst., is better
known. This is a black insect, not apterous, with long, soft,
yellowish elytra; it is about half an inch in length. The female
lays her eggs at the entrance of the nests of bees of the genus
Anthophora, Fabr., which burrow in walls, and a month afterwards,
shining greenish-black horny larvæ, with long antennæ and legs,
hatch. They remain motionless till spring, when the bees begin
to fly about, when they attach themselves to the male bees, which
appear before the females; and when the bees pair, they transfer
themselves to the latter. When the bee lays an egg, one of the
larvæ drops down upon it, and proceeds to devour the contents.
When it has finished, in some days' time, it changes into the
second larva, which is a soft white bloated maggot, destitute of
eyes or antennæ, and with very short legs. This feeds for a
month on honey, when it turns into a kind of false pupa, which is
at first soft, but soon becomes hard and yellowish; and in this
state it passes the winter. Next spring a third form of larva
emerges, very similar to the second, which takes no food, but soon
changes into the real pupa, from which the perfect insect emerges
in about a month.

Horia Maculata, Swed., is a reddish beetle, spotted with black, and about an inch long; its head is very large, and almost square; it is found in South America. *Mylabris*, Fabr., is a large genus found throughout the warmer parts of the Old World. Most of the species are black, with large yellow or red spots or bands, and are sometimes used for vesicatory purposes. The commonest species in Europe is *M. Floralis*, Pall., which is found as far north as Southern Germany; it is black, with yellow markings, and frequents flowers.

Meloetyphlus Fuscutus, Waterh., was kindly pointed out to me by my friend and colleague Mr. C. O. Waterhouse as a very remarkable insect. It occurs in Peru, and although nothing is known of its habits, it is in all probability parasitic upon ants; for it is of a dark reddish-brown colour, and almost exactly resembles the great ants of the genus *Eciton* in size and shape.

Cantharis Vesicatoria, Linn., the Blister Beetle, is too well known to need a long description. It is of a most brilliant green colour, and about half an inch in length. It is not very common in England, but is abundant in many parts of the Continent on various trees, more especially on the ash; and I have seen no beetle which presents so brilliant an appearance as this when the sun is shining on a tree upon which several are feeding.

The genus *Nematognatha*, Ill., is remarkable for having a long proboscis almost like that of a butterfly. It is widely distributed, and the South European species are black below, and yellow, more or less marked with black, above.

FAMILY XIII.—*Œdemeridæ*.

Antennæ eleven- or twelve- jointed, long and filiform, the middle joints nearly as broad as long; claws simple; body long, rather soft; front coxæ very long, intermediate coxæ contiguous.

The *Œdemeridæ* are small delicate insects which frequent flowers, and have a slight resemblance to Longicorns. The larvæ feed on dead wood or flower stalks. As an example, we may mention *Œdemera Podagrioides*, Linn., which is nearly half an inch in length, and is black, clothed with silvery hair. The base of the antennæ and the elytra are yellow, and the thorax and under-surface of the abdomen are also yellow in the female; the legs are of a reddish yellow.

SECTION X.—Xylophaga.

Tarsi four-jointed; body oblong; antennæ with the basal joint long, and more or less clubbed at the tip; head not produced into a true rostrum, and partly covered by the thorax.

FAMILY.—*Scolytidæ.*

This family, the only one in this section, includes the small brown or black beetles which the Germans appropriately name Bark Beetles. They are generally abundant and gregarious, and the larvæ form long galleries in the bark or wood of trees. Their numbers make them far more injurious than the larger insects which live on wood, and in some seasons whole avenues of elms have been destroyed by *Scolytus Destructor*, Oliv., which may be considered the type of the family. It is a black beetle about one-sixth of an inch long, with brown elytra, and reddish legs and antennæ. Two other species may be noticed for the peculiarity in their antennæ. The first is *Platypus Cylindrus*, Fabr., a long brown beetle, with reddish legs and antennæ, about one-sixth of an inch long. The antennæ are very short, and terminate in an enormous club. It lives in old dry oak wood. *Phlœotribus Oleæ*, Fabr., is a cylindrical black species, one-twelfth of an inch long, with reddish legs and ramose antennæ. It is very destructive to the olive in the south of Europe.

SECTION XI.—Rhynchophora.

Body cylindrical, rarely round; tarsi four-jointed; head produced into a rostrum, on the sides of which the antennæ are placed; antennæ six- to ten- jointed, often angulated beyond the long scape; elytra hard, horny, and covering the abdomen.

The Weevils are a very extensive and easily recognised group, though they vary considerably in structure and appearance. The elytra are frequently of almost stony hardness, perhaps harder than in any other insects. The majority of the species, though considerably varied, are not very remarkable for their size or colour, the Diamond Beetle and its allies excepted.

FAMILY I.—*Curculionidæ.*

Rostrum straight, with the antennæ on the sides, and the small mouth at the extremity; antennæ generally angulated, and often clubbed at the tip.

In so large a family we cannot do more than enumerate a few representative genera and species, as in the case of the *Carabidæ*. *Brachyderes Incanus*, Linn., is a moderately broad and oval insect, with a short broad rostrum, and the antennæ inserted near the extremity. It is about one-third of an inch in length, and is met with on various trees in summer, but passes the winter under moss.

Naupactus Longimanus, Fabr., is the type of an allied South American genus, very numerous in species. It is an oval black beetle, clothed with silvery-green scales; the thorax and elytra are streaked and spotted with brighter green. It measures half an inch in length.

Sitones Lineatus, Linn., is a black species, one-sixth of an inch in length, with a short rostrum, and three pale longitudinal stripes on the thorax. The legs and antennæ are rust colour, and the whole insect is covered with scales, which are brown, grey, greenish, or coppery in different individuals. It is very common on clover, and other plants, attacking them as soon as they begin to sprout in spring.

Several European species are covered with green scales, in a similar manner to the exotic Diamond Beetles, though they are not so brilliant. One of these is *Chlorophanus Viridis*, Linn., a green-scaled species, in which the sides of the thorax and the elytra are yellow. It is found on shrubs, and is about one-third of an inch in length.

The Brazilian genus *Cyphus*, Germ., includes species of considerable size, which are of a brilliant blue or green colour; one or two are whitish. *C. Illustris*, Guér., is pale blue, with black markings.

Otiorhynchus, Germ., includes a number of dull black species, measuring about a quarter or half an inch in length, which feed on trees and bushes. *O. Ligustici*, Linn., is injurious to the vine on the Continent.

Phyllobius, Schönh., includes a variety of species, both British and foreign, several of which are scaled with green. They are rather long beetles, about a quarter of an inch in length, with the antennæ inserted near the base of the short rostrum. They feed on the leaves of trees.

Entimus Imperialis, Forst., the splendid gold-spangled Diamond Beetle, so favourite an object for the microscope, is a native of Brazil. It is black, spangled all over with golden-green, but is said to be quite white on first emerging from the pupa.

Another interesting exotic genus is *Brachycerus*, Oliv. The rostrum is stout, of moderate length ; the thorax is provided with a spine on each side ; the wings are absent, and the elytra are soldered together, and are very convex, and frequently deeply punctured. They frequent sandy places, and although several small species inhabit the South of Europe, by far the greater number occur in South Africa. Many of the species are black, with rows of reddish or yellowish depressed spots.

Hypera, Germ., is a large genus of dull-coloured beetles, about one-third of an inch in length, which are common on various plants, and form their slender cocoons beneath the leaves. They are of an oval form, and the rostrum is as long as the thorax, and slightly curved.

Cleonus, Schönh., is another large and widely-distributed genus, including species of dull black or grey colours.

Lixus, Fabr., includes slender species of moderate size, in most of which the abdomen and elytra are produced into a sharp point. It is represented by numerous species in most parts of the world. *L. Mucranatus*, Oliv., which is slate-coloured, and about half an inch long, is common in South Europe and Algeria. It is found on thistles and other flowers.

Curculio Abietis, Linn., which is common in fir woods, is a dull black, deeply-punctured beetle, with two transverse yellowish bands on the elytra ; it measures half an inch, or rather less, in length.

Hilipus, Germ., is an extensive South American genus allied to *Curculio ;* most of the species are black, with white, grey, or yellowish markings.

The genus *Apion*, Herbst, includes a great number of small beetles, many of which do not exceed one-tenth or one-twelfth of an inch in length. They are of various colours, such as black, blue, green, red, etc., and live gregariously on various plants. They have a narrow head and thorax, a long rostrum, and broad elytra, but no wings. *A. Flavipes*, Fabr., is black, with reddish legs, and lives on trefoil.

One of the most familiar weevils in the larva state is *Balaninus Nucum*, Linn., the Nut Weevil. Its whitish grub is often found in nuts, especially filberts, but it will also attack acorns. The beetle is black, with reddish legs, and a long proboscis, and is about a quarter of an inch long.

Rhynchites, Herbst, is a genus of beautiful little beetles, about one-sixth of an inch long, several of which are of a brilliant golden-green or purple colour, while others are coppery. They live on various trees, and are sometimes very injurious in orchards.

Orchestes Alni, Linn., is a red beetle, with two black spots on each of the elytra; it is about one-eighth of an inch long, and is found on alder. The species of this genus are numerous in Europe, and frequent various trees, such as the oak, beech, and willow.

The species of *Cionus*, Clairv., are broad and oval, with a small head and pointed rostrum. They are generally found on mullein. *C. Pulverosus*, Gyll., is a South European species, about one-sixth of an inch long. It is of a brownish grey, with two black spots on the suture.

Cryptorhynchus Lapathi, Linn., is a conspicuous beetle, about one-third of an inch in length, which is found upon alders and willows. It is a convex dull black insect, thickly scaled with white on the sides of the thorax, and at the base, and for nearly half the extremity of the elytra. Its larva feeds on the pith of the willow, and the beetle appears in autumn, and lives through the winter. This is the only European representative of an extensive genus which is found in all the warmer parts of the world, but is specially numerous in America.

There are several exotic genera of weevils with small bodies and very long, sprawling, hairy legs, which gives them a curious resemblance to spiders. One of these is *Tachygonus Lecontei*, Gyll., from North America, a black species with white markings.

Among the most destructive of the *Rhynchophora* are the notorious Corn Weevils, *Calandra Granaria* and *Oryzæ*, Linn. They measure about one-eighth of an inch in length. The former is brown, with red legs and antennæ, and the latter is black, with a spot on each shoulder and on each of the elytra, and the border of the latter reddish. They sometimes commit great ravages in granaries, each larva entering a single grain, and devouring the contents.

Cossonus Linearis, Linn., is a brown or blackish insect, with red legs and antennæ, which measures nearly a quarter of an inch in length. It is met with under dead bark.

Several of the largest of the foreign *Curculionidæ* are closely allied to *Calandra*. They are generally of a black or reddish-brown colour, and the inside of the legs, and sometimes even the rostrum, is fringed with reddish hairs. *Protocerius Colossus*, Oliv., is more than two inches in length, and is common in the East Indies; while the dull black *Rhynchophorus Palmarum*, Linn., which is about an inch and a half long, is equally common in South America. Its larva feeds on the pith of palm-trees, and is considered a great delicacy by the natives. It is probable that all the large allied species are also wood-borers. In some of the genera allied to *Rhynchophorus* (*Cyrtotrachelus* and *Macrochirus*, Schönh.), the front pair of legs are very much longer than the others.

FAMILY II.—*Brenthidæ.*

Antennæ eleven-jointed, not clubbed; rostrum straight and very long; body generally long and narrow, rarely oblong; first and second segments of the abdomen very long.

This small family is almost confined to the tropics, and the species are easily recognisable by their peculiar shape. One of the largest is *Eutrachelus Temminckii*, Latr., which is black, with red spots; it is found in Java. One species of the family only is met with in South Europe. This is *Amorphocephalus Coronatus*, Guér., which is reddish brown, and about half an inch in length; it is found under bark.

FAMILY III.—*Bruchidæ.*

Antennæ straight, eleven-jointed, serrated on the inside, or thickened towards the tip, or with the three apical joints enlarged, inserted on the sides of the head in a cavity before the eyes; head generally produced into a short rostrum.

Includes two sub-families; in the *Bruchinæ* the club of the antennæ is not conspicuous, but the joints of the tarsi are distinct, while in the *Anthotribinæ* the antennæ are generally clubbed, the joints of the tarsi are indistinct, and the rostrum is generally longer than in the *Bruchinæ*. One example of each may be noticed. *Bruchus Pisi*, Linn., the Pea Weevil, is about one-sixth of an inch long, and is black, thickly covered in parts with pale grey pubescence, especially towards the end of the elytra, where it is marked with two black spots. The base of the antennæ and the front tibiæ and tarsi are of a reddish yellow. The beetles lay their eggs in spring, when the peas are quite young, and the larvæ, when hatched, feed upon the peas. Other very similar species feed on various leguminous plants; and it is said that worm-eaten peas and beans are very injurious to the animals which feed upon them.

Tropidoderes Albirostris, Herbst, is a black species, about a quarter of a inch long, with dense white hairs on the rostrum, on a large space toward the tip of each of the elytra, on the under surface, and on part of the legs. The species of this genus are found on bushes, or under bark.

Several of the exotic genera of this family have antennæ of enormous length; thus, the brown East Indian species of *Mecoceras*, Schönh., which are about an inch long, have antennæ full three inches in length. But their structure is so palpably Rhynchophorous that they could not easily be mistaken for *Longicornia*.

SECTION XII.—LONGICORNIA.

Tarsi four-jointed; antennæ long or very long, filiform; mandibles strong; tip of the abdomen produced into a short ovipositor in the female; larvæ wood-borers.

The *Longicornia* may generally be easily recognised by the characters just cited. They are divided into three very distinct families.

FAMILY I.—*Prionidæ.*

Labrum small and indistinct; mandibles very large, especially in the males; antennæ stout, of moderate length; scape very thick, inserted near the mandibles, or near, but not within, the orbits; head not flattened in front; eyes kidney-shaped.

The *Prionidæ* are much broader and bulkier in proportion than any of the other Longicorns, and some of them are among the largest beetles known. Their great mandibles give them a superficial resemblance to the *Lucanidæ*, from which the structure of their antennæ will at once distinguish them.

Parandra, Latr., is very unlike the typical species. The species are of moderate size, rather depressed, with large mandibles and short antennæ. *P. Brunnea*, Fabr., which is common in the United States, is of a shining reddish brown, and is about an inch in length.

The structure of the mandibles in the *Prionidæ* differs very much in different species, and the thorax is often armed with strong lateral spines or teeth. These latter are very conspicuous in *Cyrtognathus Walkeri*, Waterh., a black Himalayan species, which is also remarkable for its simply-formed but large and divergent mandibles, and its stout bristly antennæ and legs.

One species only of this family (*Prionus Coriarius*, Linn.) is found in England, where, however, it is by no means common. It is a pitchy-brown insect, an inch or more in length, with prominent lateral spines on the thorax, but with rather small mandibles. *Ergates Faber*, Fabr., is an allied but much larger species found in many parts of the Continent, but not in England.

Macrodontia, Serv., is a South American genus, remarkable for its pale brown colour (resembling that of dead wood), and for its enormous mandibles, which are more or less strongly toothed.

One of the largest beetles known is *Titanus Giganteus*, Linn., a native of Cayenne. It is nearly seven inches in length, and two inches across the elytra; the mandibles are short, but very thick and strong, and the thorax has a strong spine on each side, near the front. The head, thorax, and legs are black, and the elytra and abdomen of a dark reddish brown.

Acanthinodera Cumingii, Hope, is a Chilian species, remarkable for its very small head; the female is dark brown, and about two inches in length; the male is yellowish brown, and much smaller.

The genus *Pyrodes*, Serv., includes species of moderate size, but of a green or violet colour; it is confined to South America. Several other genera from the same country likewise include green or blue species, sometimes of large size, but generally of deep rather than brilliant colours. Some are of a rich golden green, but the bright metallic green colour met with in the polished *Buprestidæ*, etc., is always wanting in this family, probably because the surface of the insect is too strongly rugose or punctured to reflect such colours.

FAMILY II.—*Cerambycidæ*.

Mandibles rather small, nearly alike in both sexes; labrum well marked, occupying the whole width of the head; eyes always concave, and more or less surrounding the base of the antennæ; head produced in front, but never vertical.

An extensive family, including a great number of species of different sizes, shapes, and colours. In several genera the eyes are completely divided in two by the base of the antennæ, so that the insect appears to have four eyes, as in *Gyrinus*.

Spondylis Buprestoides, Linn., is a black beetle, about three-quarters of an inch in length, which is common in many parts of Europe. It has a small head, and comparatively short antennæ, and scarcely looks like one of the Longicorns. Like most of the species of this family, it is found in rotten wood.

The typical genus *Cerambyx*, Linn., includes several large and conspicuous European species, which are, however, believed not to

E

be truly indigenous in England, as, although they have been met with occasionally, they are thought to have been imported with timber. They are black insects, with long antennæ, and a spine on each side of the thorax. The two commonest species are *C. Cerdo,* Fabr., which is about an inch in length, and *C. Heros,* Scop., which has the elytra tipped with brown, and is sometimes nearly two inches in length, but which, like many other wood-feeding insects, varies considerably in size in different specimens. The beetles may be found on flowers, or on newly-felled timber. The latter is so attractive to beetles that when Mr. A. R. Wallace was collecting in the Eastern Archipelago, he always used to get some trees felled as soon as he established himself in a new locality, and rarely failed to reap a rich harvest.

Eburia, Serv., is a very pretty South American genus; the species are of moderate size, and are generally of a yellowish colour, with spots of an ivory white.

Pachyta, Serv., includes several moderate-sized European species, seldom reaching the length of half an inch. *P. Quadrimaculata,* Linn., has yellow elytra, with black spots. These beetles are found on flowers, especially in mountainous regions.

Leptura, Linn., is a large genus, the species of which are generally about half an inch in length, and are found on flowers; the female is provided with a short ovipositor. *L. Cordigera,* Fuessly, found in South Europe, and perhaps in South-Western Germany, is black, with more or less of the sides of the elytra red.

In *Necydalis,* Linn., and some allied genera, the elytra are exceedingly short, but the wings are not folded beneath them as in the *Brachelytra,* but uncovered. *N. Major,* Linn., is black, with yellowish pubescence, and yellowish antennæ, legs, and elytra. It measures an inch in length, and is occasionally met with on sallow-blossoms, on the Continent, but is far from common.

The commonest of the larger Longicorns in North Europe is undoubtedly the Musk Beetle (*Aromia Moschata*). It is green, with a lateral spine on the thorax, and is about an inch long. It is rather a sluggish insect, and may be found resting on the trunks of willows, on the wood of which its larva feeds. It may easily be seized with the fingers, as it is quite harmless, though it emits a peculiar, but not unpleasant odour.

Callichroma, Latr., is a very similar genus, fairly well represented in most tropical countries. Most of the species are green, and closely resemble our common Musk Beetle.

One of the prettiest European Longicorns is *Rosalia Alpina*, Linn., which is not uncommon in Switzerland. It is about the size of *Aromia Moschata*, and is covered with a delicate pale-blue bloom, with a black band and some smaller markings on the elytra. It is met with on the trunks of decaying copper-beeches throughout the summer.

Some of the smaller South American Longicorns are delicately-formed insects, with curious tufts on their bodies. Thus, *Cosmosoma Speculiferum*, Gory, is black, with the scutellum, and a large square spot in the middle of the elytra on the suture; yellowish white; the under surface is also silvery. The antennæ are very peculiar, being ciliated to the middle, beyond which is a large tuft of hair; the hind tibiæ are also slightly ciliated. In *Coremia Hirtipes*, Oliv., a slender black species, the antennæ are much shorter than in *Cosmosoma*, and are simply filiform; but the hind legs are very long and slender, especially the hind tibiæ, the middle of which is decorated with a tuft of hair greatly resembling that upon the antennæ of the other genus. Concerning this latter species, Mr. Bates remarks:[1] "Found throughout the Amazons, flying slowly over dead timber in new clearings. It resembles a large *Culex*."

The genus *Clytus*, Laich., includes a great number of beetles found in all parts of the world. The European species are sometimes called "Wasp Beetles," being about half an inch in length, with comparatively short antennæ, and generally black, with yellow bands or spots. The beetles are found on timber, or on flowers, and are not uncommon; they are active on the wing.

Purpuricenus, Serv., is a genus containing handsome species, found in most parts of the world, several of which inhabit the Mediterranean region. One species only, *P. Koehleri*, Linn., is met with as far north as the southern slopes of the Alps. It is nearly three-quarters of an inch in length, and is black, often with a red spot on each side of the thorax; the elytra are of a purplish red, with a large black spot in the middle of the suture of the elytra. Most of the other species are also of a bright red colour, varied with black.

Trachyderes Variegatus, Perty, is an example of a well-known Brazilian genus; it is black, with reddish-yellow markings. *Megaderus Stigma*, Linn., is a very similar species from Cayenne; it is black, with an oblique yellowish streak on each of the elytra.

[1] *Trans. Ent. Soc. Lond.* 1870, p. 395.

Tragocerus Fasciatus, Don., an Australian species, resembles the two last mentioned; the head and thorax are black, and the elytra of a yellowish orange, with black markings.

The curious genus *Vesperus,* Latr., inhabits South Europe and the Mediterranean district generally. The species are of a yellowish-brown colour, and measure half an inch or more in length. The male is a slender Longicorn beetle, with antennæ about as long as the body, and elytra reaching to the extremity of the abdomen; but the female, which is considerably larger than the male, has short antennæ, very short and divergent elytra, rudimentary wings (if any), and a thick heavy body; in fact, it has a very considerable resemblance to *Meloë,* except in its legs and antennæ. These beetles are nocturnal in their habits.

FAMILY III.—*Lamiidæ.*

Head vertical, flattened in front; mandibles of moderate size, nearly alike in both sexes; labrum nearly as broad as the lower part of the head; antennæ setaceous; wings occasionally absent.

The *Lamiidæ* are fully as numerous and varied as the *Cerambycidæ,* from which they may generally be easily distinguished by the position of the head. Many species far surpass the largest of the *Cerambycidæ,* both in size and in the length of their antennæ; but none of them equal the largest of the *Prionidæ* (*Titanus,* for example) in bulk.

Dorcadion, Dalm., is an extensive genus of moderate-sized species, the great majority of which inhabit the countries bordering on the Mediterranean. The species are found running about roads and walls. *D. Pedestre,* Poda., common throughout South-Eastern Europe, including Austria, etc., is black, more or less clothed with brownish or whitish down; the antennæ and legs are reddish.

The type of this family is *Lamia Textor,* a dull black, thickly-punctured insect, about an inch long. It is found in osier-beds, but is not very common in England.

Monohammus, Serv., is a rather large genus, which has representatives in most quarters of the globe. Two species, *M. Sartor,* Fabr., and *Sutor,* Linn., are common on the Continent, and are reputed British, though some writers think that all the British specimens have been accidentally introduced; they are black, with yellowish down; the first is three-quarters of an inch in length, and the second an inch and a quarter; they frequent pine forests.

Tæniotes, Serv., includes a number of handsome species found in tropical America; the antennæ are fully twice as long as the body. *T. Decoratus*, Cast., from Brazil, is black, with yellow markings.

Aristobia Horridula, Hope, is a curious reddish-brown East Indian species. There are two large black tufts of hair on the antennæ near the base, and the elytra are thickly studded with small tufts of short bristles.

The genus *Batocera*, Cast., includes some of the largest and most beautiful of the East Indian Longicorns. They have long antennæ, and strong spines on the sides of the thorax, and at the front angles of the elytra. The species are generally brown or yellowish brown, speckled or spotted with white.

Gnoma Giraffa, Schreib., is a curious species from New Guinea, in which the thorax is rather narrow, about as long as the abdomen, and constricted in the middle; it is of a uniform black colour.

Sternotomis, Westw., is a beautiful African genus, in which the species are of moderate size, rarely exceeding an inch in length. They are generally of a beautiful green, varied with black, and sometimes with yellow.

Tragocephala Formosa, Oliv., from the Cape, is black, with large reddish or orange spots, and white dots; the antennæ are much shorter in this genus than in *Stenotomis*.

Petrognatha Gigas, Fabr., is one of the largest of the African Longicorns, equalling or surpassing the species of *Batocera* in size; and instead of reproducing the beautiful colours of the two last genera, it is black, with dull grey elytra, marked with a large irregular black blotch on the outer edge of each.

We will now pass on to *Macropus Longimanus*, Linn., a common Brazilian insect, and one of the largest and most beautiful of all the Longicorns. It differs considerably in size, and a very good idea of the dimensions and general appearance of large specimens may be formed from our figure. It is black, with numerous red and grey markings on the elytra, and the legs are also varied with red and black.

Acanthocinus Ædilis, Linn., is a greyish-brown insect, with two more or less distinct darker bands; it is rather more than half an inch in length. This beetle is found more or less commonly in pine forests throughout Europe, and is remarkable among the European Longicorns for the enormous length of the antennæ in the male, which are four or five times the length of the body.

Several other European genera may now be noticed.

Agapanthia, Serv., includes black species, thickly clothed with yellowish or greyish hair on the antennæ, legs, and body.   They measure from half an inch to three-quarters of an inch in length, and are numerous in South Europe, where they may be met with on thistles and other flowers.

Saperda Carcharias, Linn., is a very common insect on the Continent, but much less so in England.   It is black, densely clothed with yellowish hair, and the elytra are narrowed towards the tip, and terminate in a short spine.   It is more than an inch in length, and frequents willows and poplars.

Phytœcia, Muls., includes many long, narrow, pubescent species, with comparatively short antennæ.   Most of them inhabit the Mediterranean Region, but several are found in Northern Europe.   They are generally black, with yellowish or reddish down; but sometimes more or less of the insect is reddish.   They vary in size from a quarter of an inch upwards.   *P. Detrita*, Fabr., is a common North African species about an inch long; it is black, with a broad suffused white line on each of the elytra.

Tetrops Præusta, Oliv., is a black beetle with yellowish-brown elytra and legs, the former tipped with black; it measures nearly a quarter of an inch in length, and is found on the flowers of the plum, etc.   It is chiefly remarkable for being the only British Longicorn in which the eyes are divided into two unequal halves by the antennæ, so that the insect has really four eyes.

SECTION XIII.—EUPODA.

Tarsi generally four-jointed; antennæ filiform, generally shorter than the body; body convex, rounded, or oval; elytra covering the abdomen; hind femora often thickened; habits herbivorous in all stages.

FAMILY I.—*Crioceridæ.*

Shape oval; antennæ filiform, gradually thickening towards the tip, and inserted near the eyes, at least as long as the head and thorax together; thorax cylindrical, narrower than the elytra; hind legs generally long, with thickened femora.

Includes four sub-families, *Sagrinæ, Donaciinæ, Crioccrinæ,* and *Megalopodinæ.*

SUB-FAMILY I.—*Sagrinæ.*

Mandibles entire, pointed; antennæ inserted widely apart on the inner front edge of the eyes; hind femora frequently much enlarged; first segment of the abdomen at least twice as large as any of the others; body rather long.

The type of this group is the beautiful genus *Sagra*, Fabr., which inhabits tropical Asia and Africa. The species are green, golden-green, purple, blue, or even black, and measure from half an inch to an inch in length; the hind coxæ are of enormous size. The most beautiful and one of the largest species is *S. Buqueti*, Less., which is met with in Java and Borneo. It is bright green, with the inner edge of the elytra along the suture of a bright coppery red or flame-colour. *S. Seraphica*, Lac., from Senegal, is a violet-blue species.

The only European genus of *Sagrinæ* is *Orsodacna*, Latr., which includes several black or yellowish species, which resemble *Sagra* in shape, but are less than a quarter of an inch in length; they are found on flowers.

SUB-FAMILY II.—*Donaciinæ.*

Mandibles indented at the tip; antennæ rather long, slender, filiform, inserted near together on the front of the head, some distance from the eyes; thorax much narrower than the base of the elytra; legs rather long; femora not dilated; first segment of the abdomen very large; body elongated or oblong; habits aquatic.

This sub-family only includes two genera—*Donacia*, Fabr., and *Hæmonia*, Latr., and most of the known species are either European or North American, though a few have been described from different parts of Asia. The species of *Donacia* are about one-third of an inch in length, and are generally of a bright green or bronzy colour. The larvæ feed under water on the roots of water-plants, and the beetles are often found basking on the leaves. The under surface of the bodies of the latter is clothed with a silvery-white down, which entangles a bubble of air, which they carry with them beneath the water when diving.

SUB-FAMILY III.—*Criocerinæ.*

Mandibles indented or bifid at the tip; antennæ inserted widely apart on the inner front edge of the eyes, rather thick, especially towards the tip, and moniliform ; thorax narrower than the base of the elytra ; first segment of the abdomen rather larger than the others ; body long, oval.

The *Criocerinæ* resemble the *Donaciinæ* in shape, but they are not aquatic ; their integuments are harder, and they are more varied in their colouring.

The type of the sub-family is perhaps *Crioceris Asparagi*, Linn., a bluish-green beetle, with a red thorax, and red edges to the elytra, which are also spotted with yellow. It measures nearly a quarter of an inch in length, and is common in gardens on asparagus.

One of the largest genera of the *Criocerinæ* is *Lema*, Fabr., which has representatives in all parts of the world, but appears to be most numerous in South America. The European species are of a shining blue, green, blackish-green, or red, and measure nearly a quarter of an inch in length.

SUB-FAMILY IV.—*Megalopodinæ*.

Mandibles pointed ; antennæ more or less thickened from the base to the tip ; dentated or pectinated ; head depressed ; front and middle coxæ contiguous ; last segment of the abdomen larger than any of the rest.

All the species of this sub-family are exotic, and a large proportion inhabit tropical America, although a few may be met with in Africa and the East Indies. They are moderate-sized insects, which live on plants and shrubs ; their flight is rather heavy, and they avoid the heat of the day. Like many other beetles, they are said to produce a sharp sound, and also to emit a yellow fluid when touched.

FAMILY II.—*Cryptocephalidæ*.

Head buried in the thorax as far as the eyes; antennæ wide apart ; mandibles pointed.

SUB-FAMILY I.—*Clythrinæ*.

Body rather long ; antennæ pectinated ; thorax as wide as the elytra at the base ; legs short.

Clythra Quadrimaculata, Linn., may serve to represent the typical genus of this family. It is about one-third of an inch in length, and is black, with yellow elytra, each of which is marked with a black spot on the shoulder, and a larger one, often divided into two, about the middle. It is found on flowers, not uncommonly, in many parts of Europe.

The species of this sub-family are found all over the world, but appear to be specially numerous in the Mediterranean region. Many of them are very similar to the species just noticed both in shape and markings.

SUB-FAMILY II.—*Chlamydinæ.*

Antennæ short, serrated, retractile; elytra not covering the tip of the abdomen, and strongly lobed at the base; legs of equal length, retractile.

An exotic family of small extent, by far the larger number of which inhabit tropical America; their elytra are usually covered with deep punctures.

Poropleura Bacca, Kirb., is a brilliant coppery-red species, with dull green ridges on the elytra; it is a native of Brazil.

SUB-FAMILY III.—*Cryptocephalinæ.*

Antennæ filiform, and rather long; elytra generally covering the abdomen to the tip.

The typical genus of this rather extensive sub-family is *Cryptocephalus*, Geoffr., one of the largest genera of the *Phytophaga.*

The species are found on flowers, and are of small size, rarely attaining a length of a quarter of an inch. They are of varied colours: black, violet, blue, green, coppery, purple, red, or yellow; sometimes unicolourous, and sometimes with black or yellow spots. They are found on various shrubs and flowers; and I remember once finding two specimens of a beautiful golden-green species (*C. Sericeus*, Linn.) in a buttercup. *C. Cicatricosus*, Luc., an Algerian species, is black, with red elytra spotted with blue-black.

FAMILY III.—*Eumolpidæ.*

Antennæ long, not compressed, the terminal joints larger than the others; head slightly separated from the thorax; thorax transverse; body oval.

This family includes a large number of exotic species, many of which are of considerable size and brilliant metallic colours. Only a few species inhabit Europe, but several of these are very injurious to cultivated plants.

Eumolpus Fulgidus, Fabr., a common South American species, is one of the most beautiful of the family. It is of a brilliant blue or green, with coppery reflections.

Many species are, however, of less brilliant colours. *Adoxus Vitis*, Fabr., is black, with the elytra, tibiæ, and base of the antennæ reddish; it is about a quarter of an inch in length, and is frequently very injurious to the vine in many parts of Europe in early spring.

Pachnephorus Cylindricus, Luc., is a handsome Algerian species, with bronzed head and thorax, and blue elytra; it is found in damp places under stones.

FAMILY IV.—*Chrysomelidæ.*

Head completely separated from the thorax; antennæ with the terminal joints hardly longer than the others; thorax transverse; elytra convex, oval, entirely covering the body.

The *Chrysomelidæ*, or Golden Apple Beetles, have received their name from the brilliant metallic colouring of some of the species, which rivals that of the *Eumolpidæ*, whereas other species are of very dull colours.

One of the most beautiful species of the typical genus *Chrysomela*, Linn., is *C. Cerealis*, Linn. It is of a brilliant golden green, with a purplish lustre, and there are three bands on the thorax, and three on each of the elytra, besides the suture, of a deep blue, bordered with green. It is about one-third of an inch in length. It is not common in Britain, but is met with sometimes on the mountains near Llanberis. It is much commoner on the Continent, where it is found under stones in spring, and, later in the year, on grass and herbs. Most of the other species of the genus are also found among grass. They differ considerably in colour; *C. Banksii*, Fabr., is of a bronzy green; *C. Limbata*, Fabr., is black, with a red border; *C. Rufa*, Duft., a rare Alpine species, is of a pale brownish red; *C. Goettingensis*, Linn., is of a dark violet; *C. Schach*, Fabr., is blue-black, etc.

A great number of genera, comprising a variety of moderate-sized, and often very pretty species, are peculiar to tropical America. One of the largest is *Doryphora*, Ill., as an example of which we have figured *D. Punctatissima*, Oliv., which is found in Cayenne. It is black, with pale yellow elytra, covered with small black spots, and is nearly an inch long.

The famous Colorado Potato Beetle was originally described

as a *Doryphora*, and is still commonly referred to that genus, though it more properly belongs to the allied genus *Leptinotarsa*, Stål.

L. Decemlineata, Say, is about one-third of an inch in length and the elytra are marked with alternate stripes of black and dull yellow; the thorax is also yellow, with a blackish V-shaped mark in the centre, and several dark spots on each side. The wings are not colourless, as in most other beetles, but red. The larvæ, which are the chief destructive agents, are reddish grubs, spotted with black. This insect was only known for many years to feed on different wild species of *Solanaceæ* in the Rocky Mountains, but in course of time the spread of civilisation led to the invasion of its haunts by the potato. This furnished the beetle with a new and almost inexhaustible supply of food, and it took to feeding on the cultivated plant, rapidly increased in numbers, and spread from one potato-field to another, till its ravages extended over the greater part of Canada and the United States, when its progress was arrested by the Atlantic Ocean. After great damage had been done in America, various remedies were proposed by American entomologists; but the only one which has proved generally successful is watering the plants with a preparation of arsenic known as "Paris Green." Hitherto the beetle has not succeeded in establishing itself on this side of the Atlantic. Some years ago, however, there was a general fear of its introduction into Europe, and more or less effectual precautions were taken against it by all the European States. Everything found in a potato-field, or even any unfamiliar annulose animal found anywhere, was at once mistaken for a Colorado Potato Beetle, and often announced as such in the local journals. Perhaps the great caterpillar of the Death's Head Hawk-Moth (*Acherontia Atropos*, Linn.), which feeds on the potato, was more often mistaken for it than anything else. But there is no doubt that single specimens of the beetle were sometimes observed at sea-ports, just as tropical insects, etc., of all kinds, some harmless and others noxious, are constantly met with in the London Docks. It is quite likely that the insect might become easily naturalised in Europe, if once fairly introduced, and prove very injurious, so that although the first panic has now subsided, it is to be hoped that the authorities will not relax their vigilance. Any one bringing over, or keeping the insect alive in England, is liable to a fine of £10, and very properly, for if a few live beetles were to escape, it might be difficult to eradicate the pest afterwards. A few years ago a colony was actually discovered in a potato-

field at Mülheim, near Cologne; how introduced was, I believe,
not ascertained.   The whole field was immediately ploughed up,
drenched with petroleum,' and burned over—a prompt measure,
which fortunately proved successful.

Professor Riley is the best authority on the Potato Beetle, and
those who wish for further information on the subject may consult
his little book, published in London in 1877.

One of the largest European *Chrysomelidæ* is *Timarcha Tene-
bricosa*, Fabr., the Bloody-nose Beetle.   It measures about half an
inch in length, and is of a dull black; roundish, convex, apterous,
and very sluggish, and when touched it emits a red fluid, from
which it derives its popular name.   *T. Turbida*, Erichs., is a black
Algerian species.

FAMILY V.—*Halticidæ*.

Antennæ long, cylindrical, inserted near together between the
eyes; body short, oval or hemispherical; hind legs longer than the
others; hind femora thickened.

The most familiar representatives of this family are the beetles
known as Turnip Flies, or Turnip Fleas.   They are of small size,
often measuring less than one-twelfth of an inch in length, and
their thickened femora enable them to leap with great agility.
The Turnip Beetles belong to the genera *Haltica*, Geoffr., and
Phyllotreta, Foudr., and are of a bronzy-black colour, often with a
yellow stripe on each elytra.   Many plans have been proposed
for their destruction; but as they feed on other plants besides
turnips, it is very desirable to keep the edges of turnip-fields as
clear of weeds as possible, as many of these would simply answer
the purpose of nurseries for the beetles.

FAMILY VI.—*Galerucidæ*.

Antennæ long and generally slender, cylindrical, inserted close
together between the eyes; body rather long, somewhat depressed;
legs rather long and slender; hind femora not thickened.

The *Galerucidæ* are generally larger and longer beetles than the
Halticidæ, and are destitute of the power of leaping.   They are
adorned with varied colours, and several species have a great
resemblance to the *Crioceridæ*, from which they may be at once
distinguished by their long filiform antennæ.

Galeruca Tanaceti, Linn., which may be taken as a representative of the family, is black (sometimes with brown elytra), coarsely

punctured, and about one-third of an inch long. It is not an uncommon species, and is found on flowers.

FAMILY VII.—*Hispidæ*.

Antennæ rather short, cylindrical, inserted close together on the front of the head ; body oval, convex, and generally spiny.

It is impossible to mistake the typical *Hispidæ*, for they are the very porcupines or hedgehogs of the *Coleoptera*. They are nearly all exotic, though one or two species are found in Europe, the best known of which is *Hispa Atra*, Linn., a black insect, about one-eighth of an inch in length. It is far from common, at least in Central Europe, but is occasionally met with running over grass growing in sandy places in the evening.

The South American genus *Alurnus*, Fabr., is very different from *Hispa*. *A. Grossus*, Fabr., from Cayenne, the typical species, is an inch in length ; the head, legs, and antennæ are black, the thorax is red, rugose, armed with a spine on each side at the base, and bordered behind with black, and the elytra are smooth and yellow ; the body is not spiny. It is a native of Cayenne.

FAMILY VIII.—*Cassididæ*.

Antennæ cylindrical, inserted close together on the top of the head ; body rounded, more or less depressed ; thorax (in the more typical species) entirely covering the head.

The *Cassididæ*, or Tortoise Beetles, are an extensive group, and may often be recognised at once by their form alone. Many of the species are brightly coloured, and some are metallic. Their larvæ are provided with a curious fork-like appendage, attached to the hinder extremity of the body, but curving forwards. On this they pile their excrement, under the shade of which they always live. The beetles are sluggish, with short legs and antennæ, and they and their larvæ feed on low plants.

The American genus *Himatidium*, Fabr., and its allies differ from the more typical genera in the antennæ being moderately long and slender, and in the head not being concealed by the thorax. They are often of small size and dull colours. *H. Latreillei*, Cast., is a Brazilian species, which measures about one-third of an inch in length. It is of an orange-brown colour, with dull bronzy-green elytra.

The genus *Calaspidea*, Hope, has longer legs and antennæ than typical *Cassida*. The species are all tropical American, and are

of considerable size. The elytra are of great breadth, half as broad
again as the thorax. *C. Grossus*, Linn., a native of Guiana, is black,
with red elytra, marked with depressed black dots, and towards
the edge with black reticulated markings.

The European species of the typical genus *Cassida*, Linn., are
rather numerous. They are of moderate size, and most of them
are green, but others are black, or red, spotted with black. *C.
Vittata*, Vill., is green above, with a golden band on each of the
elytra; the under surface is black. It is about a quarter of an inch
in length, and is not an uncommon species.

FAMILY IX.—*Languriidæ*.

Antennæ rather short, inserted before the eyes, eleven-jointed,
the four or five last joints forming a large oblong compressed
club; body long, narrowed behind.

These insects are entirely exotic, and most of the species are
found in the East Indies. The great majority of the species
belong to the typical genus *Languria*, Latr.; they measure about
one-third of an inch in length. One of the best known species is
L. Bicolor, Fabr., common in the Southern United States; it is
black, with the face and sides of the thorax red.

Some of the East Indian species are considerably larger; thus
Callilanguria Luzonica, Crotch, from the Philippines, is nearly an
inch in length. The head is black, the thorax red, and the elytra
green.

FAMILY X.—*Erotylidæ*.

Body variable in shape, oblong, oval, elliptical, or hemispherical;
head small, partly concealed by the thorax; antennæ ten- or eleven-
jointed, the last two, three, or four joints forming a compressed
club; elytra oval, elliptical, covering the abdomen; legs sometimes
five-jointed.

An interesting and rather extensive family, which, however, is
poorly represented in Europe by a few small species, which are
generally found in fungi.

Triplax Russica, Linn., is a reddish-yellow oval beetle, with
the antennæ, scutellum, elytra, and pectus black; it is a quarter of
an inch in length, and is not an uncommon species.

Erotylus Histrio, Fabr., is a handsome Brazilian species; it is
black, and the elytra are irregularly banded with yellow, with a
red spot on each shoulder, and another near the tip of each elytron.

Phricobacis Marginatus, Guér., somewhat resembles a *Cassida* in the shape of the elytra, though very different otherwise. It is violet-black, with two yellow spots on each of the elytra, and is about three-quarters of an inch in length.

SECTION XIV.—PSEUDOTRIMERA.

Tarsi generally three-jointed; antennæ generally short, with a three-jointed club; elytra covering the abdomen, and never truncated at the tips.

FAMILY I.—*Endomychidæ.*

Body oval; antennæ eleven-jointed, longer than the head and thorax, and inserted on the front of the head, the three terminal joints forming a long club; maxillary palpi filiform, a little thickened at the end, but not terminated by a large securiform joint; femora thickened; claws simple.

The beetles belonging to this family are not very numerous; they are generally of small size, and are found in fungi, or under bark. It will suffice to enumerate one or two representative species. In *Dapsa Barbara,* Luc., the antennæ are less thickened than in *Endomychus;* it is an Algerian species, measuring about a quarter of an inch in length, and is of a reddish colour.

Endomychus Coccineus, Linn., the type of the family, is a bright red beetle, with two large black spots on each of the elytra; the head, antennæ, legs, and middle of the thorax are also black. The beetle is nearly a quarter of an inch long, and is not rare in some localities.

FAMILY II.—*Coccinellidæ.*

Body hemispherical, rarely oval; antennæ inserted on the sides of the face near the base of the mandibles, concealed by the head when at rest, generally eleven-jointed and clavate, seldom as long as the head and thorax; maxillary palpi with the last joint large, and generally securiform; claws simple or bifid; habits carnivorous, at least in the typical species.

The *Coccinellidæ* or Lady-birds comprise an extensive series of beetles, generally of small or moderate size, and of varied colours. Most of the European species are black, with red or yellow spots, or red or yellow, with black spots. Two of the commonest species are the Seven-Spot Lady-bird (*Coccinella Septempunctata,* Linn.), and the Two-Spot Lady-bird (*Adalia Bipunctata*, Linn.). The first has a black head and thorax, spotted with white, and red elytra, marked with three black spots on each side, and one near the base on the suture; it is about a quarter of an inch in length. The other species is rather smaller, and is marked with one black spot only on each elytron. It is, however, exceedingly variable; sometimes the collar is bordered with yellow, and the elytra are black, with red markings. Both these species are exceedingly common, especially the first, which sometimes appears in restricted localities in vast swarms. They are very useful insects, as they feed in all their stages on the Plant Lice, or *Aphides*, which are among the worst of all the insect pests of our fields and gardens.

The genus *Scymnus*, Kug, includes a considerable number of small black species, which feed on the *Aphides* which infest fir and pine trees.

The species of *Rhizobius*, Steph., are more oval than *Coccinella* and its immediate allies. *R. Litura*, Fabr., is a yellowish-brown insect, sometimes speckled with darker, and about an eighth of an inch in length. It frequents pine and fir woods, and is not a very common insect.

One of the smallest insects of this family is *Agaricophilus Reflexus*, Motsch., which is less than one-twelfth of an inch in length. It is hemispherical in shape, black, smooth, and shining, with yellowish legs and antennæ, and is found in fungi growing on the roots of trees. It is a Russian insect.

Epilachna, Chevr., is a very extensive genus, but it has only a few representatives in Europe, one of which is *E. Chrysomelina*, Fabr., a round, yellowish insect, with three oblique pairs of small black spots on each elytron, the innermost row near the suture, but the middle ones much further from the suture than the end ones; it is about one-twelfth of an inch long, and lives on lucerne.

FAMILY III.—*Corylophidæ*.

Antennæ nine- to eleven- jointed, with several of the terminal joints thickened; tarsi with four joints, the third small, but not concealed; head completely hidden by the thorax.

The type of this small family is *Corylophus Cassidioides*, Marsh., a shining reddish-brown beetle, hardly one-thirtieth of an inch in length, which is met with, like the *Trichopterygidæ*, in decaying vegetable matter.

ORDER ORTHOPTERA.

MANDIBULATE insects, with four wings, the anterior wings (called tegmina) much narrower than the hind wings, less hard than on the Coleoptera, and leathery rather than horny in their texture; metamorphoses incomplete, the larva and pupa being active; hind legs often formed for leaping; eggs generally enclosed in a case.

These insects are exceedingly numerous and destructive in warm climates, but are only represented in Britain by about sixty species, few of which are really abundant. They include the Earwigs, Cockroaches, Crickets, Locusts, Grasshoppers, etc. They are divided into four groups and seven families, the first being sometimes regarded as a separate Order, viz. *Euplexoptera* (*Forficulidæ*); *Cursoria* (*Blattidæ*); *Gressoria* (*Mantidæ* and *Phasmidæ*); *Saltatoria* (*Achetidæ*, *Gryllidæ*, and *Locustidæ*).

FAMILY I.—*Forficulidæ*.

Tegmina very short, beneath which the ample wings are partially folded; abdomen terminating in a forceps. This family includes the Earwigs, which have so great a resemblance to the *Staphylinidæ* that Linné and his immediate followers placed them at the end of the Coleoptera; but all modern authors, except those who regard them as forming a distinct Order, have included them with the Orthoptera. The majority of the species are nocturnal, hiding themselves in cracks and crevices, or among flowers or dead leaves, during the day; some species, however, are diurnal, such as *Labia Minor*, Leach, which flies by day. *Forficula Auricularia*, Linn. (the common Earwig), feeds chiefly on vegetable matter, and is very destructive to fruit and flowers; and it is difficult to find a dahlia which does not conceal several among its closely conglomerated petals. Unlike most other insects, the female does not perish as soon as she has laid her eggs, but lives to behold her offspring, brooding over her eggs and young almost like a hen. But it is distressing to learn that if the mother should die she is immedi-

F

ately devoured by her progeny. The earwig derives its name from
its occasionally creeping into the human ear in search of concealment. This has been denied by some authors, who have argued
on *a priori* grounds that it was impossible, and have considered
the name of *earwig* to be a corruption of *ear-wing*, in allusion to
the shape of the hind wings of the insect. Although it is uncommon, I have heard of perfectly trustworthy instances in which
earwigs have entered the ear; but any insect can be driven out at
once by pouring the ear full of oil. Some few species are apterous.
The eggs are not enclosed in a capsule, and the young earwigs
resemble the perfect insect, but do not acquire wings till their last
change.

FAMILY II.—*Blattidæ.*

Tegmina overlapping; legs formed for running; head often
concealed beneath the large prothorax; abdomen with two short
slender filaments at the extremity.

This family includes the Cockroaches, which are among the
most destructive insects in warm climates, and frequently swarm
on board ship, when some species become torpid on reaching colder
climates, but reappear in abundance on the return of the vessel to
a warmer country. Unfortunately, however, this is not always
the case; and two or three large and troublesome species have
fully established themselves in England within the last few centuries. The commonest of these is *Periplaneta Orientalis*, Linn., a
reddish-brown insect, improperly called the Black Beetle by house-
keepers. But several other species are occasionally met with at
large in England, including even the great cockroach called the
Drummer in the West Indies (*Blaberus Giganteus*, Linn.) from the
noise it makes at night. There are, however, several small species
of *Blatta* which live in the woods and fields, and appear to be
really indigenous in England. A large proportion of the *Blattidæ*
are either grey or brown, reddish-brown being the predominant
colour. There are occasional exceptions; thus, the species of the
American genus *Panchlora*, Burm., are all of a light green (a colour
frequently met with in other families of the *Orthoptera*); and *Corydia
Petiveriana*, Linn., which differs from most of the species we
have mentioned in its rounded, instead of long oval form, is black,
with large whitish or yellowish spots. This latter is a common
Indian insect.

FAMILY III.—*Mantidæ*.

Body long and slender; front legs thickened and serrated; habits predatory.

The *Mantidæ*, or Praying Insects, are celebrated for their habit of resting on their four hind legs, with their front legs raised in the air in what was long supposed to be an attitude of devotion, but really in an observant attitude, and on the alert for their prey. These insects are not found in England, but are very common in warm countries, and several species are met with in South France. The best known of these is *Mantis Religiosa*, Linn., a green species measuring an inch and a half or two inches in length. Most of the *Mantidæ* are of a green colour, which doubtless helps to conceal them from their prey. One of the prettiest species is *Harpax Ocellaria*, Drury, which is found on the west coast of Africa, and measures about two inches across the wings. The tegmina are dark green, with a large yellow eye-like spot in the centre, and the tips and hind wings are transparent.

FAMILY IV.—*Phasmidæ*.

Body long and slender; all the legs fitted for walking; plant-feeders.

The *Phasmidæ* include the Stick Insects or Spectre Insects and the Leaf Insects. Many of the species have very long and slender bodies and legs, and resemble dried pieces of stick. A large number are apterous, and others have very short tegmina and wings, which must be quite useless for flight, while in others, again, the tegmina are very short, and the wings are ample. In the last case the tegmina are generally of a greenish colour, while the wings are often of a most delicate pink. Among the more interesting species we may mention *Cyphocrania Semirubra*, Serv., from Brazil, with short greenish elytra and ample pink wings, as we have just described; *Phibalocera Pythonius*, Westw., a green, stout, wingless insect, seven or eight inches long, which has a striking resemblance to a shoot of bamboo; and *Lopaphus Cocophages*, Newp., a brown slender insect, with very short wings and tegmina. The two latter species are common in the South Sea Islands, where *L. Cocophages* sometimes commits dreadful ravages in the plantations of cocoa-nut trees. When this insect is alarmed it squirts out a highly acrid fluid, which causes great pain, and sometimes blindness, if it reaches the eyes. Many other species of

Phasmidæ possess the same power to a greater or less extent; and one of the South African species is stated to be able to eject an offensive fluid to a distance of five feet. The genus *Phyllium*, Latr., includes several East Indian species which are known as Leaf Insects, the whole insect being remarkably leaf-like, and even the legs being furnished with broad leaf-like appendages. The *Phasmidæ* are sluggish insects, as may be perceived from their organisation, and chiefly inhabit tropical countries; but a few slender apterous green or brown species, measuring about two or three inches in length, and belonging to the genus *Bacillus*, Latr., are met with in South Europe. Many of the large tropical *Phasmidæ* measure nearly a foot in length.

FAMILY V.—*Achetidæ.*

Antennæ long and slender; hind legs long; the femora thickened, and formed for leaping; wings laid flat over the back, and often projecting beyond the abdomen, which is furnished with two long setæ; ovipositor prominent; tarsi generally three-jointed.

Of this family, which includes the Crickets, we have only five species in England, the best known being the House Cricket (*Acheta Domestica*, Linn.), a brown species found in houses; the Field Cricket (*A. Campestris*, Linn.), a black species, found on heaths, etc.; and the Mole Cricket (*Gryllotalpa Vulgaris*, Linn.), a brown species, twice as large as the others, which burrows in loose soil, and is sometimes very destructive in fields and gardens; it is remarkable for the peculiar shape of its front legs, which are exactly like those of a mole.

Some of the foreign species of *Achetidæ* are of very remarkable forms. *Schizodactylus Monstrosus*, Linn., which is common in India, is a brown species, measuring more than an inch and a half in length; the tegmina and wings are much longer than the body, and are rolled up in spirals when not expanded; the tibiæ are spiny, and the tarsi are provided with leaf-like expansions. Many crickets are apterous, among which are the large heavy species belonging to the genera *Callimenus*, Fisch., and *Brachyporus*, Charp., which resemble gigantic woodlice, or rather, perhaps, shells of the genus *Chiton* in shape. The largest of all the crickets are perhaps the brown species belonging to the genus *Deinacrida*, White, which are found on trees in New Zealand. They are sometimes four or five inches in length, and their legs are very large, and set with rows of very formidable spines, resembling those of a brier.

The natives are afraid to climb the trees on account of these insects, which are able to inflict a very severe bite. Another remarkable cricket, also found in New Zealand, is *Macropathus Filipes*, Walk., the body of which does not much exceed an inch in length; but the antennæ are of enormous length, many times longer than the body, and fully eight inches long. Crickets are generally of dull colours; and the brown and black of our two species of *Acheta* is typical of the colours of most of the species of the family.

FAMILY VI.—*Gryllidæ.*

Antennæ and legs as in *Achetidæ ;* wings and tegmina rooflike; abdomen furnished with a long ovipositor; tarsi generally four-jointed.

The most conspicuous British insect of this family is known as the Great Green Grasshopper (*Phasgonura Viridissima*, Linn.), which measures nearly four inches in expanse of wing, and is therefore nearly as large as the Migratory Locusts which sometimes visit us. It is not an uncommon insect in many parts of England. Many insects of this family are of a green colour, which is liable to fade to yellowish after death. *Ephippitytha Trigintiguttata*, Serv., is a very beautiful Australian species, measuring about four inches across the tegmina, which are of a greenish yellow, with a double row of black spots, the first along the front margin; the wings are slightly transparent. *Chloroscelus Tanana*, Bates, is a large green species found on the river Amazon, where the natives keep it in small wicker cages for the sake of its song. In some species of this family, as in the genus *Phyllophora*, the prothorax is of a very extraordinary shape, being formed into a sort of pointed cape, which extends backwards above the abdomen for half its length.

FAMILY VII.—*Locustidæ.*

Antennæ short; hind legs formed for leaping; wings extending along the sides of the abdomen, as in the *Gryllidæ;* abdomen nearly as long as the wings; ovipositor rudimentary; tarsi generally three-jointed.

This family includes the true Locusts and Grasshoppers, the former of which have been celebrated from the dawn of history for the ravages which they have committed in countries exposed to their attacks. The small grasshoppers which are common in

[1] The families *Gryllidæ* and *Locustidæ* are often called *Locustidæ* and *Acridiidæ*.

our fields are quite harmless, and are generally of a green, brown, or reddish colour, and about an inch long; they belong to the genus *Rhammatocerus*, Fisch., and to some allied genera. The genus *Truxalis*, Fabr., includes several species which inhabit Africa and the shores of the Mediterranean. They are remarkable for the peculiar shape of the head and antennæ, which is not very easy to describe, but which will be seen at a glance on a reference to our figure of *T. Nasuta*, Linn., the commonest species. It is a green insect, with longitudinal reddish stripes on the head and body, and transparent hind wings. The true locusts are insects of large size, with rather narrow tegmina, generally of a brown colour, varied with darker, and ample brightly-coloured hind wings, generally more or less transparent, and frequently marked with numerous angular dusky spots. Different species of locusts, about five inches in expanse of wing, often cause great destruction in various parts of Africa, Asia, and even in Southern and Eastern Europe; but in general they only appear in England singly, as rare and occasional visitors; though, when the greater part of Europe was overrun by them in the middle of the last century, a sufficient number reached England to cause considerable damage in various places. Famine and plague have often followed their ravages in more southern countries. Several species of *Locusta* and *Pachyteles* are met with in England occasionally, which have brown fore wings and green or yellow hind wings. The Rocky Mountain Locust (*Caloptenus Spretus*, Thomas), which sometimes appears in annihilating swarms in the United States, is much smaller than the destructive European species, expanding rather less than two inches. It is a reddish-brown insect, with brown spots, and the hind wings are transparent. Some of the great South American locusts (*Acridotheres Dux*, Drury, and some allied species) are among the largest insects known. They are very bulky, their bodies being nearly four inches in length, and the wings sometimes measure nearly a foot in expanse. In *A. Dux* the greater part of the body is green, the legs being varied with red, and the hind tibiæ very spiny; the wings are red, speckled with dusky arrow-headed spots. Fortunately, however, these very large species are not nearly so destructive as the smaller ones, especially in proportion to their size. Many species of this family are of great beauty, very different indeed from the dingy cockroaches and crickets. It would be difficult to find a more beautiful insect than *Titanacris Albipes*, De Geer, a native of British Guiana. It measures about seven inches across the tegmina, which are of a dull green. This colour extends to the costa of the hind wings, but soon passes into pale blue, and then into the loveliest shade of violet purple, which extends over the greater part of the large wings.

The genus *Œdipoda*, Latr., includes several common species, which, though far inferior in size and beauty to the insects we have just been discussing, are yet very pretty. They generally measure from an inch and a half to two inches across the tegmina, which are brown, with transverse dusky stripes. Several species with blue, red, and yellow wings are common on the Continent, and the blue-winged *Œ. Cærulescens*, Linn. (of which the red-winged *Œ. Germanicum*, Latr., is now considered to be a variety) has occasionally been met with in England. These brightly-coloured insects might easily be mistaken for butterflies when flying. *Œ. Carolina*, Linn., which is common in North America, measures about two inches across the tegmina, which are brown, spotted with dusky, and slightly transparent towards the tips; the hind wings are black, with a moderately broad and slightly transparent sulphur-yellow border.

One of our common English grasshoppers, *Rhammatocerus Biguttulus*, Linn., is brown or greenish, with yellowish legs, and measures about an inch and a quarter in length. Mr. Parfitt has lately published the following interesting account of its habits :—" I have frequently observed our most abundant grasshopper, *R. Biguttulus*, sounding his music in the presence of, and hopping round, a female. Some years ago I was greatly amused as well as instructed by observing several insects of the same species, both males and females. I was drawn to the spot by the extraordinary noise made by these creatures. It was a very hot day, and on a bare portion of a hedgebank between Exeter and Budleigh-Salterton. I cautiously crept up to the place from whence the sound proceeded, and there to my delight I first saw how these insects produced the sound which I had heard. In the centre of this group were several females, apparently listening to the concert; the males were, some hopping, some walking, and others gesticulating in the most ridiculous fashion around these ladies, and each playing to the best of his abilities on his peculiar musical instrument, no doubt to their great amusement and delight." [1]

[1] *Trans. Devonshire Association*, vol. xiv. pp. 370, 371.

ORDER NEUROPTERA.

WINGS four, of similar texture, generally with numerous veins; naked or hairy; mouth furnished with mandibles: female rarely with a conspicuous ovipositor, and never armed with a sting; larva with six legs; metamorphosis complete or incomplete.

It is difficult to lay down characters for this extensive Order, which is now made to include a large number of insects which many writers have treated as belonging to distinct Orders. Still the unnecessary multiplication of primary divisions is always an evil, especially as it tends to encourage the study of isolated groups which ought rather to be considered together; and, to quote an expression of Boisduval's relative to subdividing the genus *Papilio*, " we must either retain it in its entirety, or break it into " many Orders.

ODONATA.

Wings naked, not folded in repose; eyes large and prominent; jaws well developed; antennæ short, not clavate; abdominal appendages short; metamorphosis incomplete; larva and pupa aquatic, active, the latter generally resembling the imago, and with rudimentary wings; habits predatory and carnivorous in all stages.

The *Odonata*, or Dragon Flies, are among the handsomest and most conspicuous of our native insects. The larger species are to be seen chasing their insect prey over water, or along the lanes and hedgerows; and, being insects of powerful flight, may often be met with in forest glades or on heaths at a considerable distance from water, while the smaller and more delicate species are generally to be found fluttering over streams or resting on waterplants. They may be divided into two families, and these again into sub-families.

FAMILY I.—*Libellulidæ.*

Hind wings always broader than the fore wings; structure generally robust, flight powerful.

In the first sub-family, the *Libellulinæ*, the lower lip is smaller than the palpi, and the eyes are not prolonged backwards. Several species of this sub-family are very familiar insects, such as *Libellula Depressa*, Linn., a broad flattish insect, the female yellow, and the male with the abdomen dusted with blue ; the wings expand about two inches and a half. *L. Quadrimaculata*, Linn., is about the same size, but more slender ; it is yellow, and there are two dark spots on the costa of each fore wing ; this latter species is also found in North America. Several other yellow species, about half the size of these (*Diplax Scotica*, Leach, and *D. Flaveola*, Linn., etc.), are very common. Several handsome species of this sub-family are natives of North America, two of which may here be mentioned. *Tramea Carolina*, Linn., is a large blue dragon-fly, measuring nearly four inches across the expanded wings, which are transparent, except that the very broad hind wings are brown at the base for almost a fifth of their length. *Libellula Pulchella*, Drury, is a rather smaller species. The body is brown, dusted with blue in the male, and with a yellow stripe on each side, and each of the wings has a long brown spot at the base, another large spot in the middle of the wing, extending nearly across, and a third at the tip.

Libellula Variegata, Linn., is a handsome East Indian species of about the same size, but with rather short fore wings, and very broad hind wings. The body is blue, and rather short and slender, and the wings are dark yellow, varied with large reddish-brown markings ; the extreme tip of the hind wings and the apical third of the fore wings are transparent. A number of small species with partially opaque wings are very common in West Africa ; one of these is *Libellula Portia*, Drury. It is a blue dragon-fly, with a rather broad body, and expands about an inch and a half across the wings, which are blackish-brown on the front half, and transparent below ; the dark portion is considerably excavated on its lower edge, both towards the tip, in the middle, and (very slightly) at the base. This, and several other species of similar shape, but of different colours, are common in most collections of insects received from tropical Africa.

The *Corduliinæ* differ from the *Libellulinæ* in having the eyes slightly prolonged hindwards. The genus *Cordulia* includes several beautiful bronzy-green species with yellow markings, expanding from two and a half to three inches ; the abdomen is rather slender, but thickened towards the extremity.

In the *Gomphinæ* the lower lip is larger than the palpi, and the

eyes are hardly contiguous; but they are completely so in the
Æschninæ. These sub-families include the largest of the British
dragon-flies, several of which are very common. Their bodies,
however, though longer, are not so stout in proportion as in the
Libellulinæ. *Æschna Grandis*, Linn., is a reddish-brown insect, more
than two and a half inches in length, and sometimes nearly four
inches in expanse; the wings are of a smoky yellow. *Æ. Cyanea*,
Müll., and several allied species, are brown or reddish, tessellated with blue, brown, or yellow; the wings are hyaline. *Cordu-
legaster Annulatus*, Latr., is a magnificent species of equal size, but
belonging to the *Gomphinæ*; it is black, the thorax striped, and
the abdomen banded with yellow. All these species are very
strong on the wing.

FAMILY II.—*Agrionidæ*.

Eyes widely apart; fore and hind wings of equal width; bodies
long, slender, and weak.

This family is divided into two sub-families, the *Calepteryginæ*,
which includes large species, with numerous short transverse nervures on the front edge of the wings; and the *Agrioninæ*, which
are more delicate insects, with only two such nervures. The
Calepteryginæ are also often distinguished by the beautiful colours
of their wings, a character which does not occur to the same extent
in other dragon-flies We have two species of *Calepteryx* in England,
which have a low and rather heavy flapping flight over the water
of small streams. They are very conspicuous insects of a metallic
blue colour; the males of *C. Virgo*, Linn., have deep blue wings,
those of the female being greenish or brown; and *C. Splendens*,
Harr., has transparent wings, with a deep blue band across the
middle of each in the male. One of the most beautiful of the
foreign species is *C. Chinensis*, Linn., a common East Indian species,
in which the fore wings are transparent, and the hind wings are
of a brilliant green, in the male. The American genus *Hetærina*,
Hag., is allied to *Calepteryx*, but the wings are narrower, and
transparent, with a blood-red space at the base of each.

The principal genera of the *Agrioninæ* are easily distinguished
by the shape of the stigma (or pterostigma), a small opaque spot
on the costa towards the tip of the wings. Most of the species of
Lestes, Leach, are bright metallic green, and the stigma is large
and oblong; they expand about an inch and a half across the
wings. In *Agrion*, Fabr., the stigma is small and lozenge-shaped,

and the species are red, black with blue spots, or greyish brown; the smaller species expand less than an inch. They fly little, and are generally found resting on rushes and other plants by the side of water. We have but one other British species of this sub-family, *Platycnemis Pennipes*, Pall., which differs from any others in the tibiæ being slightly dilated.

In the genus *Mecistogaster*, Ramb., the stigma is of irregular shape; the wings are long, and the body is slender, and frequently of great length. *M. Lucretia*, Drury, is a common South American species (blackish, with yellow markings), which measures five inches across the wings, which are transparent, with a dusky cloud at the tips. It is six inches in length, looking as if the abdomen was twice the proper length. *M. Linearis*, Fabr., which we have figured, is rather smaller. The genus *Megaloprepes* has broader wings and a shorter body than *Mecistogaster*. *M. Cœruleata*, Drury, from Central America, measures nearly six inches across the wings, and nearly four inches in length. The body is blue above, and the wings are transparent, with a broad blue band across each near the tip. This species is one of the largest dragon-flies known in expanse of wing.

EPHEMERIDÆ.

Wings not folded in repose; hind wings much smaller than the fore wings, sometimes wanting; mouth imperfectly developed; abdomen furnished with two or three long slender filaments; larvæ and pupæ aquatic, probably feeding on decaying vegetable matter at the bottom of the water.

The *Ephemeridæ*, called otherwise May-flies, or Day-flies, or Brown and Green Drakes, are well known to every observer of Nature who has wandered by the side of a stream in summer; and they are specially interesting to anglers, as they are a very favourite food of river fish. To the entomologist also they present many points of interest. The winged insect which quits the pupa-case is not the final form of the species, but an intermediate stage, called the subimago. The insect, after flying away from the pupa, settles and casts off yet another skin before it appears in its full development. Although the perfect insect takes no food, and lives only a very short time, and in some cases only a few hours, yet the earlier aquatic stages of its life are known to last at least two or three years. The *Ephemeridæ* often appear in extra-ordinary numbers, and Dr. Hagen states that in some parts of

Germany they are used to feed the pigs. The Rev. A. E. Eaton informs me that he believes that two species of *Ephemeridæ* form a portion of the so-called "Kungu Cake," manufactured by the natives of South Africa, of gnats and probably any other insects which can be obtained in sufficient abundance. The commonest and best known species in England is *Ephemera Vulgata*, Linn., the "Brown Drake" and "Green Drake" of anglers. One of the most interesting of the foreign species is perhaps *Oligoneuria Rhenana*, Imh., a white species, which appears in such vast numbers on the Rhine after sunset as to resemble falling snowflakes. But they live a very short time, and few or none survive till morning. As already mentioned, fish are very fond of May-flies; and in some parts of the country the swarms which appear are called "fishes' manna." The remains of several very large insects allied to the *Ephemeridæ* have lately been met with in the Devonian formations of Europe and North America.

PERLIDÆ.

Four wings of equal size, folded in repose; mouth imperfectly developed; antennæ long; abdomen frequently broad at the extremity, with a moderately long straight filament (much broader and shorter than in the *Ephemeridæ*) extending from each corner; larvæ and pupæ aquatic.

The *Perlidæ*, or Stone-flies, have considerable resemblance at first sight to the Caddis-flies, from which their folded wings, broad abdomen, and caudal setæ will at once distinguish them. Our British species are brown insects, of moderate size; but some of the foreign species are more brightly coloured; thus the insects belonging to the Australian genus *Chloroperla*, Newm., are green.

TERMITIDÆ.

Social insects; males and females with four large wings of equal size (neuters wingless); mandibles well developed; body oblong and depressed.

The *Termites*, or White Ants, have a great resemblance to ants in their habits and economy, and are even more destructive insects, as some species will hollow out any woodwork about a house from the inside, never breaking through it, but leaving the surface a mere shell, so that they may do irretrievable mischief without their presence being even suspected. Fortunately no species has

yet become acclimatised in England; but as various destructive
species are either indigenous or acclimatised in some parts of the
United States, and even in Europe (at Bordeaux, for example),
every precaution should be taken to prevent any risk of their establishing themselves in our own country.

Several classes of individuals are met with in the nests of the
Termites, and their relations to each other, and their transformations, do not appear to be clearly made out.

In *Termes Bellicosus*, the habits of which were observed at Sierra
Leone by Smeathman, the males and females leave the nest for their
"marriage flight," as in the case of ants; but instead of the male
perishing, as with *Hymenoptera*, the males and females lose their
wings, and a surviving pair are led into the nest by the neuters,
after losing their wings, when the abdomen of the female becomes
enormously distended with eggs, until her bulk is equal to that
of 20,000 or 30,000 workers, and she measures about three inches
in length. The eggs are discharged by a constant peristaltic
motion, at the rate of about sixty per minute. Unlike
Hymenoptera, the greater part of the work of the nest is per-
formed by the larvæ, from which the pupæ differ in possessing
rudiments of wings. There is also another form, the soldiers,
which differ from the larvæ by their enormous heads and powerful mandibles. Some writers have regarded them as pupæ, and
others as neuters; the latter theory is most probable; but further
careful observations on these insects would be of great interest.
Smeathman describes how, when the nests are attacked, the workers
disappear, and the soldiers rush out with the greatest fury, snap-
ping blindly at every object, and if they seize a man's leg, instantly
drawing a blood-stain through his stocking an inch long. But if
the alarm subsides, the soldiers disappear, and the workers issue
forth in great numbers, and immediately set to work to repair any
damage which the nest may have sustained. This and several
allied species build nests in various parts of Africa to the height
of ten or twelve feet, formed of a species of cement so hard and
solid that they will bear the weight of three or four men at once. The
sentinels of the herds of antelopes and other wild animals use them
for watch-towers. Frank Oates, a recent traveller in South Africa,
writes:[1]—"The white ants kept tumbling over me all night, and
knocking down leaves from the roof. These white ants (*Termites*)
are the curse of all African settlers and travellers, devouring

[1] *Matabele Land and the Victoria Falls*, pp. 134 and 135.

everything except iron or tin, whilst in time even houses succumb to their ravages. They form, however, an article of food in many places amongst the natives, by whom they are much esteemed on account of their slightly acid flavour.[1] The enormous structures they erect are frequently carried up the trunk of a high tree, or may sometimes be seen standing alone at a height of eighteen feet. . . . The Dutch Boers and others make use of these ant-hills for cooking purposes, hollowing out the lower portion of the heap, and filling the hollow thus formed with wood, which is lighted, and, when consumed, renders the receptacle an admirable oven, retaining its heat for a great length of time." He gives two illustrations of these ant-hills, one of which represents just such an oven as he has described.

PSOCIDÆ.

Head very large; antennæ long and slender, setaceous, composed of about thirteen joints; tarsi with only two or three joints; hind wings smaller than the fore wings, sometimes wanting; and a few species are wholly apterous; metamorphosis incomplete; pupa active.

The *Psocidæ* are very small insects, which feed on dry vegetable and animal substances; and Dr. Hagen states that he has sometimes found neglected heaps of chaff to consist almost entirely of *Psoci*. The species are met with on the trunks of trees, under bark, in caves, on old lichen-covered walls, and in similar localities. The species figured (*P. Biunctatus*, Linn.) is a greyish-yellow insect, which measures about a quarter of an inch across the wings; it is found on the trunks of apple-trees in summer, according to Westwood. *Atropos Pulsatoria*, Linn., is a wingless whitish insect, measuring about the twentieth of an inch in length, which frequents houses, being found among old books and papers, and among collections of natural history, to which it is very injurious.

EMBIDÆ.

Head large; antennæ slender, sometimes with only eleven joints, and sometimes with as many as thirty; tarsi three-jointed; fore and hind wings of equal size; metamorphosis incomplete.

The *Embidæ* are insects resembling small Termites, and the species are not numerous, though the family appears to have representatives in most parts of the world, including South Europe. *Embia Savignyi*, Westw., a dull reddish insect found in Egypt, is the

---

[1] Another point of resemblance to ants.

longest known species of this group, which is closely allied to the two preceding families.

THRIPIDÆ.

Wings long, narrow, equal, veinless, with long fringes, laid horizontally along the back when at rest; tarsi two-jointed; metamorphosis complete; pupa active.

This is a family of uncertain position; it was originally placed by Linné at the end of the *Hemiptera* after *Coccus*, and is still regarded by some entomologists (*e.g.* Pascoe) as Hemipterous. Other authors have referred it to the *Orthoptera* or *Neuroptera*, while others again have regarded it as entitled to form a distinct Order, under the name of *Thysanoptera*. It includes very small insects, which are generally met with on plants, to which they some-times cause much injury by absorbing their juices. Some species met with in gardens and greenhouses are known to gardeners as the "Black Fly;" but the most frequently observed of any is the small black insect met with in wheat, infesting both the stalk and the ear, and often to be found nestling in the furrow of the seed itself. The female is apterous, and the larva and pupa are yellow, the latter with short wing-cases. Its name is *Thrips Cerealium*, Hal.

MALLOPHAGA.

Wingless, mandibulate insects, not undergoing a metamorphosis, and parasitic upon birds.

This group, which includes the Bird-Lice, was formerly regarded either as a separate Order by itself, or was united with the *Pediculidæ* to form the Order *Anoplura*. By modern writers it is generally treated as a degraded family of either the *Hemiptera* or the *Neuroptera*. Westwood, however, excludes the *Mallophaga*, *Anoplura*, and *Thysanura* from the insects altogether, regarding them as a distinct class, under the name of *Ametabola*, chiefly on account of the total absence of either wings or metamorphoses in these groups.

The *Mallophaga* differ considerably in structure, but are gener-ally longer and more slender than the *Pediculidæ*, to which they have a great analogical resemblance, though differing so much in structure that they are usually placed in distinct Orders. They are all parasitic on birds, feeding on the soft parts near the roots of the feathers.

THYSANURA.

Wingless, mandibulate insects, with long many-jointed antennæ; abdomen composed of ten segments ; not undergoing a metamorphosis, and not parasitic.

This group (with which the *Collembola* were formerly included) is generally classed either as a distinct Order (perhaps not truly belonging to the insects), or is treated as a degraded or perhaps a primitive form of the *Orthoptera* or *Neuroptera*. Their affinities are studied with great care and attention, because they are supposed to represent some of the oldest forms of insects, and it is thought that their study will throw light on many interesting affinities between forms now widely separated which might otherwise be overlooked. The standard work on these groups is Sir John Lubbock's "Monograph of the *Collembola* and *Thysanura*," published by the Ray Society in 1873.

The *Thysanura* are generally known as "Springtails," from possessing two or three long caudal appendages. They are divided into several families, of which the *Lepismatidæ* are the best known. Their bodies are covered with scales, while those of the other families are only covered with hairs. *Lepisma Saccharina*, Linn., which measures one-third of an inch in length, is a very common species, frequenting dark dry places ; it is frequently found among sugar-stores, between the cracks of boards, and sometimes among stored books. It is called the "Silver-fish," from its silvery white colour, and the manner in which it shoots or glides along when disturbed. I once examined a chest of books carefully, among which this creature was common, without being able to perceive that the books had sustained the slightest injury ; but I have been informed that the insect has caused great damage to a public library at Malta. It is, however, quite possible that this library was infested with several species of insects, and that the blame was laid upon the *Lepisma* as being the largest and most conspicuous, while the real offenders escaped notice. The remaining species of *Lepismatidæ* are found under stones, under bark, or in ants' nests; those of the genus *Machilis*, Latr., frequent damp places, *M. Maritima*, Leach, being common on the sea-shore. It is brown, rather larger than *Lepisma*, and instead of the three longest anal appendages being of nearly equal length, the middle one is more than twice as long as the lateral ones in *Machilis*. The *Campodeidæ* are furnished with two long caudal appendages, set

with hairs; and the *Iapygidæ* have shorter antennæ and legs than
the other families, and the caudal appendages are modified into a
pair of forceps. They are found in damp places or under stones,
and are destitute of eyes.

COLLEMBOLA.

Wingless, mandibulate insects; antennæ with few joints; abdomen composed of six segments; not undergoing a metamorphosis, and not parasitic.

The *Collembola* are small insects, the largest of which do not exceed a quarter of an inch in length, and many measure only one-twelfth of an inch, or even much less. Sir John Lubbock divides them into several families, the first of which, the *Smynthuridæ*, has four-jointed antennæ, with a long terminal segment; the head is very large, the thorax short, and the abdomen broad, short, and terminating obtusely somewhat suddenly. The species are rather gaily coloured, many being green or yellow. They are found among grass, dead leaves, or rotten wood. Lubbock gives the following account of the courtship of his *Smynthurus Luteus*, a small yellow species, $\frac{1}{33}$d of an inch in length, which is common among grass in summer: "It is very amusing to see these little creatures coquetting together. The male, which is much smaller than the female, runs round her, and they butt one another, standing face to face, and moving backwards and forwards like two playful lambs. Then the female pretends to run away, and the male runs after her, with a queer appearance of anger; gets in front and stands facing her again; then she turns coyly round, but he, quicker and more active, scuttles round her, and seems to whip her with his antennæ; then for a bit they stand face to face, play with their antennæ, and seem to be all in all to one another."— (Lubbock, p. 109.)

The *Papyriidæ* are very similar to the *Smynthuridæ*, but the terminal joint of the antennæ is short, with whorls of hair.

In the *Degeeriadæ* and *Poduridæ* the body is cylindrical, but they are distinguished by having the fourth and fifth segments of the abdomen respectively furnished with an apparatus for leaping. They frequent damp places in woods, etc. Several species of the former family are remarkable for their long antennæ; in the lead-coloured *Tomocerus Longicornis*, Müll., they are longer than the body. Several species of the genera *Templetonia* and *Seira*, Lubb.,

G

are beautifully silvery. *Isotoma Saltans*, Agassiz, is a small black species, which abounds on the glaciers of the Alps.

Two species of *Poduridæ* are likewise worth mentioning for their habits. One is *Achorutes Dubius*, Templ., found by Templeton and Lubbock on the surface of standing water, and on sand-banks; and the other is *Lipura Stillicidii*, Schiödte, which frequents caves. The former species is blue-black, and the latter white, and these colours predominate in the family.

The *Anouridæ* are a small family resembling woodlice in form. One species, *Anoura Rosæ*, Gerv., found in the Jardin des Plantes, is entirely of a rose colour.

The eyes of several of the *Thysanura* and *Collembola* are different from those of all other adult forms included with the insects. In the *Collembola* they consist of from one to eight ocelli, arranged in a series on each side of the head, thus offering an analogy with those of Lepidopterous larvæ. On the other hand, most of the *Thysanura* have two compound eyes; and one or two genera have been asserted by Nicolet to have ocelli similar to those of the *Collembola* on each side of the head, a statement which Lubbock has been unable to confirm. Several genera of both groups are believed to be entirely destitute of eyes.

NEUROPTERA PLANIPENNIA.

Head of moderate size; antennæ many-jointed, variable in length, and sometimes very long, filiform, or clubbed; wings naked, generally of equal length; hind wings sometimes with long appendages; metamorphosis complete; pupa inactive.

A very large and important group, rivalling the *Odonata* in size and beauty, and far surpassing them both in number and in the singularity of their forms. They are, however, very poorly represented in Britain, and although we have representatives of several of the principal genera, nearly all the larger and more conspicuous species met with on the Continent of Europe are absent. They are divided into three families, of which the second is by far the most important.

FAMILY I.—*Sialidæ*.

Wings large, reticulated, deflexed, more or less projecting at the anal angle; antennæ long; body short and thick.

In the first sub-family, the *Sialinæ*, the head is transverse, the prothorax broad, and of moderate length, and the larva is aquatic. The best known British species is *Sialis Lutarius*, Linn., a very abundant insect near water. It is smoky black, with numerous nervures, and measures nearly an inch and a half across the wings. Several very large insects belonging to this family are common in North America. One of these is *Corydalis Cornuta*, Linn., which measures five and a half inches across its greyish semi-transparent wings. It is quite harmless, though the huge mandibles of the male give it a very formidable appearance.

In the *Raphidiinæ* the head is long; the prothorax is long and slender, tapering in front; and the larvæ live under bark. Several dark-brown species, measuring about an inch across the wings, are common in Europe, to one of which Linné gave the name of *Raphidia Ophiopsis*, from a fancied resemblance of the long neck and head to that of a snake.

FAMILY II.—*Hemerobiidæ*.

Wings strongly deflexed; hind wings not produced at the anal angle; body usually slender; larva not aquatic.

The first sub-family, the *Myrmeleontidinæ*, includes the Ant-Lions. Their larvæ are well known to form a pitfall of loose sand, at the bottom of which they lurk, with only their jaws projecting, and feed on the insects which may happen to fall over the edge. They are not found in Britain, but the larva of our common Green Tiger Beetle has similar habits, and might be called the British Ant-Lion. Two brown species, which expand about two inches (*Myrmeleon Formicarius*, Linn., and *M. Formicalynx*, Burm.), are not uncommon on the Continent. They resemble dragon-flies, but their bodies are shorter and less tapering, and they may be immediately distinguished by their short, clubbed antennæ. The genus *Palpares*, Ramb., is found throughout Asia, Africa, and South Europe, and includes species of moderate or large size, with semi-transparent white or yellowish wings, banded or spotted with brown or black. *P. Libelluloides*, Linn., is found in South Europe and the Mediterranean region.

The *Ascalaphinæ* form another sub-family not represented in Britain. They may be distinguished from the Ant-Lions by their long clubbed antennæ, and their shorter and broader wings and bodies. Several species of the genus *Ascalaphus*, Fabr., with transparent wings, variously ornamented with brown and yellow, are

common in Switzerland and Southern Europe, where they may be
seen flying among fir-trees in the day-time.   The long clubbed
antennæ and brightly-coloured wings actually led Scopeli, a celebrated entomologist of the last century, to describe one of the
species as a butterfly, under the name of *Papilio Macaronius.*

The *Nemopterinæ* form another small group, chiefly found in the
countries bordering on the Mediterranean, and in Western Asia.
Their bodies are short, their antennæ slender, and of moderate
length, and their fore wings are broad.   Their hind wings, however, are very long and narrow, and frequently more or less dilated
towards the tip, giving the insect, when held vertically, very much
the appearance of being supported on stilts.   The Spanish *Nemo-
ptera Lusitanica*, Ramb., is yellow, with brown markings, and expands
over two inches; the hind wings being almost as long.   There is
another section of the genus with narrower and transparent wings.

The *Chrysopinæ* have long slender antennæ, delicate transparent,
reticulated wings, and beautiful golden eyes; their bodies are
generally of a green colour.   Several species of the genus *Chrysopa*,
Leach, are very common in England.   They are common in woods
and gardens, and are easily caught, as they have a weak flight; but
they exhale a peculiarly unpleasant odour, which has been compared to that of human ordure.   They generally expand about
an inch.   Their eggs have a peculiar appearance, being attached
to the surface of a leaf by a long slender stalk.   The larvæ live on
Aphides, and destroy great numbers, seizing them with their strong
mandibles, and speedily sucking out the liquid contents of their
bodies.

The genus *Hemerobius*, Linn., the type of the sub-family *Hemero-
biinæ*, includes a few brown or yellowish species, rarely expanding
more than three-quarters of an inch; their antennæ are moniliform,
and their larvæ feed on *Aphides,* and clothe themselves with the
empty skins of their prey.   *Osmylus Fulvicephalus*, Scop., the largest
of the British *Planipennia*, has broad, transparent wings, the fore
wings slightly pointed, and ornamented with a few brown spots;
it measures nearly two inches in expanse, and frequents the neighbourhood of streams, the larva being partly aquatic in its habits.
Drepanopteryx Phalænoides, Linn., a great rarity in Britain, resembles
a small brown moth, and measures nearly an inch and a half across
the wings.

The genus *Coniopteryx*, Hal., typical of the sub-family *Conio-
pteryginæ*, includes a few small white species, seldom much more

than a quarter of an inch across the wings, which are remarkable
for being always covered with a white mealy powder. The larva
is found on fir-trees, where it feeds on *Aphides.*

The sub-family *Mantispinæ* is remarkable for having the fore
legs long, thick, and serrated, as in *Mantis.* The commonest species
is *Mantispa Pagana,* Fabr., which, although not found in Britain, is
met with in many parts of Europe among trees and shrubs. The
thorax is red, and the abdomen yellow, with red lines; the wings
are transparent.

FAMILY III.—*Panorpidæ.*

Wings long, narrow, and equal, horizontal in repose; mouth
produced into a kind of beak; larvæ living underground, and
probably feeding on insects, etc., of subterranean habits.

Several species of *Panorpa,* Linn., abound along hedges; they
are brown or black insects, with transparent wings blotched or
spotted with black; the body is sometimes marked with yellow.
They are frequently called "Scorpion Flies," from the long abdomen
of the male being provided with a singular forceps. The species
of the genus *Bittacus,* Latr., which are common on the Continent,
though not British, have long, slender, transparent wings, and long
slender legs; and so much resemble *Tipulidæ* that they might
easily be mistaken for them at first sight, even in a collection, but
that they have four wings instead of two. *Boreus Hiemalis,* Linn.,
is a small greenish-brown insect about one-sixth of an inch long,
with rudimentary wings. It is found among moss, and sometimes
on the surface of the snow during the winter months, and possesses
the power of leaping.

TRICHOPTERA.

Antennæ long and slender; mouth imperfectly developed;
tarsi generally five-jointed; wings long, with but few transverse
veins, hairy, deflected; hind wings folded. Metamorphosis complete; larvæ aquatic, living in cases, in which they also assume
the pupa state; pupa inactive.

The *Trichoptera,* or *Phryganidæ,* are known as Caddis Flies,
and the cases which the larvæ construct for themselves of bits
of stick, small stones, or even shells, are perhaps better known
than the flies themselves. They are sometimes regarded as a
separate Order, but are at present usually treated as a section of
the *Neuroptera,* pending a more thorough and satisfactory rearrange-

ment of the Orders of Insects than exists at present. Our native
species are all of dull colours, grey, brown, and black predominating; and many of them, especially the smaller species, have
considerable resemblance to moths, both in general appearance and
in mode of flight. Their study is attended with peculiar difficulties, as the species greatly resemble each other, and cannot be
satisfactorily separated without an examination of the anal appendages.

Mr. M'Lachlan, in his *Monographic Revision and Synopsis of the
Trichoptera of the European Fauna*, the latest standard work on the
subject, enumerates eight families, chiefly founded on the structure
of the palpi; but we shall here confine ourselves to a notice of a
few of the most conspicuous and interesting species.

Phryganea Grandis, Linn., which may be considered typical of
the family *Phryganidæ*, is a brown insect measuring nearly two
inches in expanse. It is common in most parts of the country,
and its larva, which forms a cylindrical tube of fragments of leaves,
etc., lives in still water. There are two or three other British
species, which are very similar, but rather smaller. There are
some Chinese and Japanese species of *Phryganea* with yellow hind
wings bordered with brown; and Indian species with purplish
hind wings largely tipped with yellow.

The *Hydroptilidæ* are small dark insects with short and almost
moniliform antennæ, and long fringes to the hind wings, so that
they might easily be mistaken for *Micro-Lepidoptera*. They are
gregarious, fly by day as well as in the evening and at night, and
are very active, and frequently swarm near water.

The species of *Leptocerus*, Leach, are brown or black insects,
expanding three-quarters of an inch or an inch across the wings,
and are remarkable for the great length of their antennæ, which
are often more than twice as long as the wings, especially in the
males. The larvæ form their cases of sand. The *Leptoceridæ*, like
most of the *Trichoptera*, are gregarious insects, and are generally
met with in abundance, if at all.

The other five families admitted by M'Lachlan are the
Limnophilidæ, *Sericostomatidæ*, *Œstropsidæ*, *Hydropsychidæ*, and
Rhyacophilidæ.

ORDER HYMENOPTERA.

WINGS four, with few veins; apparently naked, but frequently clothed with short scattered bristles; mouth furnished with mandibles, and likewise with a proboscis; female with a conspicuous ovipositor, often modified into a sting; larvæ generally footless; pupæ inactive.

The Order *Hymenoptera* is one of the most interesting and extensive. The habits and structure of the insects which it includes are very various. Among these are the Ants, Bees, and Wasps, which live in communities, and exhibit an amount of intelligence far exceeding that of any other insects, except, perhaps, the Termites, which they also resemble in the work of the community being executed by imperfectly-developed females, called workers, which are sometimes of two or three kinds, with special duties, and which form the bulk of the population. The great bulk of parasitic insects likewise belong to the present Order. Linné called this Order *Hymenoptera* in allusion to the row of small hooks connecting the front and hind wings during flight; however, many species are included in it which are apterous in one or both sexes. It is primarily divided into *Hymenoptera Terebrantia*, in which the ovipositor is used as a borer, and the *Hymenoptera Aculeata*, in which it is modified into a sting. In the latter section, the antennæ are thirteen-jointed in the males, and twelve-jointed in the females.

I.—HYMENOPTERA TEREBRANTIA—PHYTOPHAGA.

Abdomen not stalked; larva with from six to twenty-two legs, feeding on plants or trees.

FAMILY I.—*Tenthredinidæ*.

Ovipositor of the female modified into a saw, and used to form incisions on leaves for the reception of her eggs; larvæ resembling caterpillars, and feeding exposed on plants.

In the first sub-family of the Saw-flies, the *Cimbicinæ*, the antennæ are short, and knobbed at the end like those of a butterfly. *Trichiosoma Lucorum*, Linn., is a very common insect on hedges; it is black, and rather hairy, and measures rather more than an inch across the wings. The larva is solitary, provided with twenty-two legs, and forms a hard cocoon attached to the branches of the hawthorn, in which it passes the winter. The Australian genus *Perga* includes many handsome species, generally of a bronzy green or tawny colour, with a conspicuous yellow scutellum. So far as is known, their larvæ, which have only six legs, live gregariously on different species of *Eucalyptus*, and form their cocoons in the ground. The female of *Perga Lewisii*, Westw., a native of Tasmania and South Australia, watches over her young for several weeks after they are hatched; but this habit has not been stated to occur in any other species.

In the sub-family *Hylotominæ*, the antennæ are only three-jointed, the joints beyond the second being fused into one, and generally very pilose. In several genera of this group the third joint is bifurcated in the males, the two branches being of equal length, and giving the insect a rather singular appearance. In several other genera belonging to different sub-families (*Pterygophorus, Lophyrus, Cladius,* etc.), the antennæ are either pectinated or branched in the males, and simple in the females, one of the most remarkable instances being a Papuan species, *Cladomacra Macropus*, Smith, which measures rather more than half an inch across the wings. The insect is reddish, with the antennæ, hind legs, and the tip of the abdomen black; the antennæ are very long and slender, with a long branch projecting from the base of each joint.

The best known of all the Saw-flies is *Nematus Ribesii*, Scop., a small yellow insect, with black spots on the thorax, the larvæ of which often strip our gooseberry and currant bushes of their leaves.

Tenthredo Atra, Linn., is a black species, with red legs, and the middle of the abdomen red in the female. I mention it to record the fact that a specimen lately received from Munich was found to be greatly infested by a red mite, specimens of which were likewise found attached to several other *Hymenoptera* from the same locality. The genus *Allantus*, Jur., includes a number of black and yellow species, some of which are predatory in their habits, and feed on other insects.

In the typical groups of *Tenthredinidæ*, the majority of the genera have nine-jointed antennæ, but in some of the less typical sub-families, such as the *Lophyridinæ* and *Lydinæ*, the number of joints is frequently much greater, often exceeding twenty.

FAMILY II.—*Siricidæ.*

Ovipositor of the female exserted, and forming a powerful awl for piercing the bark of trees, in the solid wood of which the larvæ feed.

The number of known species of this family is not large. The insects themselves are, however, large and conspicuous, and are not very uncommon in fir plantations, though much more abundant on the Continent than in England. The larvæ sometimes remain concealed in timber for years, and the flies, when arrived at maturity, have been known to issue unexpectedly from the flooring, or other timber of a house, greatly to the consternation of the inhabitants. Wood-feeding insects often vary very much in size, and these are no exception to the rule, some specimens being almost twice as large as others; but they generally measure considerably over an inch both in length and expanse. The two commonest species are *Sirex Gigas*, Linn., and *S. Noctilio*, Fabr. In both species the antennæ are filiform, and many-jointed, and the abdomen of the male is triangular at the tip, while that of the female is provided with a long ovipositor. *S. Gigas* is yellow, with two black bands on the abdomen in the female, and the tip black in the male. *S. Noctilio* is of a purplish-blue colour.

II.—HYMENOPTERA TEREBRANTIA—ENTOMOPHAGA.

Abdomen petiolated, or at least attached to the thorax only by a small portion of its base; larva footless; parasitic on the eggs or larvæ of other insects, except in the gall-producing *Cynipidæ*.

Many authors make two subdivisions in this section: *Pupivora* or *Spiculifera*, including the families *Cynipidæ*, *Chalcididæ*, *Proctotrypidæ*, *Braconidæ*, *Ichneumonidæ*, and *Evaniidæ*; and *Tubulifera*, including the *Chrysididæ*. The latter family, however, appears to me to belong rather to the *Hymenoptera Aculeata* than to the *Terebrantia*.

FAMILY I.—*Cynipidæ.*

Ovipositor concealed, sub-spiral; antennæ straight, thirteen- to fifteen-jointed; wings with few veins; either gall-producers or parasites.

This family includes the true gall-flies, a very large number of which are attached to the oak, and a few to other trees. They are, however, not the only gall-insects; for the family of gall-gnats among the *Diptera* (*Cecidomyidæ*), and several other species belonging to various Orders, are likewise gall-producers. The *Cynipidæ* are small insects (sometimes exceedingly minute), and are generally provided with large wings, though some of the alternate broods (formerly placed in the genus *Biorhiza*, Westw.) are apterous. The oak-galls are very various in shape and size, the so-called oak-apples, produced by *Aphilothrix Radicis*, Fabr., and *Teras Terminalis*, Fabr., are large and soft; the gall of *Dryophanta Scutellaris*, Hart., placed on the under side of a leaf, is about the size and shape of a White Heart Cherry, and hard; and the Artichoke Gall, produced by *Aphilothrix Fecundatrix*, Hart., really resembles an artichoke in miniature, or, more exactly, a small green fir-cone. The gall-nuts of commerce, from which ink is obtained, are produced by an exotic species of *Cynips*, as are also the so-called apples of Sodom, which are met with in the neighbourhood of the Dead Sea. Very dissimilar from any of these is the mossy excrescence called the bedeguar, which is common on the wild rose, and is the gall of *Rhodites Rosæ*, Linn.

The *Cynipidæ* present problems of great interest. For a long time it was believed that no males of many species existed, and that the race consisted wholly of fertile females. One great difficulty in investigating these insects is that the galls are so greatly infested by parasites, chiefly belonging to the family *Chalcididæ*, that the parasites bred from the galls often far out-number the real owners. At length, however, it has been ascertained that a large number of the gall-producing *Cynipidæ*, if not all, are dimorphous, and exhibit a regular alternation of genera-tions, the spring and autumn broods being so utterly different that they were hitherto always supposed to belong to different genera. The spring broods consist wholly of fertile females, and the autumn broods consist of males and females. In some cases the former are apterous, and live at the roots of trees; and the galls from which the spring and autumn broods proceed are as different as the insects themselves. Thus, according to Adler, *Neuroterus Fumipennis*, Hart., a small black insect with reddish legs and clouded wings, which appears in May, and is produced from a round flat scale-like gall on the under side of the oak leaves, is the female parthenogenetic form of *Spathegaster*

Tricolor, Hart., males and females of which appear in July from a white hairy gall on the upper side of the leaves.

Again, *Biorhiza Renum*, Hart., is a uniform reddish-brown wingless parthenogenetic female, which emerges in mid-winter from a small kidney-shaped gall on the under side of the oak leaves, which has ripened and fallen to the ground in October. After this female has laid her eggs, the results are round juicy galls, varying from the size of a pea to that of a cherry, and placed on the bark of the oak, but always arising from a small bud. These arrive at perfection in May and June, and give rise to a brood of black flies, with yellowish-red legs and abdomen, with very long wings, and consisting of both males and females.

FAMILY II.—*Chalcididæ*.

Ovipositor generally exserted; antennæ elbowed (basal joint often very long); six- to thirteen- jointed (rarely fourteen); palpi short; wings with very few veins; pupa naked; habits parasitic (with a few exceptions).

The *Chalcididæ* include a great number of small insects, few of even the larger species of which exceed half an inch in expanse. Many of them are singular in shape, and others brilliantly metallic; but, owing to their small size, they have hitherto been studied by comparatively few entomologists. Perhaps about 1200 or 1500 species have hitherto been described; but much still remains to be done, especially in foreign countries, before we know much of so extensive a group.

In the comparatively large species of *Leucospis, Smicra, Chalcis*, etc., the hind femora are of a very peculiar shape, being so much thickened as in some cases to resemble the abdomen in size. On the under surface these thickened femora are either serrated or armed with strong, and sometimes large and pointed, teeth.

The genus *Leucospis*, Fabr., includes black species with yellow spots, remarkable for the position of the ovipositor of the female, which is recurved over the abdomen as far forwards as the scutellum; they are not British. In the genus *Halticella*, Spin., the long scape of the antennæ is placed just above the mouth, instead of near the top of the head, as in most other insects. *Callimome*, Spin., includes a number of small brilliant green or bronzy species, with long ovipositors, which are mostly parasitic on galls. *Eucharis*, Latr., and some other genera have beautifully branching antennæ.

Many of the *Chalcididæ* are apterous in one or both sexes, and, according to Professor Westwood and Sir S. S. Saunders, the males of *Blastophaga* are apterous, while the females are winged; a most unusual anomaly in insects.

Several species of most extraordinary forms, belonging to the genera *Agaon, Blastophaga, Idarnes,* etc., inhabit the interior of various species of wild and cultivated figs; and as they are believed to promote the ripening of the latter, the fig-growers inoculate their young figs with the insects from infested plants by a process known as caprification. The largest genus of the *Chalcididæ* is *Pteromalus,* Swed., the species of which infest *Lepidoptera,* and sometimes emerge in great numbers from a single pupa. *Eurytoma,* Ill., and some allied genera depart from the usual parasitic habits of the *Chalcididæ* in being plant-feeders, feeding in the stalks of wheat, etc.

FAMILY III.—*Proctotrypidæ.*

Ovipositor exserted or concealed; body rather long and slender; antennæ elbowed, ten- to sixteen- jointed; wings nearly veinless; palpi long and drooping; pupa enclosed in a cocoon; habits parasitic.

The *Proctotrypidæ* are probably much less numerous than the *Chalcididæ,* but have been even less studied, being much smaller and more obscure insects; in fact some of them share with the *Trichopterygidæ* among the *Coleoptera,* the reputation of being the smallest insects. They exhibit considerable variation in structure and habits, and are usually either parasitic on very small insects, or infest the eggs of larger ones. The smallest and some of the most beautiful species among them belong to the genus *Mymar,* Curt., and allies. *M. Pulchellus,* Curt., has battledore-shaped wings, the broad part being fringed with long hairs. An allied North American species (*Pteratomus Putnami,* Pack.) measures one-ninetieth of an inch in length, and is said to be the smallest insect known. It is supposed to be an egg-parasite on *Megachile Centuncularis,* Linn., or on a parasite of that bee.

The *Proctotrypidæ* are often placed as a section of *Hymenoptera* called *Oxyura.*

FAMILY IV.—*Braconidæ.*

Antennæ not elbowed beyond the scape, generally with more than sixteen joints, second joint shorter than the first and third, and not followed by a minute rudimentary joint; abdomen with the second and third segments soldered together, the three first segments larger than the others; ovipositor exserted or concealed; habits parasitic.

The *Braconidæ* and *Ichneumonidæ* form together two closely allied families of great extent, of which about 10,000 species are supposed to be described at present; but although the European species have been discussed by many authors, very little has been published on the exotic species in a connected form.   They have been divided into a great number of sub-families and genera, which cannot here be discussed in detail.   Many of the foreign species of *Braconidæ* are rather large and handsome insects, often varied with black and yellow, as in *Bracon Bicolor*, Brullè, which occurs in South Africa.   On the other hand, our native species of *Aphidius*, Nees, and the allied genera, many of which infest *Aphidæ* and other small insects, are themselves small.   The best known of the *Braconidæ* is perhaps *Microgaster Glomeratus*, Linn., a small blackish species, with reddish-yellow legs, which destroys the larva of the common cabbage butterfly (*Pieris Brassicæ*, Linn.), round the dead body of which its little yellow cocoons may often be observed. But for these and other insect parasites, the insects which attack our field and garden crops would prove infinitely more destructive than at present.

FAMILY V.—*Ichneumonidæ.*

Antennæ not elbowed beyond the scape, always with more than sixteen joints; scape large, always followed by two small joints; abdomen sessile or petiolated, often with a long exserted ovipositor; habits parasitic.

The *Ichneumonidæ* are rather large and slender insects, and are divided into several distinct-looking sub-families.

In the typical *Ichneumoninæ* the abdomen is depressed and petiolated, the first segment curved, and generally widened near the tip, and the ovipositor is concealed, or but little prominent.   The genus *Ichneumon*, Linn., is itself a very large one; and the great majority of the species are black, either with red legs, or with the antennæ, legs, shoulders, scutellum, and legs varied with yellow, or a great part of the abdomen may be either red or yellow in one or both sexes.   The species of *Trogus*, Panz., are rather large insects, measuring an inch or more in length; they are black, with reddish legs and abdomen, and the wings are sometimes slightly dusky at the edges.

The *Cryptinæ* differ from the *Ichneumoninæ* in the exserted ovipositor, and also in the position of the spiracles; a large number of species belonging to the genus *Pezomachus*, Grav., etc., are apterous in one or both sexes, and somewhat resemble ants in appearance.

In the *Pimplinæ*, the first segment of the abdomen is usually straight; and the ovipositor is generally very long. The best known species is *Rhyssa Persuasoria*, Linn., a black insect, with the thorax, scutellum, and the sides of the long narrow abdomen spotted with pale yellow. It measures about an inch in length, but the ovipositor, which is composed of three long slender bristles, is fully twice as long as the body. This species is met with in fir woods, and uses its extraordinary ovipositor to drill holes in trees infested by the larva of *Sirex Gigas*, Linn., on which its own larva is parasitic. The insect frequently drives its ovipositor so firmly into the wood that it is unable to withdraw it, and perishes in this position. Other species of *Rhyssa* very similar to this are found in various parts of the world, one of the largest and handsomest being *R. Antipodum*, Smith, a native of New Zealand. Its habits are unknown, but it is not unlikely to feed on the large wood-feeding larvæ of the genus *Charagia*, Walk. (green moths belonging to the family *Zeuzeridæ*), which are common in that country.

In the *Ophioninæ* the antennæ are long and slender, as indeed is the whole insect; and the abdomen is very narrow and compressed, and rarely furnished with a prominent ovipositor. *O. Luteus*, Fabr., is a common species found over a great part of the world.

FAMILY VI.—*Evaniidæ.*

Antennæ not elbowed beyond the scape, thirteen- or fourteen-jointed; wings veined, no closed cells on the hind wings; abdomen attached to the upper part of the metathorax; ovipositor straight; habits parasitic.

The typical genus *Evania*, Fabr., is found in all parts of the world; and many of the recorded species are either very closely allied, or not truly distinct. They have probably been introduced into many countries with the cockroaches, on the egg-capsules of which their larvæ are parasitic. *E. Appendigaster*, Linn., is a small black insect, measuring less than an inch across the fore wings, with a very small abdomen on a long petiole, and enormous hind legs, nearly twice as long as the whole body. On the other hand, several other genera are remarkable for the extraordinary length of the abdomen of the female; thus the North American *Pelecinus Politurator*, Drury, is a shining black insect, measuring about an inch and a half across the wings; but the abdomen is very slender, and composed of very long joints, the last only being short and pointed; the entire insect not measuring much less than three inches in length. The hind legs are also long, and the tibiæ dilated.

FAMILY VII.—*Chrysididæ.*

Body nearly cylindrical; abdomen with a very short peduncle, and composed of from three to five segments, one of which is often much larger than the others, and the last of which is often furnished at the extremity with a series of large teeth, varying in number according to the species; the terminal segments of the abdomen form a retractile tube, furnished at the extremity with a small imperfect sting; and the body is hard, and the abdomen concave beneath, so that the insect, when alarmed, doubles its abdomen beneath it, and rolls itself up into a more or less globular form.

The Ruby-tailed Flies are among the most brilliant of all the *Hymenoptera*, most of the species being either of an intense green, blue, or fiery red. They are small or moderate-sized insects, which are found on walls or flowers in the full heat of the sun; for, as a rule, the most brilliantly coloured insects are diurnal in their habits. As far as their habits are known, they deposit their eggs in the nests of other insects (chiefly *Hymenoptera*), on the larvæ of which their own offspring feed. The European species are very numerous, and are divided into a considerable number of genera; but it is some years since anything of importance has been published on the exotic *Chrysididæ. Chrysis Ignita*, Linn., the commonest of the European species, varies very much in size and colour, as well as in the length and position of the four teeth at the extremity of the abdomen. It is either blue or green, or suffused with copper, or even considerably varied with black. The late Mr. F. Smith suggests that its extraordinary variability may be due to variation in food, as it is parasitic on several genera of *Hymenoptera* of different sizes and habits (*Vespa, Odynerus, Cerceris*, etc.).

As already stated, the position of the *Chrysididæ* is somewhat uncertain; they have affinities both with the *Terebrantia* and the *Aculeata.* In certain genera of the *Vespidæ*, especially *Polybia*, the abdomen is so retractile that it can almost be drawn within the first segment; and this may indicate some relationship to the retractile abdomen of the *Chrysididæ.*

HYMENOPTERA ACULEATA—HETEROGYNA.

FAMILY VIII.—*Formicidæ.*

Social insects, consisting of males, females, and neuters; the last wingless, and the two former only acquiring wings (which are ample, but soon lost) for a single flight.

The *Formicidæ*, or Ants, may be divided into three sub-families; the *Formicinæ*, many of which bite sharply, but are stingless; and the *Ponerinæ* and *Myrmicinæ*, in which the females and neuters (or workers) are generally armed with a sting. In the *Ponerinæ* the petiole of the abdomen is formed of only one node, and in the *Myrmicinæ* of two. The singular genus *Dorylus*, Latr., has been formed into a separate family, *Dorylidæ*, characterised by its fili-form instead of angulated antennæ, its small head, and long cylindrical abdomen. But it is structurally nearest related to the *Ponerinæ*, and without further observations on these exotic insects, and their habits and transformations, it is perhaps better to treat them as belonging to that sub-family.

The largest of the European *Formicinæ* is *Camponotus Hercu-laneus*, Linn., which measures about half an inch in length, and an inch in expanse of wing. It is a smooth black ant, with the thorax (or at least the metathorax), the base of the abdomen, and the legs, more or less red. The wings of the males and females are deeply tinged with smoky yellow. It is very common in many parts of Europe and North America, but is not found in England. It is a very courageous insect, and an ant-hill will sometimes send out an army, and fight a pitched battle with a neighbouring community of its own or another species. These are regular wars, and not slave-hunting excursions, which are undertaken by several species of ants, for the purpose of obtaining pupæ of another species, which are afterwards reared in their nests to do the work of the plunderers, who are too lazy in some cases to do anything but fight, and are so absolutely dependent on their slaves that they cannot even feed themselves without their help.

Camponotus Smaragdinus, Fabr., is a common Indian ant, allied to *C. Herculaneus*, but smaller. It is remarkable for its green colour (very unusual among ants, which are generally black, brown, or red). It lives in trees, and constructs a large nest of live leaves, connected as they grow on the tree by a white web. *Polyrhachi* , Smith, is another genus of East Indian ants, remarkable for the long spines placed on different parts of the body. Little is known of their habits; but *P. Nidificans*, Jerdon, is said by its describer to make " a small nest about half an inch or rather more in diameter, of some papyraceous materials, which it fixes on a leaf."

Formica Fuliginosa, Latr., is a common jet-black ant, rather less than a quarter of an inch long. According to Mr. F. Smith, its nests are generally found near a decaying tree or an old post, and its movements are unusually slow, and it seems very fond of sunning itself, instead of being constantly at work. But considering the high state of civilisation to which many ants have attained; how some keep slaves, almost all herds of much greater variety and far more numerous than our own; how others grow corn ; and others make great roads and tunnels vastly more gigantic in proportion than any human engineer would dream for a moment of attempting, we need not wonder that some communities should allow themselves an occasional holiday. It has long been known that many kinds of insects are found in ants' nests, and that many species derive much of their food from honey-dew, the sweet secretion discharged by *Aphidæ*, or Plant Lice. But, according to some recent observations of M. Lichtenstein, a French entomologist, who is making a special study of the *Aphidæ, Formica Fuliginosa* is not content to watch over colonies of *Aphidæ*, or to keep herds in its. nest, like other ants, but actually superintends their breeding in a manner which could hardly be imagined. Many *Aphidæ* exhibit the phenomenon known as alternation of generations ; that is, there is a winged sexual brood, and a wingless asexual brood; and sometimes the former lives in the open air, and the latter at the roots of plants. When, therefore, these ants meet with a winged *Aphis* about to lay eggs which will produce a subterranean brood, they first clip her wings to prevent her escape, and then open a way for her, and guide her down to the roots of the grass. But when winged *Aphidæ* are born in their nests, they do not clip their wings, but open a way for them into the air, that they may fly to the plants on which their young are to feed, and thus insure the perpetuation of the species.

It is quite possible that all the insects which frequent ants' nests do not inhabit them simply as food-producers. The remarkable beetles belonging to the genus *Paussus* (none of which are British) are usually found among ants. It is not unlikely that they may be kept in the nest to repel intruders by their artillery, for they are all crepitating insects, discharging a highly corrosive fluid with an explosion, after the manner of a *Brachinus*.

There are frequently two classes of workers observed among ants; but perhaps the most curious instance is that of the honey-ants (*Camponotus Inflatus*, Lubb., *Myrmecocystus Melliger*, Llave, and *Crematogaster Inflatus*, Smith. In the two former of these species the honey-sack is formed of the abdomen, and in the last is an appendage to the metathorax. The best known is *Myrmecocystus Melliger*, which is met with in Mexico and Colorado, and an elaborate account of its habits has just been published by Rev. Dr. M'Cook,[1] an American minister, who spends his summer holidays in the investigation of the manners and customs of the many interesting species of ants which are met with in the west and south of the United States. Although many galls have an exceedingly disagreeable flavour, there are others which exude a sweet substance, and it is from these that the ants obtain the honey. Among the ants there are large and small workers, and Dr. M'Cook's observations lead him to infer that as the former grow older they become more and more distended with honey, until they become the honey-receptacles where a large supply is stored up for the benefit of the community. Among other interesting observations relating to their habits and economy, he records that although the ants will feed on the honey, if a honey-ant is accidentally crushed, yet, if a honey-ant dies, she is carefully buried in the common cemetery of the nest, along with the honey-bag, which is detached for convenience of transport, but never opened.

Many of the *Ponerinœ* are remarkable for their form and size, as well as for their habits. The genera *Odontomachus*, Latr., and *Orectognathus*, Jerd., have enormous mandibles projecting in front of their heads. The latter genus is East Indian, and the species which belong to it feed upon other insects; but they do not always run like other ants, but, if alarmed or disturbed (and probably also in the pursuit of prey), take long leaps.

The largest ant in the collection of the British Museum is a

[1] *The Honey Ants of the Garden of the Gods*, Philadelphia, 1882.

black hairy ant, with a large head, called *Dinoponera Grandis,* Guér. It is a Brazilian species, and is an inch in length. There are no winged specimens in the Museum.

The genus *Dorylus* has been already alluded to. The males are large, heavy-looking, tawny insects, measuring about an inch in length, with a long and rather slender abdomen, and wings about an inch and a quarter in expanse. The female, which has only lately been described by Mr. Trimen, from a specimen which he obtained from a friend (Mr. Fairbridge), who had it dug out of a nest which he was destroying, is not unlike the male, but blind and wingless; while the workers are much smaller red ants, with powerful mandibles, and have been placed in quite another genus, *Anomma,* Shuck. Mr. Trimen has since informed me that the chief difficulty in investigating the domestic habits and mutual relations of these ants arises from the fact that they generally make their nests under the foundations of buildings, the owners of which are selfishly unwilling to allow their houses to be pulled down in the cause of science.

Various species of ants, including the workers of *Dorylus,* are in the habit of migrating in vast armies, both in Africa and America, devouring all the insects they meet with. The inhabitants are glad to quit their houses on their approach, when the ants enter, and make a clean sweep of all the vermin on the premises, which they attack in such numbers that neither the great cockroaches, nor even the rats and mice, can escape them. When they reach a small stream, they form a bridge of their own bodies, one clinging to another. When they pass through a forest it is said to be quite a ludicrous sight to see the stampede of locusts, grasshoppers, and other insects before them. Mr. Belt has given a very interesting account in his *Naturalist in Nicaragua* of the foraging parties of ants belonging to the genus *Eciton,* Latr., one of the *Myrmicinæ.* The spiders showed the greatest intelligence; some dropping down from the branch of a tree by a thread, so as to remain suspended, secure from the foes which swarmed above and below; while the larger ones, instead of taking refuge, like the cockroaches, with the certainty of being soon driven out again, and surrounded and devoured, would "make off many yards in advance, apparently determined to put a good distance between themselves and the foe." He also saw one of the *Phalangiidæ* (eight-legged creatures, allied to the spiders) standing in the midst of the ants, and lifting its long legs whenever any of the ants approached, sometimes having five in the air at once, and putting them down wherever there was a clear space. Another insect which escaped was a green leaf-like locust, which remained absolutely immoveable, and though many ants ran over its legs, they did not perceive that it was an insect. These ants, however, hunt by touch and smell rather than by sight, their eyes being very imperfect. Some idea of their numbers may be formed from Mr. H. W. Bates having once observed a dense column of a species of *Eciton* on the march through the forests of the Amazon, which column extended sixty or seventy yards, without any indication of either the van or the rear of the army.

We will now consider the third and last family of the Ants, the *Myrmicinæ*, to which the genus *Eciton*, as already mentioned, belongs. Probably the most troublesome of our British ants is the little yellow House Ant, *Diplorhoptrum Molestum*, Say. Fifty years ago it was almost unknown in England, but it is now abundant in houses in most of our large towns, more especially in London. Mr. F. Smith considers that it is a Brazilian species, for the Rev. H. Clark found it very annoying at Rio Janeiro : " everywhere,— in-doors, out of doors, and upon everything." It appears to have been introduced into North America (where it was first described) a few years before it appeared in London. If the nests are accessible, which is not often the case, they may be destroyed with boiling water ; and washing with a solution of carbolic acid will also go far to check their ravages. The number of the ants may be much reduced by laying down pieces of liver in places where they abound, which may be plunged into boiling water at intervals, the ants shaken off, and then laid down again. Another method has lately been mentioned to me by Dr. Murie of the Linnean Society, which seems likely to answer still better than the liver. This is to put a sponge into sugar and water, and when the ants have covered and permeated it, to rinse it with boiling water, dip it again into the syrup, and replace it.

The genus *Crematogaster*, Lund., builds its nest in trees ; *C. Inflatus*, Smith, which occurs in Borneo and Malacca, has been already mentioned as a honey-ant.

At the beginning of the present century it was warmly debated among entomologists whether ants ever store up grain, as asserted by various ancient writers. As nothing of the kind has been observed in Northern Europe, it was hastily concluded (from a prejudice that we have not yet quite outgrown, that the ancients must have been mistaken whenever their experience was unconfirmed by our own observations) that they had mistaken the pupæ for corn; for any one who has purposely or accidentally dug into an ant-hill knows that the workers immediately seize upon the pupæ, and endeavour to remove them to a place of safety. More cautious writers, however, thought it possible that ants might really store up grain in some countries, though perhaps not in our own; a view that has since been abundantly substantiated by the observations of many excellent naturalists in all the warmer parts of the globe. Lieut.-Colonel Sykes first recorded the harvesting habits of an Indian ant (which he named *Atta Providens*, but which is now placed in the allied genus *Pheidole*, Westw., in the first volume of the Transactions of the Entomological Society of London, published in 1836; and Mr. H. W. Bates and others have observed the same thing in various parts of tropical America. But the most complete and important observations on the subject have been published by Mr. J. T. Moggridge, in his *Harvesting Ants and Trap-door Spiders*, and by Rev. Dr. M'Cook, in his *Natural History of the Agricultural Ant of Texas.*

All the true harvesting ants yet observed appear to belong to the genus *Atta*, St. Farg., or to closely-allied genera. There are two orders of workers among them, large and small, generally destitute of ocelli, though the large workers, which are remarkable for their enormous heads, occasionally have one only.

The ants observed by Mr. Moggridge as storing up grain were chiefly *Atta Barbara*, Linn., a black ant, sometimes with a red head, and *A. Structor*, Latr., which is of a reddish-brown colour. They are common all round the Mediterranean, and he observed no less than fifty-four different species of seeds in their granaries, where they are laid up, carefully cleansed from the husks, which are thrown away (even seed-capsules being often detached and carried into the nest), and submitted to some treatment which still requires explanation, which, without destroying their vitality, prevents their germinating as long as they are in the nest. These ants do not appear to visit *Aphidæ*, or take them to their nests, though they will feed on other insects at times. Sometimes two nests will go to war, the weaker nest being perhaps ultimately deserted. In one case Mr. Moggridge observed a war between two nests, which lasted from January 18 to March 4, with scarcely any intermission.

A yet more interesting species is the Agricultural Ant of

Texas (*Pogonomyrmex Barbatus*, Smith), a reddish-brown species about half an inch long, with a long reddish beard on the face. Its habits have been studied by Lincecum, Buckley, and M'Cook, the last of whom has written an elaborate monograph on the species and its habits. The formicary is established on a spot well exposed to the sun, and a circular clearing is made around it, often of from ten to twelve feet in diameter, and frequently paved with small pebbles, upon which no weeds are allowed to grow. Smooth and level roads are also made through the thickets of weeds beyond the clearing, and Lincecum describes one over 300 feet long, which traversed 60 feet of thick weeds, overran heavy beds of crop grass 180 feet, and then through the weeds growing in the locks of a heavy rail fence 60 feet more. Throughout the whole extent this road was very smooth and even, and varied from a straight line only so far as to lose some thirty feet of distance in passing from the pavement to the outer terminus. The width was from two to two and a half inches. In some places, on account of insurmountable obstructions, the road separated into two or three trails of an inch in width, which united beyond the obstruction. M'Cook remarks that, at a moderate computation, such a road "would be equivalent to the construction and maintenance by man of a good hard road ten miles long and twenty-two feet wide."

Along these roads the ants pass to and fro, carrying into their nests various kinds of grass-seeds, which are cleansed from the husk, and stored up in the manner of *Atta*. But there is not always an empty clearing round the ant-hill. The space is sometimes more or less overgrown with a grass called *Aristida Oligantha*, the seed of which forms part of the ordinary stores of the ants; and it is conjectured that the ants actually sow and harvest the crop of this particular grass for their own requirements. This ant does not gather the seeds until they have fallen, although the European *Atta Barbata*, and the Floridan *Atta Crudelis*, Smith, have been observed gathering growing seeds and seed-capsules on the plants themselves.

The description of the nests, habits, structure, etc., of the Agricultural Ant is too long to quote, but a few more interesting points may be mentioned. The ants do not feed on grain alone, but hasten to gather up other insects, such as winged termites, after a heavy shower of rain has beaten them down to the ground. But, though they sometimes profit by rain, it adds to their labours, for, if their store of corn becomes damp, it is brought up into the open air to dry. They are exceedingly cleanly, shampooing themselves and each other frequently, especially after eating or sleeping, and whenever they are in ease and comfort. M'Cook has sometimes seen *Atta Crudelis* yawning and stretching itself after awaking from a sound sleep. All ants, M'Cook thinks, have cemeteries for their dead; but he records a very curious observation made by Mrs. Treat on *Formica Sanguinea*, Latr., a red, slave-making ant. The cemetery for the mistresses is near the gates of the nests, but the black slaves are buried singly, at a considerable distance! As regards the strength and speed of these ants, M'Cook calculates that one instance he observed was equivalent to a man carrying a weight of 2500 pounds a distance of 176 miles in eleven hours. Although *Pogonomyrmex Barbatus* will occasionally make war on a rival nest, it is usually of a peaceable disposition, and will sometimes even permit a small black ant (*Dorymyrmex Insana*, Buckley) to establish nests within its own territory. But, according to Lincecum, as quoted by M'Cook, if the small ants multiply so much as to make themselves inconvenient to the larger ones, the latter get rid of them by a systematic persecution, heaping wormcasts over the black ants' nests in greater quantities than these can clear away, until they force them to shift their abodes in despair.

One more genus of ants must be noticed before we quit the subject: the Cutting or Parasol Ants (*Œcodoma*, Latr.) of tropical America. These are small reddish ants about half an inch in length (the small workers being much less), and the wings of the female expand more than two inches. There are two kinds of large workers among the Saûba ants observed by Mr. Bates on the Amazons. Both have immense heads, but one kind has a highly polished head, and accompanies the small workers, as if to superintend their labours, in which, however, the larger ones take no part. But if the nest is probed with a stick, another kind of large worker, with a hairy head, and a large double ocellus in the middle of the forehead, will make its way to the surface.

These ants are chiefly remarkable for their enormous subterranean galleries and for their leaf-collecting habits. Mr. Bates records an instance of the galleries belonging to a single nest at Pará extending seventy yards; and another of their piercing and draining a reservoir. He also mentions that the Rev. H. Clark states that at Rio de Janeiro they have excavated a tunnel under a river as broad as the Thames at London Bridge. They gather

and store up immense quantities of leaves in their nests, cutting
them into pieces of a convenient size to carry, and especially pre-
ferring imported to native plants.   Mr. Belt, who has given an
account of their habits in his *Naturalist in Nicaragua*, believed that
the ants use the leaves as a hotbed for growing a particular kind
of fungus, on which they feed.   M‘Cook does not share this
opinion, but thinks that the ants live on the juices of the leaves,
and that the presence of a fungus is only accidental; he is also of
opinion that the leaves are used in the construction of a kind of
comb.   When the best authorities disagree, we can only await the
result of further and more conclusive observations.

Belt records a curious instance of their sagacity.   After several
had been crushed in crossing the tramways, they constructed sub-
ways under the rails, and one day, when the cars were not running,
Belt stopped up the tunnels, but, although many ants were thus
cut off from the nest, they would not attempt to cross the rails
again, but immediately set to work making fresh tunnels.   He
succeeded in destroying many of them by sprinkling corrosive
sublimate across their paths in dry weather, which drives them mad.
He has given a most graphic account of its effects, which I cannot
resist the temptation of quoting: "As soon as one of the ants
touches the white powder, it commences to run about wildly, and
to attack any other ant it comes across.   In a couple of hours
round balls of the ants will be found, all biting each other; and
numerous individuals will be seen bitten completely in two, whilst
others have lost some of their legs or antennæ.   News of the
commotion is carried to the formicarium, and large fellows,
measuring three-quarters of an inch in length, that only come out
of the nest during a migration or an attack on the nest or one of
the working columns, are seen stalking down with a determined
air, as if they would soon right matters.   As soon, however, as
they have touched the sublimate, all their stateliness leaves them;
they rush about; their legs are seized hold of by some of the
smaller ants already affected by the poison; and they themselves
begin to bite, and in a short time become the centre of fresh balls
of rabid ants."

Belt was once much annoyed by an attack, made by the ants
belonging to a nest at some distance, upon his garden.   He made
the nest untenable by pouring carbolic acid and water into the
formicarium, when the foraging parties were all immediately with-
drawn, and at once occupied themselves in carrying away every-

thing worth saving from the old nest to a temporary shelter on a small slope, down which they rolled their loads to others waiting below, while they themselves returned for more; they also carried out many dead ants from the nest. Soon afterwards, thinking themselves in danger so close to the old nest, they removed to a distance of 200 yards. Next year they attacked Mr. Belt's garden again, and he forced them to leave their nest in the same manner, when they returned to the old nest. Belt adds: "I do not doubt that some of the leading minds in this formicarium recollected the nest of the year before, and directed the migration to it." This is confirmed by Sir John Lubbock's discovery that ants live at least seven or eight years in the perfect state, and possibly much longer.

Limited space prevents me from noticing the habits of our North European ants, but this is of little consequence, as they are referred to in a great number of popular works; and those who wish for information on this subject will easily find a good compendium of the older observations in Kirby and Spence's *Introduction to Entomology*, while Sir John Lubbock has just summed up his own most important observations and experiments in his new book on *Ants, Bees, and Wasps*. I have therefore preferred to give an account of some of the more interesting foreign species, derived from works likely to be less known, or less accessible to the generality of my readers.

HYMENOPTERA ACULEATA—FOSSORES.

Wings not folded; species solitary, consisting of males and females, the latter sometimes apterous; generally forming their nests in the ground.

FAMILY IX.—*Mutillidæ.*

Female usually apterous, and armed with a sting; legs stout; femora not dilated; tibiæ more or less spinose; antennæ filiform; male with the tip of the abdomen generally furnished with teeth or spines.

The *Mutillidæ* are sometimes called Solitary Ants, for they somewhat resemble a large ant in shape. Smith, in fact, included them with the ants in his *Catalogue of British Fossorial Hymenoptera;* but they are too closely allied to the *Scoliidæ* to be placed in a different section of the *Hymenoptera*. The species of *Mutilla* are very numerous, about a thousand having been described from the warmer parts of the world; but very few are European, the commonest being *Mutilla Europæa*, Linn., a black or blue-black insect about half an inch long, with a red thorax, and three more or less interrupted white bands on the abdomen. This species frequents sandy places, and is believed to be sometimes at least parasitic in the nests of humble-bees. The species of *Mutilla* are generally clothed with a beautiful short down, and are mostly of a black colour, often with a red thorax, and the abdomen is frequently adorned with red, white, or golden spots, and is sometimes entirely red or yellow.

Family X.—*Thymidæ.*

Female apterous, very stout, mesothorax constricted; legs very spiny; femora compressed and dilated; male slender, winged.

The insects of this family are almost exclusively confined to Australia and South America, where they are very numerous. They are generally of a black colour, with more or less extended yellow markings. The females are very dissimilar to the males, and are very slightly pubescent in comparison with *Mutilla*, but their legs are generally much more strongly spined. Their great bloated bodies give them very little resemblance to any other insects, except perhaps to the Oil Beetles (*Meloidæ*). They are probably parasitic insects.

Family XI.—*Scoliidæ.*

Female generally winged; legs very stout, femora compressed and dilated, tibiæ very spinose; antennæ stout, shorter than the thorax.

Although this family is abundant in warm climates, we have only two small species belonging to the genus *Tiphia*, Fabr., in Britain. They are black, with more or less reddish legs, and measure from a quarter to half an inch in length. But in South Europe we meet with several large and handsome species, one of which, *Scolia Hortorum*, Fabr., we have figured; it is black, with two yellow bands on the abdomen. It provisions its nest with the larvæ of the large wood-feeding beetle, *Oryctes Nasicornis*, Linn. *Scolia Atrata*, Fabr., a black species with reddish wings tipped with violet, which is common in the West Indies, is one of the most curious in its habits of any. According to Consul Krug, who observed it at Porto Rico, it is in the habit of provisioning its nest with a large grasshopper. It first digs its nest, and then goes in search of a grasshopper. Having partially disabled it with its sting, it mounts on its back, and rides it up to its own grave, where it buries it. If the grave proves to be too small, the wasp drives the grasshopper away while it enlarges it as much as is required, and then brings it back to the hole.

FAMILY XII.—*Sapygidæ.*

Both sexes winged; antennæ as long as the head and thorax, usually more or less clavate; legs not spinose.

We have two native species of this family: one, *Sapyga Punctata*, Panz., black, with transverse white spots on the abdomen, which is black in the male and red in the female; and *S. Clavi-cornis*, Linn., which is black, with yellow markings on the abdomen. The first species measures nearly half an inch in length, and the second is rather smaller. Mr. F. Smith believed that this insect does not dig its own burrow, its legs not being adapted to the purpose, but makes use of that of some other insect, which it stores with caterpillars for the sustenance of its future offspring.

FAMILY XIII.—*Bembecidæ.*

Collar small, not prolonged backwards; lower mouth-parts much produced, forming a kind of proboscis, as in the bees; legs stout, rather short, and the front legs furnished with strong bristles.

This small family is not represented in Britain, though found in Southern Europe, and in all the warmer parts of the world; the two principal genera are *Bembex*, Fabr., and *Monedula*, Latr. Most of the species resemble large wasps, being black, with yellow belts; but the pattern of their markings is so peculiar that they may generally be recognised by that alone. The yellow bands are generally interrupted in the middle, and deeply excavated on each side in front. These insects form their burrows in the sand, scratching a hole with their fore feet like a dog, as observed by Sir S. S. Saunders in the Ionian Islands, and lay up a store of *Diptera* or *Hymenoptera*, which they sometimes capture on the wing, and sometimes fairly stalk down; they then deposit their eggs, and close up the hole. They fly rapidly from flower to flower, producing a sharp and intermittent buzzing, and many of he species exhale an odour of roses.

FAMILY XIV.—*Pompilidæ.*

Collar either transversely or longitudinally square; legs long; abdomen oval, and attached to the thorax by a short petiole.

A very extensive group, having representatives in all parts of the world; the species are black, sometimes with red legs and antennæ, and the abdomen is often red, especially at the base; the wings may be colourless, banded with brown, or marked with whitish; or yellow, or brilliantly iridescent blue. Many of the European species provision their nests with spiders, while others store up caterpillars, etc. Some of the species of the tropical genera *Pepsis,* Fabr., and *Mygnimia,* Smith, are among the largest of Hymenopterous insects, measuring three inches or more across the wings.

FAMILY XV.—*Sphegidæ.*

Prothorax narrowed in front, and the hinder angles not produced to the base of the wings; abdomen with a long round petiole, consisting of the first and sometimes part of the second segment; wings rather short.

The shape of the *Sphegidæ* will at once distinguish them from almost all other *Hymenoptera,* except some of the *Vespidæ;* but the latter have the sides of the prothorax prolonged backwards to the base of the wings. Certain Ichneumons also resemble them in shape; but, apart from other characters, the nervures of the wings are very differently arranged in these from what they are in any *Aculeata.* Different species of *Sphegidæ* provision their nests with different insects, or with spiders. They sometimes attack insects much larger and stronger, or apparently better defended than themselves, such as field-crickets, weevils, etc.; but they paralyse them by striking their sting into the principal nervous centres, and then drag them to their nests, where they bury them alive, but paralysed, so that a living but helpless prey is provided for the larvæ when they shall emerge from the eggs.

Some of the tropical *Sphegidæ,* belonging to the genera *Chlorion,* Latr., and *Ampulex,* Jur., are of a beautiful metallic blue or green; *Ampulex Compressio,* Jur., which is found at Mauritius, etc., preys on *Blattidæ. Proneus Maxillaris,* Latr., a common black West African species, is remarkable for the enormous mandibles of the male.

FAMILY XVI.—*Larridæ*.

Mandibles usually deeply emarginate on the outside near the base; four front tibiæ with a single spine at the tip; hind tibiæ with two spines.

The species of this family are generally rather small insects, few of the species measuring half an inch in length. They are usually black, sometimes with the abdomen red at the base; or the face is adorned with silvery pubescence.

FAMILY XVII.—*Nyssonidæ*.

"Mandibles not emarginate beneath; legs subspinose."— (Smith.)

This family much resembles the last. Smith, in his *Catalogue of British Fossorial Lepidoptera*, gives an account of the habits of *Mellinus Arvensis*, Linn., a black species about half an inch long, with yellow stripes on the abdomen, and yellow legs. It provisions its nest with flies, and, not being able to capture them by swiftness, runs past them when they are resting, in an unconcerned manner, till they are thrown off their guard, when they are pounced upon, and carried off to the nest.

FAMILY XVIII.—*Crabronidæ*.

Head large and square; antennæ often thickened at the tips; abdomen oval or elliptic, and sometimes clavate or petiolated; mandibles with the outer margin but slightly curved; prothorax very short.

A very extensive group, as used by Smith. Edward Saunders, however, in his "Synopsis of British *Heterogyna* and Fossorial Hymenoptera" (Transactions of the Entomological Society of London for 1880), admits three families, viz. *Pemphredonidæ*, *Mimesidæ*, and *Crabronidæ*. The species are black, with yellow spots and bands, and often with silvery pubescence on the face; they may often be seen resting on flowers. The small species of *Crabro* form their burrows in the pith of bramble, rose, etc., or in rotten wood; others burrow in the ground. The genera *Mimesa*, Shuck., and *Psen*, Latr., are black, with red legs, or with the petiolated abdomen red at the base. Some of the smaller species store up gnats or aphides.

FAMILY XIX.—*Philanthidæ.*

"Head wider than the thorax ; the intermediate tibiæ armed with a single spur at their apex ; the legs with the anterior tarsi strongly ciliated."—(Smith.)

In the genus *Cerceris,* Latr., the first segment of the abdomen is narrow, and all the segments are constricted at the extremities ; this is much less the case in *Philanthus,* Fabr. ; but in the South American genus *Trachypus,* Klug, the abdomen is petiolated. Most of the species are black, with yellow spots and bands. Some of the species provision their nests with beetles (*Buprestidæ, Curculionidæ,* etc.) or grasshoppers ; but others attack bees, and are very mischievous, destroying great numbers. *Philanthus Triangulum,* Latr., was named *P. Apivorus* by Latreille on account of this habit.

HYMENOPTERA ACULEATA—DIPLOPTERA.

Fore wings folded in repose ; species solitary or social ; both sexes winged ; sides of the prothorax prolonged backwards to the base of the wings ; four front tibiæ with one spine at the tip ; hind tibiæ with two.

The *Diploptera,* or true Wasps, are divided into three families, which we will now proceed to consider.

FAMILY XX.—*Masaridæ.*

Solitary species ; antennæ twelve-jointed in both sexes, but the terminal joints frequently so closely welded together that the antennæ appear to be only eight-jointed ; fore wings with only two sub-marginal cells ; abdomen hardly contractile, the second segment not conspicuously larger than the others.

The *Masaridæ* are a small group of black, yellow-belted wasps which are not found in Britain, though several species are met with on the Continent, chiefly in the Mediterranean region. They appear to be more numerous in Africa and Australia than in other parts of the world. They are remarkable for the great differences in the shape of the antennæ, which present every gradation between long and short, slender, or formed into a large club. The club is largest in the genera *Celonites,* Latr., and *Masaris,* Fabr. *Celonites Abbreviatus,* Vill., was mistaken by Olivier for a *Cimbex,* owing to the peculiar form of the antennæ. The wings are much less distinctly folded in this and the following family than in the *Vespidæ*.

FAMILY XXI.—*Eumenidæ*.

Solitary species; antennæ with thirteen distinct joints in the males, and twelve in the females; fore wings with three sub-marginal cells; abdomen sometimes petiolated, the second segment large, and the terminal segments often very contractile; four front tibiæ with one spine at the tip; hind tibiæ with two; claws of the tarsi bifid.

The *Eumenidæ* are very similar in their habits to the *Fossores*, forming cells of mud or clay in the ground, which they provision with caterpillars or other insects; others form their nests in rotten wood, or in the hollow stems of brambles, etc. The best known wasps of this family are those belonging to the great genus *Odynerus*, Latr., which is found all over the world; several black species with yellow markings are common in England.

FAMILY XXII.—*Vespidæ*.

Social species, consisting of males, females, and neuters; antennæ with thirteen distinct joints in the males and twelve in the females; fore wings with three sub-marginal cells; abdomen sometimes petiolated, the second segment large, and the terminal segments often very contractile; four front tibiæ with two spines at the tip; claws of the tarsi simple.

The *Vespidæ*, or Social Wasps, are poorly represented in England; but several genera of very various forms occur in other countries. The species of *Belenogaster*, Sauss., are large slender species with petiolated abdomen and long wings. They are generally of a greyish or reddish brown, sometimes nearly black, and frequently with yellow markings (but not very extended) on the abdomen. The wings are transparent, yellow, or violet. The species, which measure from one to nearly two inches across the wings, are chiefly natives of Africa.

The genus *Icaria* includes a number of smaller wasps, not usually measuring more than half an inch across the wings. They are common in Africa and the East Indies. The petiole is stout, and the hinder segments of the abdomen are generally contracted within the second so completely that it often appears at first sight as if they were broken off. These pretty little wasps are of very various colours; one species (*I. Pomicolor*, Sauss.) is of an apple green. It is found in Madagascar. The species of *Icaria* construct small open nests in trees, composed of a substance resembling thin brown paper, and containing numerous cells.

Polistes, Latr., is one of the largest genera of the *Vespidæ*, and is the only genus, except *Vespa*, which is represented in Europe, three or four species being found in the South. They are black, with yellow spots on the head and back, and are about as long as a common wasp, but much more slender; the first segment of the abdomen is bell-shaped. They construct a nest similar to that made by the wasps of the genus *Icaria*, in which they lay up a small store of honey.

The true Wasps, belonging to the genus *Vespa*, are black and yellow insects, which are too well known to need description. The smaller wasps are very similar, but are divided into species chiefly by the black markings on their yellow faces. The Hornet (*Vespa Crabro*, Linn.) is nearly half as large again as the other species, from which it may be distinguished by its redder colour, and the row of reddish spots on each side of the abdomen. Some species of wasps construct their nests in the ground, and others in trees; these nests are composed of a material resembling thin coarse brown paper. Each nest is commenced by one female, which has survived the winter; but as soon as her first eggs hatch, and the first brood is reared, the wasps help the foundress in enlarging the nest and bringing up the young; other females begin to lay, and the colony rapidly increases. Hence the necessity for killing the large wasps which appear in spring, if we wish to diminish the numbers of wasps in the succeeding summer and autumn. When cold weather sets in, the wasps rapidly perish, only a few females surviving the winter in a torpid state to continue the race during the following year.

The Hornet is less numerous than the smaller wasps; it lives in smaller communities, and is not only a much less abundant species, but appears to be almost confined to the south of England; on the Continent it is much more generally abundant. But it is not a quarrelsome insect, though its powerful sting makes it formidable if molested. It generally constructs its nest in hollow trees, but will also build under the eaves of houses. The wasps construct their nests of rasped wood, or bark; and I possess a beautiful hornets' nest, which was found fixed to the rafter of a house at Colchester which was being rebuilt. It has every appearance of being constructed of deal shavings.

The genus *Vespa* has representatives in many parts of the world; but the largest and handsomest species are perhaps those which inhabit the East Indies. One of the largest is *Vespa Mandarinia*, Smith, which is common in China and Japan, and measures fully two inches across the wings. There are several smaller East Indian species of more varied colours than ours; some are quite black, and others are black with a broad reddish band on the abdomen; or the whole abdomen may be reddish, except at the base.

The sting of some of the foreign wasps is a serious matter, and liable to produce unpleasant effects for a long time afterwards. Mitchell, during one of his exploring expeditions in Eastern Australia, was stung by a wasp from a nest built in a tree near which he passed. The pain was so severe that it made him cry out; and affected the muscles of the injured leg so much, that when he dismounted in the evening he fell on attempting to stand upon it; and the place was marked by a livid spot of the size of a sixpence, which did not disappear for six months afterwards. The species, which Mitchell calls *Abispa Australiana*, has not yet been correctly identified; the description given corresponds fairly with *Monorebia Ephippium*, Fabr., an Australian species belonging to the *Eumenidæ*; but the habits of this species, as Smith remarks, are not at all like those of Mitchell's insect; and it is evident that the latter was one of the true *Vespidæ*, though there does not appear to be any species in the collection of the British Museum which can be recognised as Mitchell's insect.

Hymenoptera Aculeata—Anthophila.

All the sexes winged; antennæ twelve-jointed in the females and thirteen-jointed in the males, the former generally armed with a sting, and with the first joint of the tarsi more or less dilated; "hairs more or less branched or plumose, at least those on the thorax."—(E. Saunders.)

Family I.—*Andrenidæ*.

Solitary species; tongue short, acute, or else obtuse and emarginate; labium and terminal maxillary lobes not forming a long proboscis; hind legs very hairy; basal joint of the hind tarsi but slightly dilated, and never externally dilated into an angle.

The *Andrenidæ* are small dark-coloured bees, often more or less

clothed with whitish hairs, or pubescence, or with fulvous pubescence. They are found all over the world, and are well represented
in England, the genus *Andrena*, Fabr., being by far the most
numerous in species among our British bees. They form burrows
in the ground, or in the crevices of walls, and the species of
Andrena appear in early spring, when they may be met with at
the flowers of the sallow. The species of the genus *Prosopis*, Fabr.,
form their nests in bramble stems, and occasionally in dock.
According to Smith, living examples of *Andrena* exhale an agree-
able odour when alive. Some species are very subject to the
attacks of the curious Coleopterous parasite *Stylops*, which may
frequently be seen slightly protruding from their bodies, and
disfigures them to such an extent that stylopised bees have frequently been described as distinct species.

FAMILY II.—*Apidæ*.

Solitary or social species; mouth-parts produced into a long
proboscis; basal joint of the hind tarsi often externally dilated.

The species belonging to this family are very numerous, and
very varied in their structure, colours, and habits. We shall
confine ourselves here to noticing a few of the most interesting
genera in systematic order.

The species of the genus *Osmia*, Panz., are black hairy bees,
generally more or less varied with reddish hairs, and measuring
about one-third of an inch in length. They form their nests in
the ground, under stones, in walls, in old trees, or in empty snail
shells. A long account of their habits is given by F. Smith in
his *Catalogue of British Bees in the Collection of the British Museum.*
Anthocopa Papaveris, Latr., a Continental species allied to *Osmia*,
which has not yet been ascertained to be British, lines its underground nest with the scarlet petals of the field-poppy; the species
of *Megachile*, Latr., which are grey, pubescent bees, are also leaf-
cutters. Many species are very common in England, especially
M. Centuncularis, Linn., which may often be seen cutting very neat
segments of a circle out of rose-leaves, etc.

There is a small section of bees the habits of which are not
yet thoroughly understood, though it has long been known that
they are parasitic on other bees; or at least they lay their eggs
in their nests, and the young larvæ are believed to feed on the
store laid up for the use of the offspring of the rightful owners.
Hence Latreille called the invaders Cuckoo Bees. They belong

chiefly to the genus *Nomada*, Fabr., and are very wasp-like in their appearance, being small bees with short tongues, hind legs simple, unfitted for collecting pollen, and nearly naked bodies. Most of the species are black, with red or yellow spots and belts; a few are reddish with black markings.

Most of our British bees are of obscure colours; but some of the large South American species belonging to the genera *Acanthopus*, Klug, *Aglaë*, St. Farg., *Chrysantheida*, Perty, etc., are of the most brilliant purple or golden green. They are larger than humble-bees, but not hairy, and must be magnificent insects when flying in the sun.

Eucera Longicornis, Scop., a black hairy bee about half an inch long, the thorax of which is covered with rust-coloured hair, is our British representative of a very extensive genus, the males of which are remarkable for their unusually long antennæ, as long as the whole body. It is a common species, and forms its burrows in the ground, sometimes in large colonies.

The genus *Xylocopa*, Latr., is not represented in Britain, though several species are found on the Continent. The beautiful Carpenter Bee (*Xylocopa Violacea*, Scop.) is abundant throughout southern and a considerable part of central Europe; it is black, with brilliant iridescent violet wings, and forms its nest in wood. The species of *Bombus*, Fabr., on the contrary, form their nests in the ground. These are the well-known Humble-Bees; large, stout, hairy bees, which are generally either black with red tails, or varied with black and yellowish bands; sometimes almost the whole insect is of a yellowish colour. This is one of the most difficult genera of all; for many species greatly resemble each other, and at the same time vary among themselves in size as well as in other characters. They form nests in the ground, resembling those of field-mice; and at other times will appropriate the nests of small birds. Here they live in small communities, consisting of males, females, and workers. They are subject to the attacks of many parasites, one of which, a mite of considerable size, may often be noticed upon their bodies. There is also a genus of bees (*Apathus*, Newm.) which greatly resemble the *Bombi* in whose nests they are parasitic; but they consist only of males and females, and their legs are not formed for collecting pollen.

There are two genera of social, honey-collecting bees found in South America: *Melipona*, Latr., and *Trigona*, Jur., which are remarkable for being destitute of stings.

Last, but not least, we must close our notice of the *Hymenoptera* with the Hive-Bee, *Apis Mellifera*, Linn., an insect now naturalised over the whole world. It is a blackish pubescent insect, with the thorax and legs more or less reddish; the males and females measure about two-thirds of an inch in length, and the workers are somewhat smaller.

The ancients were aware that the bees were governed by a sovereign, which, however, they supposed to be the king, and not the queen. Another widely-diffused error, which we meet with both among the Hebrews and Romans, was that bees were either bred from or made their nest in dead carcasses. It is only within the last few centuries that their real economy has been rationally investigated; and though numbers of good observers have devoted much time and attention to the subject, much still remains to be done before their habits are thoroughly understood. As long accounts of their economy are to be found in almost every book on natural history, we may perhaps be allowed to pass the subject over in the present work, only remarking that on the whole the habits of bees appear to be less interesting than those of ants, and that they appear to be decidedly inferior in intelligence.

ORDER LEPIDOPTERA.

[As I have already treated of European Butterflies and Moths in a separate work, the present article is devoted chiefly to foreign species.]

Wings four, clothed with scales; metamorphosis complete; larva mandibulate, most frequently with from ten to sixteen legs; pupa inactive, often enclosed in a cocoon; imago haustellate.

Butterflies and Moths have always been very favourite insects, not only with entomologists, but with all dwellers in the country, or lovers of Nature. They cannot easily be confused with any other Order than that to which they belong, except in a few instances in which Caddis-flies somewhat resemble small moths, or some of the clear-winged moths resemble *Diptera* or *Hymenoptera*.

The bright colours of these insects are due entirely to the scales with which their wings are covered, and which are doubtless metamorphosed hairs. When this clothing, which is more or less dense, is removed, we find a colourless membrane beneath, traversed by branching veins, as in other insects.

The distinction between Butterflies and Moths is purely artificial, and is more sharply emphasised in English by the use of separate words than in other languages. Thus the French and Germans generally use the words *Papillon* and *Schmetterling*, which correspond to *Lepidoptera* in general, and instead of using distinct words, use expressions corresponding to Day-Butterflies and Night-Butterflies. Still, the term Butterflies is conveniently employed to include the first five families of *Lepidoptera*, the fifth of which, the *Hesperiidæ*, is so widely separated from all the true Butterflies on the one hand, and from all the true Moths on the other, that there is little real danger of a butterfly being mistaken for a moth, or *vice versâ*, by any one at all acquainted with the subject, though those who proceed on the axiom that a butterfly is a brightly-coloured insect with a slender body, and a moth a dull-coloured insect with a thick body, will fall into many mistakes.

Linné divided the *Lepidoptera* into three genera only,—*Papilio Sphina*, and *Phalæna*, or Butterflies, Hawk-Moths, and Moths. These he divided into sub-genera and sections, most of which represent families, in the arrangements followed by modern authors.

SECTION I.—RHOPALOCERA, OR BUTTERFLIES.

Antennæ terminating in a more or less gradually-formed club ; fore and hind wings not linked together by a bristle at the base ; flight generally diurnal.

FAMILY I.—*Nymphalidæ.*

Front pair of legs more or less rudimentary ; pupa attached by the tail only.

This is by far the largest of the five families of Butterflies, and includes nearly half of all the known species. It is divided into several sub-families.

SUB-FAMILY I.—*Danainæ.*

Discoidal cells of the wings closed ; costal nervure short, not extending to the tip of the wing ; hind wing-cells large, and irregular in shape ; wings rounded, or very slightly scalloped, never ocellated ; head small ; palpi slender ; larvæ not spiny, but furnished with fleshy tubercles, or with two or three pairs of long, slender filaments ; imago frequently provided with scent-producing organs.

The typical *Danainæ* are inhabitants of Asia and Africa ; most of the American species are rather different. The largest species belong to the genus *Hestia*, Hübn., which is confined to India and the Eastern Islands. They are butterflies with very slender bodies and broad greyish-white wings, with black lines and markings. They often measure six inches across the wings, and their flight is said to be very elegant. Some Anglo-Indians give them the name of Spectre Butterflies.

Danaus Chrysippus, Linn., is the only European species of this family. It is tawny, with black borders, spotted with white ; the apical half of the fore wings is black, with a white transverse macular band. The cell of the hind wing is marked with three black spots, and, besides these, the male is provided with a dense patch of raised scales nearer to the inner margin, which is considered to be a scent-producing apparatus. Most of the species of *Danaus* are either coloured like this, or else are black, with longitudinal green markings. Their larvæ generally feed on different species of *Aristolochia*, and are furnished with a pair of long fleshy filaments at each extremity of the body, and sometimes also in the middle.

Many species of *Danaus* are met with in Asia and Africa (*D. Chrysippus* being common in both continents), and several others (all belonging to the tawny group of the genus) inhabit America.

Amauris, Hübn., is an African genus, which resembles *Danaus* in size and shape, except that the fore wings are rather narrower and more pointed. The species are black, with white spots and markings on the fore wings, and more or less of the base of the hind wings white.

Euplœa, Fabr., is a very large genus, especially numerous in the Eastern Islands, though several species are found in India, Eastern Africa, Madagascar, etc. Most of the species are velvety black or brown, more or less marked with round white or pale-blue spots; many are shot with rich purple. They vary from two to five inches in expanse of wing; their wings are generally rather long and narrow, and rounded off at the extremity.

The American section of this sub-family includes a great number of very delicately-formed insects belonging to *Ithomia*, Hübn., and allied genera. The wings are generally very long and slender, and either adorned with varied colours, in which black, yellow, and tawny predominate, or transparent, except at the edges. They vary from an inch and a half to four inches in expanse; and several of the larger species of *Lycorea* and *Tithorea*, Doubl., etc., much resemble butterflies of the genus *Heliconius*, Linn., with which they were invariably classed until about twenty years ago.

SUB-FAMILY II.—*Satyrinæ.*

Discoidal cells of the wings closed; wings rounded or scalloped, very rarely tailed, but nearly always with ocellated spots; palpi compressed, hairy; larvæ without spines, but with a bifid tail.

The species of this sub-family are generally of moderate size and dull colours. Their larvæ feed on different species of grasses, and the butterflies frequent meadows and woods. They are very numerous in Europe, where nearly one-third of the known butterflies belong to this group; but in tropical countries, as well as in North America, they are far less numerous, especially in proportion to the number of other butterflies. Many genera are almost confined to mountainous countries; and the disappearance of these

and other Alpine butterflies from South Spain and Italy, where
several of our common Central European butterflies take their
places as purely mountain species, is one reason why the South
European faunæ are so much poorer than those of Alpine Europe.

Some South American species are perfectly transparent except
on the veins and borders; but their much broader and shorter
wings will prevent them from ever being mistaken for *Danainæ*.
These belong to the genera *Cithærias*, Hübn., and *Hætera*, Fabr.
The species of *Cithærias* are exceedingly delicate and beautiful
insects, and are often adorned with an oblong blotch of deep
crimson or violet near the inner margin of the hind wings.

Melanitis Leda, Linn., is a rather large butterfly, common over a
great part of Africa and Southern Asia. It is two or three inches
in expanse, and is brown, with angulated hind wings; towards the
tip of the fore wings are two large contiguous round white spots
surrounded with black, and frequently with fulvous also. This
species is very common and widely distributed, and is interesting
from its habit of flying at dusk, or after dark, instead of in the
day-time.

A larger and handsomer species allied to this is the black and
white *Neorina Lowii*, Doubl. and Hew., a native of Borneo and
Sumatra.

The smaller South American *Satyrinæ* belong principally to the
genus *Euptychia*, Hübn. The species vary in size from one to
nearly two inches, and are of various shades of brown, though
some are whitish, and others bright blue. There is generally at
least one "eye," or ocellated spot, near the tip of the fore wings,
which is most distinct on the under surface. The wings, especially
the under surface, are often adorned with transverse lines; and
the hind wings are occasionally dentated.

The genus *Maniola*, Schrank, includes the brown butterflies
known as Mountain Ringlets. They are very numerous in the
Alps, and may be known by the black marginal spots, more or
less surrounded with red, and often with a white dot in the
centre. Some of these species, as well as other blackish or dark
brown *Satyrinæ*, exhibit greenish or bluish reflections in certain
lights. Two or three species are found on low ground, but even
these are rarely met with except in hilly districts. Two species
only (*Maniola Epiphron*, Knoch, and *Æthiops*, Esp.) are found in
the north of England and Scotland.

The genus *Œneis*, Hübn., is remarkable for the great majority of the species being Arctic, though one or two are Alpine. They are generally of a pale tawny colour, with marginal spots or eyes. The curious silvery *Argyrophorus Argenteus*, Blanch., a native of Chili, is allied to these butterflies; as are also the Marbled Whites, which belong to the genus *Melanargia*, Meig. These are of a black and white colour above, though the wings are sometimes more or less marked with reddish on the under surface along the nervures. They are most numerous in Southern Europe, though one or two species are met with throughout Europe, North Africa, and Northern and Western Asia.

The largest and handsomest of the European *Satyrinæ* belong to the genus *Hipparchia*, Fabr. Our common Grayling (*Hipparchia Semele*, Linn.) is the only British species. It is brown, with a black eye near the tip of the fore wings, bordered by a square tawny blotch on each side; the female has a second eye, surrounded with tawny, near the hinder angle; the hind wings have a tawny submarginal band, and a small black eye near the anal angle. It frequents dry hill-sides or heaths, especially in chalky localities; and I first met with it on the Great Orme's Head, in Wales. It measures about two or two and a half inches in expanse. Several of the European species of this genus are very simply marked, such as *H. Phædra*, Linn., which is dark brown, with two black eyes, with large blue pupils, on the hind wings. It is found in open places in woods, but is not common everywhere. The handsomest species of this genus is *H. Parisotis*, Koll., which is a dark-brown insect about the size of *H. Phædra*, but is ornamented with a broad white or very pale blue border to all the wings. It is met with from Armenia to North-Western India.

The greater number of the smaller *Satyrinæ* of Asia and Africa belong to the genus *Mycalesis*, Hübn. They are black or brown, and, like so many butterflies of this family, are generally adorned with three eyes, two on the fore wings, and one at the anal angle of the hind wings. Many of the males are adorned with a large fan-like tuft of hair at the base of the hind wings above. One peculiarity by which a brown butterfly may often be recognised as a *Mycalesis* at a glance, is that the eye near the hinder angle of the fore wings is generally much larger than that at the tip, whereas the reverse is the case in other genera of *Satyrinæ*. The species are generally of small size, rarely exceeding an inch and a half in expanse.

Yvthima, Hübn., another genus common in Asia and Africa,

includes small brown butterflies, often not exceeding an inch in expanse, with a large black eye in a yellow ring at the tip of the fore wings, with two white pupils.

The larger and handsomer South American *Satyrinæ* belong to the genera *Taygetis*, Hübn., and *Pronophila*, Westw., and their allies. The latter are most numerous in Western South America. They are brown insects, with more or less dentated hind wings, and are generally adorned with tawny markings.

Several of the most recent writers include the East Indian genus *Elymnias*, Hübn., with the *Satyrinæ*. The species of this genus measure about three inches across the wings, and they have all a superficial resemblance to different species of *Danainæ* and *Satyrinæ*, from which their more or less dentated wings, which are generally irregularly mottled with brown or grey beneath, would at once distinguish them.

SUB-FAMILY III.—*Morphinæ*.

Hind wings with the discoidal cell open; size large; wings broad, rounded, or very slightly scalloped; hind wings sometimes lobed at the anal angle, but never tailed; wings generally adorned beneath with a row of moderate-sized eyes; flight diurnal; larvæ with forked tails.

The *Morphinæ* are nearly always of a blue, brown, white, or tawny colour, and are exclusively confined to the East Indies and tropical America. Several genera are met with in the former region, but the typical genus *Morpho*, Fabr., is exclusively confined to the latter.

The species of *Tenaris*, Hübn., are very singular-looking butterflies, brown or white, according to the species, with two large black eyes with white pupils, and more or less surrounded with yellow, on each hind wing, most distinct on the under surface. They are confined to the Papuan Islands and the Moluccas.

Amathusia Phidippus, Linn., is a brown butterfly with a large lobe on the hind wings; it is found in Java.

The genus *Thaumantis*, Hübn., which is met with in India, China, and Malayana, is nearly allied to *Morpho*. The species are of large size, with rounded wings; and several, such as *T. Diores*, Doubl., are brown, with a large suffused blue spot in the middle of each wing. One of the finest North Indian species is *T. Camudeva*, Westw., which is dark brown, dull red, and bluish white above, and yellow beneath.

The South American species of *Morpho* are magnificent insects. The great long-winged orange species (*M. Hecuba*, Linn., and *Cisseis*, Feld.) are fully nine inches in expanse, and have a lofty sailing flight, while some of the species with broader and shorter wings, such as the black bordered *M. Menelaus*, Linn., have a lower, but very rapid flight through the forest, and settle occasionally. The high-flying species very rarely come within reach; and Mr. Bates has informed me that although he often saw the beautiful *M. Rhetenor*, Cram., one of the most richly blue Amazonian species, he was only able to obtain two specimens in eleven years. This, and several blue species, have an orange female, while others have two forms of female, one orange and the other blue; and others again have females resembling the males. Among the latter are several species of a very delicate blue, or even whitish colour, and generally with no black border. *M. Polyphemus*, Doubl. and Hew., a Mexican species, is one of these.

The high-flying species of *Morpho* which inhabit the mountainous districts of Western America, are much easier captured than those which frequent the plains, though their capture is often attended with difficulty and danger. I have heard of one naturalist in Bogota, who fell over a precipice, and broke his arm, and then found that he had a three days' journey to make on horseback before he could meet with a doctor to set it. Another naturalist, who was collecting in Bolivia (the well-known Mr. Buckley), found that *Morpho Godartii*, Guér., a beautiful species of a rather light blue, which was previously almost unknown to entomologists, frequented an inaccessible ledge in the mountains; and he was obliged to have himself lowered by ropes over the precipice before he could obtain it.

SUB-FAMILY IV.—*Brassolinæ.*

Discoidal cells of the wings closed; hind wings with a pre-discoidal cell; size generally large; body very robust; wings broad, rounded, or scalloped, never tailed or lobed; hind wings with three more or less fully-formed eyes, one of which is often very large; flight crepuscular; larvæ with bifid tails.

The species of this sub-family are large insects, much resembling the *Morphinæ*. They are nearly always of a brown or tawny colour, and although several species are more or less suffused with blue or purple, it is always of a dark tint, rarely, even at the brightest, resembling the colour of any *Morpho*. These insects are exclusively confined to tropical America.

One of the commonest species is *Caligo Teucer*, Linn. The borders of the wings are broadly velvety black, and the base of the fore wings is yellowish grey, shading into bluish on the hind wings. The under surface of the hind wings is finely reticulated with grey or brown, and marked with three eyes, the last of which is very large and oval, black, and surrounded with a moderately broad buff ring.

Another very handsome species of this family is *Dynastes Napoleon*, Doubl. and Hew. It is black, with an oblique white macular band on the fore wings, and a broad tawny band on the hind wings. It is found in South Brazil, and is considered a great rarity.

Sub-Family V.—*Acræinæ*.

Discoidal cells of the wings closed ; wings long and narrow ; palpi thick, not very hairy ; larvæ spiny.

The species of *Acræa* are chiefly natives of Africa, only a few being found in India, Australia, etc. Most of the species are red, with black spots, and several are more or less transparent. Some few, however, are brown, with black spots, and red or white markings, or tawny with black markings.

In the allied South American genus *Actinote*, the colours of the species are more varied, but brown and fulvous generally predominate. Black spots are wanting, but the hind wings are nearly always longitudinally striated beneath.

Sub-Family VI.—*Heliconinæ*.

Discoidal cells of the wings closed, those of hind wings small ; wings long and narrow, costal nervure extending to the tip of the fore wing ; head broad ; palpi thick, hairy ; larvæ spiny.

The *Heliconinæ* are exclusively confined to tropical America, and are very varied in pattern and coloration, although there is no group in which a greater variety is obtained from simple materials by the substitution of one colour for another in insects otherwise similar. A very common and simply marked species is *Heliconius Melpomene*, Linn., which is black, with a broad red band across the fore wings. Another section of the genus resembles *Mechanitis*, a genus of *Danainæ* allied to *Ithomia*, in its markings. *Heliconius Eucrate*, Hübn., is an instance of this. It is black and tawny, with a large white spot near the tip of the fore wings.

Discoidal cells of the hind wings open ; structure both of the larva and imago very variable.

The typical *Nymphalinæ* are a very extensive group, which it is not easy to divide satisfactorily into smaller sections ; and, indeed, most authors do not consider even the *Morphinæ* sufficiently distinct to be separated from them. But these two groups are distinguished from all the other *Nymphalidæ* by the open hind-wing cells.

The genus *Colænis*, Hübn., has long and rather narrow wings. The species are about four inches in expanse, and are usually of a tawny colour ; but *C. Dido*, Linn., is black and green. These butterflies frequent plantations and clearings throughout tropical America.

Dione, Hübn., a genus of similar habits, includes species with shorter wings, of a rich tawny, spotted, but not bordered with black. The under surface is splendidly spotted with silver, to a much greater extent than in any of our own fritillaries.

The East Indian genus *Cathosia*, Fabr., includes species with rounded and dentated wings, which are remarkable for the elegant festooned markings of the under surface of the wings. Above they are of a pale salmon colour (or sometimes white in the females), with black spots and borders.

These and several other tropical genera, which we have not room to notice, are allied to the genus *Argynnis*, Fabr., which includes fulvous, black-spotted and black-bordered butterflies, with silver spots or streaks on the under surface of the hind wings. These are very numerous throughout Europe, Asia, and North America, and are known to collectors as Fritillaries. Some of the smaller species extend to the extreme limits of animal life in the Arctic regions ; but the genus is not found south of the Sahara, in Africa, where it is replaced by *Acræa ;* nor in South America (except a few small species confined to the mountains of the west), being there replaced by *Colænis*, and allied genera.

The species of *Melitæa*, Fabr., much resemble those of *Argynnis*, but do not exceed the dimensions of the smaller species of that genus, rarely measuring more than an inch and a half across the wings, whereas many species of *Argynnis* expand three inches and upwards. They are tawny, and are rarely marked with black spots, which are replaced by black lines ; and the under surface

of the hind wings is tessellated with straw-colour or pale red.
They are found throughout Europe, Asia, and North America,
but not in Africa or South America; nor do they extend to the
very high Arctic latitudes, where we still meet with *Argynnis*.
Some of the North American species are black, with white and
red spots.

Most of the smaller tawny *Nymphalinæ* of America belong to
the genus *Phyciodes*, Hübn. Many resemble *Melitæa* above, but
the under side of the hind wings is yellowish or greyish, without
sharply defined markings. Others have very long wings, and
closely resemble small *Heliconinæ*, being marked with black and
tawny in a similar manner, while others again are black, with
white spots on the fore wings, and a broad white band on the
hind wings. The short-winged species are usually smaller than
an average *Melitæa*, but the largest of the other group occasionally exceed two inches in expanse. This genus, though occurring also in North America, entirely replaces *Melitæa* in tropical
America, and has given rise to Mr. Bates's observation that representative tropical forms of temperate groups rarely surpass, and
are often inferior to the latter, both in size and beauty.

All these genera have spiny larvæ, and so likewise has the
next group of *Nymphalinæ*, that represented by *Vanessa*, Fabr.,
and its allies, which may be distinguished from most of the other
Nymphalinæ by their more or less dentated wings. This character reaches its acme in the genus *Polygonia*, Hübn., the species
of which are rich tawny, spotted with black, and marked with a
white C on the under surface of each wing. This genus is most
numerous in North America, but is represented in Britain by the
Comma Butterfly (*P. C.-Album*, Linn.).

Eleven species of the *Vanessa* group are found in Europe, seven
of which are British, a larger proportion than obtains among other
butterflies; but most of the *Vanessæ* are strong-winged insects,
feeding on nettles, thistles, and other common weeds; and this
may help to account for the wide distribution of many of the
species. They are richly-coloured butterflies, and most of the
species are common; one of the most beautiful is the black and
scarlet "Red Admiral" (*Pyrameis Atalanta*, Linn.), which is
common in most gardens in autumn.

The *Vanessæ* are represented in Asia and Africa by the genera
Junonia, Hübn., *Precis*, Hübn., *Salamis*, Boisd., and a few others.
Junonia Orithya, Linn., a common East Indian species, is black

or brown (the hind wings generally blue), with buff markings towards the tip of the fore wings, and two black eyes with bluish pupils, in red rings, on the hind wings.

One of the largest and handsomest butterflies of this group is *Salamis Anacardii*, Linn. It is found in most parts of Africa, and frequently exceeds three inches in expanse of wing. It is of an iridescent greenish white, like mother-of-pearl, with several black spots and markings.

The genus *Kallima*, Westw., also includes large and handsome butterflies, which are generally of a greyish-blue colour, with the tip of the fore wings black, bordered on the inside by an oblique tawny band. They are called "Dead Leaf Butterflies," for there is a lobe at the inner angle of the hind wings which simulates the stalk, from which a dark stripe runs obliquely across both wings beneath to the tip of the fore wings; and the entire under surface is mottled with lighter or darker brown, in order to complete the resemblance. One or two of these butterflies are met with in Africa, but the greater part inhabit the East Indies; *K. Paralekta*, Horsf., is a native of Java.

Napeocles Jucunda, Hübn., is a large black butterfly with hooked fore wings and rounded hind wings; a broad blue band crosses all the wings, and there is a blue spot near the tip. This is a Brazilian species representing *Salamis* in South America.

The butterflies of the South American genus *Anartia*, Hübn., closely resemble *Vanessa* in appearance and habits. They are of moderate size, with slightly dentated and angulated wings, and the hind wings are rendered almost square by a slight projection at the outer angle. *V. Amalthea*, Linn., is black, broadly banded with red in the middle of the wings, and is marked with white spots towards the margins.

We have now reached an extensive series of butterflies of moderate or small size, but beautiful colours, which are almost exclusively natives of South America.

The species of *Cybdelis*, Boisd., measure about an inch and a half across the fore wings. The hind margin of the fore wings projects slightly below the tip, and is somewhat concave below the projection. The hind wings are scalloped, and curved strongly outwards in the middle. The commonest species is *C. Mnasylus*, Doubl. and Hew., which is rich brown, with white spots, those on the hind wings broadly surrounded with blue.

The species of *Eunica*, Hübn., are brown or velvety black

butterflies of moderate size, sometimes spotted with white, and
generally more or less adorned with rich purplish blue.

Catonephele, Hübn., is remarkable for the disparity of the sexes.
The males are black, with broad markings of the richest orange,
and the females are also black, but are marked with yellow bands
and spots arranged nearly as in the East Indian genus *Neptis*, or
in the allied South American genus *Myscelia*, Doubl., in which
latter they were formerly included, as it was not until their habits
had been carefully studied in their native countries that it was
supposed that there was any specific identity between such dissimilar butterflies.

The smallest of the true *Nymphalinæ* belong to the genus
Dynamine, Hübn. Several are white, with the costa and hind
margin black, spotted with white; the costa is often shaded with
bluish or greenish, and there is frequently a dark transverse stripe
near the base of the hind wings. On the under surface, the dark
portions of the wings are lined and blotched with reddish and
bluish grey. Some of these white species scarcely exceed an inch
in expanse; but there is another group of rather larger species in
which the males are bluish, greenish, or brassy, with dark borders,
and sometimes spots; and the females are brown, spotted and
banded with white. On the under side of the hind wings are two
large black eyes, with blue pupils and yellow rings, placed on a
reddish band, which is edged with white on both sides. In
other species, the males are bluish or greenish, spotted with white,
and with black tips and borders, and the females are black and
white. The under side of the hind wings is silvery grey, with
reddish lines or stripes, but without eyes. These pretty little
butterflies are found flying about hedges, or at the edges of woods.

The genera *Callicore* and *Perisama*, Hübn., are velvety black
above, with more or less extended blue or green markings. On
the under surface the fore wings are broadly scarlet at the base;
and the hind wings in *Callicore* are grey or brown, with two pairs
of black spots (frequently united), each pair enclosed by an oval
black figure; and both then enclosed by two more or less complete
black concentric circles. The English residents in Brazil call these
butterflies "Eighty-eights," from the peculiar markings on the
under surface of the hind wings. In *Perisama* the hind wings are
of different colours beneath, and are marked with two black lines,
between which runs a row of black dots.

Catagramma, Boisd., is closely allied to the last two genera, but here the greater number of the species are black and scarlet above, though some are marked with blue, green, or yellow. The under surface varies; several species are marked nearly as in *Callicore*, but more heavily, while in others the under surface of the hind wings is covered with alternate stripes of black and yellow.

Gynæcia Dirce, Linn., is a very common and widely distributed butterfly in South America, where it is fond of settling on the trunks of trees with its wings raised, like *Ageronia* and several other allied genera. It is a robust insect, and measures upwards of two inches across the wings. The fore wings are triangular and obtusely pointed, owing to the hind margin being rather oblique; and there is a projecting lobe on the lower part of the hind wings. The upper side is uniform brown, with a broad yellow band running obliquely across the fore wings. On the under side the transverse band is paler, and the whole of the wings are beautifully striped and reticulated with brown and grey.

The species of *Pandora*, Westw., are large insects, expanding about three inches. The hind margin of the fore wings is more or less concave, but the hind wings are not dentated. They are black, with a brassy-green band beyond the middle on all the wings; towards the base they are darker green, intersected by numerous rather broad black lines. The under side of the hind wings is red. They inhabit the west of South America, and their flight is very rapid.

Ageronia, Hübn., is chiefly remarkable for the crackling noise which several species make with their wings during flight. The butterflies are tesselated with black and grey, green, or blue, according to the species; they measure upwards of two inches in expanse, and the wings are slightly dentated; but the hind margin of the fore wings is hardly concave.

The genus *Didonis*, Hübn., includes a few brown butterflies, expanding about two and a half inches. The fore wings are rounded, and the hind wings dentated; the latter are marked with a conspicuous red submarginal band, and are spotted with red at the base beneath.

The genus *Megalura*, Blanch., includes several brown or tawny species, with black transverse lines running across both pairs of wings. In another section, represented by *M. Corinna*, Latr., the species are brown, with a broad tawny band across the fore wings and a large blue blotch at the base of the hind wings. The species

K

expand two inches, or over, and are remarkable for having a long tail on the hind wings, similar to that found in many species of *Papilio.*

Victorina Steneles, Linn., is a common South American butterfly, much resembling *Colænis Dido* at first sight, but with shorter and broader wings. It is brown, with a broad greenish band, entire on the hind wings, and broken into spots on the fore wings. There is an outer row of green spots, and the anal angle of the hind wings is marked with a red or orange spot.

On quitting South American insects, we arrive first at the genus *Cyrestis,* Boisd. The species are allied to *Megalura,* but are smaller, much more delicately formed, and with shorter tails; they are generally white or tawny, and, except two African species, they are all East Indian. *C. Thyodamas,* Boisd., is a native of North India.

The genera *Hypolimnas,* Hübn., *Pseudacrœa,* Westw., and some of their allies, are remarkable for the singular resemblance of many of the species included in them to species of *Danaus, Euplœa,* and *Acrœa.* The most remarkable of these is *Hypolimnas Misippus,* Linn., a common species in Africa and the East Indies, as well as on the north coast of South America, where it has doubtless been introduced, as no other species of the group is known to occur in America. It measures about three inches in expanse, and the male is black, with slightly dentated wings. On each wing is a large bluish-white spot, and there is a smaller white spot near the tip of the fore wings. But the female is a tawny insect, marked almost exactly like *Danaus Chrysippus,* except that the hind wings are rather more dentated, and that there is only one black spot in the middle, instead of five.

The African species of *Hypolimnas* are very handsome; *D. Salmacis,* Drury, not an uncommon species, is black, blue, and white, and considerably larger than *D. Misippus.*

Adelpha, Hübn., is a genus which replaces *Limenitis* in tropical America, extending as far north as California. They are middle-sized dark-brown butterflies, with a white or pale-greenish band running from the middle of the fore wings to the inner margin of the hind wings, and there is an orange mark, varying in size and shape in different species, towards the tip of the fore wings. This is the general coloration, but there are exceptions. Some species have a large round or oval white spot in the middle of the hind wings, instead of a band; and others are brown, with the greater part of the fore wings filled up with red or tawny.

The White Admiral (*Limenitis Sibylla*, Linn.) is not a very common insect in the south of England, but is more abundant on the Continent. It is dark brown, with a white macular band, interrupted on the fore wings, running from the middle of the costa of the fore wings to the middle of the inner margin of the hind wings. Its larva feeds on honeysuckle, and is green, with rust-coloured hairy tubercles, and a red head. The butterfly averages about two inches in expanse of wings, and has a sailing flight along the edges of glades in woods. Many larger species of *Limenitis* inhabit North America, the most interesting being *Limenitis Archippus*, Cram., which resembles the common North American *Danaus Erippus*, Cram., being tawny, with black nervures. It is, however, smaller, not exceeding three inches in expanse.

Neptis, Fabr., and *Athyma*, Westw., are genera which include many East Indian species; and the former has a few representatives in Africa and Eastern Europe also. They are black butterflies, with white or yellow markings, similar to those of *Limenitis Sibylla*, but there is generally a more or less interrupted pale streak running from the base of the fore wings; and *Neptis* has more rounded wings than either *Limenitis* or *Athyma*.

One of the most characteristic genera of African butterflies is *Euphædra*, Hübn. They are rather large insects, averaging about three inches in expanse, and the hind wings at least are dentated. Most of them are of a velvety black above, with the greater part of the hind wings and the adjacent portion of the fore wings green. There is a broad white or yellow transverse band near the tip of the fore wings. The under side of the hind wings is generally of a more yellowish green, with a variable number of black spots differently arranged according to the species. Many species are of the richest crimson at the base beneath; and in *E. Xypete*, Hew., this coloration extends over the greater part of the hind wings. In another section of the genus the species are red, the fore wings being black at the tip, with an oblique white band; the hind wings have a black border spotted with white. The latter species have a general resemblance to *Danaus Chrysippus*.

The Purple Emperor (*Apatura Iris*, Linn.) is considered one of the finest of our British butterflies. It is brown, and the male is shot with rich purple. The fore wings are spotted with white, and there is a white band across the middle of the hind wings; near the anal angle of the hind wings is an orange ring. The genus *Apatura* is well represented in Asia and America. The Indian

A. Namouna, Doubl., is shot with much brighter blue; but most of the other Indian species, and several of the South American too, are much inferior to our own in size and beauty. But others from the latter country are of a bright blue or greenish blue above; and in *A. Laurentia*, Godt., the under surface of the hind wings is of a brilliant silvery white. The larvæ of *Apatura* and its allies are smooth, with horns on the head, and sometimes a slightly bifid tail. The butterflies fly round the tops of the highest trees, and rarely descend to the ground.

Agrias Ædon, Hew., is the type of a magnificent genus confined to the west of South America. The species have black and scarlet fore wings, and stout bodies, and resemble gigantic *Catagrammæ* in appearance, measuring nearly four inches in expanse. There is generally a large blue spot on the brown hind wings. The species are always rare, and difficult to obtain, generally settling on the trunks or branches of trees at some height from the ground. But, like other butterflies of this group, they may sometimes be found on pathways, settled on dung.

The genus *Charaxes*, Ochs., includes a large number of very handsome African and East Indian butterflies much resembling *Apatura* in their habits. They are lofty flyers, and difficult to capture. One species only (*C. Jasius*, Linn.) is European; for it is common all round the Mediterranean wherever the Strawberry Tree (*Arbutus Unedo*), on which the larva feeds, is plentiful. It is reddish-brown above, with yellow borders; the under surface is beautifully reticulated with dark red and white. It measures about three inches across the wings. Several of the African species are similarly marked; others are brown, with red or blue markings; and one of the smallest species, *C. Eupole*, Drury, which does not exceed two inches in expanse, is of a peculiar, slightly yellowish, green colour. The East Indian species are either of a deep tawny or orange brown, with black borders, or of a creamy white. In South America this genus is represented by *Megistanis*, Westw., the commonest species of which, *M. Bæotus*, Doubl. and Hew., is common on the Upper Amazons, and in Bogota, and is black, with blue markings; it expands about four inches. Mr. Bates notes this species as appearing at the commencement of the dry season in June, flying about the moist sediment left by the retreating waters of the river. Although abundant, it is a difficult insect to capture, as it is very wary, and its flight is very wild and rapid. In both these genera the hind wings are strongly dentated, and are usually adorned with at least two tails. In several South American genera placed near the end of the *Nymphalinæ*, the hind wings are adorned with a moderately broad spatulate tail. *Hypna Clytemnestra*, Hübn., a brown butterfly with a yellowish-white band across the fore wings, is one of these; it is common in most parts of South America, or else there are a number of closely-allied local forms in different localities.

The species of *Anæa*, Hübn., are of moderate size, not much exceeding two inches in expanse, and are generally of a dark brown, more or less blue at the base, this colour frequently extending over a great part of the wings; in other species the prevailing shade is red.

The genus *Protogonius*, Hübn., is remarkable for its singular form; the wings are long, and of a black and tawny colour, as in some of the *Heliconinæ*; but the fore wings are strongly arched, and there is a projection in the middle, extending further than either the tip or the hinder angle; the hind wings are furnished with a rather long spatulate tail. The species are confined to tropical America.

Before finally quitting the *Nymphalidæ*, we must not forget to notice the genus *Siderone*, Hübn., which has pointed fore wings, and rounded and slightly dentated hind wings, with a short projection at the anal angle. The under surface is mottled, and there is an oblique stripe as in *Kallima*, which this genus probably represents in America; the under surface of all the species has more or less resemblance to a dead leaf; but the upper surface differs considerably in the two principal sections of the genus. In one it is black, with rich scarlet markings, and in the other it is varied with tawny and yellowish. Like *Kallima*, too, the species which most resemble dead leaves are very variable; and variability appears to be a usual accompaniment of this peculiar form of protective mimicry.

FAMILY II.—*Lewoniidæ*.

Front pair of legs rudimentary in the male, and fully developed in the female; species of small size and delicate formation; pupa attached by the tail.

SUB-FAMILY I.—*Libytheinæ*.

Palpi contiguous, four times as long as the head, and forming a kind of beak; wings angulated; pupa suspended by the tail.

With the exception of one or two South American *Nymphalidæ* allied to *Eunica*, no other butterflies resemble the genus *Libythea*, Fabr., in the extraordinary development of the palpi. The species are of small size, seldom measuring as much as two inches across the wings. They are all very similar, being brown, with fulvous markings, and, though not numerous in species, yet representatives of the genus are met with in South Europe, the East Indies, West Africa, Mauritius, North and South America, the West Indies, and the Moluccan and Papuan Islands. Those found in the Papuan Islands are larger than the others, with less strongly angulated wings, and differ also in coloration, being brown or blue.

Sub-Family II.—*Nemeobiinæ*.

Palpi of moderate length; subcostal nervure with four branches.

Mr. H. W. Bates has divided the *Erycinidæ* of authors into three sub-families by the neuration. These butterflies are almost entirely confined to tropical America, a few genera and species only occurring in Africa and the East Indies, and only one in Europe. Even in temperate North America very few species are met with, and those chiefly in California and the adjacent Western States.

Nemeobius Lucina, Linn. (the Duke of Burgundy Fritillary), is a somewhat local species in England, though not uncommon throughout the greater part of Europe. It measures about an inch in expanse, and is brown, with rows of dull orange spots, which give the fore wings the appearance of being tessellated. It derives its English name from its general resemblance to the species of *Melitæa*.

Zemeros Flegyas, Cram., is a common East Indian species, measuring about an inch and a half across the wings, which are slightly dentated. It is brown, covered with irregular black spots, marked with white.

In some species the hind wings are so strongly dentated as to be slightly tailed. *Abisara Tepahi*, Boisd., may be taken as an example. It is brown, with numerous white lines on the under surface, and is a native of Madagascar.

The largest of the *Nemeobiinæ* belong to the genus *Eurybea*, Hübn. They expand about two inches, and are of a light brown, sometimes glossed with violet, with a large blue eye surrounded with tawny, near the middle of the fore wings, and a row of white, and often of red spots near the borders of all the wings. This genus, and all the following genera of the *Erycinidæ*, are American.

The genus *Mesosemia*, Hübn., is one of the easiest recognised genera of this family, as well as one of the largest. The species are brown or blue, and are generally striated with darker brown and white or blue on the hind wings. The fore wings are sometimes marked with a white transverse bar; but in almost every species, a large round black eye, with two white pupils, and surrounded by a pale ring, is situated near the middle of the fore wings.

Sub-Family III.—*Euselasiinæ*.

Palpi of moderate length; subcostal nervure, with from two to four branches; lower radial nervure emitted straight from the subcostal, or connected with it by an oblique perfect discocellular nervule.

The typical genus *Euselasia*, Hübn., includes a number of small species, not much exceeding an inch in length, with short, rather broad wings, and bright colours. They are blue, brown, orange, tawny, or reddish, in various combinations, and the under surface is generally more or less striated. Some species have a superficial resemblance to other butterflies belonging to widely different genera, such as *Euptychia* and *Thecla*, from which their structure will at once distinguish them.

Sub-Family IV.—*Lemoniinæ*.

Palpi of moderate length; subcostal nervure with three branches; lower radial nervure of both wings connected with the subcostal at a right angle by a more or less rudimentary discocellular nervule.

Two-thirds of the family *Lemoniidæ* belong to this sub-family, which is divided into upwards of fifty genera, most of which are of small extent. A few of the more interesting may here be mentioned.

The species of *Lymnas*, Blanch., are black or brown, with rather large red spots near the base, on both sides of the wings, and often with a yellow bar across the fore wings, and a yellow border to the hind wings.

Several very beautiful tailed species belong to the genus *Diorhina*, Mor., and its allies. *D. Butes*, Linn., is black, with bluish-white stripes, and one or two scarlet spots near the anal angle of the hind wings.

The species of *Zeonia*, Swains., are transparent-winged insects, with black borders and stripes; the hind wings are more or less marked with crimson.

Barbicornis, Latr., is a singular black and yellow tailed insect, with pectinated antennæ like a moth. Some authors include it with the *Lithosiidæ*.

The species of *Helicopis*, Fabr., are very delicately-formed insects, which are among the commonest of the South American *Lemoniidæ*. They are of a creamy white, yellow towards the base, with black borders, and the under side of the hind wings is adorned with silvery spots. Mr. Bates found two species of this genus common in damp shady places near Pará, and observes: "Their flight is very slow and feeble; they seek the protected under surface of the leaves, and in repose close their wings over the back, so as to expose the brilliantly-spotted under surface."[1]

The species of *Emesis*, Fabr., are rather dingy insects. They are brown insects, with more or less pointed fore wings, near the tip of which is often a white spot, and they are traversed by darker lines. The under surface is generally reddish yellow, with the lines more distinct.

Lemonias, Hübn., includes a number of small species, which are generally of a black colour, more or less of the wings, especially towards the base, being red or blue, spotted with black, at least on the under surface.

The genus *Nymphidium*, Hübn., is not unlike *Dynamine*, among the *Nymphalidæ*, in appearance. Many of the species are white or yellowish white, with brown or yellowish-brown borders.

Theope, Westw., includes small species, with broad truncated fore wings; they are blue, more or less bordered with brown, and the under surface is brown or yellowish, and is in most cases absolutely uniform in colour, being often destitute of any markings whatever.

The genus *Aricoris*, Westw., includes several rather long-winged black and yellow butterflies; and *Stalachtis*, Hübn., contains several species not unlike *Heliconinæ* in shape and colour. They are about two inches in expanse, and are black, with reddish or yellowish markings; other species are partly transparent, thus resembling *Ithomiæ*.

[1] *Naturalist on the Amazons*, i. p. 23.

FAMILY III.—*Lycænidæ*.

Front legs perfect in the female; the front tarsi more or less imperfect in the male; pupa attached by the tail, and a belt round the body; larva short and broad.

These are insects of small size and delicate structure, and various shades of blue, brown, or red preponderate in their coloration. Most of the genera are of great extent, and the family has not yet been satisfactorily divided into sub-families.

Miletus Symethus,[1] Cram., a common East Indian species, measures about an inch and a half across the wings, which are brown, with a large white spot in the middle of the fore wings. This butterfly is remarkable for having very thick legs, and is said to be frequently found in ants' nests, a circumstance which need no longer puzzle us, as it has lately been discovered that the larvæ of several *Lycænidæ* exude a liquid of which ants are very fond.

Axiocerces, Hübn., is a genus with more or less dentated wings; the species are brown, with red or tawny markings, and are especially numerous in South Africa. This genus replaces *Lycæna* in Africa, for the latter is not met with south of the Mediterranean region.

The genus *Lycæna*, Fabr., to which we have just alluded, includes the beautiful coppery-red butterflies known to all collectors as "Coppers." Some of the European species are shot with purple; but this is not the case with *C. Virganreæ*, Linn., which is one of the most brilliant species, and is not uncommon on the Continent in many places, though a doubtful species in England.

The small genus *Thestor* is black and orange above, and the hind wings are frequently green beneath, as in the typical species, *T. Ballus*, Fabr., which is not uncommon in the Mediterranean region.

Polyommatus, Latr., in which the small blue butterflies which frequent meadows and heaths may be placed, is a very extensive genus; but the species are nearly all of some shade of blue or brown. Frequently the male is blue, and the female brown. A row of red spots often runs round all or part of the wings; and the under surface is usually grey or brown, and marked with numerous black spots surrounded with white. In one group of the genus, represented in Britain by *P. Bæticus*, Linn., which is

[1] It is now believed that the statement that it is found in ants' nests applies to some other Lepidopterous insect.

occasionally captured on the south coast, the hind wings are furnished with a short and slender tail, and are striped instead of spotted beneath.

Hypochrysops, Feld., is a genus confined to Australia and the adjacent islands, and remarkable for the beauty of the markings of the under surface of the wings. *H. Polycletus*, Linn., is blue (or brown, with the base blue, in the female), and the under surface of the hind wings is brown, with rows of bright red spots bordered with black and golden-green. It measures about an inch and a half across the wings, which are slightly dentated. It inhabits Amboyna.

The genus *Thecla*, Fabr., is a very extensive group, which includes the butterflies known as Hair-streaks. The European species are brown, sometimes with a marginal row of red spots, and are adorned with a slender white line across both pairs of wings, which forms a more or less distinct W at the anal angle of the hind wings. Our smallest species, the Green Hair-streak (*Thecla Rubi*, Linn.), which is not uncommon among brambles in spring, does not much exceed an inch in expanse. It is brown and tailless, and the under surface is green, with some indistinct white dots. By far the larger proportion of the extra-European species of this genus are American. They are generally blue, with or without black borders, and are nearly always furnished with a short tail. Many are marked beneath like our own Hair-streaks; but some of the larger species have the under surface of the wings dusted with brilliant golden-green; and the largest species of all, *T. Marsyas*, Linn., a common South American insect, which sometimes measures nearly three inches in expanse, is of a pale blue above, and the under surface is of a pale shining violet blue, with several black spots slightly surrounded with white.

Our Brown Hair-streak (*Zephyrus Betulæ*, Linn.), which is found flying along hedgerows in the south of England, and the Purple Hair-streak (*Z. Quercus*, Linn.), which is common in oak woods, represent a distinct genus, which has representatives throughout Europe, Asia, and the west of North America. Several of the East Indian and Japanese species, which closely resemble our own beneath, are green or orange above, instead of brown or blue.

Tailed *Lycænidæ* of various genera are very numerous in Africa and the East Indies. As an example we may notice *Myrina Silenus*, Cram., an African species, which is rich blue, with black borders.

Amblypodia, Horsf., is a genus which includes a great number of rather large *Lycænidæ*, which chiefly inhabit India and the Eastern Islands. They are of different shades of blue, and the under surface is brown, more or less divided into large spots by white lines. There is frequently a green band towards the hind margin of the hind wings beneath. *A. Apidanus*, Cram., is a native of Java.

Eumæus, Hübn., is a small genus of interesting butterflies found in Mexico, Cuba, and Central America. *E. Minyas*, Hübn., is black, shaded with greenish blue, and the hind wings are bordered with a row of large golden-green spots. The under surface is dark brown, covered with golden-green spots.

FAMILY IV.—*Papilionidæ.*

Both sexes with six perfect legs; larva long, cylindrical, not spiny; pupa attached by the tail, and a belt of silk round the body.

SUB-FAMILY I.—*Pierinæ.*

Inner margin of the hind wings not concave; larvæ clothed with short hair, but with no retractile fork on the second segment.

The *Pierinæ* are insects of moderate size, and white and yellow are the prevailing colours of the upper surface of the wings. Their wings are rarely dentated, and are very rarely tailed, and even then the tail is confined to a slight projection on the hind margin of the hind wings, or a more or less pointed lobe at the anal angle.

Two or three South American genera at the beginning of this sub-family are very dissimilar from any of the others. The species of *Pereute*, Herr.-Schäff., resemble *Heliconius*. *P. Charops*, Boisd., from Mexico, is black, with an oblique red or bluish-white stripe across the fore wing. *Archonias*, Hübn., includes black species with white or yellow markings, and dentated hind wings, which somewhat resemble certain genera of South American *Nymphalinæ*; while *Dismorphia*, Hübn., is remarkable for the resemblance which many of its long narrow-winged species bear to *Ithomia*, and other genera of American *Danainæ*, though others may be distinguished from them at a glance by their broad hind wings. *D. Eumelia*, Cram., is a black and yellow species, which is very similar indeed to an *Ithomia*, while *L. Thermesia*, Godt., is a white, black-bordered species that could hardly be mistaken for anything but a Pieride.

The smallest and most delicately formed of the European *Pierinæ* is the Wood White (*Leucophasia Sinapis*, Linn.), a white butterfly with an ash-coloured spot at the tip of the fore wings, which are comparatively long and narrow, and expand about an inch and a half. It is found in shady woods, and has a very weak flight, and although abundant in other parts of Europe, is always scarce and local in the north-western countries.

Nychitona, Butl., is a genus very similar to this, but with shorter and broader and much rounded wings. It is found in Africa and the East Indies.

Eurema, Hübn., is an extensive genus to which most of the smaller white and yellow black-bordered butterflies of the Tropics belong. They measure from an inch to an inch and a half in expanse, and are frequently very common, but are often neglected, both by collectors and authors, on account of their small size and general uniformity of colouring.

The White Cabbage Butterflies of our gardens belong to the genus *Pieris*, Schrank. Three species are abundant in every garden : the Large and Small White Butterflies, and the Green-veined White Butterfly (*Pieris Brassica, Rapæ*, and *Napi*, Linn.). The first is easily known by its large size, and the deeper black tip to the wings ; in the third species, the under surface of the wings is more or less heavily veined with greenish. The Black-veined White Butterfly (*P. Cratægi*, Linn.) likewise hardly needs a description. It is about the size of the Large White Butterfly, and is local in the south of England. It is generally abundant on the Continent, but there is only one brood in early summer, so that it rarely appears much longer than a month on the wing, while there is a succession of broods of the other species, which are to be found almost all the year round. Our only other British species of *Pieris* (*P. Duplidice*, Linn.) is a rarity in the southern counties ; the under surface is tesselated with green.

The species of *Tuchyris*, Wall., have rather pointed wings, and are confined to the East Indies. Several are white ; but others, such as *T. Nero*, Fabr., and *T. Celestina*, Boisd., are red or blue.

Delias, Hübn., is another beautiful East Indian genus allied to *Pieris*. The butterflies resemble *Pieris* in shape and size, and are often white above with black borders; but the hind wings are generally bordered beneath with a row of red spots.

The genus *Pieris* has several representatives in South America ; but one very singular allied genus is confined to that country.

This is *Perrhybris*, Hübn. On the upper surface the males are white with black borders; but the upper surface of the females, and the under surface of both sexes, is striped with tawny, black and yellow, as in some species of *Heliconius*, etc.

Catopsilia, Hübn., includes most of the larger yellow butter-flies of the Tropics, several of which closely resemble our Brim-stone in appearance, except that all the wings are rounded; or if there is any projection on the hind wings at all, it is at the anal angle. Some of the East Indian species are white, irrorated with brown beneath. But the finest species of the genus is perhaps the Cuban *C. Avellaneda*, Herr.-Schäff. It measures four inches across the wings, which are of a rich orange colour, with a large red blotch in the middle of the fore wings, and a wide border of the same colour to the hind wings; and the coloration is so peculiar that the insect looks as if it had been artificially painted.

The Brimstone Butterfly (*Gonepteryx Rhamni*, Linn.) is common in woods in most parts of England. It measures about two and a half inches across the wings, which are of a bright sulphur colour in the male, and whitish sulphur in the female. There is a pro-jection on the hind margin, and an orange spot in the middle of each wing. There are several South American species very similar in shape and colour, but about twice the size.

Colias, Fabr., is a genus distributed over most parts of the world, though in tropical countries the species are found, if at all, in the mountains. Several species, however, are Polar. They are moderate-sized butterflies, with rounded wings, and are white, yellow, or orange, with black borders, which are generally veined in the male and spotted in the female. There is a black spot on the fore wings, and an orange one on the hind wings; on the under surface, which is often green, the spots are generally centred with silver. The orange species are sometimes shot with violet or purple; and they have generally two varieties of females, one orange and the other whitish. These butterflies are known as Clouded Yellows by collectors.

The Orange Tip (*Euchloe Cardamines*, Linn.) is a common spring butterfly, with rather long delicate wings. The male is marked with a bright orange spot near the tip. The under surface of the wings is tesselated with bright green, and the female has sometimes been mistaken for the Bath White. But in the Orange Tip the fore wings are merely tipped with brown, whereas they are partially bordered with brown in that species; and the markings of the under surface are much duller in the Bath White. The Orange Tip frequents meadows, gardens, and open places in woods. Several of the allied European species are yellow instead of white, and others are not marked with orange, but are streaked or spotted with silvery on the under surface of the hind wings.

Orange Tips belonging to the genera *Teracolus*, Swains., and *Ixias*, Hübn., are common in Africa and the East Indies, to which the latter is confined; but those belonging to the genus *Hebomoia*, Hübn., measure five inches in expanse, and are among the largest of the *Pierinæ*. They are white or yellow insects, and are confined to India and the adjacent islands. One of the finest species is *H. Leucippe*, Cram., a native of Amboyna and Ceram. Almost the whole of the fore wings is of a reddish orange, and the hind wings are of a sulphur-yellow. The common Indian species, *H. Glaucippe*, Linn., is white, with a large triangular orange blotch bordered with black near the tip of the fore wings.

SUB-FAMILY II.—*Papilioninæ*.

Inner margin of the hind wings concave; larvæ naked or hairy, always with a retractile fork on the second segment.

This sub-family includes the true Swallow-tailed Butterflies, which derive their name from the long tail on the hind wings. But many genera and species do not exhibit this peculiarity, and sometimes two closely-allied forms exhibit it in one case, and not in the other. There are even some species in which one sex only is tailed. They are insects of moderate or large size, and some of the species are among the largest butterflies known. In several the inner margin of the hind wings of the males is provided with a longitudinal fold, lined with long fluffy hair.

Parnassius, Latr., the first genus, considerably resembles the *Pierinæ* in appearance. The species are all white, marked with black spots, and large red spots surrounded with black. They are all very similar, and inhabit the mountains of Europe, Asia, and western North America. The best known species is *P. Apollo*, Linn., a fine butterfly, averaging three inches in expanse, which is common in the Swiss Alps. It has been reputed British, but there appears to be no authentic instance of its capture in England; and some of the localities where it is said to have been taken (Dover, for example) are so unlikely, that it could only have reached them by being brought over alive, and then set at liberty; for the species is quite unknown north-west of the Lower Moselle; though it is met with in Eastern Germany as well as in Norway and Sweden. Extraordinary captures may sometimes be accounted for in the manner suggested; but it by no means follows that the entomologist who captures an insect brought over and set at liberty is the same person who brought it over. Many insects are introduced into England with shipping, chiefly from the continent of Europe, and from North America; but a mountain species like *P. Apollo* could scarcely reach a locality like Dover unless purposely introduced.

Euryades Corethrus, Boisd., is a handsome black species, with yellow and red markings, which inhabits Uruguay and the adjacent countries; it is still rare in collections.

Thais, Fabr., is a genus of rather small butterflies, with dentated wings, which are met with on the shores of the Mediterranean. They are yellowish white, with black and red spots, and festooned markings.

Sericinus, Westw., is met with in North China, and derives its name from the silky white colour of the males; in the females the wings are heavily banded with brown. Towards the anal angle of the hind wings is a red streak on a black ground, marked below with blue. The hind wings are furnished with a long tail; but the antennæ are so much shorter in *Sericinus* than in *Papilio* that the two genera cannot possibly be confounded.

Teinopalpus Imperialis, Hope, is one of the finest North Indian species of this family. It is spangled with golden-green, varied above with pale lilac, and below with black and bright yellow. The male is smaller, more uniform in colour, and has only one tail on the hind wings, instead of three.

Ornithoptera, Boisd., though hardly sufficiently distinct from *Papilio*, is a group which includes a series of very large species, peculiar to the Eastern Islands. The males are of a velvety black, with a broad green band along the costa, and another along the hind margin; the hind wings are green, with a row of black submarginal spots. The females are large brown butterflies, with white spots and markings. In some species, the green of the males is replaced with blue (as in *O. Urvilliana*, Boisd.), or rich orange (as in *O. Crœsus*, Wall.). These butterflies are found in the Eastern Archipelago; but there is another section which extends to the Indian Peninsula and Ceylon, which is black, with the hind wings more or less yellow. The finest of the yellow species is *O. Magellanus*, Feld., from the Philippines, in which the yellow hind wings change in certain lights to pale iridescent green. The *Ornithopteræ* vary from three to nine inches in expanse of wing.

The great genus *Papilio*, Linn., is one of the most varied and beautiful of all the butterflies. The species are usually, but not always, inferior to the largest *Ornithoptera* in size. Few of the latter surpass *P. Antimachus*, Drury, the rarest of the African species. Its wings are still longer and narrower than in *Ornithoptera*, but the fore wings are dark brown, with many tawny yellow spots and markings towards the base, and the hind wings are of a tawny yellow, with black spots and a black border. Nothing is known of its habits, and although it was figured by Drury as long ago as 1782, it was not till 1864 that a second specimen was brought to Europe. Since then it has been received occasionally, but is still one of the rarest butterflies in collections.

Several groups of this genus are peculiar to South America. *P. Polydamas*, Linn., and its allies are green or dark brown, often with a yellow band on the hind wings, which is narrower and broken into spots on the fore wings. A very extensive group is dark brown, with dentated hind wings and a large dull green or creamy-white mark on the fore wings, and a bright crimson band or row of spots on the hind wings, which frequently changes to iridescent blue or green in different lights. *P. Triopas*, Godt., a common insect on the Lower Amazons, is allied to these, but is black, with large yellow spots.

Some of the East Indian species of *Papilio* resemble *Danainæ*. One of the commonest is the large black and buff *P. Dissimilis*, Linn. *P. Paradoxa*, Zink., from Java, has a most deceptive resemblance to a *Euplœa*.

Some species present very little resemblance to any others. One of these is *P. Antenor*, Drury, a large tailed butterfly, five inches in expanse, which is found in Madagascar. It is black, with several rows of large white spots on the wings; and the head, abdomen, and a row of large submarginal lunules on the hind wings, are bright scarlet. It is not rare, but is difficult to capture, as its flight is very lofty. It was figured by Drury in 1773; but it was sixty years before a second specimen was brought to England, and thirty more before the real locality was known. *P. Hector*, Linn., is a common Indian species. It is black and tailed, with white markings on the fore wings, and two rows of large blood-red spots on the hind wings.

Some of the South American species have very strongly dentated hind wings ; so much so as occasionally to appear to have
several short tails. This is the case with *P. Grayi*, Boisd., and to
a less extent in *P. Androgeos*, Cram., both of which are black, with
yellow markings, but which represent two different sections of the
genus.

P. Demoleus, Linn., is a very common African butterfly. It is
brown, with yellow markings, and two bluish eyes on the hind
wings. *P. Erithonius*, Cram., a very closely-allied species, but with
a broader and more irregular band on the hind wings, is one of
the most abundant butterflies in India.

Papilio Helenus, Linn., and its allies are large black East Indian
butterflies, three or four inches in expanse, with a large cream-
coloured palmate spot on the hind wings. These lead us on to
Papilio Paris, Linn., and its allies, which are black, spangled with
golden green, and are frequently marked with a large blue spot on
the hind wings, instead of a cream-coloured one.

Many handsome species of *Papilio* inhabit the Eastern Islands
and North Australia, one of the most remarkable of which is
P. Ulysses, Linn., which is of a deep blue, with black borders. A
great contrast to this is *P. Nox*, Swains., a dark-brown species
from Java, with only a faint purple reflection.

Black and green is a very prevalent colour among East Indian
and African species. One of the commonest species in the former
locality is *P. Sarpedon*, Linn. Other very common colours in the
genus, especially among the tailed species, are white, cream colour,
and yellow. Our only British species, *P. Machaon*, Linn., is black
and yellow, with a large red eye at the anal angle of the hind
wings. In England it is confined to the fen districts in the south-
east, but it is a generally distributed insect on the Continent, and is
likewise met with over a considerable part of Asia. Many species
more or less resembling this in colour are found in the northern
hemisphere ; the finest being perhaps *P. Daunus*, Boisd., which
inhabits California and New Mexico. It measures nearly six
inches across the wings, and has three tails on the hind
wings.

The Scarce Swallowtail (*P. Podalirius*, Linn.), though now
extinct in England, is common in many parts of the Continent.
The fore wings are more pointed, and the hind wings are more
triangular, with longer and slenderer tails, than in *P. Machaon*. It
is a pale yellow butterfly, with black transverse bands ; and the

L

submarginal band on the hind wings is marked with blue
crescents.

The curious genus *Leptocircus*, Swains., with its peculiarly
shaped wings and long tails, has no resemblance to any other
genus of *Papilioninœ*, but might readily be mistaken for one of the
Lemoniidœ. The fore wings are longer than the hind wings, which
are produced longitudinally instead of laterally into a very long
tail. The wings are black, and the outer half of the fore wings
is marked by a broad transparent band, divided into spots by
the veins ; and a green stripe runs from the costa of the fore wings
near the base, parallel to the body, to beyond the middle of the
hind wings. The few known species are all very similar, and
are confined to India, Siam, and some of the adjacent islands.

FAMILY V.—*Hesperiidœ*.

Body robust ; head broad ; antennæ inserted widely apart, and
often hooked at the tips ; hind tibiæ spurred ; larva generally
with a prominent head ; pupa enclosed in a slight cocoon.

The *Hesperiidœ*, or Skippers, are an isolated family, having no
great affinity to any of the other butterflies, and not very much
more with the moths. They are poorly represented in Europe,
and are specially abundant in tropical America, though they are
fairly numerous in other parts of the world. They derive their
English name from the short jerking flight of most of the European
species. They are generally of small size, the great majority of
the species averaging from an inch to an inch and a half in
expanse, though some few are much larger. Many are of a brown
colour, marked with small transparent spots towards the tips of
the fore wings ; and brown and fulvous are the most prevalent
colours in the family.

Thymele Proteus, Linn., is the type of an American genus, which
may be recognised at a glance by its long and rather broad tails.
It is brown, with tawny spots on the fore wings, and the hind
wings are thickly clothed with greenish hair towards the base.
Telegonus, Hübn., is another allied American genus, but the species
are furnished with a strong lobe at the anal angle of the hind
wings, instead of a tail.

Casyapa Thyrsis, Fabr., is a large brown Indian species, with
three or four yellow spots in the middle of the fore wings. It
measures three inches in expanse, but the largest known species
of the family is *Ismene Iphis*, Drury, which is common on the

west coast of Africa. It measures four inches in expanse, and is of a bluish black, with the head and the tip of the abdomen scarlet.

Pyrrhopyga versicolor, Latr., is a representative of a beautiful South American genus of *Hesperiidæ;* it is black, with red and yellow markings.

The extensive genus *Pamphila*, Fabr., includes a great number of brown and tawny species of moderate size, many of which much resemble our Large Skipper (*P. Sylvanus*, Linn.). The oblique patch of brown scales which will be noticed on the fore wings of this species is met with in all the species of this genus, but only in the males.

The genus *Hesperia*, Fabr., includes a number of small, white-spotted species, very similar to our own Grizzled Skipper (*H. Malvæ*, Linn.), a common insect in woods. The species of *Erynnis*, Schrank, several of which are found on the Continent, may be distinguished from *Hesperia* by their slightly dentated wings. *Erynnis* is remarkable, too, as being the only European genus in which the small apical transparent spots appear.

Heteropterus Morpheus, Pall., one of the largest European *Hesperiidæ*, is brown, with one or two yellow spots near the tip; the under surface of the hind wings is yellow, and is marked with several white spots surrounded with black.

Among the more remarkable South American species we may mention *Pythonides Cerialis*, Cram., a small brown species, with the under surface of the hind wings blue; and several species of the genera *Achlyodes* and *Antigonus*, Hübn., and *Helias*, Fabr., which are very dingy, brown insects, and look more like moths than butterflies.

SECTION II.—HETEROCERA, OR MOTHS.

Antennæ variously formed, but very rarely terminating in a club; fore and hind wings often linked together by a bristle at the base; flight generally crepuscular or nocturnal.

The number of known moths far exceeds that of the butterflies. Four or five times as many species of the former are known as of the latter; but they have been far less assiduously collected and studied, and as yet we have no reliable classification of the group, for all recent attempts made hitherto in this direction have been only partial and tentative; and there is much difference of opinion as to the real affinities of many groups. Many of the families of moths are perfectly distinct, it is true; but their mutual relationships have not been satisfactorily worked out; and the great mass of species classed as *Bombyces*, especially those formerly referred to the *Lithosiidæ*, in its widest sense, are perhaps more difficult to deal with than any.   The arrangement of the Moths here adopted is based on the general lines which are usually accepted by entomologists in default of something better; but must be looked upon as wholly provisional.

SUB-SECTION I.—*Sphinges.*

Antennæ more or less thickened before the tip; abdomen often extending beyond the hind wings; flight often diurnal or crepuscular.

Excluding the *Zygænidæ*, which, though included by Linné in his genus *Sphinx*, are certainly *Bombyces*, this group contains five very dissimilar families, three at least of which hardly belong to it.

FAMILY I.—*Sphingidæ.*

Body stout; abdomen extending far beyond the hind wings; wings narrow; fore wings generally much longer than the hind wings, and rather pointed; wings generally opaque; abdomen rarely tufted; larva generally with a horn near the tail; pupa in a subterranean cell.

SUB-FAMILY I.—*Macroglossinæ.*

Size small; wings sometimes transparent; abdomen with a large expansile tuft at the extremity; flight diurnal.

The present group includes the Bee Hawk-moths and Humming-bird Hawk-moths.   The Bee Hawk-moths belong to the genus *Hemaris*, Dalm.   The species measure from an inch and a half to two inches and a half across the wings, which are transparent, with brown, reddish, or greenish borders; their bodies are generally green or brown, and, if green, belted with red; and the anal tuft is usually red or brown.

The genus *Macroglossa*, Ochs., is very similar to this in shape; many of the species resemble our common Humming-bird Hawkmoth, which has dark-brown fore wings, reddish-brown hind wings, and a black apical tuft.   It is a very rapid insect on the wing, flying from flower to flower, and sucking the nectar with its long proboscis, in the manner of a humming-bird.   It is not easily captured on the wing without practice, and it never rests except upon a wall; under a bank; or in some similar situation where its colour is a protection. It flies both by day and at dusk, but the Bee Hawk-moths fly only by day, with less rapidity, and are almost always met with in or near woods, while the Humming-bird Moth, when abundant, will frequent any locality where it can find flowers.

Several genera of this sub-family have strongly dentated wings. As an instance we may mention the North American *Sphecodina Abbotii*, which is dark brown, with the costal half of the hind wings yellow.

The prettiest genus of this family is *Calliomma*, Walk., which includes several South American species with slightly dentated wings, expanding about two and a half inches. Several of these are fawn colour, with two or three silvery spots in the middle of the fore wings.

SUB-FAMILY II.—*Chœrocampinæ*.

Wings long and narrow, pointed at the tip, and generally brightly coloured; larva with the front segments tapering, and often retractile.

The Elephant Hawk-moths derive both their English and Greek appellations from the peculiar tapering retractile form of the caterpillar. The name of the typical genus *Chœrocampa*, Dup., means Hog-Caterpillar. *Chœrocampa*, even after many species have been separated from it under other names, still remains one of the most extensive genera of *Sphingidæ*. We have two species in Britain, the commonest of which is *C. Elpenor*, Linn., a green and pink insect, with the base of the hind wings black; its larva feeds on willow-herb. Our other species, *C. Celerio*, Linn., the Vine Hawk-moth, has brown fore wings with an oblique silver stripe, and black and rose-coloured hind wings. Although always rare with us, and possibly only a casual visitor in England, it is found with the vine everywhere throughout the warmer parts of Europe, Asia, and Africa.

Several of the tropical American species of *Chœrocampa* are green, with a row of yellow spots on the hind wings. One or two Indian species are similarly marked.

The species of *Deilephila*, Ochs., are shorter and broader, and the fore wings are rather broader and less pointed than in *Chœrocampa*, and the front segments of the larvæ, though con-siderably narrowed, are hardly contractile. They are all rare in

England. The fore wings are generally green, intersected by white, grey, or silvery markings; and black hind wings, with a rosy band in the middle, and a narrow rosy border. We have figured *D. Hippophaes*, Esp., a common South European species.

Philampelus, Harr., is a beautiful genus which derives its name from most of the American species feeding on the wild vine. But they are not all American; *P. Megæra*, Linn., is an African species, measuring three inches and a half across the fore wings, which are bright green; the hind wings are yellow, black at the base and across the middle.

It is curious how species closely resembling each other, but not very closely allied, are sometimes met with in the same localities in pairs. Our own Large and Small Elephant Hawk-moths are very much alike, though belonging to distinct genera; and one of the commonest African *Chœrocampinæ* is *Basiothia Medea*, Fabr., a green moth, with orange-coloured hind wings, about half the size of *P. Megæra*.

The genus *Ambulyx*, Westw., includes species of large size, and with long pointed wings. They are found in the East Indies, Africa, and America, but are not numerous in species. *A. Strigilis*, Linn., a common South American insect, exceeds five inches in expanse; it is brown, with pale orange hind wings, crossed by several narrow brown lines.

SUB-FAMILY III.—*Smerinthinæ*.

Antennæ slightly pectinated in the male; wings generally more or less dentated; proboscis short or wanting.

The insects of this sub-family have a rather heavy flight, and exhibit some resemblance to the *Notodontidæ* among the *Bombyces*. Our British Eyed Hawk-moth (*Smerinthus Ocellatus*, Linn.) may be regarded as typical; it has brown fore wings and pink hind wings, and towards the anal angle of the hind wings is a black space marked with a blue ring. North America is peculiarly rich in species allied to this.

Cœquosa Triangularis, Don., is a large Australian moth which is referred to this sub-family. It is fawn-colour, slightly varied with whitish, and the fore wings are marked with a large brown triangle.

SUB-FAMILY IV.—*Acherontiinæ*.

Head, body, and antennæ very stout; proboscis short and thick; wings hardly pointed.

The type of this sub-family is *Acherantia Atropos*, Linn., the Death's Head Hawk-moth, which is the largest Lepidopterous insect found in England, expanding nearly six inches. The fore wings are dark brown, varied with tawny, and the hind wings are brown, with black bands; the markings on the back of the thorax have been thought to resemble a skull. The larva is yellow, varied with green, and striped with violet; it feeds on the potato. This insect is widely distributed in the Old World, and is often taken at sea, many miles from land; but it probably flies late at night, as it is rarely observed on the wing.

SUB-FAMILY V.—*Sphinginæ*.

Wings not dentated, of moderate width, rarely acutely pointed; proboscis long, often enclosed in a convoluted sheath in the pupa.

The South American genus *Cocytius*, Hübn., includes the largest known *Sphingidæ*, some of which expand as much as eight or nine inches across the wings. In *S. Antæus*, Dru., the fore wings are brown, and the hind wings are yellow at the base and transparent in the middle, with a black border.

Anceryx, Walk., *Isognathus*, Feld., and *Dilophonota*, Burm., include American species about three inches in expanse, which are not closely related to any European *Sphinges*. The fore wings are grey or brown, and the hind wings are red or yellow, with black borders.

The type of the Linnean genus *Sphinx* is our common Privet Hawk-moth (*S. Ligustri*, Linn.), easily recognised by its light brown fore wings, and black and pink hind wings and abdomen. Its green larva is often met with on privet and lilac.

FAMILY II.—*Ægeriidæ*.

Size small; wings long and narrow, always more or less transparent; abdomen generally slender, always longer than the hind wings; larvæ feeding in the stems or roots of plants.

The genus *Sphecia*, Hübn., includes sluggish stout-bodied insects, with black bodies banded with yellow, and transparent wings, which gives them much resemblance to wasps.

Trochilium, Scop., includes a number of smaller species, with slender bodies belted with red or yellow, and tufted tails. They are active day-flying insects, but most of the species are scarce in collections, probably on account of their resemblance to various *Diptera* and *Hymenoptera*.

T. Scoliæforme, Lasp., one of the largest species, has transparent wings, with steel-blue borders; the abdomen is belted with yellow; it is a rare Welsh insect.

The *Ægeriidæ* have more resemblance to the *Pyralidæ* or *Gelechiidæ* than to the *Sphingidæ*, and Mr. Butler has recently proposed to remove them to the neighbourhood of the *Pyralidæ*.

FAMILY III.—*Thyrididæ*.

Size small; body slender; wings moderately broad, with transparent spots; body longer than the hind wings.

A family containing only a few discordant species of very doubtful affinities. *Thyris Vitrina*, Boisd., here figured, is a North American species. It is brown, with a small transparent spot in the middle of the fore wings, and a large one on the hind wings; the tips of the borders of all the wings are spotted with red, and the base and inner margin of the hind wings are of the same colour.

FAMILY IV.—*Uraniidæ*.

Size large; antennæ filiform, scarcely thickened; wings broad, tailed; abdomen moderately stout, never extending beyond the hind wings.

The older writers on Entomology regarded these insects as butterflies, associating them at first with the *Papilionidæ*, and subsequently with the *Hesperiidæ*. They exhibit affinities to several distinct groups of moths; and many recent authors place them next to the *Geometræ*.

The species of *Urania*, Fabr., are banded with black and green, tinged with golden in some species, as in the Cuban *U. Boisduvalii*, Guér., and with coppery red in the Jamaican *U. Sloanus*, Linn. The species of *Urania* are all American. *Thaliura Rhipheus*, Cram., an allied Madagascar species, is half as large again, and has the hind wings tricaudate, and splendidly suffused with coppery red, much deeper than in *U. Sloanus*, and is varied with yellow on the under surface.

Nyctalemon Orontes, Linn., is the type of a handsome genus which is met with in North Australia and the adjacent islands. It is velvety black, with green bands.

Coronis, Latr., is an American genus, easily recognised by the peculiar shape of the wings. *C. Egina*, Boisd., has dark-brown fore wings, with paler transverse waved markings, and a large red blotch on the hind wings.

FAMILY V.—*Castniidæ*.

Size moderate or large; wings generally broad and brightly coloured; antennæ considerably thickened; abdomen as long or longer than the hind wings; body stout.

The genus *Castnia*, Fabr., is confined to tropical America, and includes a number of large day-flying moths which were long classed with the butterflies. *C. Licus*, Drury, is one of the commonest species. It is brown, with a yellow band on the fore wings, and a broad white one on the hind wings, which are also marked with a row of orange sub-marginal spots. The species differ considerably in shape; one, *C. Linus*, Stoll, about four inches in expanse, has long, rather narrow, rounded wings, and is black, with yellowish hyaline spots, and much resembles some of the larger transparent American *Danainæ*.

The Australian genus *Synemon*, Doubl., though placed here, has strongly-clubbed antennæ, and resembles the *Hesperiidæ* in its general appearance. The type *S. Sophia*, White, is dark brown, with yellow spots on the hind wings: it expands nearly two inches.

Cocytia D'Urvillii, Boisd., is a pointed-winged insect, with a stouter and more obtuse abdomen than *Castnia*. The wings are transparent, with black borders, reddish nervures, and a red space at the base of the fore wings. It inhabits New Guinea.

SUB-SECTION II.—*Bombyces*.

Antennæ often pectinated, especially in the males, or filiform, rarely thickened; body generally stout; wings ample; hind wings not differing much from the fore wings in texture, often gaily coloured; larva with sixteen legs; pupa enclosed in a cocoon.

FAMILY I.—*Agaristidæ*.

Antennæ long, slightly thickened; fore wings moderately broad, not much longer than the hind wings; abdomen of moderate thickness, and tufted at the extremity.

A family of handsome moths, which has no representative in Europe, if we except the Cinnabar Moth (*Callimorpha Jacobæa*, Linn.), which Guénée was inclined to refer to it. This is a moth with blackish fore wings, marked with a broad scarlet stripe, and

two red spots; and scarlet hind wings. It is common among
ragwort, and expands a little more than an inch. Most authors,
however, class it with the *Arctiidæ*. *Alypia Octomaculata*, Fabr.,
which is destructive to the vine in North America, is a rather
more robust insect, and slightly smaller. It is black, with two
bright yellow spots on the fore wings, and two white ones on the
hind wings.

Ægocera Venulia, Cram., is the type of a genus which includes
several black and yellow species from the East Indies and Africa.
It is from the former locality, and the fore wings are brown, with
an irregular white bar, partly bordered with reddish, and the hind
wings and abdomen are yellow, the former bordered with brown,
and marked with a brown central spot.

But the largest and handsomest species of this family are those
belonging to the genera *Eusemia*, Dalm., which is found throughout
the tropics of the Old World, and *Agarista*, Leach, which is confined to Australia and the adjacent islands. *E. Pales*, Boisd., is
black, with white markings on the fore wings, and a large blue
spot on the hind wings; it is a native of Madagascar.

FAMILY II.—*Chalcosiidæ*.

Antennæ moderately long, thickly and closely pectinated;
wings moderately broad, and brightly or richly coloured.

The moths of this family are almost confined to the East
Indies. They have longer and narrower wings than the *Agaristidæ*, and many resemble butterflies rather than moths. The
species of *Cyclosia*, Hübn., resemble the genus *Euplœa* both in
shape, size, and colour, being dark brown, with small white and
blue spots. *Heterusia*, Hope, is another beautiful genus, in which
the fore wings are pale bronzy green and white, and the hind
wings are black, banded with white or yellow, and spotted with
blue. It is not surprising that the older entomologists, who were
acquainted with very few of these insects, should have mistaken
them for butterflies.

The genus *Epicopeia*, Westw., is one of the most remarkable.
It includes dark-brown insects, with darker veins, greatly resembling some of the common East Indian species of *Papilio ;* the hind
wings are strongly dentated, angulated outwards, and often furnished with a short broad tail; and the head, tip of abdomen,
and generally some spots near the extremity of the hind wings,

are bright red. The hind wings are generally marked with a large white blotch at or beyond the middle. The species are all East Indian.

FAMILY III.—*Zygænidæ.*

Antennæ more or less thickened beyond the middle ; sometimes pectinated ; wings long and narrow, always extending beyond the abdomen when closed, though the abdomen generally reaches far beyond the hind wings when the wings are expanded ; flight diurnal.

This extensive family includes the small brightly-coloured day flying moths known as Burnets and Green Foresters. It may be divided into several sub-families, but we will confine ourselves here to noticing a few of the more representative genera.

The Green Foresters belong to the genus *Procris*, Fabr., and are most abundant in South Europe. In nearly all the species the fore wings are green and the hind wings brown, and they are not easily distinguished from one another. They are generally harmless, but *P. Ampelophaga*, Bayle, is destructive to the vine in South Europe.

The Burnet Moths (*Zygæna*, Fabr.) have greenish-brown fore wings variously spotted or streaked with red, and red hind wings. They are very numerous in South Europe, but only six species are known to occur in Britain. It has, however, lately been stated that a streaked species, distinct from the Scotch and Irish, *Z. Minos*, W. V., has been captured in Cornwall, but I have not seen the insect, and do not know to what species it belongs. *Z. Angelicæ*, Ochs., is a large variety of our common Six-spot Burnet (*Z. Filipendulæ*, Linn.), which is met with south of the Alps.

Syntomis, Hübn., is an extensive genus common in Asia and Africa, and with one or two representatives in Europe ; the species may be known by their belted bodies and dark wings with transparent spots. *S. Latreillei*, Boisd., a common East Indian species, is black, with a large yellow spot in the middle of the thorax, and a smaller one at the base of each wing ; the wings are marked with large transparent spots, and the abdomen is belted with white.

Many beautiful species of this family are met with in foreign countries, among which we may mention those of the genus *Phalanna*, Walk., which abound in India and Africa. The wings are black, spotted with yellow, and the abdomen is variously belted with blue, green, red, or yellow, according to the species. *P. Formosa*, Boisd., is not uncommon in Madagascar.

FAMILY IV.—*Arctiidæ*.

Antennæ moderately long, often pectinated, at least in the male ; body generally stout ; wings and abdomen brightly coloured ; larvæ hairy.

The Tiger Moths are among the most brightly-coloured of the European *Lepidoptera*, and are among those which most frequently attract attention ; for several species are easily disturbed by day, and others frequent gardens and weedy places. Many species have dark fore wings, spotted or reticulated with red and yellow, and the hind wings are red or yellow, with black spots. But they are not all brilliantly coloured ; some are white or yellowish, often spotted with black. The three commonest species are the White and Buff Ermines (*Spilosoma Menthastri* and *Lubricipeda*, Linn.), and the Tiger Moth (*Arctia Caja*, Linn.). These insects are common in every garden, where their larvæ feed on a variety of plants ; the long-haired reddish caterpillar of the Tiger Moth is often seen among lettuces, etc., or running on paths ; it is frequently called the Woolly Bear. *Hypercompa Hera*, Linn., a rare species in the south of England, though abundant on the Continent, is a day-flying species, and has a very gay appearance on the wing. In the South European genus *Trichosoma*, Ramb., the wings of the female are rudimentary ; *T. parasitum*, Esp., is a grey species with darker spots.

We may mention a few foreign genera. *Pericopis*, Hübn., and its allies are rather long-winged species, some of which resemble *Heliconiidæ*; they are all natives of America. *Thalaina Selenæa*, Doubl., is of a shining white, with an oblique red stripe bordered with black across the fore wings, and the borders partly red ; towards the hind margin of the hind wings is a blackish spot. It is, however, uncertain whether this species does not rather belong to the *Geometræ*.

Ecpantheria Scribonia, Stoll, is the largest and handsomest species of an extensive American genus. It is white, with many black rings on the thorax and fore wings ; the abdomen is blue, with three rows of yellow spots, and there are some submarginal white spots on the hind wings. This species measures about three inches in expanse.

Aloa Lactinea, Cram., is one of the commonest East India species. It is white, with the head, collar, costa of the fore wings, and femora scarlet ; the abdomen is yellow, spotted with black, and the hind wings have also two or three black spots.

FAMILY V.—*Lithosiidæ.*

Antennæ filiform; body slender, rather short; wings, especially the fore wings, generally long, slender, and overlapping; colours generally uniform and obscure.

These moths are called "Footmen" by collectors. They require searching for, or they are very liable to be overlooked, on account of their dull colours and retired habits. They are sometimes beaten from thickets, when they let themselves drop down, simulating death. The species of *Lithosia*, Fabr., are all very much alike; *L. Depressa*, Esp., has brown fore wings, with the costa and hind wings grey.

The South American genus *Josioides*, Feld., includes black species of moderate size, with yellow spots and stripes. It is rather an extensive group, and has been confounded with *Chrysauge*, Hübn., a somewhat similarly coloured genus of *Pyralidæ.*

Bizone, Walk., is a very pretty East Indian genus. The fore wings are white, with red fringes, and slightly zigzag red stripes; near the middle is a conspicuous black dot; the hind wings are often tinted with rosy.

Lycomorpha Pholus, Dru., is a common North American species; it expands about an inch and a quarter across the wings, which are orange yellow on the basal half and black at the tips.

Atolmis Rubricollis, Hübn., is a European moth of almost a uniform black, except the tip of the abdomen, which is yellow.

The genus *Deiopeia*, Steph., is widely distributed; but only one species is found in Europe, which is very rare in England. This is *D. Pulchella*, Linn., which is white, with black borders to the hind wings, and sometimes an irregular black mark in the middle. The fore wings are marked with rows of black and red spots; it expands about an inch and a half. In some species, as in the North American *D. Bella*, Linn., the hind wings are bright red.

Several genera of *Lithosiidæ* are yellow, with black streaks or spots, and we have one example in England. This is *Setina Irrorella*, Linn., a local species, but often common where it occurs; it is generally met with near the coast.

FAMILY VI.—*Hypsidæ.*

These insects are confined to the East Indies and Africa; they resemble large *Lithosiidæ* (averaging about two inches in expanse), but the wings are broader and more robust, and the antennæ are sometimes pectinated in the males. One of the commonest Indian species is *Hypsa Caricæ*, Linn. The body, hind wings, and base of the fore wings are yellow, spotted with black, and the fore wings are otherwise grey, with a longitudinal white dash, varying in size.

FAMILY VII.—*Nyctemeridæ.*

Another small group, allied to the *Lithosiidæ*, but with broader wings, and usually with pectinated antennæ. Most of the species are Indian or African. In the genus *Nyctemera*, Hübn., the fore wings are generally dark brown, with white streaks radiating from the base, and the hind wings are white, with brown borders. *N. Annulata*, Boisd., however, a common Australian species, is black, with white spots. A very similar species (*N. Doubledayi*, Walk.) occurs in New Zealand.

Pterothysanus Laticilia, Walk., is a North Indian insect, measuring two and a half inches across the wings. This is more than the usual size of the species of *Hypsa*, and the wings are broader. The fore wings are dark brown, marked with many white spots of different sizes, and the hind wings are white, with three macular brown bands. The antennæ are remarkably short, and not pectinated, and the hind wings are fringed with very long hairs. This insect is of rather doubtful position. It has some resemblance to the *Euschemidæ*, which are now proved to be *Geometræ*, but its position will probably be decided by the discovery of the larva.

FAMILY VIII.—*Liparidæ.*

Antennæ short, generally pectinated in the males; males often much smaller than the females, with comparatively slender bodies; females sometimes apterous, at other times winged, often with a large tuft of down at the tip of the abdomen; wings broad, dull-coloured; larvæ often with projecting tufts of hair.

Several species of this family fly by day. The most familiar of these is the male of the Vapourer Moth (*Orgyia Antiqua*, Linn.), a brownish tawny moth about an inch in expanse, with a large white spot near the anal angle of the fore wings. It is common in England, and is frequently to be seen even in London, wherever trees grow; the wings of the female are rudimentary. The males of the Gipsy Moth (*Liparis Dispar*, Linn.) are equally abundant on the Continent, where their caterpillars are sometimes very destructive. They are brown, and measure about an inch and a half across the wings;

but the females, which are an inch larger, are white, with blackish markings on the fore wings, and are generally to be found resting on hedges and on the trunks of trees.

Dasychira Pudibunda, Linn., is a common species allied to this, which measures about two inches across the wings. It is grey, with a darker transverse band.

The species of *Euproctis*, Hübn., *Stilpnotia*, Steph., and *Leucoma*, Steph., are generally of a silky white; the commonest are the Brown and Gold-Tail Moths (*E. Auriflua*, Fabr., and *Chrysorrhœa*, Linn.), which may be found on hedges in the evening, and the White Satin Moth (*S. Salicis*, Linn.), which is more often met with resting on the trunks of trees. The white African *Liparidæ*, belonging to the genus *Cypra*, Boisd., are remarkably delicate insects.

Darala, Walk., includes a number of moderate-sized Australian species. They are brown, generally with one or more transverse dark lines (brown or red) on the fore wings, and two black spots or eyes on the fore wings in a line from the base.

Psilura Monacha, Linn., has white fore wings, with blackish zig-zag markings; the hind wings are dull brown, and the tip of the abdomen is reddish; the female is provided with a short ovipositor. The larva feeds on trees, and is sometimes injurious on the Continent, but is not sufficiently abundant in England to be mischievous.

It is perhaps doubtful whether one or two large exotic genera which are placed in this family really belong to it. *Dreata Edulis*, Boisd., is a brown moth, with four double blackish bands on the fore wings. It expands nearly four inches, and is common in South Africa, where its pupa is eaten by the Hottentots. Several allied species are found in India.

Jana, Herr.-Schäff., is another genus peculiar to Africa and the East Indies. The species measure upwards of four inches across the wings, which are brown or fawn colour, with slender undulating bands, which are usually broader on the hind wings.

Chelepteryx Collesi, Gray, is a very large Australian moth, expanding from five to seven inches across the wings, which are rather long and narrow. The male has reddish-brown fore wings, with three transverse black lines, and two transparent spots near the tip; the hind wings are brown, with a reddish line in the middle, and an indented yellowish one towards the hind margin; the female is grey, with whitish lines.

FAMILY IX.—*Psychidæ.*

Size small; male with broad wings, and strongly pectinated antennæ; female always apterous, and with simple antennæ; larva living in a case.

The males are black, brown, or white moths, rarely exceeding an inch in expanse, which are found in meadows flying weakly among the grass like *Zygænidæ.* The female is always apterous, and in some genera is almost destitute of limbs, never quitting the case. The larvæ construct cases for themselves from scraps of vegetable matter, like the Caddis-worms, in which they change to pupæ.

FAMILY X.—*Notodontidæ.*

Size moderate; antennæ generally pectinated in the males; wings moderately broad, larvæ frequently humped, or with the claspers (or last pair of pro-legs) converted into long caudal appendages.

The genus *Cerura,* Schrank, includes several white species with darker markings. The largest British species, which sometimes expands three inches, is known to collectors as the Puss Moth, and the smaller species are called "Kittens." Their green larvæ are marked on the back with reddish brown and white, and the tail is furnished with two tubular appendages, from which the insect can protrude red filaments. These larvæ feed on willow, poplar, etc.

Several genera of this family are of rich dark colours, such as the Pebbles (*Notodonta,* Ochs.) and Chocolate Tips (*Clostera,* Schrank). Others, like the Swallow Prominents (*Pheosia,* Hübn.), are white, with brown markings. One of the prettiest species of this family is *Spatalia Bicolora,* W. V., a great rarity in England; it is snow-white, with two orange spots in the middle of the fore wings, and expands about an inch and a quarter. *Staurepus Fagi,* Linn., also a somewhat uncommon species in England, is a brown moth, two inches and a half in expanse; but the larva, from which it derives its name, is reddish brown, with very long sprawling legs, and has sometimes been compared to a lobster, and sometimes to a spider.

Edema Albifrons, Abbot and Smith, is a grey North American moth, with a broad white stripe along the costa.

Cnethecampa Processionea, Linn., is a greyish-brown moth about an inch and a quarter in expanse. It is not British, and is

not always common on the Continent; but it is famous for the
large nests which its larvæ make upon the oak, from which they
emerge to feed in a regular procession. The hairs of the larvæ
and the fine dust in the nests are terribly irritating to the skin,
so much so that it is hardly safe to approach the nests.

FAMILY XI.—*Drepanulidæ.*

Size small; body slender; antennæ pectinated in the males;
wings broad; fore wings pointed and sometimes hooked at the
tip; larvæ with fourteen legs.

These small moths somewhat resemble *Geometridæ. Platypteryx
Falcatoria*, Linn., which may be regarded as the type, is yellowish,
with darker lines; it is not an uncommon species.

FAMILY XII.—*Saturniidæ.*

Size large; body stout, not extending beyond the hind wings;
wings broad, nearly always with a transparent spot in the middle,
or with a dark eye or lunule, surrounded with different-coloured
borders; larva spiny, or fasciculate; pupa enclosed in a cocoon.

The *Saturniidæ* are by far the finest group of *Bombyces*, and
many are among the largest moths known. Nearly all the
silkworms of any commercial value (except the mulberry silkworm) belong to this family. The larvæ of many species are gregarious, and live on trees. Several larvæ secrete a white waxy
powder, which may be analogous to the waxy secretion produced
by many *Homoptera.*

Attacus Atlas, Linn., the great Atlas Moth of the East Indies,
varies considerably in size and shape; the largest specimen in the
British Museum measures eleven inches and three quarters across
the wings. It is of a yellowish tawny, with brown and white
zigzag lines, very large transparent spots, and a yellowish blotch
and black spot near the tip of the fore wings. Many similar but
smaller species are found in South America, and one or two in
India. Another section of the genus, which is confined to the
East Indies, is represented by *Attacus Cynthia*, Drury, and its
allies, some of which are almost naturalised in Europe. They are
greenish or olive-yellow, with white bands bordered with brown and
pink, and a pale lunule on each wing, instead of a transparent spot.

The handsomest of the North American species is *Samia
Cecropia*, Linn. It measures over six inches across the wings,
which are brown, with a very thick white lunule in the middle of

M

each; the body and part of the base of the fore wings are red, and the usual transverse stripes are white, bordered with red. It is not an uncommon insect, and gloves and stockings were made of its silk a century ago; but these experiments have not been continued in recent years.

The African genus *Bunæa*, Hübn., has rather long fore wings, which are marked with a square transparent spot. This leads us on to the genus *Antheræa*, Hübn., a genus with moderately long and often rather falcate fore wings; it is found in Africa, the East Indies, and Australia. Several of the Indian species are used to produce silk, especially *A. Mylitta*, Drury, which has a large round transparent spot in the middle of each wing. The male is reddish fawn-colour, and the female yellow; each wing is crossed by a white pink-bordered stripe. It measures five or six inches in expanse of wing.

The genus *Tropæa*, Hübn., includes green or yellowish tawny species, which are met with in Spain, the East Indies, Africa, and North America. All these species have shorter or longer tails; but some of the West African and South American species of the genus *Eudæmonia*, Hübn., have longer tails than any other Lepidopterous insects, sometimes fully twice as long as the breadth of the fore wings.

The only British species of this family is *Saturnia Pavonia-Minor*, Linn., the Emperor Moth. The male has brown fore wings, and yellowish hind wings; and the female is grey; the borders are brown and white, and the wings are traversed with several white lines; in the middle of each wing is a large black eye. Its green, pink-spotted larva is common on heath. The moth measures two and a quarter inches across the wings; but there is a South European species, *S. Pavonia-Major*, Linn., very similar to this, but much darker, which is nearly twice as large; its larva feeds on fruit-trees, etc.

Hyperchiria, Hübn., is a very extensive genus, which is confined to America. The species are generally brown or yellow, and are of moderate size, seldom exceeding two or three inches in expanse. Most of them have a large oval eye on the hind wings, which is sometimes so large as to fill up a considerable portion of the wing. This eye is generally black, and is often marked with blue or white; it sometimes contains two or three smaller blue spots.

Hemileuca Maia, Drury, is a North American species, about the size of our Emperor Moth. It is black, with a broad white band on each wing, marked with a small black eye, which stands near the inside of the band on the fore wings, and near the middle on the hind wings; the tip of the abdomen is reddish.

Ceratocampa, Harr., is a genus hardly belonging to this family. The species are five or six inches in expanse, and have moderately long and pointed wings. *C. Imperialis*, Drury, is yellow, speckled with black; the body is marked with red, and the wings are clouded and barred with brown and reddish; there is a small eye in the middle of all the wings, that on the upper side of the fore wings being almost obliterated. All the species of this genus are American, and *C. Imperialis* is not uncommon in the Southern United States.

Brahmœa, Walk., is another genus of somewhat doubtful position, which has been referred to the *Saturniidœ*, but which probably belongs to the *Lasiocampidœ*. The species all inhabit different parts of Asia, except the north-west; and the west coast of Africa. They are very handsome dark-brown insects, about five or six inches in expanse, with very numerous undulating black lines, and a large round mark on the inner margin of the fore wings, which has a raised appearance by an optical effect similar to that observed in the spots of the Argus Pheasant.

FAMILY XIII.—*Bombycidœ.*

Size moderate; antennæ pectinated; wings broad; fore wings slightly falcate; larva naked, somewhat resembling that of a *Sphinx.*

Bombyx Mori, Linn., the common Mulberry Silkworm, is the type of this small family. The moth is about an inch and a half in expanse, and is of a yellowish white, with two transverse brown lines. It is very sluggish, and the domesticated insect is incapable of flight. The larva is of a dirty white, but in the original wild stock it was probably brown. The cocoon is about the size of a pigeon's egg, and is of a white or yellow colour.

The silkworm was originally a native of China, but has been reared in the south of Europe for about 1300 years.

The Kentish Glory (*Endromis Versicolor*, Linn.) has brown fore wings, with white lines and markings; and the hind wings are yellowish brown in the male, and white in the female, with brown markings. It expands about two inches and a half, and is a local insect, nowhere very common, though widely distributed; the male flies rapidly in search of the female, by day, like several of the

Saturniidæ and *Lasiocampidæ.* Its naked green white-striped larva considerably resembles that of a *Sphinx ;* it feeds on birch. This insect appears to be nearly allied to *Bombyx Mori ;* and even if it does not belong to the same family, it must be placed in juxtaposition with it. Schrank actually placed the two species in the same genus; and when recently discussing the position of *Endromis* with my friend and colleague Mr. A. G. Butler, we came to the conclusion that the genus should not be widely separated from *Bombyx.*

<h3 style="text-align:center">FAMILY XIV.—Lasiocampidæ.</h3>

Insects of moderate size; antennæ generally pectinated in the male; wings moderately broad, sometimes dentated; larva hairy.

These moths are known as Eggars, on account of the hard firm egg-shaped cocoon. They are usually of a reddish-brown colour in the male, and yellow in the female, and there is sometimes a great disparity in the size of the sexes, the female, as usual in insects, being much the largest.

The genus *Gastropacha,* Ochs., may be known by its dentated wings. In repose, the costa of the hind wings projects far beyond the closed fore wings, and the whole insect has a general resemblance to a withered leaf, a peculiarity commemorated in the name given to several of these Lappet Moths, as they are termed —*G. Quercifolia, Ilicifolia, Betulifolia,* etc.

The Australian genus *Opsirhina,* Walk., includes reddish species which are remarkable for the great length of the palpi. The wings are moderately long, and a little pointed, but not dentated.

Lasiocampa Quercus, Linn., the Oak Eggar, may be considered the type of this family. It expands nearly three inches, and the males, which are rich brown, with a yellowish band in the middle of the wings, fly very wildly in the day-time in search of the yellow females; the shaggy blackish-brown larva feeds on oak and heath, and is not very difficult to rear.

The Lackey Moths (*Clisiocampa Neustria,* and *Castrensis,* Linn.) are smaller insects, not expanding more than an inch and a half. They are reddish brown, or ochreous yellow, with two brown lines on each fore wing.

<h3 style="text-align:center">FAMILY XV.—Zeuzeridæ.</h3>

Antennæ moderately long; palpi very short, or absent; female with a short ovipositor; larvæ lignivorous.

A small family, including rather discordant genera. The European species of *Xyleutes*, Hübn., are brown, reticulated with black; the Goat Moth, *X. Cossus*, Linn., is a very heavy-looking moth, three or four inches in expanse. Its great dark-red naked larva feeds in the wood of old willows, etc., and takes three years to arrive at maturity.

Some of the South European species allied to *Cossus* are of very small size, scarcely exceeding an inch in expanse; these belong to the genera *Endagria*, Boisd., and *Stygia*, Latr.

Phragmatœcia Arundinis, Hübn., is a light-brown insect, which frequents marshy localities. The wings and abdomen are longer and narrower than in the other genera of this family.

Zeuzera Æsculi, Linn., is a white, rather woolly-looking insect, adorned with numerous steel-blue spots; it is called the Wood-Leopard Moth. The larva feeds in the smaller branches of several forest and fruit trees. Many of the foreign species are of large size and splendid colours, the wings being frequently marked with blue or green. The largest species is *Z. Eucalypti*, Herr.-Schäff., a brown Australian species, with a broad white longitudinal stripe on the fore wings; the female sometimes measures seven or eight inches in expanse.

FAMILY XVI.—*Hepialidæ.*

Antennæ short; wings rather long and narrow, rounded at the tips; abdomen generally extending far beyond the hind wings.

The typical genus of this family is *Hepialus*, Fabr. The largest British species is *H. Humuli*, Linn., the Ghost Moth, which flies with a peculiar hovering flight. The male is white above and brown below; and the female has yellow fore wings, with brick-red markings, and the hind wings are of a pinky red. The smaller species are brown or red, with white markings on the fore wings, and are known as Swifts.

Some of the foreign species, like those of *Zeuzera*, are large and handsome. The genus *Charagia*, Walk., includes several beautiful species from Australia and New Zealand, with green markings.

Another large and beautiful species is *Leto Venus*, Stoll., a native of South Africa. It is fawn-coloured, elegantly spotted with silver.

Imago generally of moderate size; body stout, hairy, often extending beyond the hind wings, and sometimes tufted; proboscis moderately long; antennæ setaceous, sometimes pectinated in the male; wings moderately broad, hind wings more slender than the fore wings, often uniform brown, grey, or white, with a brown submarginal border, and a brown central dot; frequently iridescent; occasionally coloured like the fore wings, or adorned with bright colours; larva generally with sixteen legs, slightly pubescent; pupa often naked. This extensive group comprises a great number of families, which it is perhaps unnecessary to characterise here in detail. We shall therefore confine ourselves to noticing one or two representative species in some of the principal families. The genera of the *Noctuæ* are frequently very large, and the species included in them are often very similar.

Thyatira Batis, Linn., the Peach Blossom Moth, is greenish brown, with several brown and rosy spots, bordered with black and white, on the front wings; the hind wings are brown and white (Fam. *Cymatophoridæ*).

Acronycta Psi, Linn., the Dagger Moth, has grey fore wings, with several blackish marks, the most conspicuous being one near the anal angle of the hind wings, resembling a dagger, or the Greek letter *ψ* (Fam. *Acronyctidæ*).

The Wainscots (Fam. *Leucanidæ*) have grey or reddish fore wings, sometimes marked with longitudinal white lines, or with a few small black dots; the hind wings are paler. They are most abundant in marshy places, and many of their larvæ feed in the stems of the reed, and other water plants; the larva of a species doubtfully belonging to this family (*Nonagria* (?) *Sacchari*, Sepp) feeds on the pith of the sugar-cane.

Polytela Gloriosæ, Fabr., is a common East Indian species. The thorax is bluish in front, and the head and hinder part of the thorax are spotted with yellow; the tip of the abdomen is yellow; the fore wings are dark grey, with denticulated black lines, and red and yellow stripes and markings, and the hind wings are grey, with yellow fringes (Fam. *Glottulidæ*).

Xylophasia Polyodon, Linn., the Dark Arches, is a brown moth, about two inches in expanse, which is common everywhere in gardens. The fore wings are varied with black, and have a pale W-shaped submarginal line, a mark which reappears in a great many genera of *Noctuæ;* the abdomen is rather long, and tufted at the extremity (Fam. *Apamidæ*).

The genus *Prodenia,* Guén., is remarkable for the beautiful pearly-white hind wings of most of the species; the fore wings are generally brown or fawn-coloured. One species is found in Southern Europe; the others are Indian or American (Fam. *Apamidæ*).

The Cabbage Moth (*Mamestra Brassicæ,* Linn.) is brown, with transverse black markings on the fore wings, the centre of which is marked with white. *M. Persicariæ,* Linn., is a similar, but much darker species, and the white mark on the fore wings comes out much more conspicuously (Fam. *Apamidæ*).

The genus *Agrotis,* Ochs., one of the most typical of the *Noctuæ,* includes a great number of moderate-sized species with brown fore wings, and grey or white hind wings. But the most conspicuous species of the *Agrotidæ* are the Yellow Under-wings, belonging to the genus *Triphæna,* Hübn., which have brown or reddish fore wings, and bright yellow hind wings, with a black border, and sometimes a black spot in the middle. Several are very common, and are frequently disturbed from strawberry-beds and weedy places in the day-time, when they escape with a rapid but rather heavy flight, resembling that of some grasshoppers. Another handsome species is *Ochropleura Plecta,* Hübn., which has reddish fore wings, with a broad white bar on the costa, and whitish hind wings.

The *Orthosiidæ* include a number of spring and autumn moths, which are taken at the blossoms of the sallow and ivy. They are either of a light uniform brown, or reddish brown, or yellow, in the latter case frequently with orange markings. Some of the American species have green fore wings.

Cosmia Diffinis, Linn., is a conspicuous reddish-brown moth, about an inch and a quarter in expanse, with two white spots on the costa of each fore wing. An allied species, *C. Trapezina,* Linn., is brown or reddish, with two pale lines on the fore wings.

The larvæ of this genus are green, and feed on trees, but will often attack and devour other caterpillars (Fam. *Cosmidæ*).

Agriopis Aprilina, Linn., has pale-green fore wings, with transverse zigzag black white-bordered marks. The hind wings are brown, with two rather obscure white bands (Fam. *Hadenidæ*).

The genus *Cucullia,* Ochs., includes a variety of brown or grey moths, with rather narrow and pointed fore wings, and a long pointed abdomen; the thorax is crested. They are called "Sharks" by collectors, and fly over flowers in the evening in the same manner as the *Sphingidæ*, which they considerably resemble in shape. The larvæ are adorned with various colours, and feed gregariously on the leaves of mullein and other plants. Some of the foreign species are beautifully marked with green and silver (Fam. *Cucullidæ*).

Heliothis Dipsacea, Linn., is greyish brown, with darker markings on the fore wings; the hind wings are black and white. It flies in clover-fields by day in the south of England (Fam. *Heliothidæ*).

Anarta Myrtilli, Linn., has red fore wings with whitish lines; the hind wings are yellow, with a broad black border; it expands about an inch, and flies by day on heaths. The other species of the genus have either yellow or white black-bordered hind wings; and many of them are Alpine or Polar insects (Fam. *Heliothidæ*).

Acontia Albicellis, Fabr., is a brown and white moth, which flies by day, like several of the species of *Acontidæ* and the allied families, which are of smaller size and more variegated colours than most of the other *Noctuæ*. It is a very rare species in the south of England, though commoner on the Continent.

The species of *Brephos*, Ochs., have brown fore wings, with some slight pale markings; the hind wings are orange and black. They are met with in woods by day in early spring (Fam. *Brephidæ*).

Palindia, Guén., is a genus of rather small moths, exclusively confined to tropical America. Many are brown and white, in varying proportions, and the hind wings are frequently yellowish, as in *B. Dominicata*, Guén. The hind wings of this species are marked with a large black spot on the front angle, and with a smaller one at the lower angle; between the two, the wing is edged with a silvery line. Other species are green, varied with white along the costa and inner margin of the hind wings, while the species of the allied genus *Dyomyx*, Guén., are brown, with a black eye in a yellow ring near the hinder angle of the fore wings. They generally frequent the depths of the forest, and have a short rapid flight by day, and settle on leaves with their wings a little sloping, when their shape resembles an equilateral triangle (Fam. *Palindidæ*).

The genus *Plusia*, Ochs., includes a great number of rather pretty species, of moderate size. The fore wings are generally brown, some-

times a little suffused or marked with purplish or reddish, and are
nearly always marked with a silvery or yellowish figure resembling
a letter ; or else they are brown, more or less extensively blotched
with brassy green, which sometimes fills up a great part of the
wing. The hind wings are pale brown, with a darker submarginal
band, or, in a few foreign species, yellow (Fam. *Plusidæ*).

In the *Calpidæ* the palpi are very large. But their chief peculiarity is the shape of the inner margin of the fore wings, which is
excavated and dentated. The genus *Gonodanta*, Hübn., is entirely
American ; the species are of moderate size, and the hind wings
are nearly always yellow, with black borders or lines. *Calpe
Ophideroides*, Guén., is a much larger species. The fore wings are
brown, with an oblique white black-bordered stripe running from
the tip to the cavity on the inner margin ; the hind wings are
yellow. It is not uncommon in India.

The *Hyblæidæ* are a small family of pretty species, almost confined to the East Indies. The only exception is *Hyblæa Puera*,
Cram., which is found in Africa, Central America, and the West
Indies, as well as in India and China. It has brown fore wings,
and black hind wings, with orange-red bands. In *H. Constellata*,
Guén., the fore wings are varied with paler, and the hind wings
are spotted with yellow.

The *Gonopteridæ* are moths of moderate size, with the hind
margin of the hind wings angulated outwards, and sometimes
dentated. The only European species is the Herald Moth (*Gono-
ptera Libatrix*, Linn.), which may be known by its strongly dentated
brown fore wings, with brick-red blotches, and some pale transverse markings. It is a common species, and is found in the
northern parts of North America as well as in Europe. It is often
found in houses. The species of *Cosmophila*, Boisd., are not unlike
Orthosiidæ, except for the projecting angle on the fore wings. One
of the commonest is *C. Stigmatizans*, Fabr., which is found in
India, Australia, and West Africa. It is yellowish grey, the fore
wings with four angulated transverse lines, the third and fourth
connected, and the hind wings are pale yellow.

One of the commonest of the larger British *Noctuæ* is *Mormo
Maura*, Linn., the Old Lady, a dark-brown insect with grey markings, which frequently flies in at the windows of country houses
in the evening (Fam. *Amphipyridæ*).

Stilbia Anomala, Haw., is an insect with rather narrow brown
fore wings, and broad whitish hind wings ; the body is unusually

slender for a *Noctua*. It is not a very common species (Fam. *Stilbidæ*).

Polydesma, Boisd., includes several African and Indian species, of moderate size. They are brown or reddish, with numerous denticulated black transverse lines (Fam. *Polydesmidæ*).

The *Homopteridæ* are a group of very dull-coloured species, chiefly American; the hind wings are generally marked with pale lines. The species are very similar, and are not easily distinguished from each other.

Cocytodes, Guén., is a handsome Indian genus of rather large moths. They are dark brown, with blue markings on the hind wings. The type of the family *Catephidæ*, to which this genus belongs, is *Catephia Alchymista*, Fabr., which has black fore wings with paler borders; the hind wings are white, with a broad white-spotted black border. It is a common species in Southern and Central Europe, and has once been found in England.

The same contrast of black and white is common in the American genus *Bolina*, Guén. But the species of *Syneda*, Guén., which are most numerous in the Southern and Western United States, are much prettier insects, frequently with yellow hind wings (Fam. *Bolinidæ*).

The great genus *Catocala*, Ochs., is far more abundant in Europe and North America than in other parts of the world. The fore wings are brown or grey, with zigzag lines, and are assimilated in colour to the bark of trees, on which the insects usually rest. But the hind wings are banded with pale blue, red, or yellow; or else, in some of the North American species, are quite black. The larvæ of this and several allied families are called "Half-loopers," the pro-legs being imperfectly developed, which causes them to arch their backs in walking, though not to the same extent as in the *Geometræ* (Fam. *Catocalidæ*).

The *Ophideridæ* are a small family of large and handsome species, entirely confined to the Tropics. In *Ophideres*, Boisd., the fore wings are brown, generally with an oblique line running from the tip, and more or less varied with white, and sometimes with green. The hind wings are always yellow, with a black border on the upper half, and a thick curved black mark in the middle. The proboscis is very strong, and is used for perforating and sucking oranges, and doubtless other fruits also. *Miniodes Discolor*, Guén., is a beautiful West African moth, with rose-coloured hind wings. The fore wings are brown, varied with

yellow in the male, aud greyish brown in the female. *Phyllodes,*
Boisd., includes East Indian species, often measuring six inches
across the rather pointed fore wings. The hind wings aro frequently marked with a very large white and rosy spot near the
anal angle. *Potamophora Manlia,* Cram., is a smaller East Indian
species, with a transverse blue bar on the hind wings; but the
dullest-coloured genus of the whole family is *Lygniodes,* Guén.
(also East Indian), the species of which are blackish brown, with
the hind wings partly bordered with white.

The *Erebidæ* are insects of large size, with long ascending
palpi. They have some resemblance to *Geometræ,* their bodies
being only moderately stout, and the hind wings being frequently
marked almost like the fore wings. They are insects of rather
dull colours, and most of the species are American. *Thysania
Agrippina,* Cram., is one of the largest moths known, measuring
nearly a foot across the wings, which are, however, not broad
in proportion, but rather long, slightly pointed, and dentated.
It is whitish, with many dentated transverse blackish lines, and
is no rarity in Brazil; the genus *Letis,* Hübn., contains much
smaller species. *Erebus Odora,* Linn., the type of the family, is
a dark-brown moth about seven or eight inches in expanse; the
wings aro marked with black and pale indented lines; the fore
wings have a rather irregular black eye in a yellow ring, and
there is a bluish mark, like a thick double crescent, near the anal
angle of the hind wings; the female has a pinkish band near the
borders of the wings.

The allied family *Ommatophoridæ* is more varied in colour, and
is nearly always marked with a large eye on the fore wings. The
species inhabit the tropics of the Old World, and do not attain
the gigantic size of the larger *Erebidæ.* The largest species is
Patula Macrops, Linn., a common African and Indian moth, about
six inches in expanse. It is dark brown, with blackish markings
and dentated wings, and there is a very large eye on the fore
wings, marked with reddish, black, white, and blue. The species
of *Nyctipao,* Hübn., are more elegant insects, being extensively
marked with white. Several of the species are more or less
suffused with purple, and the ocellus is sometimes marked with
blue. All the species are East Indian. In the allied African
genus *Cyligramma,* Boisd., the ocellus on the fore wings is much
smaller.

Culliodes Orbigera, Guén., is a pretty brown and white

Australian species. In the allied East Indian genus *Spiramia*, Guén., the ocellus on the fore wings assumes a peculiarly irregular form (Fam. *Hypopyridæ*).

Lagoptera, Guén., is an East Indian genus with rather pointed fore wings, with an oblique line running from the tip. The hind wings are very varied in colouring, being red, with a short blackish dash in one species; yellow, with two black bands, in another; and black or brown, with a blue or white band, in others. They are the largest of the *Ophiusidæ*, measuring three or four inches across the wings. The species of *Ophiodes*, Guén., are smaller insects, with green or brown fore wings; the hind wings are generally yellow, with a black dash towards the borders. They inhabit the tropics of the Old World; but one or two species are found in Europe. A great number of species of smaller size, belonging to this family, inhabit the Tropics; these chiefly belong to the genera *Ophisma*, Guén., *Achæa*, Hübn., and *Ophiusa*, Ochs.

The *Amphigonidæ*, with two allied families, have been called *Pseudodeltoidæ*, from their resemblance to the *Deltoidæ*, a family formerly included with the *Pyrales*. They have rather slender bodies, and triangular fore wings; and the legs are frequently adorned with a fan-like tuft of hair, a character often met with in the *Catocalidæ*, and in several of the other less typical families of *Noctuæ*. The *Pseudodeltoidæ* are entirely exotic. The borders of the wings are often of very irregular shapes in the *Amphigonidæ*, but less so in *Amphigonia*, Guén., than in some allied genera. *A. Hepatizans*, Guén., is an Indian species, with white and violet markings. *Hypernaria Miniopila*, Guén., may be taken as our representative of the extensive family *Thermesiidæ*, which is almost entirely American. It is violet grey, with an oblique brown line dusted with greenish yellow, and there is a pale-red tuft of hair at the base of the intermediate tibiæ. It is a native of Cayenne.

The *Deltoidæ* derive their name from the triangular appearance of many of the species when at rest. Their bodies are slender, their wings ample, and their palpi are often very long. They were formerly included with the *Pyrales*, but are now generally placed at the end of the *Noctuæ*. They are divided into three sub-families.

The species of *Macrodes*, Guén., are South American insects, with very long antennæ, ascending palpi, and broad wings, expanding about two inches. The type is *M. Cynara*, Cram., which is of a bluish grey, with several denticulated black and white lines; it is a native of the north of South America. This insect may be taken as a representative of the *Platydinœ*.

In the *Hypeninœ*, the wings are narrower, the antennæ shorter, and the palpi porrected. The type of this family is the "Snout," a brown moth about an inch and a half in expanse, which is common among nettles. The genus *Hypena* is widely distributed, and the species are very numerous.

The East Indian genus *Dichromia*, Guén., deserves notice. The fore wings are brown or grey, and are often marked with a large triangular black spot, and the hind wings are yellow, with black borders.

The *Herminina* are an extensive group of rather small species, which are often remarkable for the peculiar tufts on their antennæ and front tibiæ; in some genera the palpi are very long, and of extraordinary shapes. The typical genus of this sub-family is *Herminia*, Latr., of which several species are common in England.

Sub-Section IV.—*Geometræ*.

Body generally slender; antennæ often pectinated in the males; wings broad, similarly coloured; larvæ with only ten legs, the first two pairs of pro-legs being undeveloped; species of moderate size.

This extensive group may always be distinguished at once by the structure of the larva, to which, however, we find some approach in several families of *Noctuæ*, such as the *Catocalidæ*. Many of the perfect insects, however, so much resemble *Bombyces*, that they were long classed with them; and there is no doubt that many more genera will be removed from various families of *Bombyces* to the *Geometræ*, as soon as their transformations are known. The largest species do not exceed four inches in expanse, and the smallest measure more than half an inch. From an inch to an inch and a half is the usual size. The *Geometræ* are divided into many families, of which we must proceed to notice the most important.

The *Urapterydæ* are rather large species, frequently with an angular projection on the hind wings. The type of this family is the Swallow-tailed Moth (*Urapteryx Sambucaria*, Linn.), the largest

British *Geometra*, measuring about two inches across the wings. It is of a pale yellow, with two dark stripes and a short line between on the fore wings, and one stripe on the hind wings. At the base of the short projecting angle of the hind wings are one or two dark spots.

Among the foreign species we may notice *Cyclidia Substigmaria*, Hübn., a common East Indian species, which expands about three inches. It is white, with rather pointed fore wings, and is marked with several black dentated lines and black submarginal spots; towards the tip of the fore wings is a brown space. The hind wings are not angulated, but are marked with a large black spot.

The *Ennomidæ* include many handsome species of moderate size, in most of which the prevailing colour is some shade of yellow. Some species, however, are brown, and a very few green. In some genera the wings are entire, and in others they are angulated or dentated. One of the commonest is the Brimstone Moth (*Rumia Cratægata*), Linn., a yellow moth, with reddish spots on the costa, and some brown lines on the wings.

Selenia Illustraria, Treitschke, is a larger and much scarcer species. It is of a purplish grey, with a slight rosy tinge, and much clouded with brown towards the base; in the middle of each wing is a small white lunule.

Crocallis Elinguaria, Linn., a third example of this family, is pale yellow, with a broad brown band on the fore wings; it is not uncommon.

The *Œnochromidæ* are an entirely exotic family, and most of the species are found in Australia. The body is rather stout, the wings entire, and the fore wings pointed. Most of the species are of considerable size. One of the handsomest species is *Gastrophora Henricaria*, Guén., which is whitish, dusted with black; the hind wings are yellow, with a broad whitish border; the under side of the fore wings is yellow at the base, and marked with a very large blue-black spot.

The *Amphidasidæ* have thick, hairy bodies, and are all of dull colours; in many species the female has rudimentary wings. One of the commonest species is the Pepper and Salt Moth (*Amphidasis Betularia*, Linn., in which the female resembles the male. *Nyssia Zonaria*, W. V., one of the species with apterous females, is found on sandhills on the coast in spring.

The *Boarmidæ* are a very extensive family of moths, generally of moderate size, with slender bodies and dentated wings, and usually of dull colours, being of some shade of grey or brown, or dull green, with darker markings. The most interesting of the exotic genera is *Hypochroma*, Guén., which has rather short fore wings and long hind wings, with very sharply-defined markings on the under surface. They are generally grey or greenish above, with darker lines and markings, and paler, with black markings below. *H. Occultaria*, Boisd., a common Australian species, is grey, with black dentated lines above, and white with black markings below; each wing is also marked beneath with a slender scarlet line.

The *Geometridæ* include species of moderate or large size, of a bright green colour, whence they are commonly known as "Emeralds." It is rather an extensive family, and the species are not likely to be mistaken for those of any other. The wings are generally entire or angulated, and are simply marked with transverse lines, or occasionally with larger masses of colour, but are never speckled.

The *Palyadæ* are a small exotic group, with slender bodies, and unusually long legs and antennæ. One of the commonest species is *Eumelea Rosalia*, Cram., an East Indian species, of a yellow colour, striated all over with reddish; it is a very variable insect. The South American genus *Ophthalmophora*, Guén., is decorated with submarginal silvery lines, and generally with a black eye with metallic markings on the hind wings.

The *Acidalidæ* are a very large family of small moths, generally with rounded wings, and often with a conspicuous black dot in the centre of each. Many are white, yellowish, or tawny, with transverse brown lines. The species of *Argyris*, Guén., are remarkable for having a large irregular eye, more or less marked with silver, on the fore wings. They are met with in south-eastern Europe, Africa, and the East Indies.

Micronia, Guén., the type of the exotic family *Micronidæ*, includes a number of white species from the East Indies, Australia, and Africa. They are marked with black transverse lines, and resemble small *Urapterydæ*, the hind wings having a slight tail, which is generally marked with a black spot.

The *Caberidæ* are a small family of white species (rarely brown or yellowish), in which the antennæ of the males are more decidedly pectinated than in the *Acidalidæ*. The most conspicuous species is *C. Taminata*, W. V., a white moth, measuring an

inch across the wings; there are two conspicuous black spots on
the costa of each fore wing.

The *Macaridæ* are moths of moderate size, in which the hind
margin of the fore wings is frequently notched below the tip,
and the hind wings are angulated or dentated.   The number of
described genera is small, but the typical genus *Macaria*, Curt.,
is exceedingly numerous in species.   *M. Notata*, Linn., the Small
Peacock Moth, is grey, with blackish markings; towards the
extremity of the costa is a fawn-coloured blotch.   It is not an
abundant species.

The *Fidonidæ* are an extensive family, many species of which
frequent heaths.   The antennæ are strongly pectinated in the male,
and the wings are rounded, generally of a pale colour, speckled
with dark atoms, and marked with darker bands; some few
species are white, with black veins, such as *Scoria Dealbata*, Linn.
One of the most conspicuous European species is *Eurranthis Plumis-
toria*, Borkh., which has yellowish-white fore wings, and yellow
hind wings, with blackish markings; it is not a British insect.

The *Zerenidæ* are rather large insects, and are generally of a
white colour, with conspicuous black and tawny markings.   One
of the most familiar of our British moths belongs to this family;
the Magpie Moth *(Abraxas Grossulariata)*, Linn., which is common
in every garden and thicket, where its larva feeds on various fruit-
trees.   The genus *Abraxas* has very numerous representatives in
Asia.

Panthera Pardalaria, Hübn., is common in tropical America.
It is of a bright yellow colour, with large black spots, and
measures two inches across the wings.

Some species, like the common *Lomaspilis Marginata*, Linn., an
insect measuring about an inch in expanse, are white, with brown
or blackish markings only, which here assume the form of a broad
border.   Another variety of coloration is met with in *Percnia
Felinaria*, Guén., a long-winged insect from North India, which
expands nearly three inches.   It is of a greyish white, with
numerous rows of black spots.

Orthostixis, Hübn., includes a few South European and North
American moths, expanding about an inch and a half across the
wings.   They are white, with central black dots, and one or two
rows of black dots on each wing.

The *Hybernidæ* are a small family of moths, which appear very
late in the autumn, and very early in the year.   As in most winter

moths, the females are apterous, and the colours of the males are brown or yellow, so as to assimilate them to dead leaves. *Hybernia Defoliaria*, Linn., is of a dull yellowish, dusted and varied with brown.

The *Larentidæ*, one of the largest families of the *Geometræ*, includes species of small or moderate size, which are known as "Pugs" and "Carpets." In many the hind wings are without markings, but in others they are coloured like the fore wings. In the former case, the fore wings are generally marked with a simple or compound transverse band, broader above than below, and darker than the rest of the wing, or else of quite a different colour.

Lorentia Cyanata, Hübn., one of the prettiest species of this family, is an Alpine insect. It is pale grey, with the base and central band of the fore wings blue. A great number of species are very similar to this in pattern, though not in colouring.

Eupithecia, Curt., includes a number of small species, most of which expand considerably less than an inch. The fore and hind wings are generally marked nearly alike, and are brown or grey, with central dark spots, and three or four dark transverse lines; a few species are marked with tawny or green. Many of the species resemble each other very closely, and are very difficult to determine.

The genus *Lobophora*, Curt., is remarkable for the small size of the hind wings, which are provided with an additional lobe at the base in several species, giving them the appearance of having six wings. *L. Sexalisata*, Hübn., is pale grey, with brown markings, and pale hind wings.

Many of the largest and most conspicuous species of this family belong to *Cidaria*, Treitschke. *C. Fulvata*, W. V., is yellow, with a rust-coloured band, bordered with black in front on the fore wings; the hind wings are whitish. It is not an uncommon species.

Another handsome species of this family is *Melanippe Hastata*, Linn., which has finely contrasted black and white markings.

Eubolia Cervinaria, W. V., may be taken as our representative of the *Eubolidæ*. It is reddish brown, with darker bands on the fore wings; the hind wings are greyish brown, with an ill-defined paler band in the centre.

Tanagra Chærophyllata, Linn., the Chimney Sweep, is a sooty black moth with a narrow whitish fringe at the tip of the fore wings. It expands about an inch, and is common in most localities. It belongs to the family *Sionidæ*.

The *Erateinidæ* are a beautiful family, confined to tropical

N

America. The hind wings are long and narrow, and are often tailed, and, but for the simple antennæ, they might easily be mistaken for butterflies of the family *Lemoniidæ*, which inhabit the same countries, and to which they have a great general resemblance.

Sub-Section V.—*Pyrales.*

Wings long and rather narrow, not folded round the body in repose; antennæ and legs long and slender; palpi short; abdomen generally long and pointed, extending considerably beyond the hind wings.

The *Pyrales* are the first group of the *Microlepidoptera*, a collective term used for the *Pyrales, Crambi, Tortrices, Tineæ, Pterophori,* and *Alucitæ,* on account of the small size of most of the species belonging to these groups. The *Pyrales* are divided into several families, which, however, are not very clearly defined, and are not recognised by all entomologists. We will confine ourselves to noticing a series of representative genera and species.

Pyralis Farinalis, Linn., the Meal-worm, may be regarded as the type of the *Pyralidæ.* The fore wings are reddish, with a paler band in the middle, edged with white lines; the hind wings are bluish grey. It measures about an inch across the wings, and is common over a considerable part of the world. It is often met with in houses, as well as the dull brown Tabby Moth (*Aglossa Pinguinalis,* Linn.).

Cardamyla Carinentalis, Walk., is an Australian species measuring about an inch and a half across the wings; the fore wings are black, veined with white, and with three waved white lines; there is also a pale-green band marked with a round black spot; the hind wings are orange, with a black spot and a black border.

The species of *Pyrausta,* Schrank, are small purplish-red moths with yellow spots or lines; *Ennychia,* Treitschke, is a very similar genus, but the species are black, with white markings. Most of the species frequent dry sunny slopes.

Hyalea Glaucopidalis, Guén., is a violet-black species, with yellow markings, and very long slender body. It is a native of America, and is very similar to some of the American *Zygænidæ.*

Megaphysa Herbiferalis, Guén., is a large South American moth, remarkable for its hooked wings. The body is green, and the fore wings are brownish grey, with semi-transparent markings; the hind wings are semi-transparent, with yellowish borders.

Hydrocampa Nymphæata, Linn., is an example of a small family of *Pyrales* whose caterpillars feed on water-plants; it is brown with white spots, and is common everywhere near water.

Margaronia, Hübn., includes species of moderate size (from an inch to an inch and a half in expanse), and generally of a pure white or green colour, with a yellowish line running along the costa of the fore wings.

Botys, Latr., is a genus of very great extent, but the species are not very varied, being generally of a grey or yellow colour. The Small Magpie Moth (*Botys Urticata*, Linn.), which is common among nettles, is an exception, being white, with two marginal rows of almost confluent black spots, and some tawny and black spots towards the base of the fore wings. *Botys Amplalis*, Guén., is a yellow South American species, with black and brown markings, and a purplish blotch towards the tip of the fore wings.

Megastes Grandalis, Guén., is a large species more resembling a *Noctua* than a *Pyralis ;* it is brown, with semi-transparent markings, and is found in South America.

Scoparia, Haw., is a large genus of rather small grey species, with brown markings; they are generally found resting on the trunks of trees, on walls, etc.

Sub-Section VI.—*Crambi.*

Wings long (fore wings narrow, hind wings broad) and folded round the body in repose; palpi long; antennæ, legs, and abdomen long and slender.

The larvæ of the first family (the *Galeriidæ*) are parasitic in the nests of bees. *Aphomia Sociella*, Linn., one of the commonest species, is brown, with the costa broadly green; it expands about an inch and a half. This family is of very small extent.

The *Phycidæ*, or Knot-Horns, derive their name from the males of several species being provided with a conspicuous tuft near the base of the antennæ. *Zophodia Convolutella*, Hübn., figured as an illustration of this family, is grey, with two zigzag white lines, broadly surrounded with blackish, on the fore wings. Its larva lives between leaves of bramble and gooseberry, but feeds on the unripe fruit. It is, however, not a very abundant insect on the Continent, and is unknown in Britain.

The *Chilonidæ* are a small family of long-winged brown or grey moths, the larvæ of which feed in the stems of the reed and of other water-plants.

The *Crambidæ*, or Grass Moths, most of which belong to the genus *Crambus*, Fabr., are a very extensive family. They are of small size, rarely exceeding an inch in expanse, and are tolerably uniform in colour. The fore wings are sometimes silvery white, but are more often brown or yellowish, generally with white or silvery lines, or brown transverse lines; the hind wings are uniform white or brown. These moths have ample hind wings, and appear comparatively large when flying, but when at rest they fold their wings round them in an almost tubular form. They frequent meadows, and are easily disturbed, but only fly a few yards, and then drop down into the grass, and seem to vanish suddenly, from the small compass which their wings occupy when closed.

SUB-SECTION VII.—*Tortrices.*

Body slender, not extending beyond the hind wings; fore wings rather short, generally broad, and truncated at the extremity; hind wings rather broad; larvæ inhabiting rolled-up leaves, seed-capsules, and seed-heads, etc.

The *Tortrices*, or Bell Moths, are an extensive group of small moths, expanding from half to three quarters of an inch. They are generally recognisable at once by their broad truncated fore wings. Their classification is still in a somewhat unsettled condition.

Halias Quercana, Linn., a green moth, with two oblique lines and white hind wings, is included by some writers with the *Tortrices*, though others place it with the *Noctuæ*, or with the *Bombyces*. The species of *Halias* are of much larger size than any of the true *Tortrices*.

Tortrix Viridana, Linn., is a moth with green fore wings and brown hind wings, which abounds among oaks in summer, and may almost be regarded as the typical species of the *Tortrices*.

The hind margin is seldom indented, but *Teras Caudana*, a very variable grey or yellowish-brown species, is remarkable for the costa being deeply excavated.

Xanthosetia Zoegana and *Hamana*, Linn., are pretty species with sulphur-yellow fore wings with brownish-red markings, which are very common among thistles.

Carpocapsa Pomonella, Linn., a brown species, with a dark patch slightly marked with coppery towards the hinder angle of the fore wings, is very injurious to apples, in which its larva feeds. Other allied species feed in plums, acorns, etc.

Sub-Section VIII.—*Tineæ*.

Body slender; wings rather long and narrow, with long fringes, not wrapped round the body in repose; larvæ variable.

The *Tineæ* are very numerous in Europe, and one-third of our British moths belong to this section; but they do not appear to be proportionately abundant in foreign countries. These moths are frequently of very small size, and few of our largest species equal an inch in expanse, while the greater part are much smaller. Some of the foreign species, however, measure an inch and a half or two inches across the wings. They have been divided into several families, most of which appear to be natural. We will proceed to mention most of the more important ones.

The *Atychiidæ* are a small family peculiar to Southern and Eastern Europe. They have some resemblance to *Zygænidæ*, with which they were formerly classed. *Atychia Pamila*, Ochs., is dark brown, with some white marks on the hind wings.

The *Tineidæ* include the Clothes Moths, several kinds of which are abundant everywhere; and their caterpillars cause considerable damage by feeding upon animal fabrics of various kinds. One of the commonest and most conspicuous species is *Tinea Tapetzella*, Linn., which is black to the middle of the fore wings, and white mixed with brown beyond.

Euplocamus Anthracinalis, Scop., is a large and conspicuous black species with white spots, which is common in Central and Southern Europe, but is not British.

The *Adelidæ* are remarkable for their beautiful colours, and the great length of their antennæ; they are generally met with in woods in spring, flying by day. *Nemotois Latreillellus*, Fabr., has golden violet wings, with two small yellow spots; it inhabits Southern Europe.

The genus *Hyponomeuta*, Zell., typical of the family *Hyponomeutidæ*, includes the Small Ermine Moths. They are much alike, having white or grey fore wings, rather less than an inch in expanse, and rows of small black spots. Their larvæ live gregariously under a web on hawthorn, sloe, apple, spindle, etc., and are sometimes very destructive.

The *Plutellidæ* are a small family with rather long wings, which are frequently pointed or slightly hooked at the tip. The largest species is *Theristis Mucronella*, Scop., a yellowish-grey insect which measures more than an inch across the wings.

Chimabacche Fagella, Fabr., which belongs to the family *Chima-bacchidæ*, is a brownish-yellow moth, often seen in woods in spring, which is remarkable for the fore wings of the female being rudimentary, and the hind wings absent.

The *Gelechiidæ* form one of the most extensive and varied families of the *Tineina ;* and the great genus *Gelechia*, Zell., alone included upwards of a hundred British species, until it was subdivided by Von Heinemann. Many of the largest and handsomest *Tineæ*, both British and foreign, belong to the *Gelechiidæ*.

Depressaria, Haw., is a large genus of dull-coloured moths with rather broader wings than most of the *Tineæ*, which the older writers regarded as *Tortrices*. They are generally grey or brown, with one or two black dots, but with no varied or conspicuous markings. Most of the species expand nearly an inch; and, having a somewhat flattened appearance, are called "Flat Bodies" by collectors.

Carcina Quercana, Fabr., is a very pretty moth, with rather long antennæ, found in woods in summer. It is pale reddish, with two yellow spots on the costa of each fore wing.

Harpella Geoffrella, Linn., another very conspicuous species, likewise found in woods, is yellow, shading into brownish towards the tip; it is also marked with bluish lines, and two yellow spots.

Cryptophasa, Lew., is an Australian genus of very large species, measuring an inch and a half or two inches across the wings. The fore wings are generally white, sometimes with a large dark spot in the middle, and the hind wings are brown. The comparatively long fringes will prevent their being mistaken for *Noctuæ*, which they otherwise considerably resemble.

Endrosis Fenestrella, Linn., the most familiar representative of the family *Œcophoridæ*, is a small grey moth about three-quarters of an inch in expanse, with a conspicuously white head and thorax. It is constantly met with in houses, but is not injurious. Some authors include it in the family *Elachistidæ*.

Gracilaria Syringella, Linn., is a peculiarly delicate pale-grey moth, about half an inch across the wings, which is abundant in gardens, where its larvæ feed in blotches of the leaves of lilac and privet. It represents the family *Gracilariidæ*.

The *Coleophoridæ* are small moths, about half an inch in expanse, with rather long narrow and pointed fore wings. Many of their larvæ live in cases, like the *Psychidæ* and *Phryganidæ*. They are of very various colours, but a large proportion are white, grey, or yellow, or of some other pale colour. *C. Vibicella*, Hübn., which we have figured, is not a very common species ; it is bright ochre-yellow, with silvery-white stripes on the fore wings.

Elachista, Staint., typical of the family *Elachistidæ*, is remarkable for the habits of the larvæ, which mine in the leaves of grasses. The perfect insects are pretty little moths ; some are white or grey, but most of them are of dark colours, with white or silvery markings ; they measure about one-third of an inch across the wings.

The smallest species of the *Tineæ* belong to the families *Lithocolletidæ*, *Nepticulidæ*, etc., and their larvæ mine in the leaves of various plants. Many are very beautiful, being of rich dark colours, relieved by metallic spots. The smallest moth known is *Nepticula Microtheriella*, Staint., the larva of which mines in the leaves of the nut. The moth only measures about one-eighth of an inch across the wings. The species of *Nepticula* are black, brown, or purplish brown, with white or yellow markings.

SUB-SECTION IX.—*Pterophori.*

Antennæ, legs, and abdomen very long and slender ; fore wings generally split into two distinct feathers, and hind wings into three.

This section consists only of the single family *Pterophoridæ*, including the Plume Moths. They are probably allied to the *Pyrales*, but have much outward resemblance to the *Tipulidæ*, among the *Diptera*, especially when standing with their wings extended, but folded into narrow compass. They are generally of dull colours—brown, grey, or white. The commonest, and one of the largest species, is the White Plume Moth (*Pterophorus Pentadactylus*, Linn.), which is common in gardens ; it is nearly pure white, and expands rather more than an inch. In one genus (*Agolistis*, Hübn.) the wings are not cleft. *A. Adactyla*, Hübn., is a native of Eastern Europe.

SUB-SECTION X.—*Alucitæ.*

Body slender ; abdomen not extending beyond the hind wings ; each wing split into six distinct feathers.

Alucita Hexadactyla, Linn., the Twenty-plume Moth, is the only species of this group found in England, though several others are found in Southern Europe. It is a small brownish insect ; and when seen at rest the division of the broad wings is not always apparent, and it might easily be mistaken for a small *Geometra*.

ORDER HEMIPTERA.

HAUSTELLATE insects; wings four, membranous, naked; the fore wings (in the *Heteroptera*) of a parchment-like consistency (except sometimes at the tips), or (in the *Homoptera*) similar to the hind wings; metamorphosis incomplete; and in one group (*Aphides*) exhibiting alternation of generations.

The two great groups into which the *Hemiptera* are divided are not unfrequently regarded as Orders.

HEMIPTERA HETEROPTERA.

Fore wings horny; hind wings, and usually the tips of the fore wings, membranous; antennæ generally long, four- or five-jointed; head generally free.

The *Hemiptera Heteroptera* include the true Bugs, an extensive group of very varied structure and habits. The greater part of the terrestrial species feed on plants; a few, however, are carnivorous, feeding on other insects, or sucking the blood of animals and birds, and most of the aquatic species are likewise carnivorous. Several systems of classification have been proposed for this section by various authors; but they differ little, except as regards the names of the principal families; and our limits will not permit us to notice the numerous sub-families into which the larger groups have been divided.

FAMILY I.—*Scutelleridæ.*

Beak prominent; antennæ not longer than the body, generally five-jointed; ocelli present; body oval; mesothorax larger than the prothorax and metathorax together; scutellum large or very large, in some cases covering the whole of the wings and abdomen; elytra coriaceous, with more or less of the extremity membranous; tarsi short.

This extensive family includes the greater proportion of the largest and handsomest species of the Land Bugs. The typical *Scutelleridæ*, or Shield Bugs, most of which are tropical, are not unlike beetles, the wings being entirely covered by the enormous convex scutellum, which is sometimes black or brown, but is often red or of a brilliant green, spotted with black, and resembles the closed elytra of a beetle.

The name *Pentatomidæ*, which is sometimes employed instead of *Scutelleridæ*, is inapplicable, as many genera of this family have four-jointed instead of five-jointed antennæ.

One of the handsomest representatives of the typical *Scutelleridæ* found in Europe is *Graphosoma Lineatum*, Linn. It measures nearly half an inch in length, and is red, with six longitudinal black lines on the prothorax, and four on the scutellum; it is common on flowers, especially *Umbelliferex*, in the south of Europe, and is sometimes met with as far north as Paris.

In *Pentatoma* and its allies the scutellum is much less developed than in the insects which we have just been considering. This section of the family is numerous in all parts of the world, and is much better represented in Europe than the former group. The species live on plants, but will also suck the juices of the many defenceless insects which are exposed to their attacks. Many of the European and exotic species are of a bright apple-green, and the latter are not unfrequently adorned with a long thick spike projecting at a right angle from each shoulder.

Edessa Cervus,[1] Fabr., which we have figured, is a native of South America. One of the commonest species in China is *Tessaratoma Papillosa*, Dru., a light-brown insect about an inch long, which forms a very large proportion of the contents of all boxes sent by unscientific collectors from that country. Its curious flat, yellowish, or reddish larva is likewise common in such collections.

Perhaps the most beautiful species of this section of the family are those forming the genus *Catacanthus*, Spin., which are natives of the Eastern Archipelago. One species (*C. Viridissimus*, Dist.), from the Tonga Islands, is almost entirely green; its larva is yellowish, with the centre more or less filled up with rich purplish blue. *C. Aurantius*, Sulz., and *Incarnatus*, Dru.; from Java, etc., are much commoner in collections; they are red or orange, with a large black spot on each elytron, and smaller ones elsewhere. The name of the genus is derived from the short strong projection directed forwards from the under surface of the base of the abdomen.

[1] By an oversight no figures have been prepared of *Edessa Cervus* and a species of *Phyllomorpha*.

FAMILY II.—*Coreidæ.*

Scutellum rather small, triangular ; antennæ generally four-jointed, last joint large, long, or flattened, and inserted above or upon an imaginary line drawn from the eyes to the base of the rostrum ; ocelli present ; membranous part of the elytra with more than five nervures.

This family includes a number of plant-feeding native and exotic species, varying considerably in shape and structure. *Menenotus Cornutus*, Pert., is a curious Brazilian species. It is about an inch long, and is of a light brown ; the elytra are yellowish. The sides of the thorax project in front almost like a pair of horns. *Machtima Crucigera*, Linn., is another rather smaller Brazilian insect. It is black, with four yellow longitudinal lines on the prothorax, and two lines of the same colour forming a cross on the closed fore wings.

The genus *Neides*, Latr., includes small yellowish or brownish species, several of which are common in Northern Europe ; they are remarkable for their very slender form ; the genus *Phyllo-morpha*, Lap., however, is very broad, and is remarkable for its curious resemblance to a leaf. A few species are found in the south of Europe, but that figured is from Madagascar.

FAMILY III.—*Lygæidæ.*

Scutellum short ; antennæ four-jointed, inserted below an imaginary line drawn from the eyes to the base of the rostrum ; ocelli present ; membranous part of the elytra never with more than five nervures.

The species of this family are nearly all vegetable-feeders, and are generally of a red, black, or yellow colour. In many species both of this and of some other families of *Hemiptera Heteroptera* there are two forms of imago, called the macropterous and micropterous forms. In the first the wings are fully developed, and in the second they are rudimentary or absent.

Several species are very injurious to cultivated plants. One of the most destructive of all is *Blissus Leucopterus*, Say, a black insect with white fore wings, each of which is marked with a large black triangular spot on the outer edge ; it measures about an eighth of an inch in length. The young larva is red. This insect is called the Chinch Bug in the United States, where it sometimes abounds to such an extent as almost to annihilate the corn crops over large districts.

Anthocoris Nemorum, Fabr., is a small black species, with pale elytra marked with two transverse black lines. It is met with on various plants, including hops, and the hop-growers, who call it the " needle-nosed flea," accuse it of destroying their crops. It is, however, supposed to be a carnivorous insect, in which case it would probably be only waging war upon the small insects which are the real destroyers of the hops.[1]

FAMILY IV.—*Pyrrhocoridæ*.

Ocelli absent; membrane of the fore wings coriaceous, with more than five nervures; otherwise resembling the *Lygæidæ* in their most important characters. A representative European species is *Pyrrhocoris Apterus*, Linn., a red insect, with a black head and scutellum, a black spot on the middle of the thorax, and two black spots on each of the fore wings. Both winged and apterous individuals occur, and the insect is sometimes very abundant.

FAMILY V.—*Capsidæ*.

Body soft; ocelli absent; antennæ four-jointed, pubescent; scutellum small, triangular; female with a distinct ovipositor.

This family includes a great number of small species of variegated colours, which feed exclusively on the sap of plants or the juice of fruit. As a representative of this family we have figured *Capsus Intermedius*, Sahlb., a shining black species, with silvery pubescence and reddish legs.

FAMILY VI.—*Tingididæ*.

Body broad, depressed; antennæ not thinner towards the tip, sometimes clubbed; rostrum three-jointed, very short.

The species of this family differ considerably among themselves in size, structure, and habits, and although the majority of the species are carnivorous, others, especially among the smaller species, are herbivorous. Our native species are generally small; and *Tingis Pyri*, Fabr., a brown insect about one-eighth of an inch long, is sometimes very injurious to pear-trees.

[1] Compare M'Lachlan, *Proceedings of the Entomological Society of London*, 1879, p. xliii; and 1880, pp. xxix and xxx.

FAMILY VII.—*Cimicidæ*.

Body broad, depressed ; antennæ four-jointed, the apical joints slender ; rostrum rather long ; wings generally rudimentary ; habits carnivorous.

The type of this family is *Cimex Lectularius*, Linn., the common Bed-Bug, which is unfortunately too well known to need description. It has always abounded in Africa, where it is possibly indigenous, but has now been conveyed with merchandise over almost the whole world. Westwood mentions that the first record of its appearance in England was in 1503. At that time it excited great alarm, some ladies having mistaken its bites for plague-spots. They sent for the doctor in consternation, but were highly amused when he detected and showed them the insect. At the present day the insect often leads to consternation, but hardly to a doctor's visit, and its discovery certainly never gives occasion for amusement.

The bed-bug, however, continued to be of very rare occurrence in Britain till after the Fire of London in 1666, when great numbers were imported in foreign timber, since which time it has been only too plentiful. But there are several interesting questions in its habits, etc., which still require investigation. Fowls, pigeons, swallows, and bats are infested by closely-allied species, or perhaps by slightly modified forms of the common bug. It will breed and multiply in empty houses, and probably feeds on the various insects which are found in such localities. Blood-thirsty as it is, it is far too abundant for man to be its sole, or even its ordinary prey, though it is sufficiently sagacious to climb to the ceiling, and drop upon the bed, if it is unable to obtain access to it from the floor. However, since the introduction of iron bedsteads, bugs can no longer multiply in the substance of the very bedstead itself, as was formerly the case ; and washing with a solution of carbolic acid will help to destroy these as well as many others of the insect pests which infest our houses. They are very subject to the attacks of various other insects, and are a favourite delicacy with the Cockroach and the Wheel Bug, though neither of these insects are to be regarded as desirable household companions.

In hot countries the bug occasionally acquires wings ; and it is stated that the negro cabins in the Southern States of America are infested by a bug two or three times larger than the ordinary species, but which does not yet seem to have fallen under the notice of entomologists.

FAMILY VIII.—*Reduviidæ*.

Head long, narrowed behind into a neck; eyes large, prominent; ocelli present; rostrum thick, curved, and naked; antennæ long, or moderately long, and slender towards the tip; legs long, strong, and often hairy; habits carnivorous.

An extensive family, easily recognisable by the peculiar shape of many of the species. The typical species is the Wheel Bug, or Masked Bug (*Reduvius Personatus*, Linn.), a black insect, three-quarters of an inch long, which is common in outhouses in the country. It feeds on other insects (including the bed-bug, as already mentioned), but although it rarely attacks man, its bite, like that of most of the larger *Reduviidæ*, is very painful. The larva of this species, as well as those of several of its allies, is also carnivorous, and is in the habit of encasing its body with particles of dust, in order to conceal itself from its insect prey.

Some of the foreign species of this family are most formidable insects, such as the great black *Conorrhinus Renggeri*, Herr.-Schäff., of Chili, which attacks travellers who are camping out, or who are sleeping in outhouses, as mentioned by Darwin in his *Journal of the Voyage of the Beagle*, and as I have lately been assured by Mr. T. Edmonds, who lived for some years in that country, where he made a fine collection of insects of all Orders.

Pirates Stridulus, Fabr., is a black insect, about half an inch long, with red fore wings spotted with black, and a red border to the abdomen. It is common in South France under stones, and is remarkable for the loud sound which it produces by rubbing its neck against the front concavity of the prothorax.

Acanthaspis Sexmaculata, Fabr., a brown yellow-spotted species, common in collections from Java, is a good representative of some of the exotic forms allied to *Reduvius;* among the more aberrant forms, *Zelus Quadrispinosus*, Linn., may be mentioned. It is a large red South American species, with two strong spines projecting from the back of the thorax on each side, as shown in the figure.

FAMILY IX.—*Emesidæ*.

Body long and slender; front coxæ long, and front legs raptorial; hinder legs very long; habits carnivorous; wings in many species only developed occasionally, or not at all.

The best-known species of this small family is *Plœaria Vaga-*

bunda, Linn., a brown very delicately-formed insect, which frequents trees, and has reminded many observers of a *Tipula,* both
from its form, and the manner in which it is continually balancing
itself on its long slender legs. This forms the last family of the
true Land-Bugs, the species belonging to the remaining families
of *Hemiptera Heteroptera* being all either water-insects, or found
only in the immediate neighbourhood of water.

Family X.—*Saldidæ.*

Body long, slender, depressed; legs long and very slender;
eyes large and prominent; head not narrowed into a neck behind;
habits carnivorous.

The species of *Salda* are small dull-coloured insects, always
found near water. They are very active, running and jumping
with great agility, and feed upon the small insects which are met
with in the localities which they frequent.

Family XI.—*Hydrometridæ.*

Body slender; head twice as long as the prothorax, forming
nearly one-third of the total length of the body; all the legs
slender and of equal length; habits probably herbivorous.

Hydrometra Stagnorum, Linn., is a black or brown insect, more
or less tinged with reddish, and about half an inch long. It is
found running on the surface of water, or else on the banks, or
among water-plants, but is not very active.

Family XII.—*Gerridæ.*

Head short; body and legs long and slender; claws of the
tarsi inserted in a notch before the extremity of the last joint;
habits carnivorous.

These are long narrow insects, generally of a black or brown
colour, and about half an inch in length, which run upon the
surface of the water. In many species the wings are only
developed occasionally. The principal European genera are *Gerris*
and *Velia,* Fabr.; but the most remarkable genus of this family is
Halobates, Esch., which is truly pelagic, the few known species
having been met with running on the surface of the ocean itself,
often at a distance of hundreds of miles from land. *Aëpophilus
Bonnairei,* Sign., is a small brownish-yellow or reddish-yellow
insect, found between tide-marks on the coasts of England and

France, in company with small beetles of similar habits, belonging to the genus *Aëpus*, Leach, which it most resembles.

FAMILY XIII.—*Galgulidæ*.

Head and body broad, the latter short and flattened; eyes pedunculated; ocelli present; antennæ four-jointed, placed below the eyes; hind legs formed for running; habits carnivorous.

This family only includes a few American species, which are brown, sometimes spotted with yellow. They are found among aquatic plants, or on the edge of the water, but are not, strictly speaking, aquatic insects, any more than the *Saldidæ*, which they somewhat resemble in their habits.

FAMILY XIV.—*Nepidæ*.

Body flattened, rather long; head of moderate size; front legs raptorial; hind legs long and slender, formed for swimming; habits aquatic and carnivorous.

The species of this family are not very numerous, but are of considerable interest. They are of large size, and very fierce and voracious. The genus *Belostoma*, Latr., found in the East Indies and America, includes the largest species of *Hemiptera Heteroptera*, some of which measure four and a half inches in length, and nearly six in expanse of wing; the front wings are of a light brown colour, varied with yellowish, and the hind wings are whitish. There is no doubt that their food partly consists of small fish, frogs, etc., as well as of water-insects. These insects are of a depressed oval form, and about three times as long as broad, but the genus *Zaitha*, Amyot, includes much shorter and broader species. *Belostoma* deposits its eggs in a cluster by the side of the water; and the natives of Mexico and South America employ them as articles of food. The females of *Zaitha* and of several allied genera pack their eggs into a compact layer on their backs, and carry them about with them.

Naucoris Cimicoides, Linn., is a greenish-yellow insect about half an inch long, which is common in pools and streams. It swims with great rapidity by day, but quits the water and flies about at night.

Two other species of this family are likewise British, both of which are remarkable for the long breathing-tube at the extremity of the body. One is *Nepa Cinerea*, Linn., the Water Scorpion, a brown insect, with the abdomen red beneath. It measures nearly an inch in length, and is common in stagnant water. Its large front legs, somewhat resembling the claws of a scorpion, have given rise to the name by which it is popularly known.

Ranatra Linearis, Linn., which measures about two inches in length, including the respiratory tube, is our largest Hemipterous insect. It is of a brownish-yellow colour, and its body is long and narrow, differing very much in shape from that of any other genus of this family, although its large front legs and long respiratory tube show it to be closely allied to the water-scorpion. Unlike other species of this family, it is by no means an active insect, creeping rather slowly at the bottom of the water. It is not very abundant in England. Notwithstanding its sluggish habits, it is just as voracious as any of its allies, being very destructive, not only to fish-spawn, but even to small fish, which it pierces with its powerful rostrum, grasping them firmly at the same time with its claws.[1] This insect is nearly always more or less infested with a small red water-mite belonging to the genus *Leptus*, Latr.

FAMILY XV.—*Notonectidæ.*

Body rather convex; eyes very large; front legs not raptorial, rather short, middle legs longer, and hind legs still longer, shaped like oars, and fringed with long hairs.

These insects are called Water Boatmen, from their habit of rowing themselves about on their backs with their long hind legs. They are carnivorous, feeding on small insects, etc. At night they leave the water, and fly about like the species of *Naucoris*. The most typical species is perhaps *Notonecta Glauca*, Linn., a yellowish insect about half an inch long, which is not uncommon in England.

HEMIPTERA HOMOPTERA.

Wings four, membranous, roof-like (one or both pairs occasionally wanting); head generally soldered to the thorax; antennæ generally short.

This extensive sub-order includes the Cicadas, Lantern Flies, Plant Lice, Scale Insects, etc. All our British species are of moderate or small size, and are generally rather inconspicuous insects, but the *Homoptera* of warmer climates are often very remarkable for their size and beauty, some species of *Cicadidæ* even surpassing the gigantic *Belostoma* in their dimensions, while many of the

---

[1] *Entomologist*, xi. pp. 95, 119, and 120.

Fulgoridæ and *Membracidæ* are remarkable for their strange forms and bright colours, and several of the latter family strongly resemble *Lepidoptera* in appearance. Nor are the smaller species to be undervalued, for the *Coccidæ* provide us with shellac and cochineal, and the *Coccidæ* and *Aphidæ* are among the most destructive insects which ravage our fields and gardens. The *Aphidæ* are interesting for other reasons also. Their extraordinary cycle of alternating generations, and the relations between ants and *Aphidæ*, are problems which have excited the attention of naturalists for several generations, and are still far from being completely understood. All the *Homoptera* are plant-feeding insects.

Family I.—*Cicadidæ*.

Antennæ short, seven-jointed; tarsi three-jointed; ocelli three; legs not fitted for leaping; male provided with abdominal drums, and female with an exserted ovipositor.

The *Cicadidæ* are inhabitants of warm climates, and our only British representative of the family (*C. Anglica*, Curt.) is one of the smaller species, the wings only expanding about an inch and a quarter, though even thus it is our largest Homopterous insect.

With a few exceptions, the species are of a black, green, or yellowish colour, and the wings are either transparent or marked with a row of moderate-sized black spots on the nervures. The drums vary considerably in size in the males of different species, but are generally very conspicuous, and are sometimes nearly as long as the abdomen itself.

Three conspicuous species are almost always to be observed in abundance in collections of insects from China. One is a large black species with transparent wings, having the extreme base blackish and coriaceous; it measures about three and a half inches in expanse (*Fidicina Atrata*, Sign.). The second species is black, but in this the wings are smoky black, and both body and wings are spotted with yellow (*Geana Maculata*, Fabr.). The third species is much smaller, not expanding more than two inches, and its body is much longer and more slender in proportion than in any other of the two preceding species. It is black, with smoky-black wings, and the head, abdomen, and two large spots on the mesothorax are of a blood-red colour (*Huechys Sanguinea*, Amyot).

Platypleura Stridula, Linn., from South Africa, is a very pretty species; it is greenish, spotted with black, the fore wings are grey, with green, brown, and transparent spots and blotches. The hind

o

wings are yellow, bordered with brown. It measures nearly three
inches across the wings.

One of the largest species of this family is *Dundubia Impera-
toria*, Westw., which measures above eight inches across the wings.
It is met with in the East Indies.

One of the most interesting species is the North American
Cicada Septemdecim, Linn., which is said only to appear in abundance
every seventeen years. It is black, with transparent wings veined
with reddish. "The young larvæ feed on the roots of the oak and
apple, clustering upon the roots, and sucking the sap with their
beak-like mouths. They live seventeen years. Different broods
appear in different localities, so that each year they are seen in
some part of the country."[1]

The larvæ and pupæ of the *Cicadidæ* resemble the imago in
general form, except that the wings, etc., are undeveloped. The
empty pupa-skin is frequently found still clinging by its legs to
bushes, etc., and is often sent home in collections.

The Cicadas are improperly called "locusts" both in America
and Australia. In countries where they abound, the larger species
keep up a perpetual chirping, and they and other insects make the
woods resound with their song at almost all hours of the day and
night. Hence I have been assured by travellers who have spent
some years in the Tropics, that nothing struck them so much on
their return to England, as what seemed to them the death-like
stillness of our woods, and that it was months, or even years,
before they were able to divest themselves of the impression that
it was always winter.

FAMILY II.—*Fulgoridæ.*

Antennæ three-jointed, inserted below the eyes; front of the
head more or less prolonged; ocelli two, placed between the eyes;
thorax not prolonged; wings deflected.

This is an extensive family, which exhibits so much variation
in structure that many authors divide it into several.

The typical *Fulgorinæ* have the prothorax generally as long
and at least as broad as the thorax; the fore wings are opaque,
and the head is furnished with a very large hollow appendage in
front. This sub-family includes the genus *Fulgora*, Linn., and its
allies, comprising the Lantern Flies and Candle Flies, which are
remarkable for their combination of large size, bright colours, and

[1] Packard's *Guide to the Study of Insects* (6th ed.), p. 535.

strange forms, and are entirely exotic. Several of the species are
reputed to be luminous, but this statement has been often and
strenuously denied, and never affirmed on what would appear to
be conclusive evidence. It is now generally discredited, but it is
so difficult to prove a negative in such a matter, especially with
reference to insects which are not natives of our own country, that
we are seldom justified in pronouncing a more positive verdict than
" Not Proven."

Next to the great *Cicadidæ*, the South American Lantern Fly
(*Fulgora Laternaria*, Linn.) is the largest Homopterous insect known.
It is nearly three inches long, and measures more than four inches
across the wings. The head bears an immense hollow projection
in front, which bends upwards at about half its length, and is then
continued forwards ; the end is rounded. The insect is greenish-
yellow, varied with black, and there is a large yellow ocellated spot
near the tip of the hind wings, with a black pupil, and enclosed
in a brown ring.

Hotinus Candelarius, Linn., the commonest of the Chinese
species, is generally called the Candle Fly. It measures about two
inches and a half across the fore wings, which are black, banded
with green, and spotted with yellow ; the hind wings are yellow,
with brown borders ; the long curving-up snout is of a reddish-
brown ; in other species it is green.

Pyrops Clavata, Westw., from India, is about the same size, but
is of a chalky-white colour; the fore wings are varied, and the
hind wings bordered with black. Its long curved snout ends in
a round knob, the extremity of which is of a bright red.

Phrictus Diadema, Linn., is a South American species in which
we observe another curious modification of the frontal prominence,
which is here rather short, broad, and trifid at the extremity.
The fore wings, which expand about three and a half inches, are
greenish, varied with yellow and brown. The hind wings are
dark red, with the border broadly brown.

The second sub-family, *Lystrinæ*, much resembles the *Fulgorinæ*,
and likewise contains many large and handsome species, but may
be distinguished from it at once by the absence of the curious
prolongation of the head. The species are all exotic, and are
chiefly found in South America. *Aphæna Variegata*, Guér., from
Cochin China, is olive-brown, with black and brown spots on the
fore wings, and two yellow ones beyond the middle ; the hind
wings and abdomen are bright red, the former with some black

and orange spots. It expands nearly two inches. The genus *Lystra*, Fabr., includes rather smaller species, all American.

In the *Cixiinæ* the prothorax is much shorter than the mesothorax, and the elytra are generally transparent. *Cixius Nervosus*, Linn., the commonest European species, measures one-third of an inch in length; it is of a reddish yellow, with black abdomen, and transparent wings.

The sub-family *Caloscelinæ* have leaf-like appendages on the front femora and tibiæ, and a spine in the middle of the hind tibiæ. The typical species is *Caloscelis Bonellii*, Latr., a Sardinian insect an eighth of an inch long. It is black, with yellow thorax and fore wings, the latter bordered with black.

The *Delphacinæ* may be distinguished by the long spine at the tip of the hind tibiæ, and by their comparatively long antennæ. The species are capable of leaping. *Delphax Flavescens*, Fabr., is one-sixth of an inch in length; it is yellowish, with transparent wings, and is a common European species.

The *Derbina* differ from the last sub-family by their unarmed hind legs. The species are all foreign, and *Derbina Coccinea*, Guér., may be mentioned as a uniform bright-red insect, measuring one-sixth of an inch in length, which inhabits New Zealand.

In the *Issinæ* the prothorax and mesothorax together are somewhat bell-shaped, but much broader than long. The humeral angles of the elytra are prominent, the legs not foliaceous, and the antennæ short. *Issus Coleoptratus*, Fabr., is a small greenish or brownish insect, a quarter of an inch long; it is not uncommon.

The *Flatinæ* are generally provided with streaks or transverse parallel nervures on the hind margin of the fore wings, and their wings fall perpendicularly on each side of the body in repose. *Flata Limbata*, Fabr., is a green species from Western Africa, which measures nearly an inch to the extremity of the closed wings.

The *Tettigometrinæ* are distinguished from all the preceding groups by the absence of a raised ridge on the sides of the face. *Tettigometra Virescens*, Panz., is a common greenish-yellow species with reddish legs, about a quarter of an inch long.

One peculiarity of the *Fulgoridæ*, to which we have not previously referred, is that many of the species exude a white waxy powder, with which they are sometimes completely covered, and which is collected for sale in some parts of China. It is probably analogous to a similar substance exuded by the larvæ of some *Lepidoptera*,—*Attacus Cynthia*. for example.

FAMILY III.—*Membracidæ.*

Antennæ very short, three-jointed, inserted in front of the eyes; ocelli two; prothorax prolonged beyond the abdomen, and sometimes covering the whole body.

This family is chiefly remarkable for the extraordinary shapes assumed by the prothorax. It would be useless to attempt to describe them; but some of the most curious are figured here. *Membracis Foliata,* Linn., is dark brown, varied with yellow; it occurs in Brazil, and is about half an inch in length. *Smilia Fasciata,* Amyot, is greenish brown, with a yellow band on the enlarged thorax; it is North American, and measures one-third of an inch in length. *Œda Inflata,* Fabr., from Brazil, is reddish yellow, reticulated with brown, and with a row of black dots on each side; and is of about the same size.

FAMILY IV.—*Cercopidæ.*

Head triangular; ocelli two; antennæ placed just in front of the eyes, three-jointed, terminating in a bristle; scutellum large, triangular, and exposed; prothorax not projecting above the abdomen, hind legs spineless, or with from one to three spines in a single line.

The Froghoppers are small insects, common among grass and bushes in the summer; they much resemble *Cicadidæ* in miniature. One of the prettiest species is *Triecphora Sanguinolenta,* which is about a quarter of an inch in length, and varied with black and red. A much commoner insect is the Cuckoo-spit (*Aphrophora Spumaria,* Linn.), which is about the same size, but yellowish grey, with two paler bands on the fore wings. This insect can make a prodigious leap in proportion to its size. Some say that it can spring to a distance of two yards. Its yellow larva may often be seen on grass or other low plants, enveloped in a mass of froth, which has given rise to the name of Cuckoo-spit. The extreme vagueness of the notions which many people possess of Entomology is amusingly illustrated by a paragraph which I met with recently among the answers to correspondents in some horticultural journal: "The cuckoo-spit is the soft or larval body (!) of a brown jumping insect of the Homopterous Order, named *Aphrophora Spumaria*" !!

FAMILY V.—*Tettigonidæ.*

Hind tibiæ with a double row of spines beneath; body narrow, elongated; ocelli, when present, placed on the vertex.

214 HOMOPTERA.

The most familiar insect of this family is *Tettigonia Viridis*, Linn., a green insect about half an inch long, with a yellow head.

FAMILY VI.—*Ledridæ*.

Hind tibiæ with a double row of spines beneath ; body broad, oval ; ocelli placed on the vertex.

Ledra Aurita, Linn., which may be regarded as the type of this family, is a greenish insect about three-quarters of an inch long, which is found on oaks. *Penthimia Atra*, Fabr., is a very broad black insect, somewhat resembling a beetle in appearance

FAMILY VII.—*Iassidæ*.

Hind tibiæ with a double row of spines beneath ; body rather long and broad, but narrower than in the *Ledridæ* ; ocelli, when present, placed on the front of the head.

A considerable number of small species are included in this family. The genus *Eupelix*, Germ., is remarkable for its large flattened head. In *Bythoscopus*, Germ., the head is also very broad, but is much shorter than in *Eupelix*, while in the typical genus *Iassus*, Fabr., the head is still less produced.

FAMILY VIII.—*Psyllidæ*.

Tarsi two-jointed ; antennæ eight- or ten- jointed, terminated by two slender bristles ; ocelli three ; wings transparent, with few nervures ; legs formed for leaping ; larva covered with a cottony secretion.

These small insects subsist on the sap of plants, to which they are sometimes injurious ; a few species produce galls. Like the *Aphidæ*, to which they are allied, they discharge a fluid of which ants are very fond. *Livia Pyri*, Linn., a red, long-winged species, abounds on pear-trees in all its stages.

FAMILY IX.—*Aphidæ*

Tarsi two-jointed ; antennæ long, five- to seven- jointed ; ocelli absent ; wings transparent, with few nervures (generally absent in the asexual forms) ; legs not formed for leaping.

The *Aphidæ* or Plant Lice are among the most destructive of all insects. They exist in enormous numbers, smothering the plants on which they feed, both by their mere abundance, and by draining them of their sap, which they discharge in the form of a sweet sticky substance called honey-dew, of which ants are very fond.[1] They are generally green or brown, and the fully mature sexual forms have large wings ; but they are also propagated asexually. Some species feed on the leaves, while others attack the roots of plants ; and one form of the same species will sometimes live in one situation, and another form in another. In some parts of the country they are called Smotherflies, and their sudden appearance was formerly attributed to the blighting influence of the east wind, and they are therefore still frequently called Blight. The extraordinary cycle of their development has lately been studied in several species by M. Lichtenstein of Montpellier and others. It has long been known that wingless *Aphidæ* propagate their race asexually, but the anomalies presented by their different stages are very curious. In some species there are two winged forms, in addition to the two wingless forms, of plant-feeders and root-feeders. One winged form is perfect, and does not feed, being destitute of a rostrum ; but the other, like the wingless forms, is sexless, and is provided with a rostrum.

One of the most destructive insects of this family is the *Aphis* of the vine (*Phyllozera Vastatrix*, Planch.), which has committed great ravages in most of the vine-producing countries of the Continent for several years past. They attack both the roots and the leaves, on which they produce small galls. The various forms are yellowish or reddish, more or less shading into brown or green.

FAMILY X.—*Aleyrodidæ.*

Both sexes with four wings of nearly equal size, opaque ; fore wings with a single nervure ; body covered with a white powder ; antennæ filiform, six-jointed ; pupa inactive, enclosed in the dried skin of the larva.

The typical species *Aleyrodes Proletella*, Linn., is a very small reddish-yellow insect, which the older writers on Entomology considered to be a moth.

FAMILY XI.—*Coccidæ.*

Antennæ filiform, eight- to eleven- jointed ; tarsi with one or two joints ; male with two wings, destitute of a rostrum, but provided with anal setæ, as in the *Ephemeræ ;* female wingless, scale-like.

The *Coccidæ* or Scale-Insects are sometimes very injurious to cultivated plants ; but they are also useful, producing cochineal,

---

[1] Compare p. 113.

shellac, manna, and other substances of considerable importance. After impregnation, the female remains attached to a leaf or branch, and her dried body serves as a protection for her eggs. Many of these insects are very small, and the males of several species have not yet been observed. *Coccus Cacti*, Linn., is a scarlet species which lives upon a Mexican species of *Cactus*, and yields the well-known dye called Cochineal. *C. Lacca*, Kerr, a West Indian species, yields shellac; while the manna is the gummy secretion discharged by the tamarisk when punctured by *C. Manniparus*, Fabr.[1]

Among the most curious of our native *Coccidæ* are the species of *Orthesia*, Bosc., which are small round white creatures resembling small woodlice rather than insects, which are sometimes met with on various low plants.

HEMIPTERA ANOPLURA.

Antennæ filiform, five-jointed; mouth suctorial; tarsi two-jointed; wings absent; abdomen large; habits parasitic on mammalia.

The *Pediculidæ* or true Lice, are now usually considered to be degraded *Homoptera*, though some writers have treated them as a distinct Order, either alone, or in conjunction with the *Mallophaga*. They are exclusively parasitic on various species of mammals, and although the same animal may support more than one species, the same louse is rarely found infesting two different animals. Three species infest man: the Head Louse (*Pediculus Capitis*, Linn.), found on the head, especially in children; the Body Louse (*Pediculus Vestimenti*, Nitsch), found in the clothes, which, though clearly a distinct species, so closely resembles the first that it is difficult to detect any satisfactory specific difference between them; and the Crab Louse (*Phthirius Inguinalis*, Leach), a broader and shorter insect, found in the hair on the face and body. The lice infesting different races of men differ a little in colour, etc., but it has not yet been positively determined whether they are distinct species, or only varieties of the common ones. Other species of lice infest elephants, monkeys, pigs, dogs, cats, mice, etc.

[1] Compare Westwood, *Modern Classification*, ii. p. 449.

ORDER DIPTERA.

WINGS two, with few veins, not clothed with scales or hair; hind wings replaced by rudimentary battledore-shaped organs, called *halteres*, or poisers; mouth furnished with a proboscis; female stingless, rarely provided with a conspicuous ovipositor; metamorphosis complete; larvæ most frequently worm-like maggots, without feet; pupæ inactive.

Few Orders of insects have been less studied than the *Diptera*, and consequently our knowledge of them is very imperfect, especially as regards foreign species. The number of recorded British species, however, is not inferior to that of the *Coleoptera* and *Hymenoptera*; and although a much smaller total number of species is at present known from all parts of the world, and although experienced entomological travellers assert that *Diptera*, in some tropical countries at least, are far less abundant in comparison than in England, yet we may fairly assume that, when all the Orders of insects have been equally well worked out, the *Coleoptera*, *Hymenoptera*, and *Diptera* will stand on about an equal footing as the three largest of all. Osten-Sacken has lately expressed an opinion that the real number of *Diptera* existing in North America will ultimately prove to fully equal if not to exceed that of the *Coleoptera*.

The food, habits, and structure of the *Diptera* vary so much that it is better not to allude to them in these introductory remarks. The Order has been divided into a great number of families, many of which will fall into the typical family *Muscidæ*, though this is subdivided into two large sections, and these again into numerous sub-families.

Although the *Diptera* are commonly spoken of as having only two wings, the hind wings are always represented by two small organs, called *halteres*, or poisers, which somewhat resemble a battledore in shape. If these are removed, or seriously injured, the insect becomes quite incapable of directing its flight. In addition to these, some species are provided with two more or less conspicuous lobes at the base of the wings, called *alulæ* or winglets.

DIPTERA APHANIPTERA.
FAMILY I.—*Pulicidæ*.

Parasitic insects, with scale-like rudiments of wings; legs long, especially the hind legs, which are formed for leaping, and provided with very large coxæ; larva vermiform.

The fleas are too well known to need description. A variety of species, very similar in appearance and habits, have been described as infesting various animals and birds. The eggs are laid in the dust, where the larvæ are said to feed on congealed blood, feathers, or other particles of animal matter which they find near them. But, like some other parasitic animals, they are able to accommodate themselves to a variety of food, and, in warm countries, colonies of fleas are often met with in sandy places living on the bare ground. Some light has, however, been thrown upon this subject by the recent discovery that fleas will attack caterpillars (and doubtless other insects also), and suck their blood. When they cannot meet with vertebrate food, it is clear that they will attack any other animal which may happen to fall in their way.

A second genus of this family (*Sarcopsylla*, Westw.) contains the Jigger or Chigoe (*S. Penetrans*, Linn.), which burrows into the skin of men and animals in the West Indies and South America, where the body of the gravid female swells to the size of a pea, and a most dangerous wound is produced if the creature is not carefully removed intact.

The *Pulicidæ* were formerly treated as a distinct Order under the name of *Aphaniptera* (Invisible Wings), so called from the rudimentary wings with which they are provided. They are now, however, generally regarded as a slightly aberrant family of *Diptera*. *Platypsylla Castoris*, Ritsema, the type of Westwood's Order *Achreioptera*, a beaver parasite resembling a small flattened cockroach, and alluded to on p. 12 as possibly belonging to the *Diptera*, is now referred by the best Coleopterists to the *Coleoptera*, and is considered to be related to the *Silphidæ*.

DIPTERA NEMOCERA.

Oviparous, two-winged flies; antennæ composed of more than six joints; palpi with four or five joints.

The arrangement of this and the following groups is chiefly taken from Osten-Sacken's *Catalogue of the Diptera of North America*, 2d ed., and Schiner's *Diptera Austriaca*.

FAMILY II.—*Cecidomyiidæ.*

Small delicate species, clothed with long hair; antennæ more
or less moniliform, with a few hairs, generally composed of twenty-
four joints in the males, and from twelve to fourteen in the
females; wings horizontal, with but few nervures; vegetable
feeders.

The species of this family are often called Gall Gnats. They
attack various plants, especially wheat and willow, generally more
or less distorting or stunting the plant, even when they do not
produce one of the abnormal excrescences to which the name gall
would be strictly applicable; some species, too, attack rotten wood
The best known and most mischievous species, however, are per
haps the Wheat Midge (*Diplosis Tritici*, Kirb.), and the Hessian Fly
(*Cecidomyia Destructor*, Say). The former is a small yellow fly,
with a long telescope-like ovipositor, with which it lays its eggs in
the blossom of the wheat. These hatch into small maggots, which
become yellow with age, and render the plant abortive by devouring the pollen.

The Hessian Fly derives its name from its having been introduced into the United States (as was supposed) by the Hessian
troops during the War of Independence. It is, however, still a
much-disputed point among entomologists as to whether this story
of its origin is correct, for it is thought to be an indigenous American species, and distinct from the various allied European forms
which some suppose to be the same. So excellent an authority as
Dr. Packard is, however, thoroughly convinced of its European
origin. It is a brown fly, which lays its eggs on the leaves of the
wheat, and the maggots, when hatched, creep down to the base of
the sheath, where they feed upon the sap, and, if numerous, soon
destroy the stalk. These maggots are at first semi-transparent,
but gradually darken with age, and, when full-grown, resemble so
many flax seeds imbedded in the substance of the stalk.

For more than a century this insect has proved exceedingly
destructive to wheat in America, but is somewhat uncertain in
appearance and locality, not proving itself equally abundant and
destructive in the same district at all times.

Before dismissing the *Cecidomyiidæ* it must be mentioned that
a few species are dimorphous, or rather exhibit alternation of generations, certain larvæ actually bringing forth living larvæ, a mode
of reproduction somewhat resembling that observed in *Aphidæ.*

FAMILY III.—*Mycetophilidæ.*

Small species; antennæ short or long, filiform or compressed, usually sixteen-jointed, sometimes setaceous, and occasionally forked; eyes separate, generally round; two or three ocelli present; wings with few nervures; hind tibiæ spined; vegetable feeders.

The larvæ of this family live gregariously in fungi, rotten wood, under bark, or in similar situations. Those of the genus *Sciara*, Meig., sometimes congregate in dense masses when full-grown, which has led to their being called "Army Worms" on the Continent and in America, a name sometimes applied in the latter country to the larva of a moth (*Leucania Unipuncta*, Haw.). The flies are remarkable for their power of leaping.

FAMILY IV.—*Simuliidæ.*

Small species; antennæ cylindrical, eleven-jointed; no ocelli; first joint of the tarsi as long as all the rest together; wings broad.

This small family includes only the genus *Simulium*, Latr. It is widely distributed, and some of the species are frequently called Sandflies, and are exceedingly annoying both in hot and cold countries by their painful bites; they also live on honey-dew. They are very restless insects, and continually vibrate their front legs, which they use as feelers when at rest.

FAMILY V.—*Bibionidæ.*

Eyes of the male large and contiguous, occupying most of the head; those of the female small; three ocelli; prothorax large; antennæ short, nine-jointed; legs and body rather short and stout.

Several species of this group are very common, among them St. Mark's Fly (*Bibio Marci*, Linn.), which is black, with transparent wings in the male and blackish ones in the female; and *B. Hortulanus*, Linn., in which the male is black, and the female red, with the head, collar, sides, scutellum, and legs black. These flies appear in spring, and their larvæ live in dung or damp earth.

FAMILY VI.—*Blephariceridæ.*

Eyes of the male large, contiguous, and hairy; in the female widely separated; three ocelli; antennæ long and slender, fourteen-jointed; wings broad and long; legs long.

The type of this family is *Blepharicera Fasciata*, Westw., a dark-brown fly with transparent wings and yellow legs. It measures about one-third of an inch in length. It is by no means a common insect. A South American species (*Paltostoma Torrentium* of F. Müller) exhibits a very peculiar form of female dimorphism. The male lives on flowers, like that of other gnats, and one of the female forms is adapted to a similar life, while the other is furnished with a lancet-like arrangement like that of the female gnats, and sucks the blood of animals.

FAMILY VII.—*Culicidæ.*

Head small; eyes round or kidney-shaped; ocelli wanting; antennæ long, fifteen-jointed, pectinated in the male; abdomen, wings, and legs, all long and slender; larva often aquatic.

This family contains the small delicate dull-coloured insects too well known in all parts of the world as gnats and mosquitoes. They are most abundant in the neighbourhood of water; for the female constructs a sort of raft of her eggs, which floats on the surface. When the larva is hatched, it floats tail upwards, being provided with respiratory organs at the extremity of its body, and rises occasionally to the surface to breathe. The pupa, however, which is of a somewhat conical shape, floats with its head upwards.

FAMILY VIII.—*Chironomidæ.*

Head small, retracted, often partly covered by the thorax; eyes generally kidney-shaped or crescent-shaped; ocelli absent or rudimentary; antennæ with from six to fifteen joints, densely pectinated in the males, and simple, and often composed of fewer joints, in the females; abdomen and legs long and slender.

The *Chironomidæ* are small delicate insects, much resembling the gnats. The females of several species are bloodsuckers. The larvæ of some species are aquatic, and those of others live under bark, in dung, or among decaying vegetable matter. The larva of *Chironomus Plumosus*, Linn., which is common in stagnant water, is called the Bloodworm, from its bright red colour. The larvæ of several species are actually marine, feeding on seaweed, etc., at low-water. *Clunio Marinus*, Hal., is far from uncommon on our British coasts, and *Chironomus Oceanicus*, Packard, has been met with by that author in Salem Harbour.

FAMILY IX.—*Orphnephilidæ.*

Head small, round; eyes round, contiguous in front; ocelli absent; antennæ shorter than the palpi, placed near the mouth;

apparently three-jointed, but eleven-jointed under the microscope; abdomen cylindrical, narrower than the thorax; legs rather short.

The typical species, *Orphnephila Testacea*, Macq., is a small fly, measuring only about one-tenth of an inch in length, which is sometimes found in bakehouses. It is of a rusty yellow colour, with brown head and abdomen, and the wings are slightly tinged with yellow.

FAMILY X.—*Psychodidæ*.

Head small, retracted; proboscis short, except in the genus *Phlebotomus*, Rond.; antennæ rather long, sixteen-jointed; eyes kidney-shaped; ocelli wanting; legs rather long; wings very broad and hairy; larva living in fungi and among rotten vegetable substances.

A small family, consisting of small brown or yellowish species, remarkable for their resemblance to moths. The species of *Phlebotomus* are troublesome blood-suckers in Southern Europe; the other genera are harmless.

FAMILY XI.—*Tipulidæ*.

Head round; proboscis rather prominent; antennæ long, composed of from six to nineteen joints; eyes large; ocelli wanting; abdomen long, cylindrical; legs generally very long and slender, breaking off at the least touch; wings long and rather narrow; larvæ phytophagous, living on rotten wood, fungi, or the roots of plants; those of a few species live in water.

The Crane Flies, or Daddy Longlegs, are familiar to every one. They are a very extensive family, and it is impossible to do more here than allude to a few of the most interesting species. The largest and most important belong to the typical genus *Tipula*, Linn., and *T. Oleracea*, Linn., a grey species with transparent brown-veined wings, and about an inch long, is common in every field, and frequently very destructive, the larva destroying the roots of grass. A larger species, *T. Gigantea*, Schrank, has a broad brown indented band on the costa. It is not rare, though much less common than *T. Oleracea*, and is generally found in the neighbourhood of woods. The giant of the genus, and probably the largest of all known *Diptera*, is *Tipula Brobdignagia*, Westw., from North China, which measures an inch and two-thirds in length, and four inches across the wings; but there is nothing remarkable about it but its size. A much more interesting species

is *Eriocera Lunata*, Westw., from Borneo. The brown wings
expand nearly an inch, and in the middle stands a large white
crescent, and there are several smaller white spots, especially
towards the hind margin of the wings. But the most singular
feature of this insect is its antennæ, which, although only five-
jointed, bear about the same proportion to the size of the insect
as in the genus *Adela* among the small moths, being fully an inch
and a half in length.

Several of our smaller *Tipulidæ* are winter insects. On most
fine sunny days, even when the snow is on the ground, we may
see the little Winter Gnat (*Trichocera Hiemalis*, Meig.) dancing in
swarms in sheltered places, although no other insect may be
visible. It is a brownish-grey, transparent-winged insect, and
measures about a quarter of an inch in length. Many other
species of this family dance in swarms in a similar manner.

Chionea Araneoides, Dalm., is a yellowish-brown, wingless,
spider-like insect, measuring less than a quarter of an inch in
length, which is sometimes common on the surface of frozen snow;
the larva lives in damp earth. Its systematic position is somewhat uncertain, and some authors regard it as an aberrant form of
Bibionidæ.

FAMILY XII.—*Dixidæ*.

Head rounded; proboscis rather prominent; antennæ long,
twelve-jointed (?); basal joint very thick, the flagellum slender
and hair-like; eyes round, distant; ocelli wanting; abdomen long
and slender, clavate behind in the male and pointed in the
female; wings rather large; legs long and slender; larva aquatic.

The species of *Dixa*, Meig., are small reddish-yellow or blackish
gnats, measuring about one-sixth of an inch in length. The wings
are generally transparent, but in some species are more or less
spotted with brown. These gnats frequent damp places in woods,
and are occasionally seen dancing in swarms before sunset.

FAMILY XIII.—*Rhyphidæ*.

Head round; proboscis rather prominent; antennæ sixteen-
jointed, about as long as the thorax; eyes large, oval; ocelli
present; abdomen cylindrical; legs slender, moderately long; wings
rather large and broad; larvæ feeding on rotten vegetable matter.

The species of *Rhyphus*, Latr., are grey or yellowish-brown
flies, about a quarter of an inch in length, which may be found

resting on leaves in damp shady places; but they may also be seen on windows, or dancing in the air.

DIPTERA BRACHYCERA.

Antennæ short; usually three-jointed (the last joint sometimes subdivided), generally with a terminal bristle (or seta); palpi with only one or two joints.

FAMILY XIV.—*Xylophagidæ.*

Head short, as broad as the thorax; antennæ with the third joint angulated; terminal bristle wanting; eyes naked, more or less widely separated; ocelli present; legs slender, naked; tibiæ with terminal spines; scutellum unarmed.

The *Xylophagidæ* are rather slender flies, from a quarter to half an inch in length. They are generally black, with the legs, scutellum, tip of the abdomen, and sometimes other marks on the latter, more or less yellow or reddish. The larvæ live in rotten wood, and the flies are often to be seen resting on the trunks of trees.

FAMILY XV.—*Cœnomyiidæ.*

Head narrower than the thorax; eyes of the male contiguous in front; scutellum with two spines; other characters nearly as in the *Xylophagidæ.*

The typical European species of this family, *Cœnomyia Ferruginea*, Scop., is a large stout fly, three-quarters of an inch in length, varying from rusty yellow to black, with pale markings on the scutellum and abdomen. The larva feeds in rotten poplars; and the fly, which is not uncommon in South Europe, especially in sub-Alpine districts, is generally met with in the neighbourhood of water.

FAMILY XVI.—*Stratiomyiidæ.*

Head short, as broad as the thorax; antennæ with the third joint annulated, and usually furnished with a terminal bristle; ocelli present; thorax and scutellum spined or spineless; legs moderately long, slender, with neither bristles nor spines.

These are small or moderate-sized flies, and the larvæ live in rotten vegetable substances, or in the water, and assume the pupa state within the larval skin. The species of *Sargus*, Fabr., are of a bright metallic blue, green, or violet. They are rather slender, nearly half an inch in length, and are found resting on low plants. The females also frequent cow-dung, heaps of garden refuse, etc., in which the larvæ feed. Several other genera of this family exhibit a metallic coloration, while others are black, often more or less varied with white or yellow.

FAMILY XVII.—*Acanthomeridæ.*

Antennæ with the third joint long, conical, annulated, tapering at the extremity, but not provided with a bristle; eyes not contiguous; abdomen very broad and compressed, last three joints small, forming the oviduct; legs slender; intermediate tibiæ with two small apical spines; hind femora with one spine beneath in the male.

The genus *Acanthomera,* Wied., is met with throughout the warmer parts of America, from Mexico to Chili. The typical species, *A. Picta,* Wied., is found in Brazil, and measures rather more than an inch in length. The head is brown, and the thorax grey, with three darker bands; the scutellum is black, with whitish sides, and the abdomen is black, with two white spots on each side, both above and below.

FAMILY XVIII.—*Tabanidæ.*

Head short, quadrangular, as broad or broader than the thorax, more or less convex in front; antennæ approximating at the base, the third joint annulated; proboscis strong, and very prominent; eyes contiguous in the male, and separated in the female; ocelli absent or present; scutellum unarmed; abdomen rather long and broad, slightly depressed; legs moderately long and thick. The larvæ live in damp earth, and the males frequent flowers, while the females live on the blood of animals.

The Gad-Flies are moderate-sized or large flies, found in all parts of the world, and are often conspicuous and handsome insects. The habits of all the species are very similar, and they are exceedingly annoying to animals, and do not scruple to attack man himself, especially in bushy places, or near water. Their bites, though painful and annoying, are not usually dangerous; but it is believed in most parts of the Continent that they frequently convey the infection of a most dangerous cattle-disease, variously known as anthrax, splenetic apoplexy, or Siberian plague. This, however, is questioned by some recent authors.

Our largest British species is *Tabanus Bovinus,* Linn., which

P

measures nearly an inch in length. It is blackish above, and reddish beneath and on the sides of the abdomen. The species of *Chrysops*, Meig., are much smaller insects, about the size of a common house-fly. They are black, with yellow markings on the abdomen, and the wings are black in the males, and transparent, banded with black, in the female. They have beautiful golden-green eyes, varied with purplish dots and lines. But in spite of their beauty, these flies are among the most troublesome of the family, frequently settling on the hand, and making their presence known by a sharp puncture which draws blood immediately.

FAMILY XIX.—*Leptidæ.*

Head short, flattened in front, often narrower than the thorax; antennæ rather short, last joint rounded or conical, and furnished with a terminal bristle; eyes contiguous, or nearly so, in the male, and separated in the female; ocelli present; abdomen rather long and narrow, or broad at the base, and gradually narrowed; legs long and slender, without bristles; larvæ and perfect insects predatory, the former sometimes parasitic.

The species of this family are rather slender, of moderate size, and of dull colours, black, grey, or yellowish predominating. They are frequently found at rest on tree-trunks, on the look-out for prey. The larva of *Vermilio Degeerii*, Macq., lives in sand, and feeds on such insects as fall in its way; those of the genus *Leptis*, Fabr., are parasitic on cockchafers and other large beetles, and those of *Chrysopila*, Macq., and *Atherix*, Meig., live in water.

FAMILY XX.—*Asilidæ.*

Head short and broad; eyes prominent, separate; ocelli present; antennæ with third joint not annulated, with or without a terminal bristle; thorax narrowed in front into a slight neck; abdomen long; legs moderately long, stout, and often hairy and bristly; larvæ in damp earth; perfect insects predatory.

The *Asilidæ*, or Robber-Flies, are a family of considerable extent, and include many large and conspicuous insects. They feed on other insects, and are very courageous, sometimes attacking even dragonflies. One of our most conspicuous species is *Asilus Crabroniformis*, Linn., which I have taken on the cliffs between Brighton and Rottingdean. It measures nearly an inch in length, and has a long tapering yellow body, with the basal half of the abdomen black, and reddish legs; the long and rather narrow wings are deeply tinged with yellowish brown. The North American *Trupanea Apivora*, Fitch, feeds on honey-bees, of which it destroys great numbers; and it is known to American bee-keepers as the Bee-Killer.

FAMILY XXI.—*Midaidæ*.

Head broad and short, distinctly separated from the thorax; antennæ four- or five- jointed, with no terminal bristle, but more or less clubbed at the tip; ocelli indistinct; legs stout and strong, hind femora thickened and spiny below; larvæ parasitic; perfect insects predatory.

The *Midaidæ* are large insects, resembling the *Asilidæ* in their habits, and are nearly all tropical; a few species, however, inhabit Spain, Portugal, and Sicily. *Midas Lusitanicus*, Meig., which inhabits Spain and Portugal, is black, with white hairs on the face, and on the sides of the thorax; the second segment of the abdomen is orange, and the hinder segments are bordered behind with yellowish white; the wings are also yellowish. It measures two-thirds of an inch in length. Among the foreign species we may mention *M. Clavatus*, Drury, from North America, which is also black, with the second segment of the abdomen deep yellow above, and coppery-brown wings. This species is an inch and a quarter long; but the Brazilian *M. Giganteus*, Wied., far surpasses it, both in size and beauty, and often measures more than an inch and a half in length. It is black, with a whitish tuft on the face, and the abdomen, except the first segment, is blue, with green shades; the wings are black.

FAMILY XXII.—*Nemestrinidæ*.

Head not broader than the thorax; ocelli present; antennæ distant at the base, not annulated, with a terminal spine; legs moderately long.

The species of this small family chiefly inhabit the warmer parts of the world. They are generally of a black colour, sometimes with red legs, or with paler hairs on the sides or at the base of the abdomen. They measure about half an inch in length. They suck the nectar of flowers through a long proboscis, but nothing is yet known of their transformations.

Family XXIII.—*Bombyliidæ.*

Head rounded, closely appressed to the thorax; abdomen clothed with woolly hairs; antennæ with the third joint not annulated, and generally provided with a bristle or tuft at the extremity; ocelli present; proboscis generally very prominent· legs rather long and slender.

The Bee-Flies are small or middle-sized, densely hairy, and very active insects, with long tongues, with which they suck honey from flowers; but the larvæ, like many other *Diptera*, are parasitic on the earlier stages of other insects, like *Ichneumons*. Many are known to attack the larvæ and pupæ of *Lepidoptera* and *Hymenoptera*, while several species which inhabit Cyprus and North America make themselves very useful by diminishing the numbers of the locusts, in the egg-capsules of which their larvæ feed.

Family XXIV.—*Therevidæ.*

Head semicircular, nearly as broad as the thorax; antennæ with a very short terminal bristle; eyes contiguous in the male and separated in the female; abdomen generally long and pointed; larvæ in fungi and rotten wood.

The species of the typical genus *Thereva*, Latr., are rather numerous. They are slender middle-sized black species, with the incisions of the abdomen white or yellow, and are often densely clothed with black, yellow, or white hair; they are generally found about trees or bushes.

Family XXV.—*Scenopinidæ.*

Head semicircular; antennæ with the third joint rather long, with no terminal bristle; eyes generally contiguous in the male, and separated in the female; ocelli present; thorax somewhat convex; abdomen flattened; legs short, unarmed; larvæ in fungi or trees.

This family includes a few small black flies, not exceeding a quarter of an inch in length. They are not very common, but are sometimes found on windows.

Family XXVI.—*Acroceridæ.*

Head small and round; antennæ two- or three- jointed, with a bristle at the extremity, and placed on different parts of the head in different genera; eyes contiguous in both sexes, occupying a great part of the head; two or three ocelli also are generally present; abdomen large, convex; legs rather thick, and without spines; metamorphoses unknown.

Little more need be said of the present family. Schiner speaks of the species as resting lazily on dry branches of trees, or flying around some particular point, but as usually rare. They are best recognised by the very small head.

FAMILY XXVII.—*Empidæ.*

Head round, rather small; antennæ with the two first joints very small, hardly distinct, the third not annulated, but generally with a terminal tuft; eyes generally contiguous in the male, and separated in the female; ocelli present; legs of various structure. Flies rapacious; larvæ living in mould.

The *Empidæ* are not unlike the *Asilidæ* in their carnivorous propensities, but the species are to be met with among bushes and resting on flowers, and, being much smaller, they are forced to content themselves with smaller insects than the *Asilidæ* will sometimes attack. Several genera are found near water. As in most *Diptera*, the females are much more bloodthirsty than the males, and Macquart, writing of *Empis Livida*, Linn., a common yellowish species about one-third of an inch in length, observes: "Among the thousands of pairs which I have noticed resting on bushes or hedges, nearly all the females were engaged in sucking some insect, sometimes small *Phryganidæ* or *Ephemeridæ*, but more often *Tipulidæ*. They busy themselves with feeding and perpetuating their species at the same time."

FAMILY XXVIII.—*Dolichopodidæ.*

Head semicircular, about as broad as the thorax; antennæ close together, sometimes almost jammed between the eyes in the male, which are approximate, but rarely contiguous; antennæ with the third joint not angulated, with a bristle at the tip or above; abdomen laterally compressed, and cylindrical, or elliptical and flattened; legs slender, bristly; hind legs long; larvæ in damp earth; flies often predaceous.

The *Dolichopodidæ* are small flies, often of brilliant colours, metallic green being the prevailing tint. Many of them frequent the neighbourhood of water, and are often found resting on water-plants, while others prefer fields and woods; the majority are very rapid in their movements. The family is extensive, including a considerable number of genera and species.

FAMILY XXIX.—*Lonchopteridæ.*

Head egg-shaped, as broad as the thorax; first two joints of the antennæ very small, setaceous, the third rounded, finely pubescent, with a slender terminal bristle; eyes prominent, green in life; ocelli present; abdomen long, narrow, and compressed; legs long, with slender spines. Metamorphoses unknown.

The species of *Lonchoptera*, Meig., are small, yellow, brown, or greenish flies, with lanceolate wings, which frequent the banks of shady streams, and are often found resting on the wet stones.

FAMILY XXX.—*Syrphidæ.*

Head semicircular, as broad as the thorax; antennæ close together at the base, third joint variously formed, but generally somewhat compressed, with a tuft on the back; eyes rather large, generally contiguous in the males; ocelli present; legs and abdomen various in structure; habits, both of larvæ and perfect insects, very various.

The *Syrphidæ* are moderate-sized flies, often of brilliant colours, many being very common. Except the enormous family of the *Muscidæ*, the present is one of the largest families of the *Diptera Brachycera*. Many of the species may be recognised at once as belonging to the *Syrphidæ* by their mode of flight alone, for they hover motionless in the air, and, if alarmed, dart off with a rapid motion that the eye cannot follow, and hover again as soon as they stay their course. It is no easy matter to capture the larger species on the wing.

The species of *Syrphus*, Fabr., are black or metallic green species, with a rather long abdomen, marked with yellow bands, often interrupted in the middle; the larvæ feed on *Aphidæ*. The flies are about half an inch long, and are common in gardens.

Several of the largest and handsomest species of European *Syrphidæ* belong to the genus *Volucella*, Geoffr. They are sometimes found on leaves and flowers, and at other times may be seen suspended in the air in the glades of woods. The flies themselves are more robust, and usually more hairy than the species of *Syrphus*, though some few, like the latter, are nearly naked. The larvæ are parasitic in the nests of wasps and humble-bees. The flies vary considerably in colour; some are yellow, with black bands and markings, or *vice versâ*, and *V. Pellucens*, Panz., is black, with a dull white band at the base of the abdomen.

The species of *Eristalis*, Latr., much resemble the *Volucellæ*, but are more slender, and the abdomen is rather longer and more pointed. The flies are black, or metallic green, or reddish, and often varied with whitish hairs; the wings in some species are marked with a brown cloud. The larvæ live on rotting animal or vegetable matter, and frequently live in stagnant water. They are often met with in drains, cesspools, and in similar situations, and are remarkable for having a very long appendage at the end of the body resembling a rat's tail.

Milesia Crabroniformis, Fabr., is a large species, common in Southern Europe, with a black head and thorax, a yellow spot on each shoulder, and a long yellow abdomen banded with black. It sometimes measures nearly an inch in length; its transformations are unknown.

FAMILY XXXI.—*Conopidæ.*

Head large, always broader than the thorax; antennæ long, third joint clubbed, and ending in a bristle; eyes not contiguous; ocelli present or absent; abdomen cylindrical, more or less contracted at the base, and expanded behind; legs moderately long and thick; larvæ parasitic on *Orthoptera* and *Hymenoptera*.

The species of *Conops*, Linn., are black slender flies, nearly half an inch long. They are marked with yellow spots and bands, and have some resemblance to wasps. *Myopa*, Fabr., is typical of another section of the family; they are reddish-brown species about a quarter or half an inch in length, with a broad depressed abdomen.

FAMILY XXXII.—*Pipunculidæ.*

Head large, round, broader than the thorax; antennæ short, third joint egg-shaped, with a bristle inserted near its base; eyes large, not quite contiguous in the males; ocelli present; abdomen narrow, round, or slightly compressed; legs with a few short spines; larvæ parasitic on other insects.

The species of the typical genus *Pipunculus*, Latr., are black or dark-brown insects, which swarm in shady places near hedges, sometimes resting on leaves, but never on flowers.

FAMILY XXXIII.—*Platypezidæ.*

Head round, as broad, or broader, than the thorax; antennæ with a terminal bristle; eyes contiguous, at least in the male; ocelli present; abdomen and legs short, the latter stout; the larvæ inhabit fungi.

The *Platypezidæ* frequent shady places under hedges or near water. One genus, *Callomyia*, Meig., includes very beautiful species, which, however, are not very abundant. They are black flies, about one-sixth of an inch in length, and the females are marked with silvery-white and orange-yellow.

FAMILY XXXIV.—*Œstridæ.*

Head large and prominent, about as broad as the thorax; antennæ short, third joint with a terminal bristle; eyes rather small, not contiguous; ocelli present; abdomen short; legs long; larvæ parasitic on various species of Mammalia.

The Bot-Flies are not remarkable in their perfect state, but are interesting from the habits of the larvæ. The principal European genera are as follows: *Gastrophilus*, Leach (larvæ in the stomach of the horse); *Œstrus*, Linn. (larvæ in the frontal sinus of sheep, buffaloes, etc.); *Pharyngomyia*, Schin., and *Cephenomyia*, Latr. (larvæ inhabiting the nasal and pharyngeal cavities of deer); *Hypoderma*, Clark (larvæ in swellings called "bots" on the skin of oxen, etc.); and *Œstromyia*, Brauer (larvæ supposed to be parasitic on the chamois).

Œstridæ do not always confine their attacks to the same species or even the same groups of animals, and in tropical countries man himself is sometimes attacked by them, though the worst Dipterous parasites on man are *Muscidæ* of the genus *Sarcophila*. It has occasionally happened, however, even in Europe, that men have been attacked by one or other of the indigenous species of *Œstrus*; but such cases are extremely rare. Even the smallest animals are liable to be infested by them. At a recent meeting of the Entomological Society, Mr. C. O. Waterhouse exhibited the larva of an *Œstrus* which measured nearly an inch and a half in length, and was found in the body of a common mouse from Peru, of which it occupied almost the whole of one side. He also stated that several other mammals received in the same collection from Peru were found to be similarly affected.[1]

[1] *Proceedings of the Entomological Society of London,* 1881, pp. xxii and xxiii.

FAMILY XXXV.—*Muscidæ*.

Antennæ with the third joint more or less oval, always compressed and provided with a terminal bristle; proboscis ending in a double fleshy lobe; abdomen nearly always soft, very rarely horny.

The *Muscidæ* form the most typical and by far the largest family of the *Diptera*, and nearly half the known species will fall under this heading. It may be divided into numerous subordinate groups, which some authors regard as distinct families, while others treat them only as sub-families, dividing the *Muscidæ* into two main sections, called *Muscidæ Calypteræ*, and *Muscidæ Acalypteræ*. In the former, the alulæ are more or less well developed, and in the latter they are rudimentary or absent. We will now proceed to consider some of the most important sub-families, genera, and species of the *Muscidæ*.

MUSCIDÆ CALYPTERÆ.

SUB-FAMILY I.—*Tachininæ*.

Antennal bristle almost naked, or clothed with very short and fine hairs; forehead generally broad; eyes straight, naked, or hairy. Abdomen more or less oval, and set with long bristles, especially on the hinder segments.

The larvæ of this sub-family, like those of most of the *Calypteræ*, are parasitic on the larvæ and pupæ of *Lepidoptera*, in the same manner as the larvæ of the *Ichneumonidæ*. The largest of the *Muscidæ* found in Central Europe is *Echinomyria Grossa*, Linn., a black and very bristly fly, with a very broad abdomen. It measures about three-quarters of an inch in length. It is sometimes found resting on dandelions in clearings in woods, and has been bred from *Lasiocampa Trifolii*.

SUB-FAMILY II.—*Dexinæ*.

Antennal bristle pectinated; forehead broad in both sexes; eyes straight, naked; abdomen with long bristles on at least the two last segments.

Our European species are not specially remarkable, but this sub-family includes the Australian genus *Rutilia*, Desv., the species of which are half an inch in length, and of the most splendid metallic green or blue, the most brilliant of all the *Muscidæ*.

SUB-FAMILY III.—*Sarcophaginæ.*

Antennal bristle pectinated at the base, and naked at the tip; forehead broad.

The species of *Sarcophila*, Rond., are moderate-sized grey flies, which occur in many parts of the world, but are fortunately not often common. They attack man and beast, laying their eggs in or near the nose, mouth, ears, or other external apertures, and the larvæ burrow in the flesh, causing the most frightful injuries, which often prove fatal. This is especially the case with *S. Wohlfahrti*, Portch., found in South Russia. The larvæ of another insect or insects, probably belonging to the same genus, are sometimes exceedingly troublesome in Texas, where they are known as "screw-worms." The "screw-worms" are now stated to be the larvæ of *Lucilia Macellaria*, Fabr., a species of *Muscinæ;* but I cannot give fuller particulars, as no competent American entomologist has yet inquired into the subject scientifically.

The flies of the genus *Sarcophaga*, Meig., much resemble those of *Sarcophila*, but are much more abundant. One of the commonest and most conspicuous species is *Sarcophaga Carnaria*, Linn., a black fly with grey longitudinal stripes on the thorax, and the abdomen tesselated with white, grey, and dark brown. It measures about half an inch in length. The larva is said to be parasitic on earthworms.

SUB-FAMILY IV.—*Muscinæ.*

Antennal bristle pectinated to the tip; eyes often contiguous or nearly so in the males; straight, naked or hairy; abdomen without bristles, or very slightly bristly towards the tip.

The *Muscidæ* include the genus *Musca*, Linn., as restricted by modern authors, and are the most typical of all the *Diptera.* Several species are common in houses almost throughout the year.

Stomoxys Calcitrans, Linn., much resembles the common housefly, but has a more pointed proboscis, with which it is able to inflict a rather sharp puncture. It is grey, the thorax with three whitish stripes, and the abdomen yellowish brown, with three rather indistinct brown spots on the second and following segments. The larvæ probably live in dunghills, and the flies are common in houses, especially in rainy weather, as well as out of doors.

Closely allied to this species is the famous African Tsetse Fly (*Glossina Morsitans*, Westw.). It is a brown fly, rather larger than a house-fly, and the abdomen is marked with several yellow stripes. The bite is harmless to man and to wild animals, being scarcely more severe than that of a mosquito, but a very few bites are sufficient to kill an ox, horse, or dog; not immediately, but by inducing a peculiar and incurable disease within a very few days. Although some still dispute the assertion that the fly is the real cause of the death of cattle, yet the natives of the regions in which it is found, and nearly all travellers, are unanimous on the subject. Packard (writing in America) appears to have strangely misunderstood the accounts of this fly, for he speaks of its killing animals by its *painful* bite; whereas it is the poisonous nature of the bite which produces death, if African travellers are correct.

Mesembrina Meridiana, Linn., is a very conspicuous black fly with the base of the wings bright yellow. It measures about half an inch in length. The larvæ live in dunghills, on which the flies will sometimes settle; at other times they may be seen swarming round the trunk of a tree, and settling occasionally. They delight in broad daylight, and are seldom or never seen in houses.

Several blue and green flies belonging to the genera *Calliphora* and *Lucilia*, Desv., are produced from larvæ which feed on more or less putrid flesh. Such are the Blow-Fly or Blue-bottle (*Calliphora Vomitoria*, Linn., which frequently comes into our rooms in summer; and the smaller Green-bottle Fly (*Lucilia Cæsar*, Linn.), a brilliant golden-green fly, about the size of a common house-fly, which is often common about hedges, settling on the leaves. A French species resembling this (*L. Bufonivora*, Méncer.) is parasitic on toads, which its larvæ attack in the head, like those of the genus *Sarcophila*.

Musca Domestica, Linn., our common house-fly, is grey, with the abdomen more or less yellowish in the male, and darker in the female. It is very common in houses, especially in summer and autumn. The larvæ live in dunghills. Our house-flies have many enemies. They may often be observed with a small animal resembling a scorpion without the sting clinging to one of their legs. This is a species of the genus *Chelifer*, and is one of the *Arachnida;* but it is not certainly known whether it causes any injury to the fly, or whether it simply avails itself of the fly's wings to convey itself from place to place. It is very common, too, to find flies fixed to the glass of a window with a whitish film around them: this is a parasitic fungus (*Empusa Muscarum*) which has germinated in the body of the fly, and has finally caused its death.

SUB-FAMILY V.—*Anthomyiinæ.*

Antennal bristle naked or pectinated; forehead narrow in the males; eyes straight, naked, or hairy; abdominal bristles often absent.

A rather extensive family, much resembling the true *Muscidæ*, and generally including dull-coloured and inconspicuous species. Some species, not unlike the common house-fly, are common in houses, especially in spring; and others are annoying by flying round our heads out of doors, and trying to settle on our faces. Most of the species breed in dung, or in decaying vegetable matter; but the larvæ of several species of the great genus *Anthomyia* mine in the leaves of plants, like those of *Tineæ*, while others again are parasitic on other insects.

MUSCIDÆ ACALYPTERÆ.

SUB-FAMILY I.—*Scatophaginæ.*

Head of moderate size; forehead bristly; antennæ short, third joint rather long; abdomen rather short and broad, not thickened behind; wings very large and broad, extending far beyond the abdomen; legs of moderate length; male often clothed with woolly hair.

These flies frequent dunghills, etc., but will also feed on other insects. One of the commonest and most familiar species is the yellow downy dung-fly (*Scatophaga Stercoraria*, Linn.), several of which may be seen resting on almost any patch of freshly-dropped dung.

SUB-FAMILY II.—*Ortalinæ.*

Head semicircular, rather large, only the vertex bristly; forehead broad; antennæ short, third joint rather long; abdomen moderately long; ovipositor of the female somewhat projecting; wings large.

The *Ortalinæ* are flies of small or moderate size, often with banded wings, which are met with in woods and fields. Little is known of their transformations.

SUB-FAMILY III.—*Trypetinæ.*

Head semicircular, often hairy, but not bristly near the mouth; forehead broad, bristly; antennæ generally short; ovipositor always more or less prominent in the female; wings rather large; legs moderately long; tibiæ without terminal spines.

The species of the typical genus *Trypeta*, Meig., are yellowish-grey flies of small or moderate size, and often with banded or spotted wings. The flies are frequently gregarious, and are often met with in abundance resting on flowers and flowering shrubs.

The largest genus of this family is *Tephritis*, Latr., which may be known from any other by its reticulated wings, and by its scutellum being provided with two or four bristles. The species are of small or moderate size, and are usually of a yellowish or greyish colour. Their larvæ feed on a great variety of plants.

Some few species of this sub-family feed on fruits, and that of *Ceratitis Hispanica*, Brême, is very destructive to oranges in the south of Europe, etc.

SUB-FAMILY IV.—*Piophilinæ*.

Head round; borders of the mouth and vertex generally bristly; forehead broad; abdomen often petiolated and curved; wings large or small; legs sometimes bristly; tips of tibiæ generally unarmed.

The typical species of this sub-family is *Piophila Casei*, Linn., a black fly, about the size of a common house-fly, but more slender; it is not abundant in the perfect state, but may be reared in any quantity from the " jumpers " which abound in cheese or bacon after being left exposed for a short time, especially in summer.

SUB-FAMILY V.—*Diopsinæ*.

Head provided with two long horns, at the extremities of which the eyes are placed; antennæ inserted towards the tips of these horns; face, sides of thorax, and scutellum spiny.

The species of this family are not numerous, and are entirely exotic; they are chiefly remarkable for their very singular structure. They are met with in various parts of Africa and the East Indies, and are black or yellow, and the wings are generally more or less spotted with brown. One species (*Sphyrocephala Brevicornis*, Say) is met with in North America. They are insects of moderate size, rarely exceeding a quarter of an inch in length.

SUB-FAMILY VI.—*Chloropinæ*.

Head semicircular; mouth and vertex generally without bristles; forehead broad; abdomen oval; legs and wings short.

Most of the flies belonging to this sub-family are of small or very small size, and are black or yellow, more or less striped with the opposite colour; their wings also are often black or yellow. The two principal genera are *Chlorops*, Meig., and *Oscinis*, Latr., the larvæ of which live in the stems of various grasses, and are sometimes extremely injurious to corn.

SUB-FAMILY VII.—*Drosophilinæ*.

Head semicircular; eyes not prominent; forehead broad; mouth and vertex bristly; third joint of antennæ rather long; terminal bristle generally pectinated or pubescent; abdomen short and broad; wings long, and generally broad; legs short and stout; larvæ feeding on decaying vegetable matter.

These are small dull-coloured flies, the larvæ of which feed on fungi, rotten fruit, and similar substances. *Drosophila Cellaris*, Linn., is a reddish species, about the tenth of an inch in length; its larva is almost omnivorous, being often met with in stale beer and wine; and it has even been found in a pickle-jar, feeding on pickled cauliflower.[1]

SUB-FAMILY VIII.—*Agromyzinæ*.

Head semicircular; forehead broad; vertex and mouth generally bristly; antennæ short, third joint rounded; bristle naked or pubescent; abdomen oval, convex; wings longer than the abdomen; legs short.

An extensive family; but the majority of the species belong to the two genera *Agromyza* and *Phytomyza;* their larvæ mine in the leaves of plants like those of the *Tineæ*. One of the commonest species is *Phytomyza Ilicis*, Kalt., the larva of which forms large brown blotches on the leaves of the holly. The perfect insect is a very small black fly, scarcely one-twelfth of an inch in length.

FAMILY XXXVI.—*Phoridæ*.

Head small, compressed, not broader than the thorax; forehead broad in both sexes; eyes large; ocelli present; antennæ always placed close to the mouth, third joint rounded, with a naked or pubescent bristle at the tip or on the upper surface; abdomen short, broad in front, and narrowed behind; ovipositor of the female prominent; coxæ long; femora (especially the hind femora) widened and compressed; hind tibiæ often curved, and hind tarsi very long; wings large; larvæ feeding on dead or living

[1] *Proceedings of the Entomological Society of London*, 1877, p. xv.

snails and insects, or on decaying vegetable matter, such as fungi or potatoes.

These flies are of small or moderate size, and are generally of a black or rusty yellow colour. They are very active, and may be observed on plants, and less frequently on windows.

DIPTERA HOMALOPTERA.

The insects belonging to this section much resemble spiders by their hairy sprawling legs and general appearance. They are all parasitic, and are remarkable for the perfect insect producing its young singly, and that not in the egg state, as in most other insects, but either in the pupa state, or as a mature larva, ready to become a pupa immediately.

FAMILY XXXVII.—*Hippoboscidæ*.

Body horny and flattened; antennæ composed of one joint only, and furnished with a terminal bristle; eyes and ocelli large or small, or absent; abdomen often very broad; legs short and strong.

Several interesting insects are comprised in this family. The first is the Forest Fly (*Hippobosca Equina*, Linn.), a brown species, about one-third of an inch in length, which attacks the horse, and is exceedingly annoying to the animal, but more from the irritation it produces by creeping about under the belly than by the actual puncture which it inflicts to suck the blood. The deer and the camel are likewise subject to the attacks of similar parasites.

The species of *Ornithomyia*, Latr., infest birds, living beneath the feathers. They are of a yellowish or greenish colour, and are about half the size of *Hippobosca*.

The preceding species are all winged, but every one who has ever seen a sheep-shearing must have seen a brown wingless insect rather less than a quarter of an inch in length among the freshly-clipped wool. This is *Melophagus Ovinus*, Linn., and is generally, but improperly, called the sheep-tick in England. In this species the eyes are very small, and the ocelli are wanting.

The genus *Braula*, Nitsch, is considered by some writers to belong to this family, while others regard it as forming a family by itself. The only species (*B. Cæca*, Nitsch) is a very small, blind, and wingless reddish-brown insect, parasitic upon the hive-bee, and known as the bee-louse. It is not exactly pupivorous, but the larva assumes the pupa state very shortly after quitting the egg.

Family XXXVIII.—*Nycteribidæ.*

Head very small; antennæ very short, two-jointed; wings absent; legs very long.

The *Nycteribidæ* are all parasitic on bats; they are of a brown or yellowish colour, and the largest species do not exceed one-sixth of an inch in length.

They are much more spider-like in their appearance than the *Hippoboscidæ*. Kolenati states that they possess eyes and two ocelli; but Schiner was unable to detect them in two species which he examined; possibly they are present in some species and absent in others.

PLATES.

THE figures of some species are more or less enlarged. These are shown by an asterisk affixed to their names in the explanation attached to each plate. In many cases the natural size is indicated by a line drawn against the figure of the insect itself. The pages referred to are those of the book on which some account of each insect (or at least of the genus or family to which it belongs) will be found. The species mentioned in the text are generally, but not always, the same as those figured on the plates.

PLATE I.

COLEOPTERA.

Cicindelidæ.

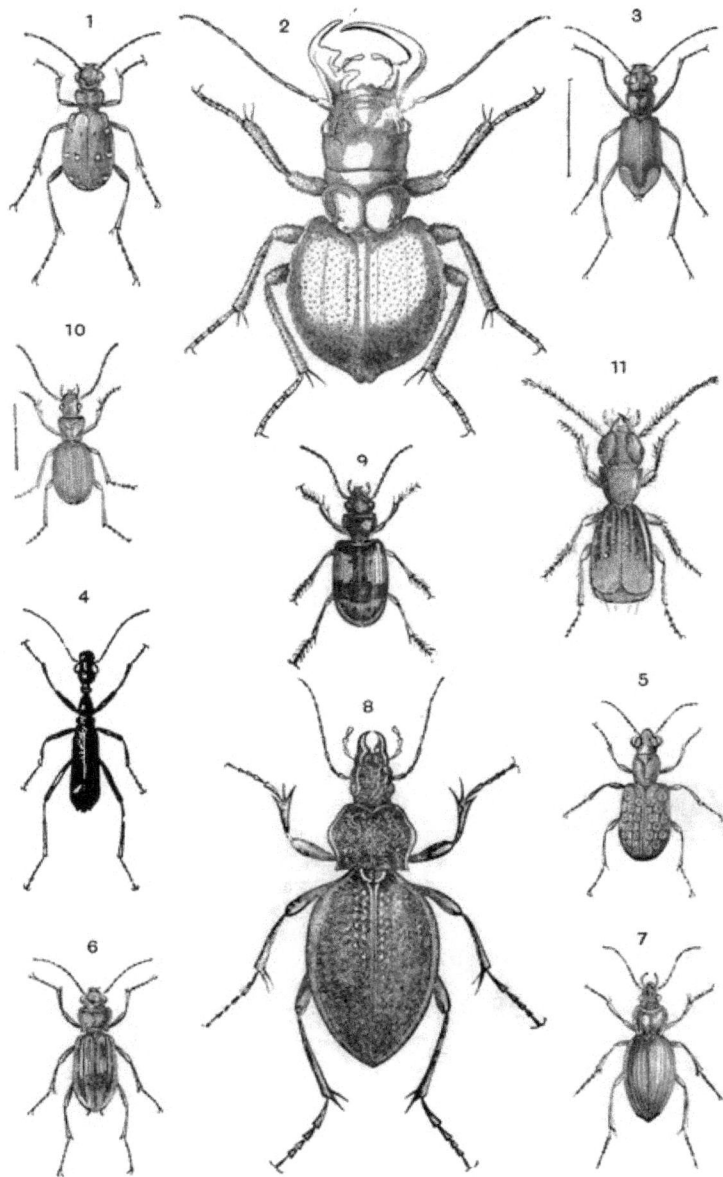

Plate I.

PLATE II.

COLEOPTERA.

Carabidæ.

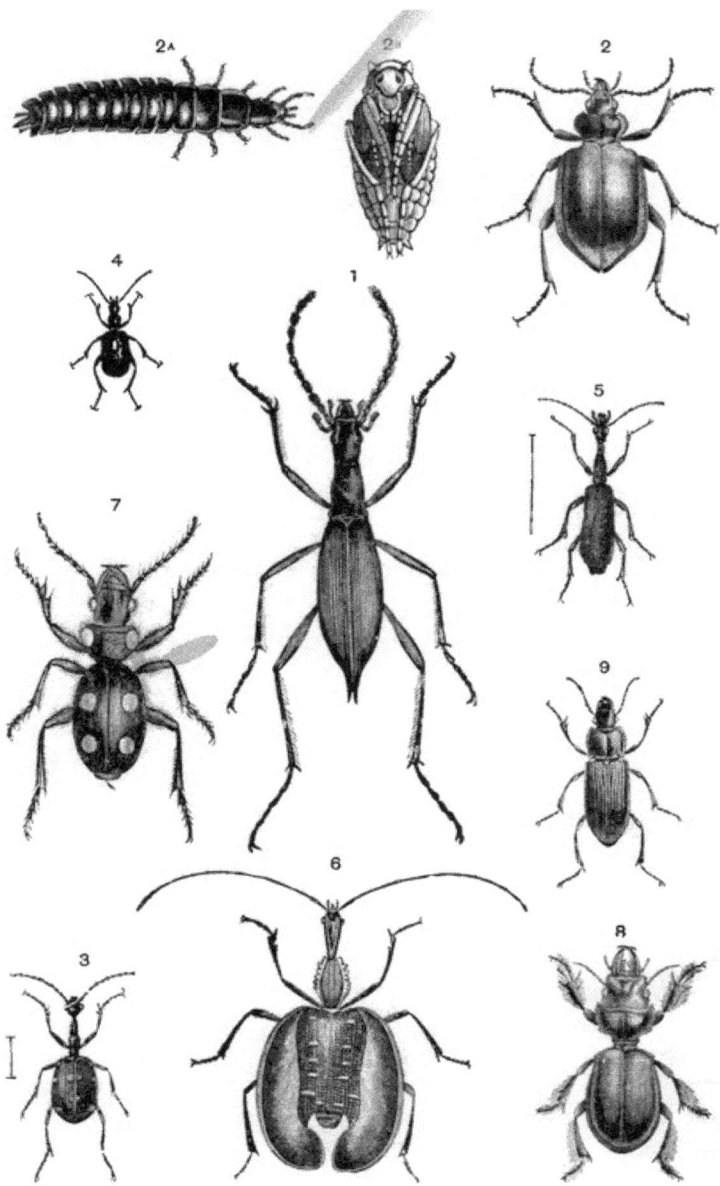

Plate 11.

PLATE III.

COLEOPTERA.

Dytiscidæ.

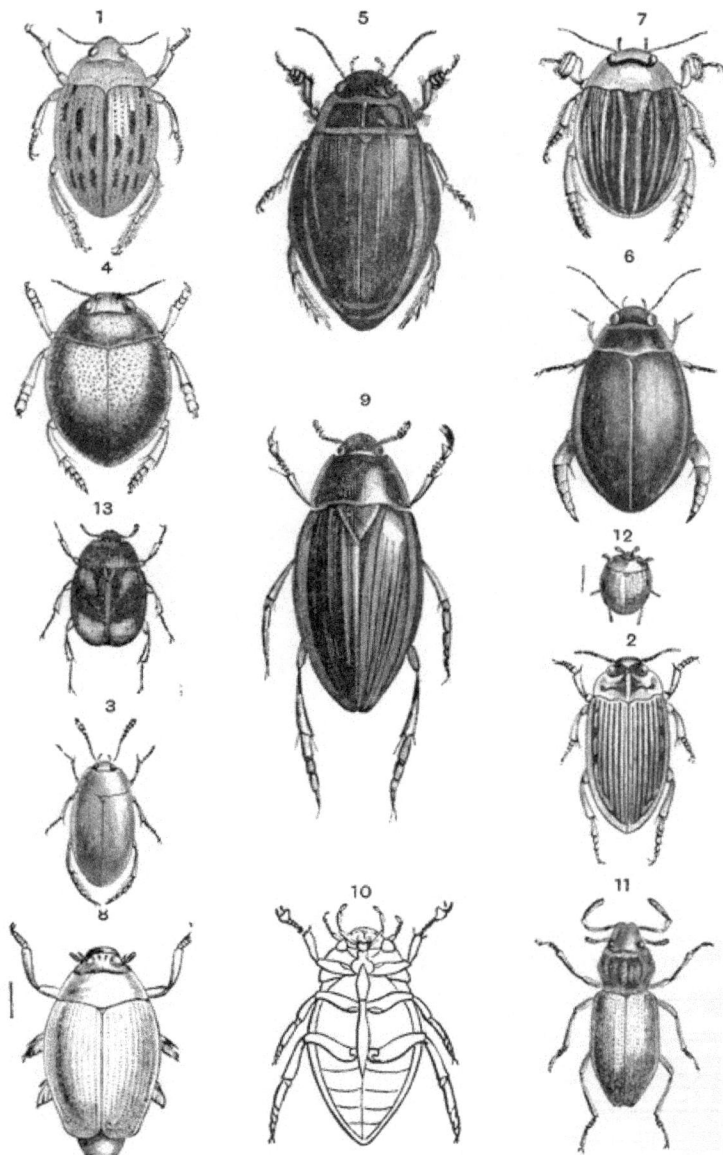

Plate III.

PLATE IV.

COLEOPTERA.

Staphylinidæ.

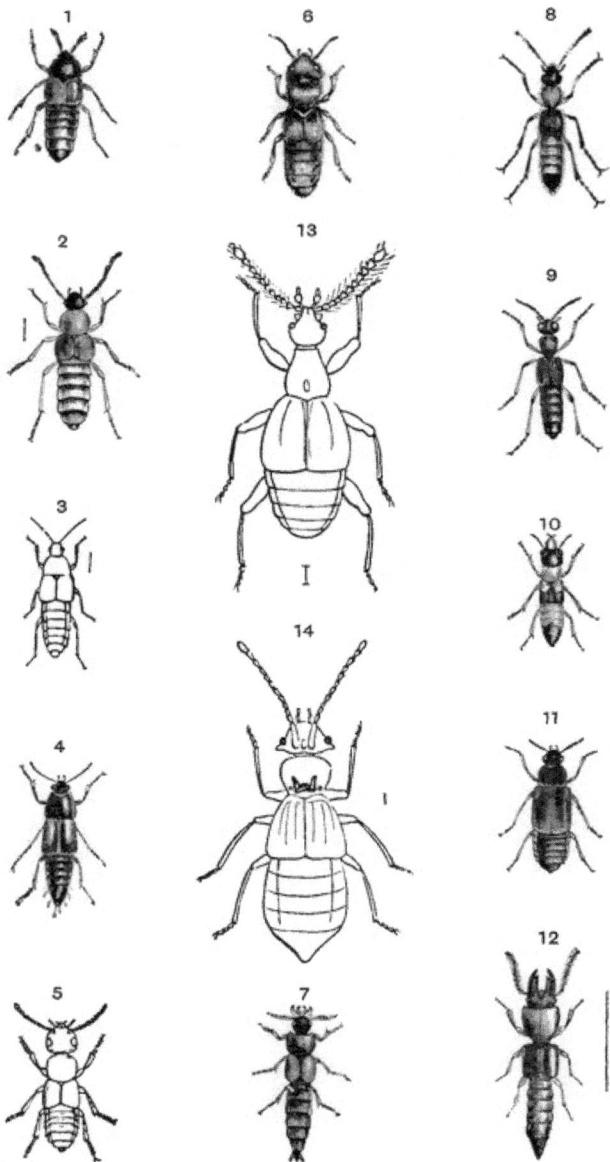

Plate IV.

PLATE V.

COLEOPTERA.

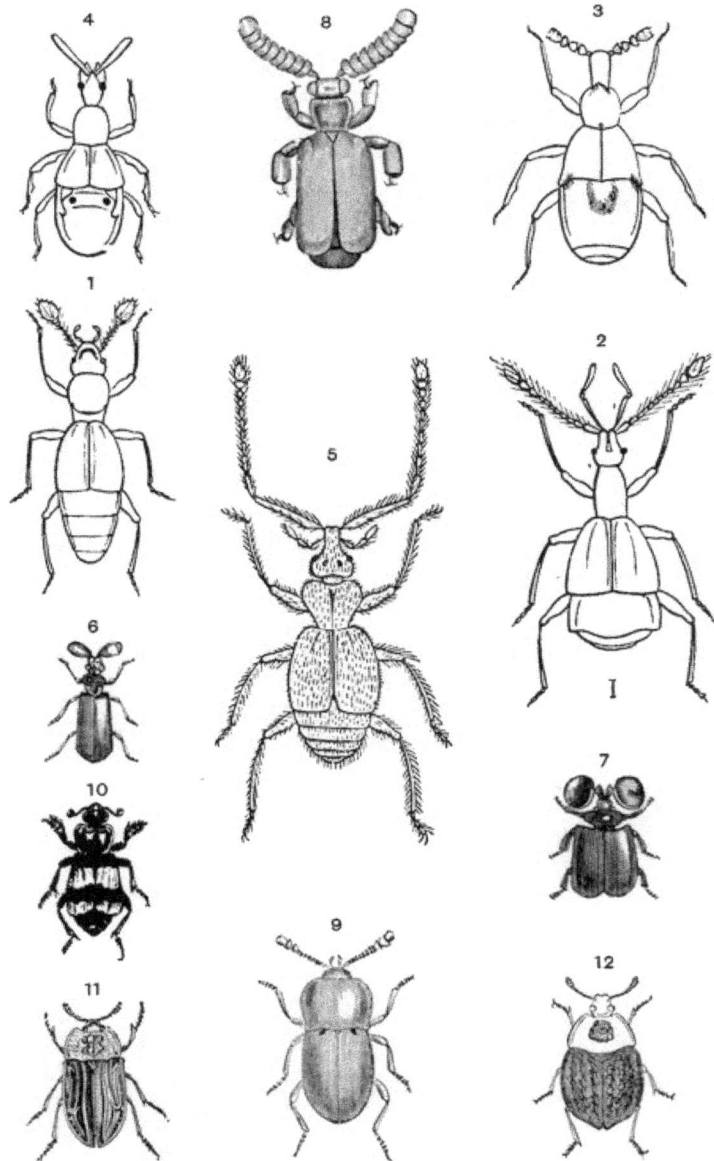

Plate V.

PLATE VI.

COLEOPTERA.

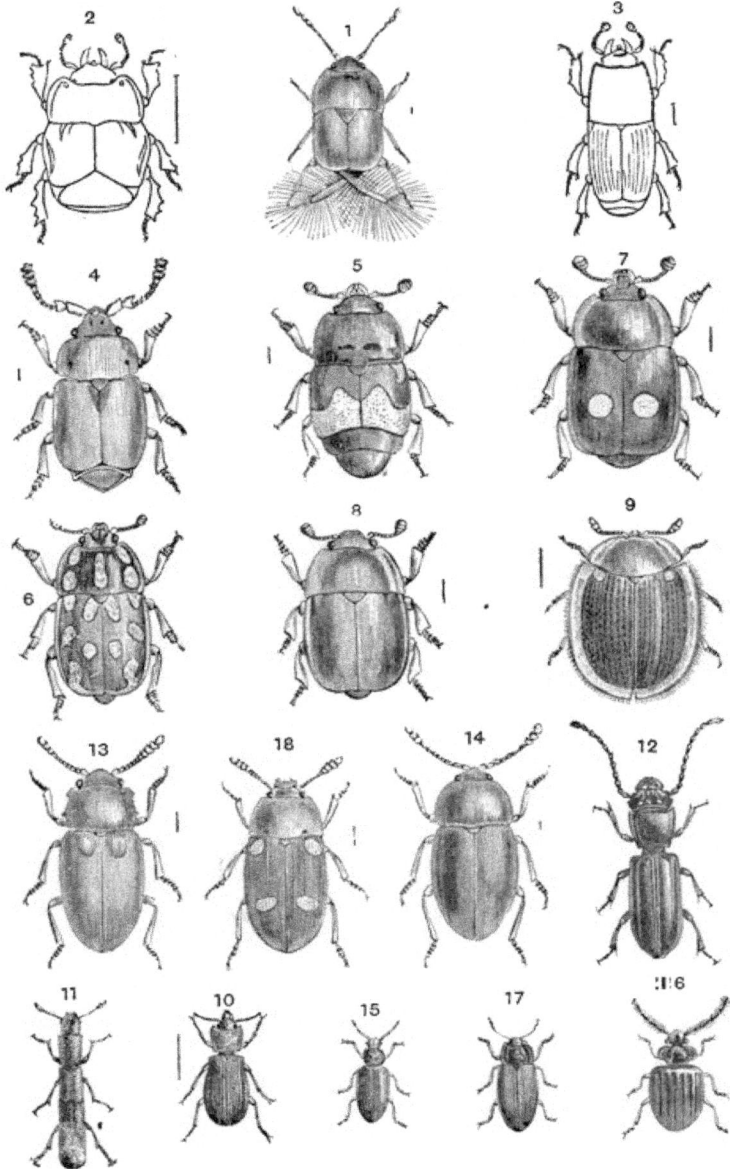

Plate VI.

PLATE VII.

COLEOPTERA.

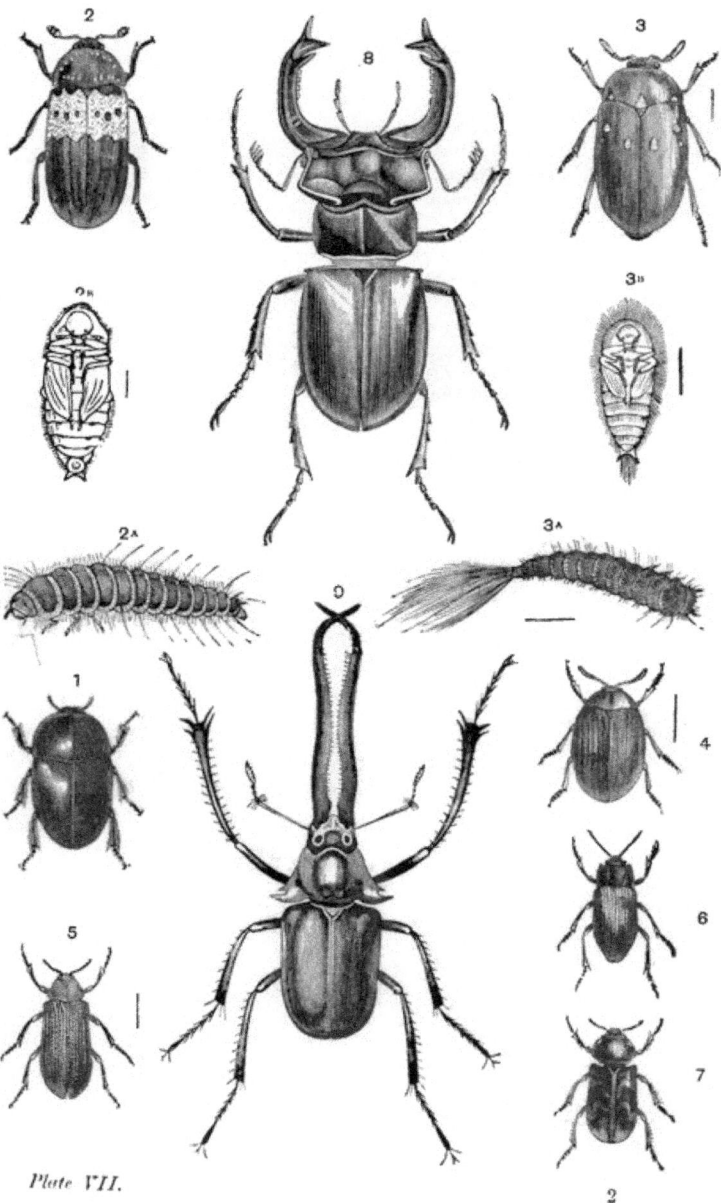

Plate VII.

PLATE VIII.

COLEOPTERA.

Lucanidæ.

Scarabæidæ.

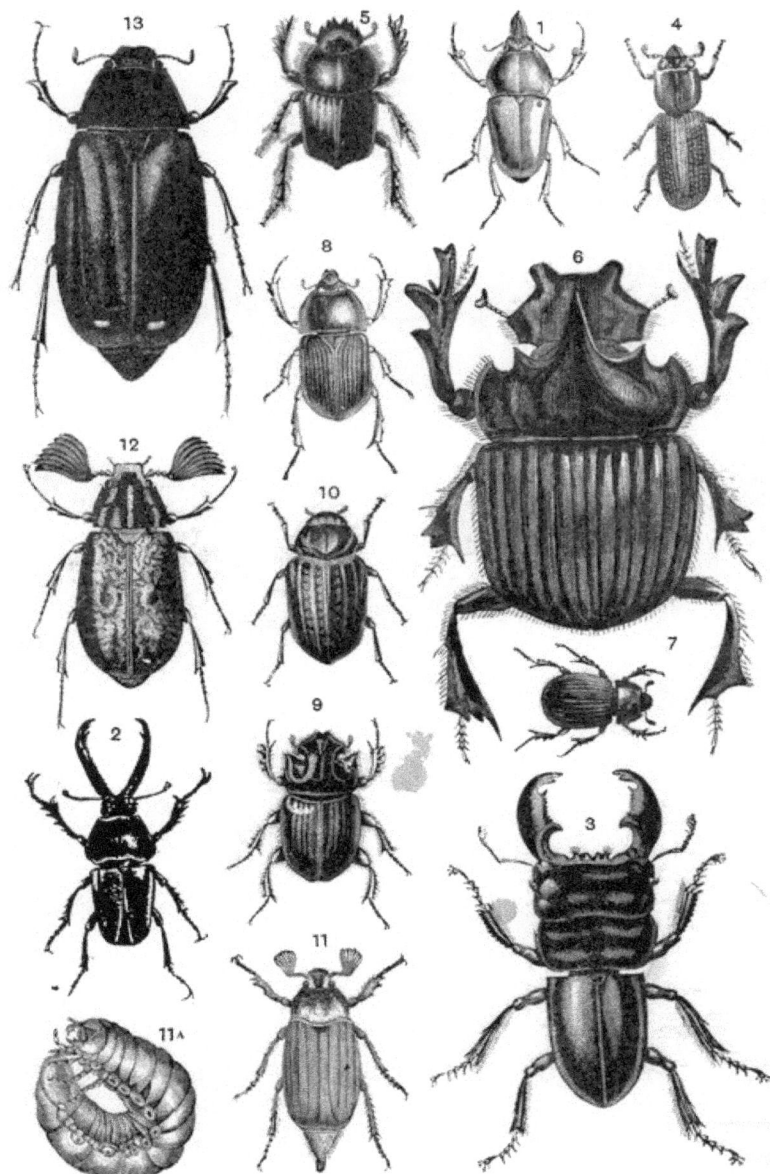

Plate VIII.

PLATE IX.

COLEOPTERA.

Scarabæidæ.

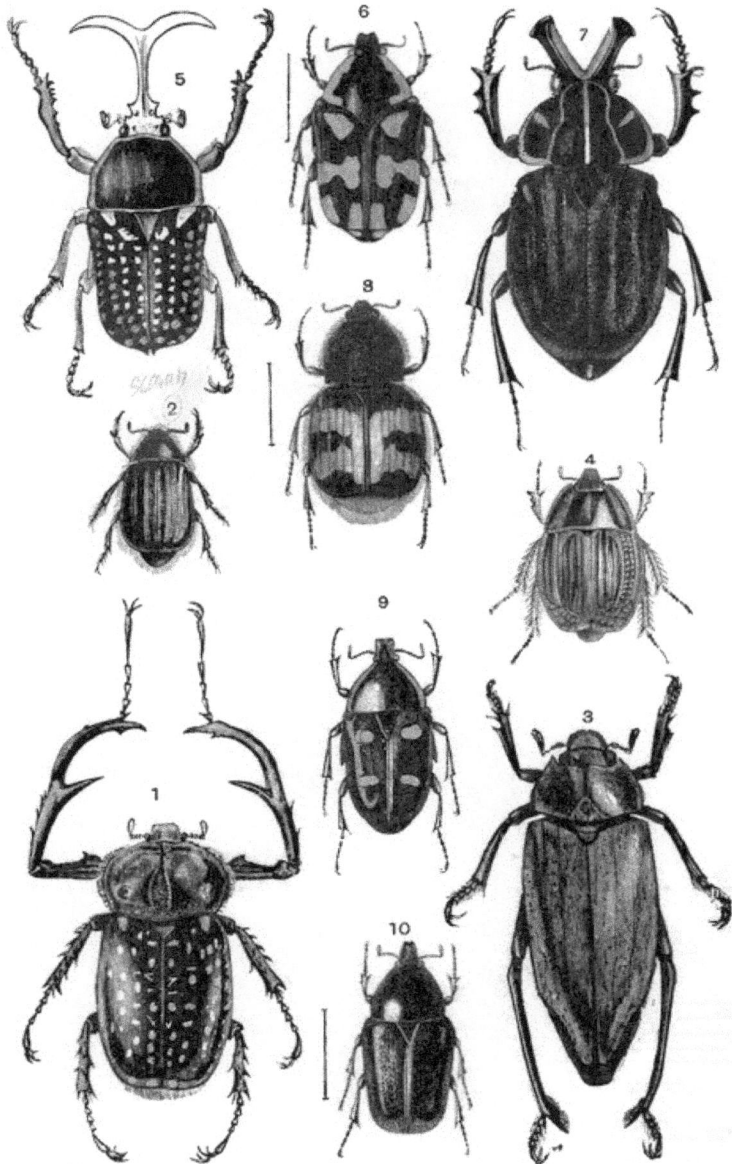

Plate IX.

PLATE X.

COLEOPTERA.

Buprestidæ.

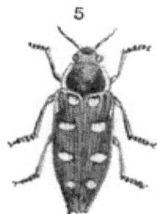

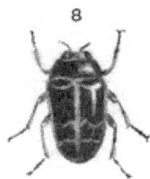

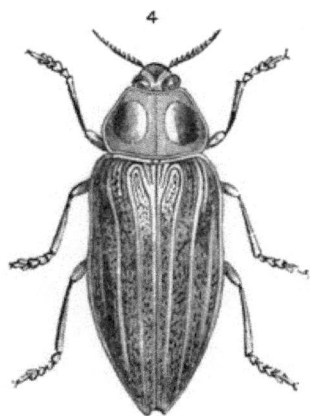

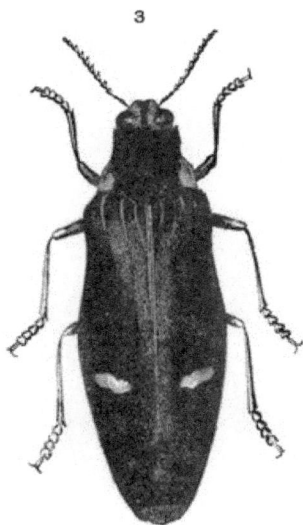

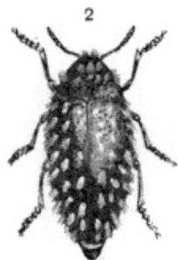

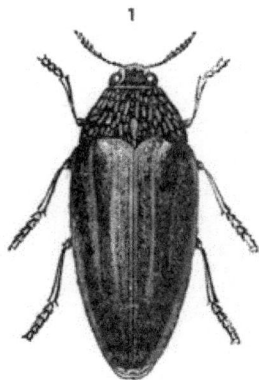

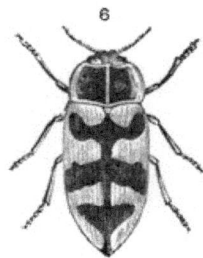

Plate X.

PLATE XI.

COLEOPTERA.

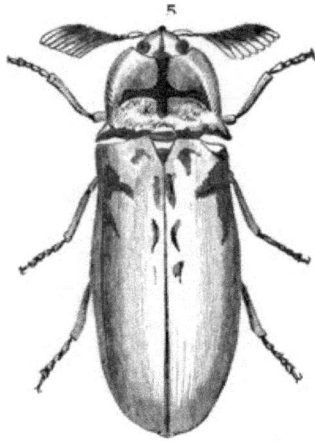

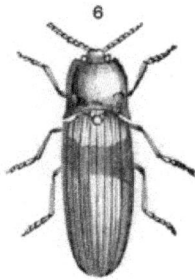

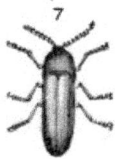

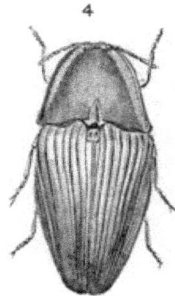

Plate XI.

PLATE XII.

COLEOPTERA.

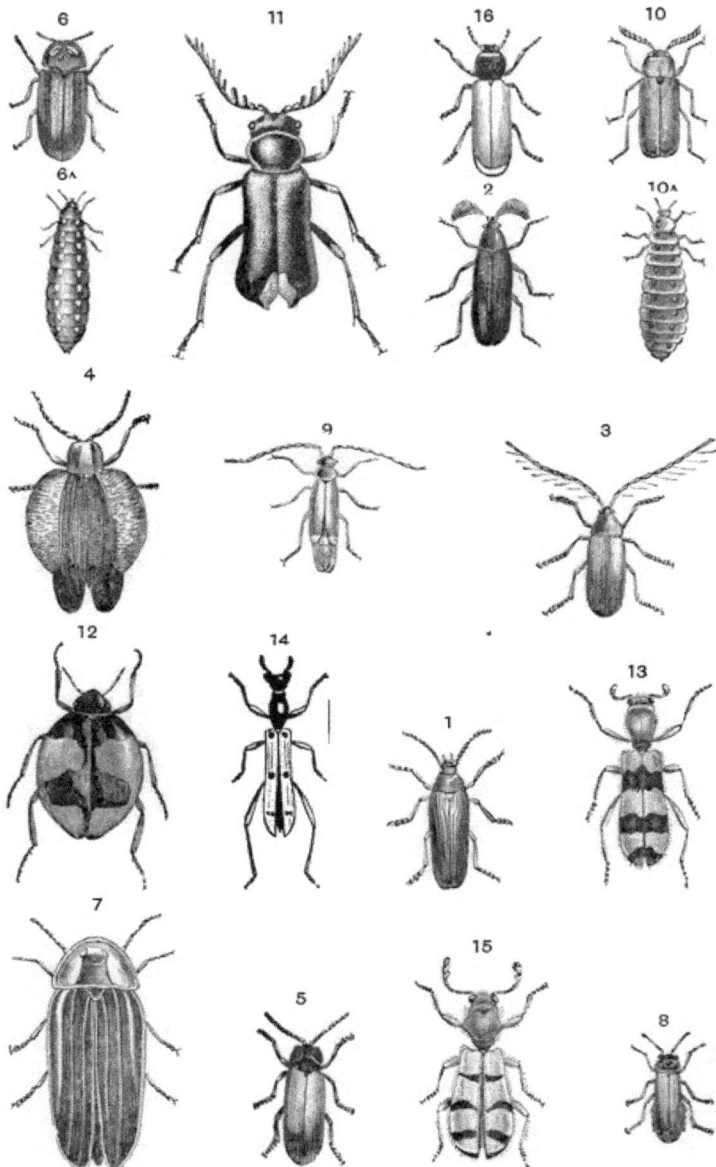

Plate XII

PLATE XIII.

COLEOPTERA.

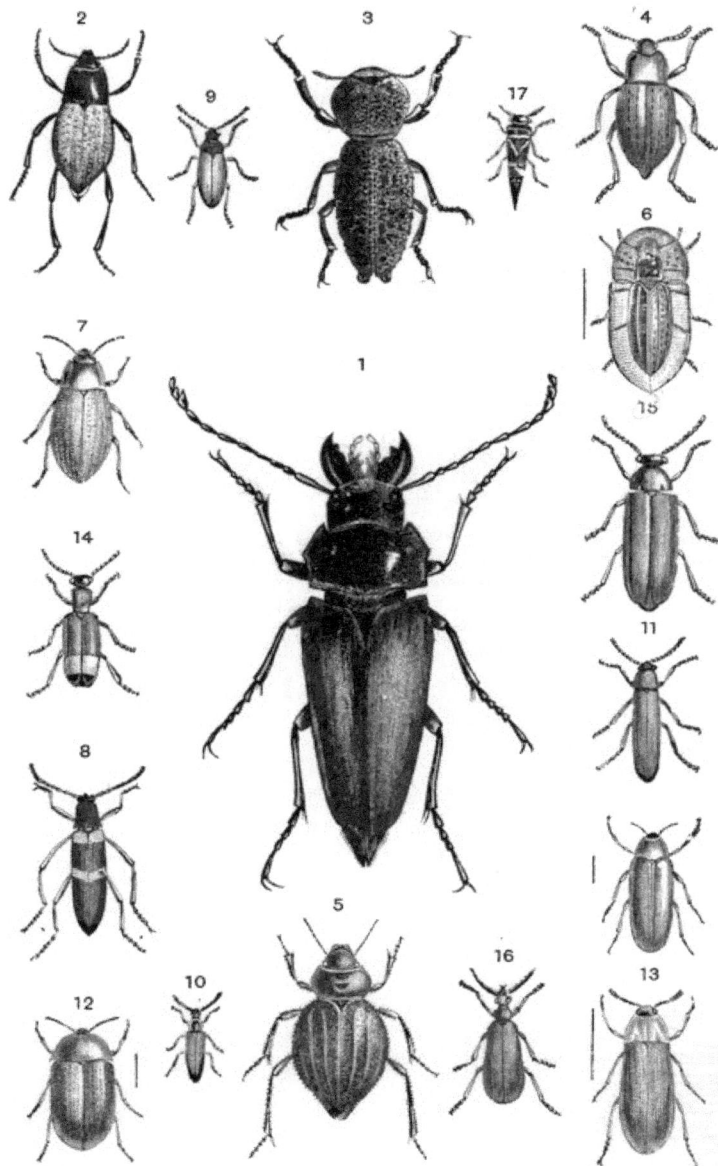

Plate XIII.

PLATE XIV.

COLEOPTERA.

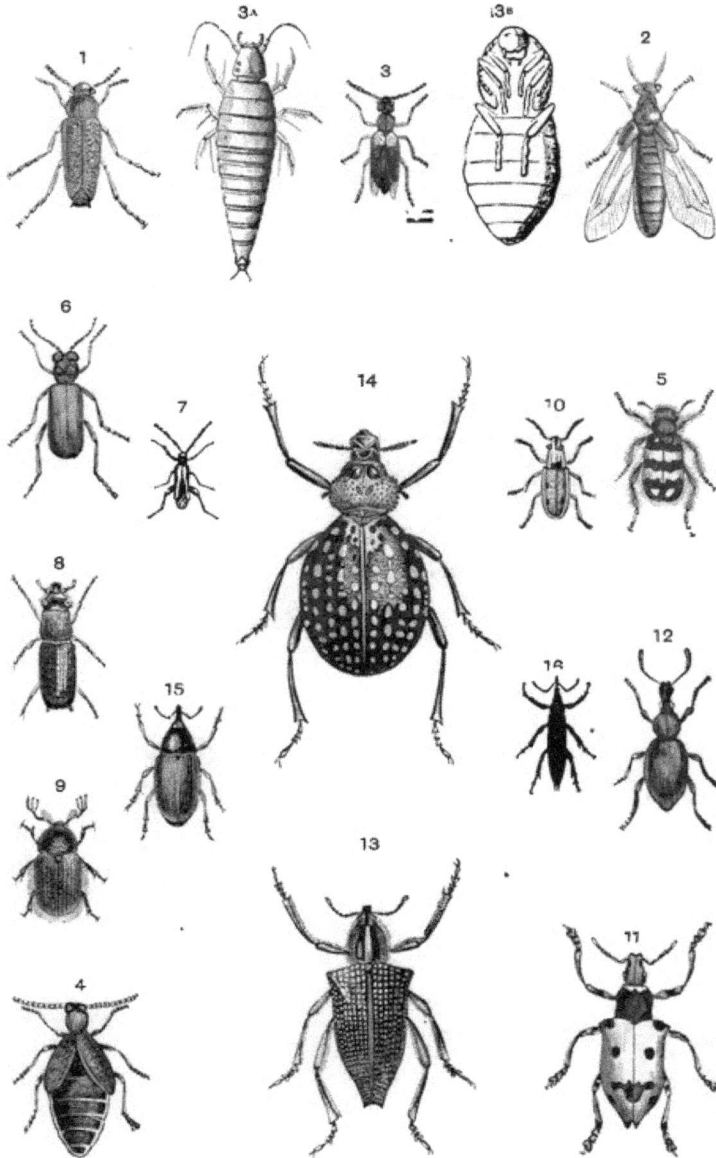

Plate XIV.

PLATE XV.

COLEOPTERA.

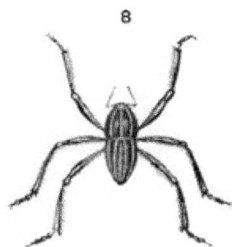

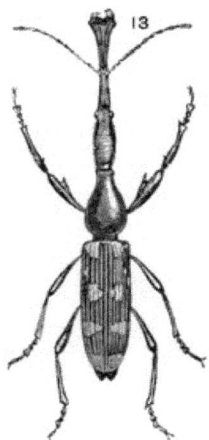

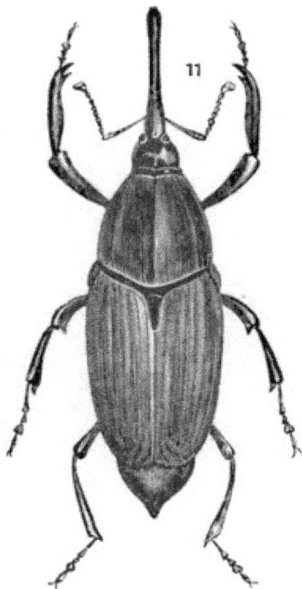

8

13

9

3

4

10

12

5

2

7

11

1

15

14

6

Plate XV.

3

PLATE XVI.

COLEOPTERA.

Prionidæ.

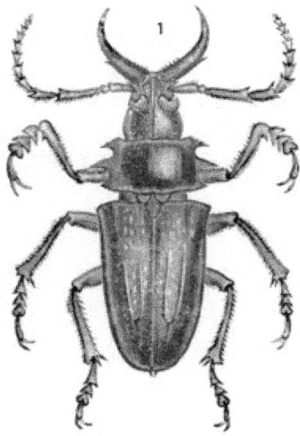

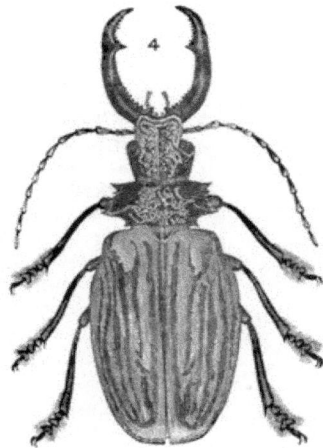

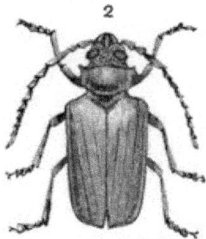

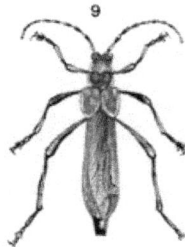

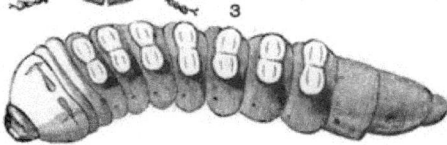

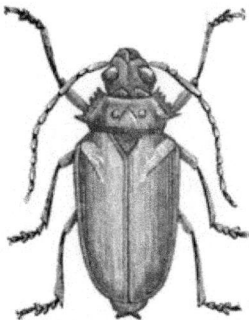

Plate XVI.

PLATE XVII.

COLEOPTERA.

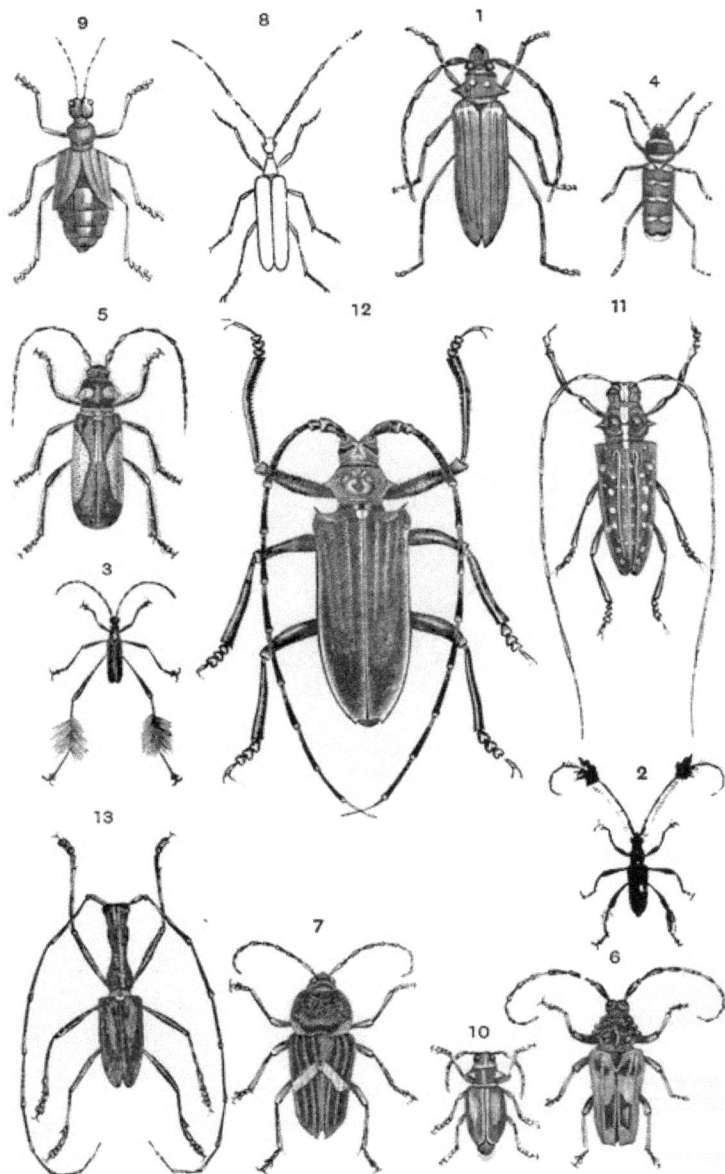

Plate XVII.

PLATE XVIII.

COLEOPTERA.

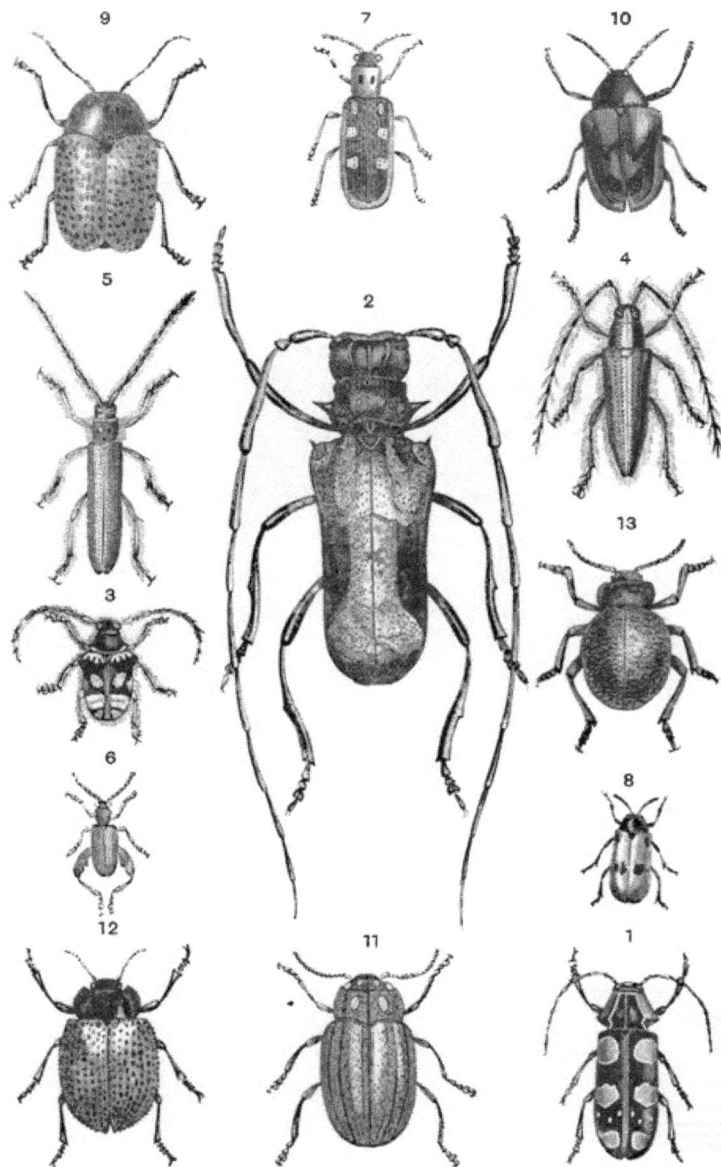

Plate XVIII.

PLATE XIX.

COLEOPTERA.

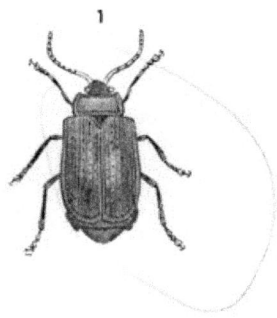

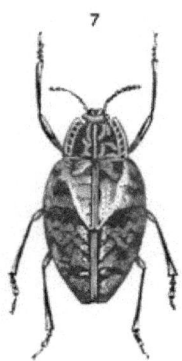

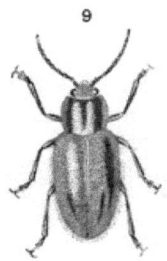

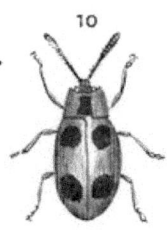

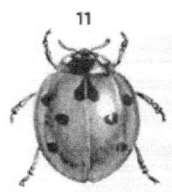

Plate XIX.

PLATE XX.

ORTHOPTERA.

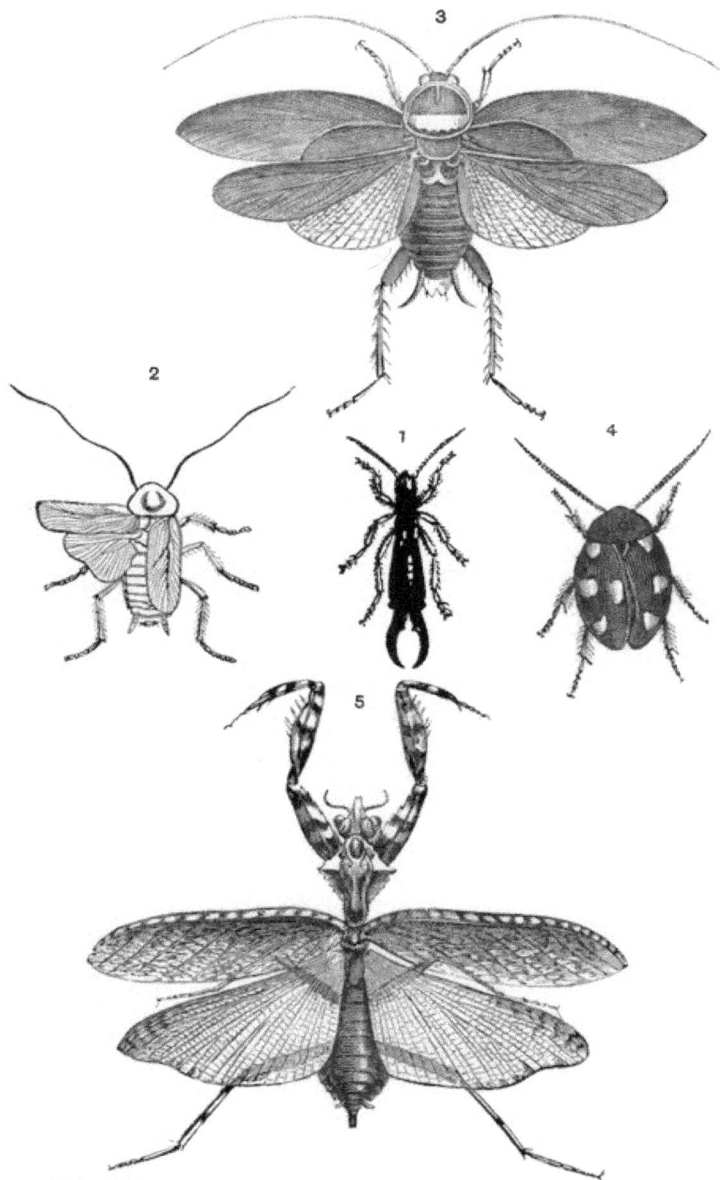

Plate XX.

PLATE XXI.

ORTHOPTERA.

Mantidæ.

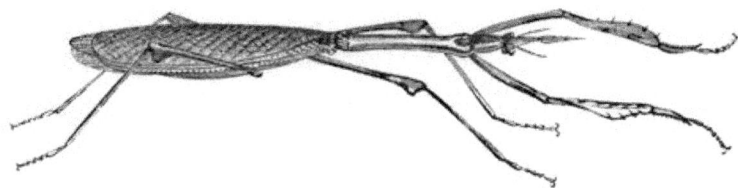

2

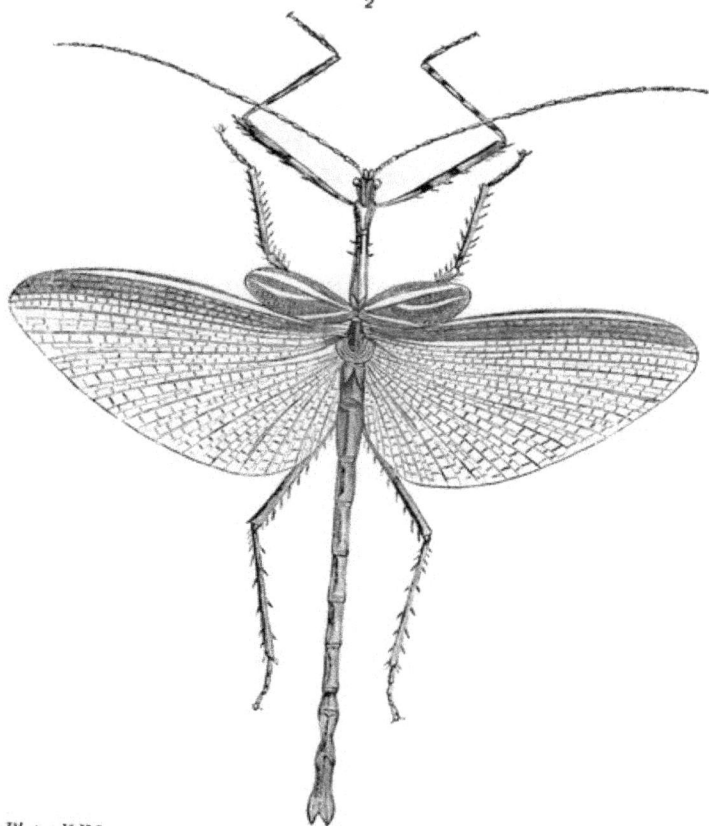

Plate XXI.

PLATE XXII.

ORTHOPTERA.

Phasmidæ.

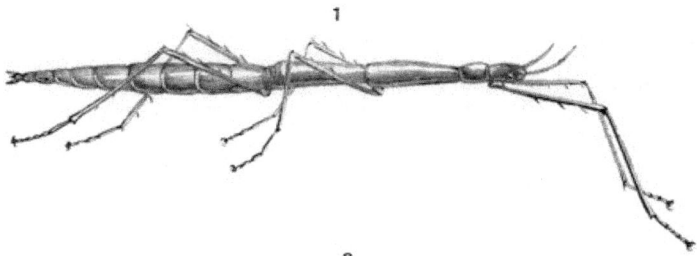

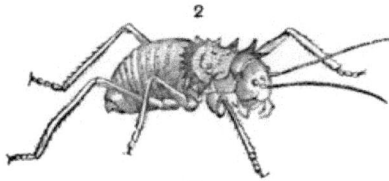

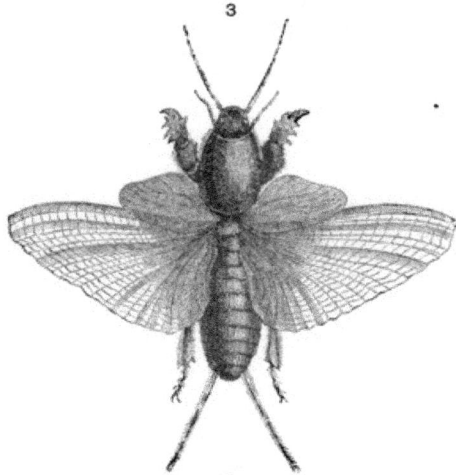

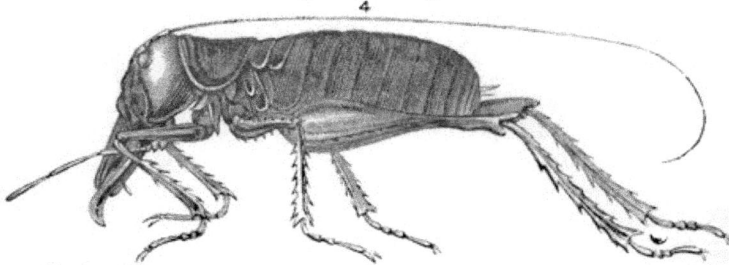

1

2

3

4

Plate XXII.

PLATE XXIII.

ORTHOPTERA.

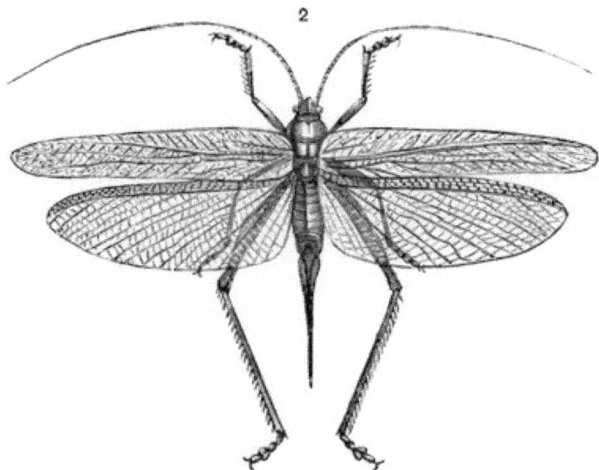

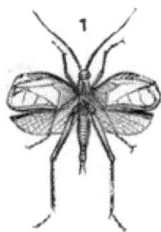

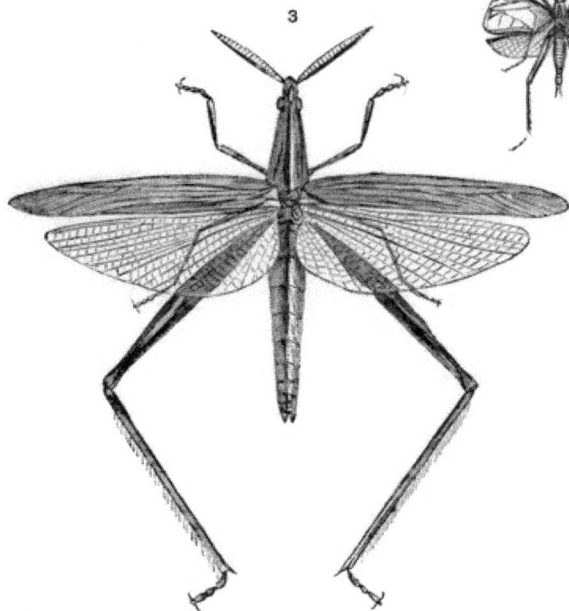

Plate XXIII.

4

PLATE XXIV.

ORTHOPTERA.

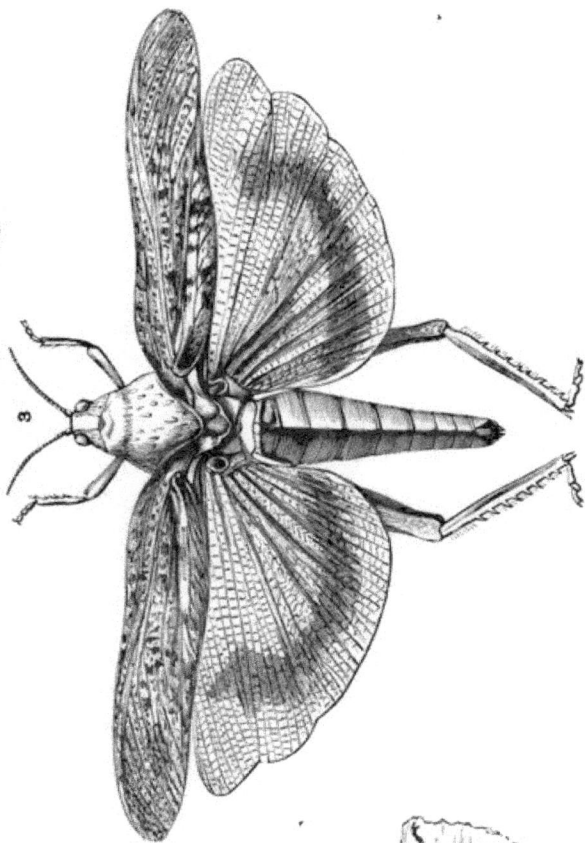

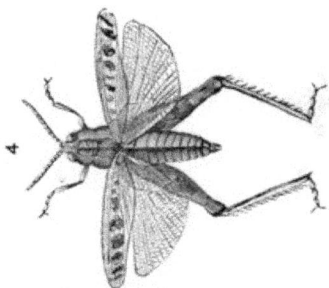

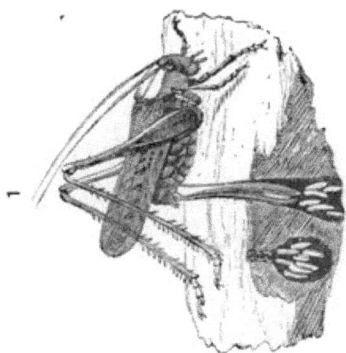

Plate XXIV.

PLATE XXV.

NEUROPTERA.

Libellulidæ.

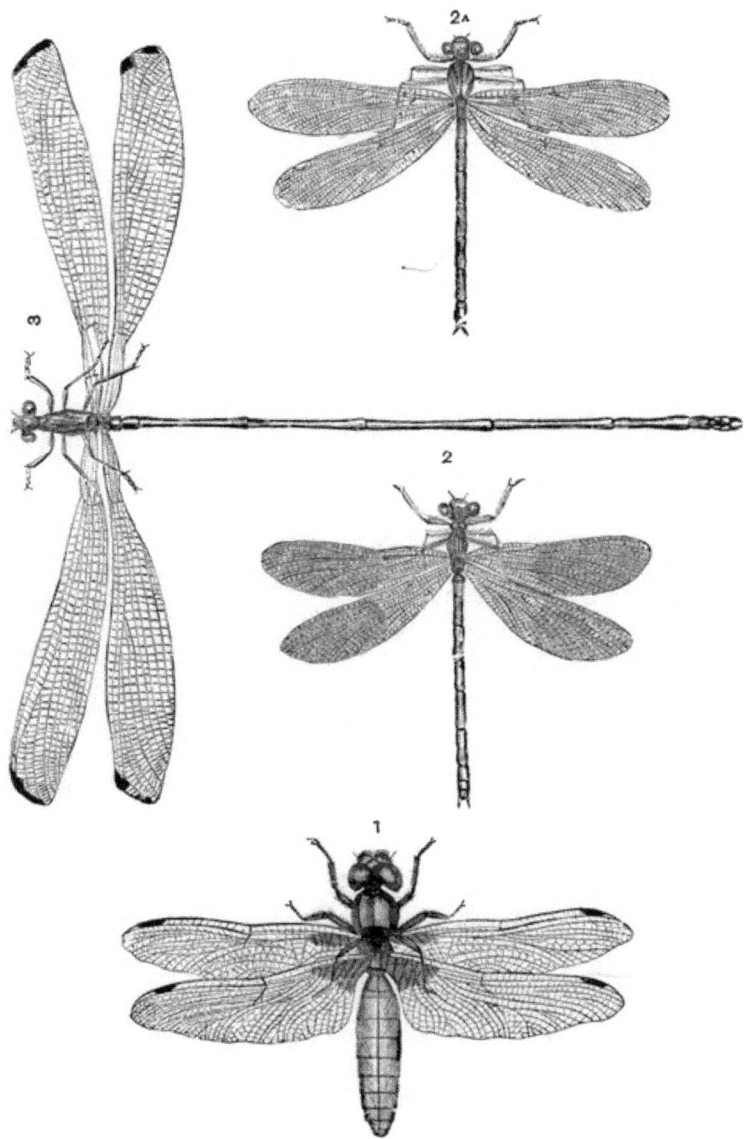

Plate XXV.

PLATE XXVI.

NEUROPTERA.

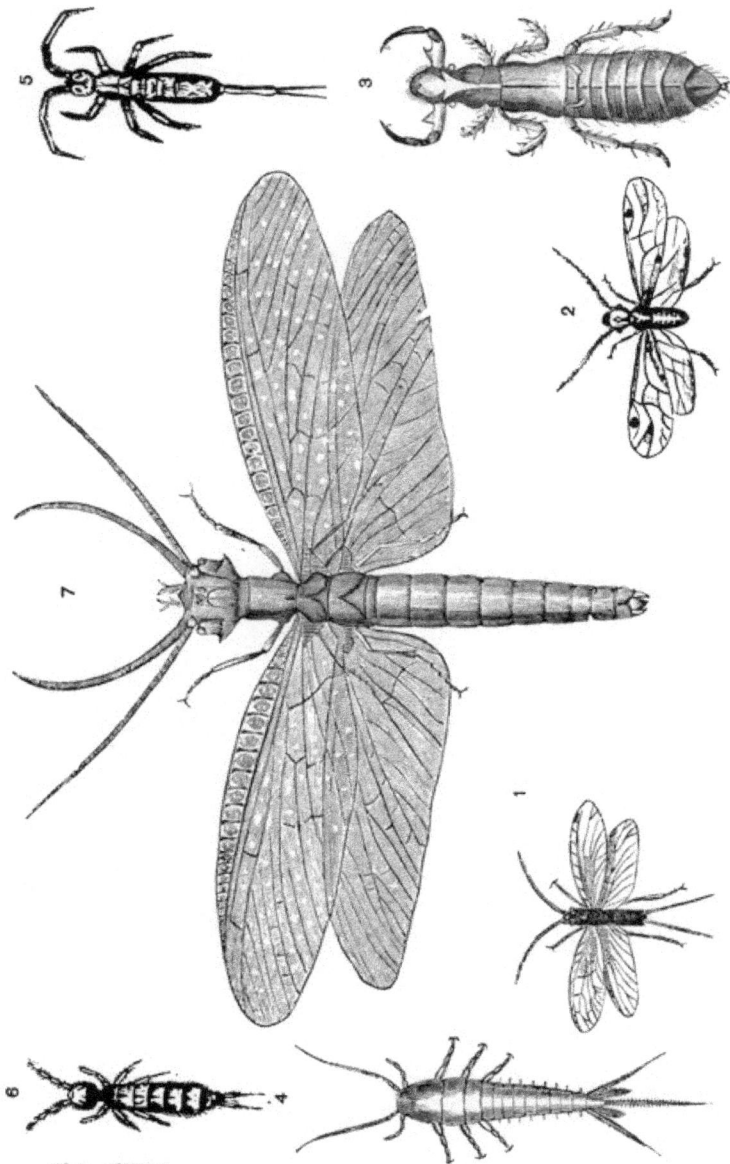

Plate XXVI.

PLATE XXVII.

NEUROPTERA.

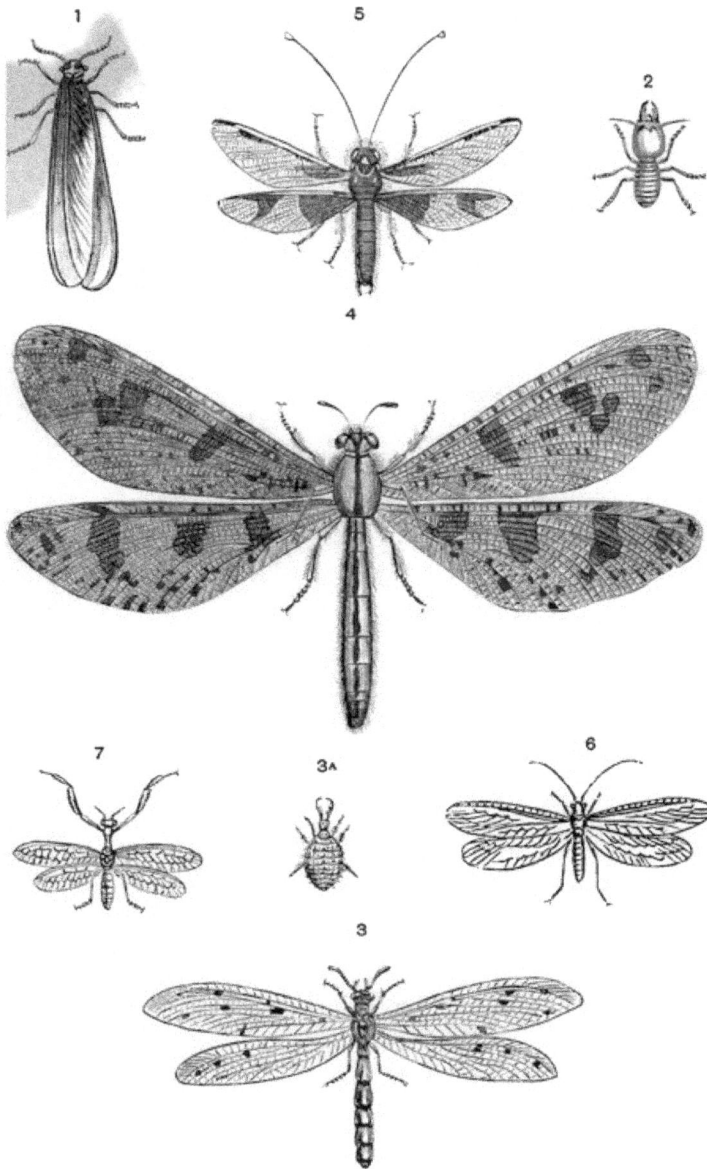

Plate XXVII.

PLATE XXVIII.

NEUROPTERA.

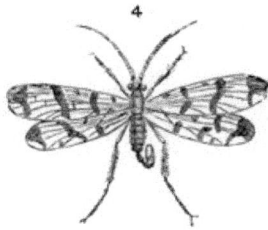

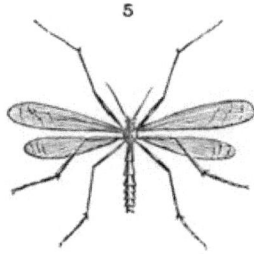

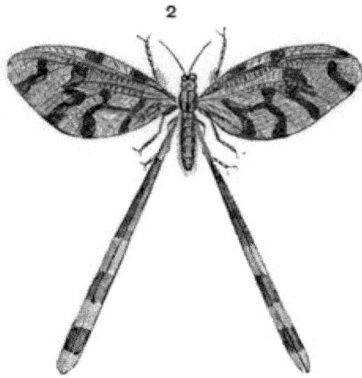

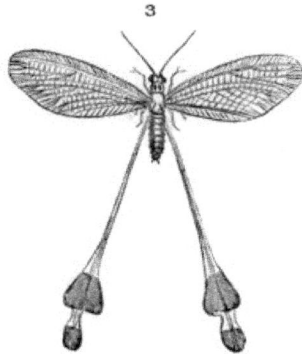

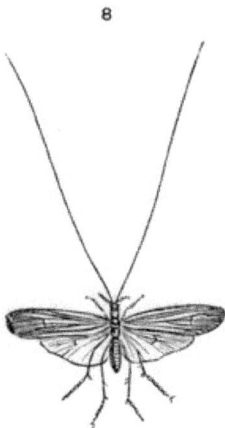

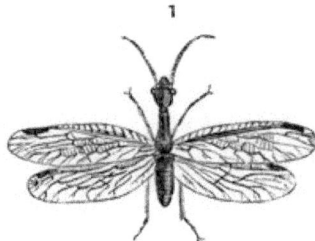

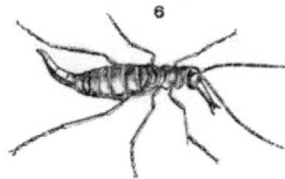

Plate XXVIII.

PLATE XXIX.

HYMENOPTERA.

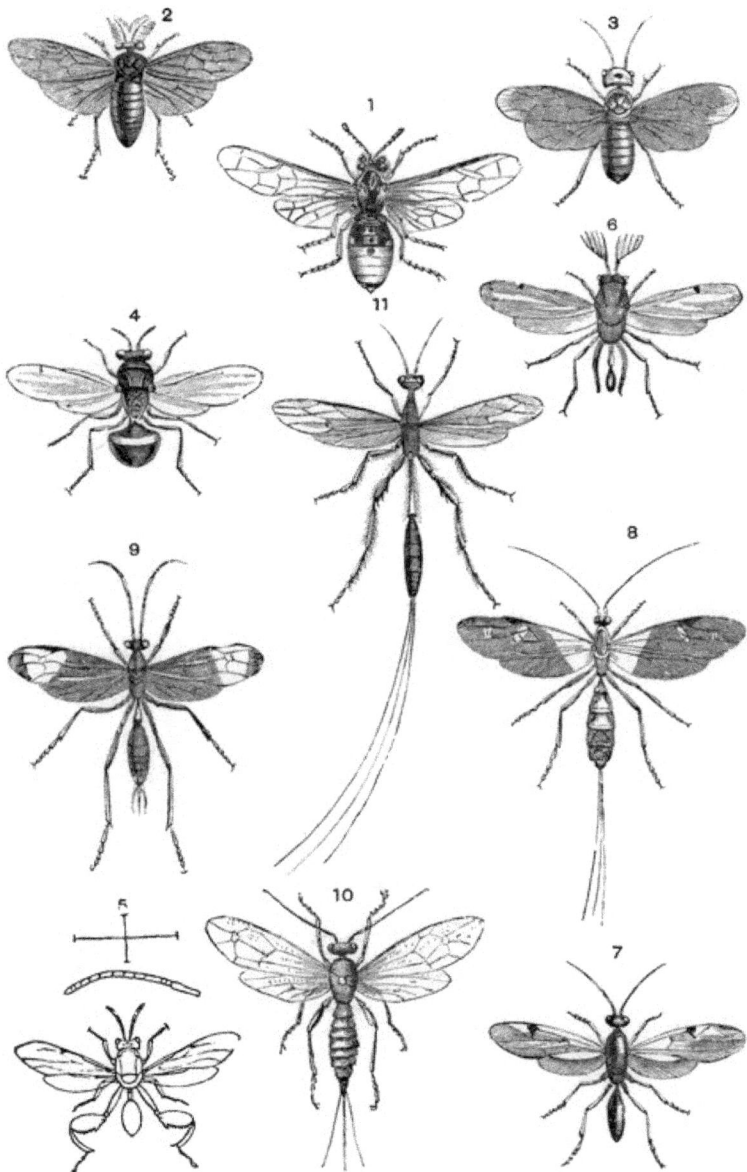

Plate XXIX.

PLATE XXX.

HYMENOPTERA.

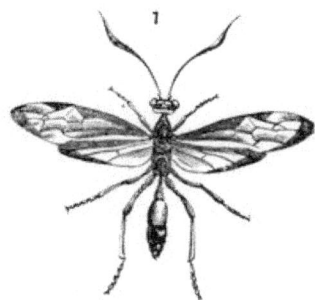

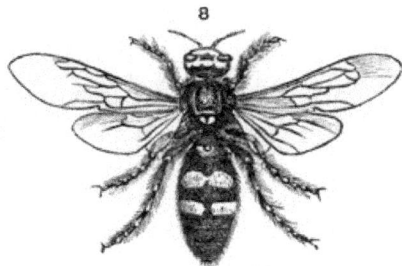

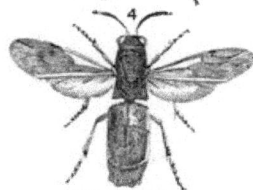

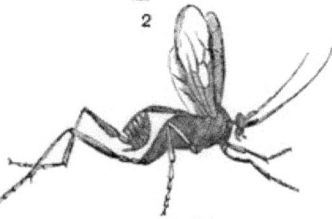

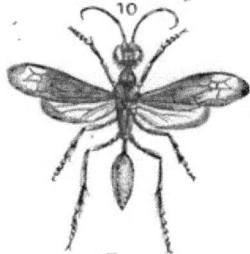

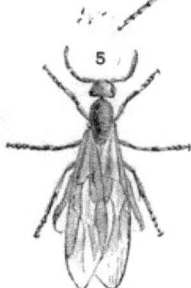

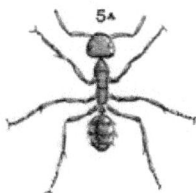

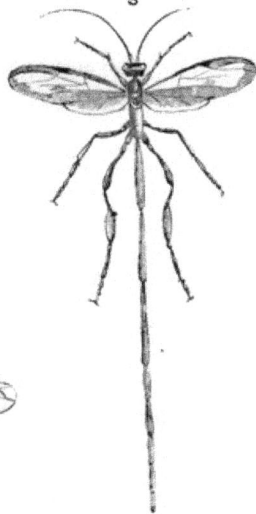

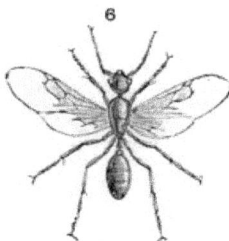

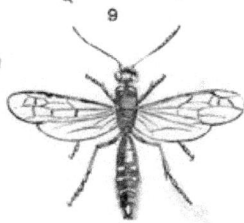

Plate XXX.

PLATE XXXI.

HYMENOPTERA.

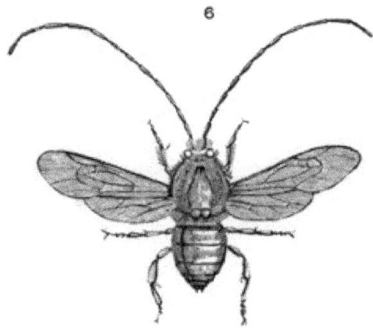

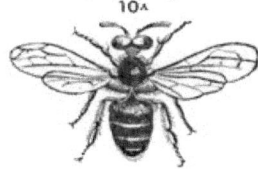

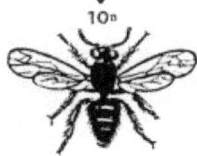

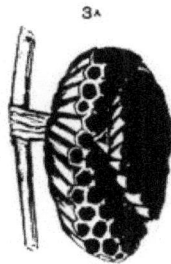

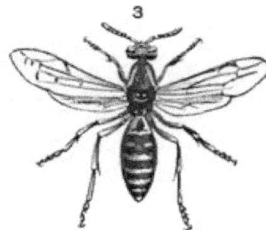

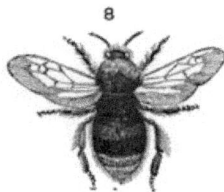

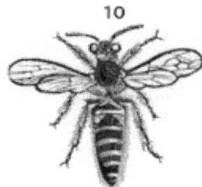

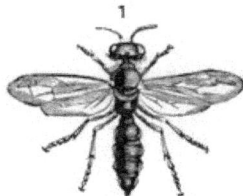

Plate XXXI.

PLATE XXXII.

LEPIDOPTERA RHOPALOCERA.

Nymphalidæ—Danainæ.

Plate *XXXII.*

PLATE XXXIII.

LEPIDOPTERA RHOPALOCERA.

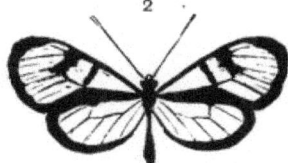

1

2

3

4

Plate XXXIII.

PLATE XXXIV.

LEPIDOPTERA RHOPALOCERA.

Nymphalidæ—Satyrinæ.

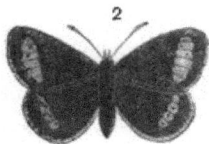

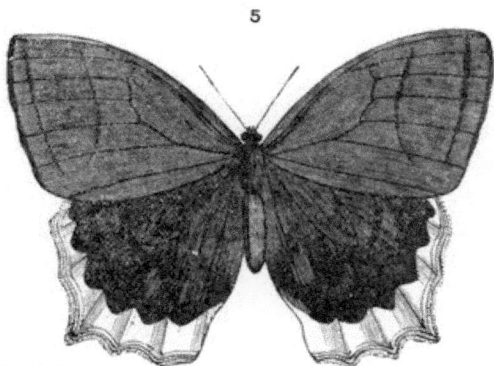

Plate XXXIV.

PLATE XXXV.

LEPIDOPTERA RHOPALOCERA.

Nymphalidæ—Morphinæ.

FIG.		PAGE
1.	Thaumantis Camadeva, *Westw.*	136

Nymphalidæ—Acræinæ.

2.	Acræa Perenna, *Doubl.*	140
3.	Actinote Hylonome, *Doubl.*	140

Plate XXXV.

PLATE XXXVI.

LEPIDOPTERA RHOPALOCERA.

Nymphalidæ—Morphinæ.

1

2

Plate *XXXVI*.

PLATE XXXVII.

LEPIDOPTERA RHOPALOCERA.

Nymphalidæ—Brassolinæ.

	PAGE
Dynastor Napoleon, *Doubl. and Hew.* .	140

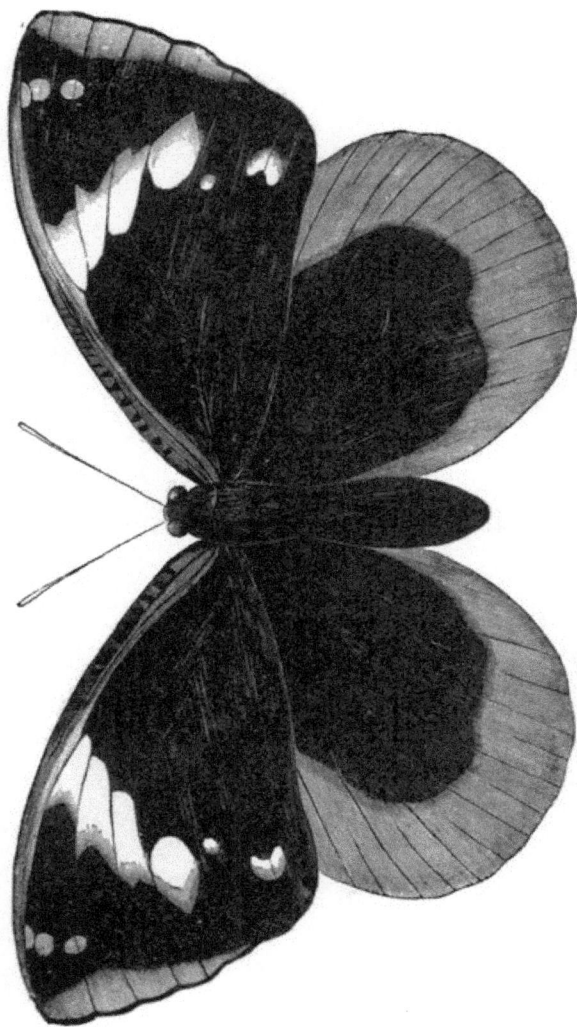

Plate XXXVII.

PLATE XXXVIII.

LEPIDOPTERA RHOPALOCERA.

Plate XXXVIII.

PLATE XXXIX.

LEPIDOPTERA RHOPALOCERA.

Nymphalidæ—Nymphalinæ.

Plate XXXIX.

PLATE XI.

LEPIDOPTERA RHOPALOCERA.

Nymphalidæ—Nymphalinæ.

Plate XL.

PLATE XLI.

LEPIDOPTERA RHOPALOCERA.

Nymphalidæ.—Nymphalinæ.

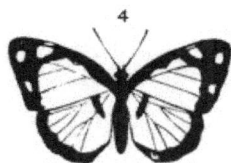

Plate XLI.

PLATE XLII.

LEPIDOPTERA RHOPALOCERA

Nymphalidæ—Nymphalinæ.

Plate XLII.

PLATE XLIII.

LEPIDOPTERA RHOPALOCERA.

Nymphalidæ—Nymphalinæ.

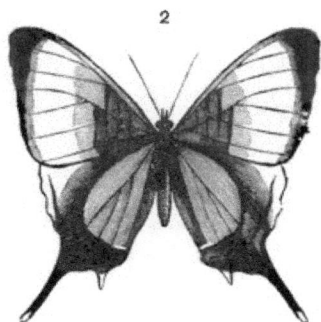

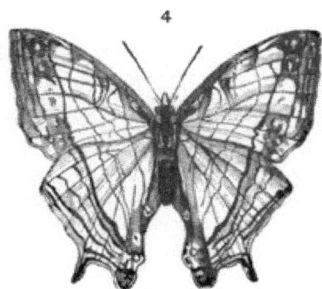

Plate XLIII.

PLATE XLIV.

LEPIDOPTERA RHOPALOCERA.

Nymphalidæ—Nymphalinæ.

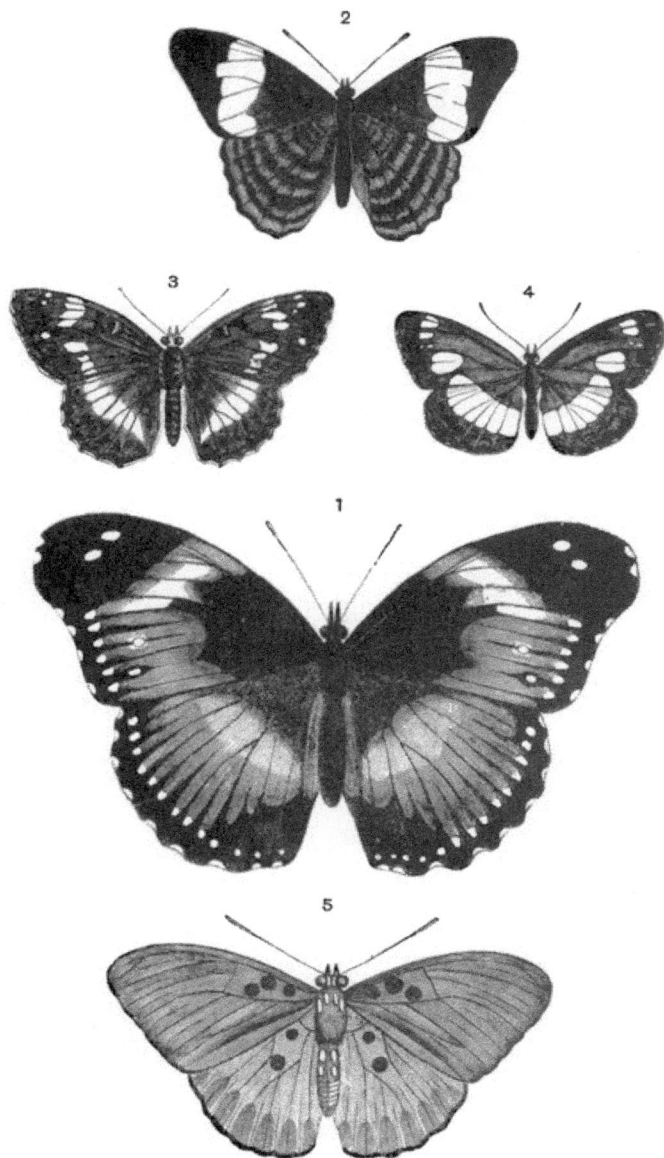

Plate XLIV.

PLATE XLV.

LEPIDOPTERA RHOPALOCERA.

Nymphalidæ—Nymphalinæ.

Plate XLV.

PLATE XLVI.

LEPIDOPTERA RHOPALOCERA.

Nymphalidæ—Nymphalinæ.

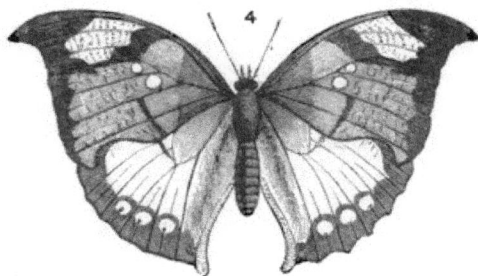

Plate XLVI.

PLATE XLVII.

LEPIDOPTERA RHOPALOCERA.

Lemoniidæ.

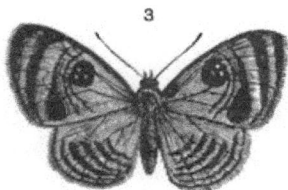

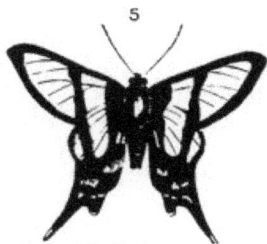

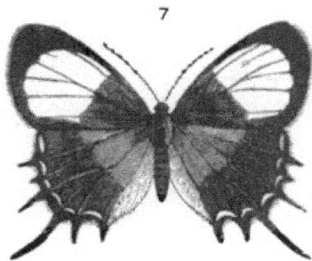

1

3

2

6

8

4

5

7

Plate XLVII.

7

PLATE XLVIII.

LEPIDOPTERA RHOPALOCERA.

Lycænidæ.

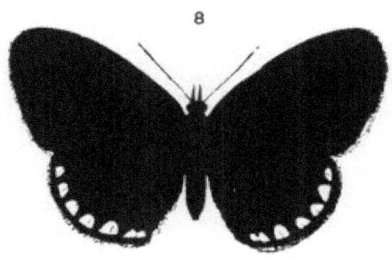

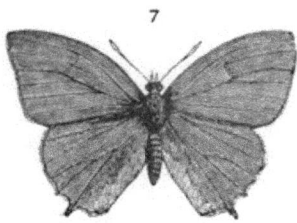

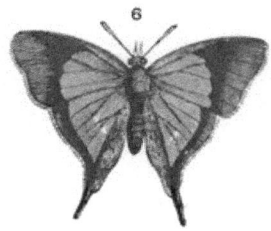

Plate XLVIII.

PLATE XLIX.

LEPIDOPTERA RHOPALOCERA.

Papilionidæ—Pierinæ.

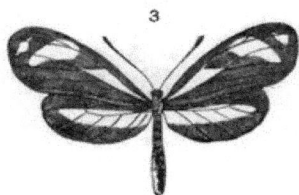

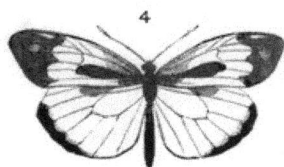

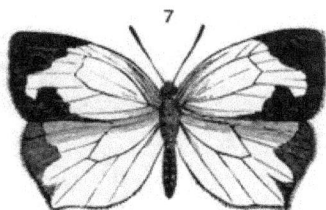

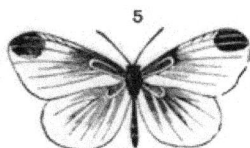

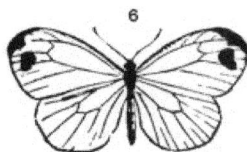

Plate XLIX.

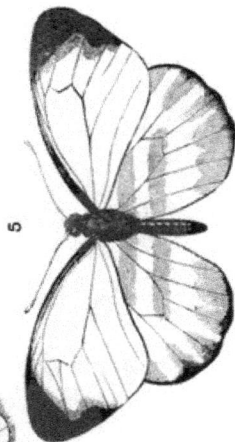

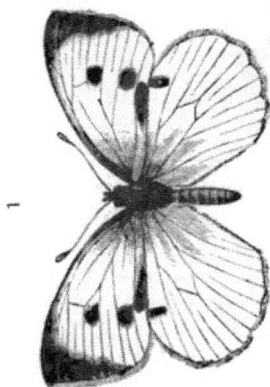

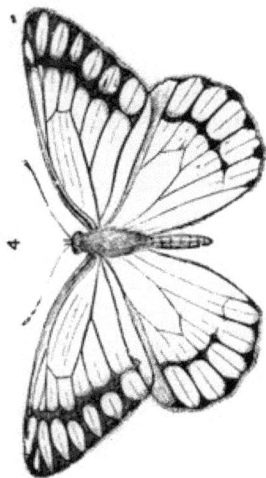

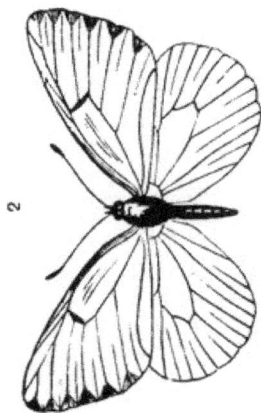

Plate L.

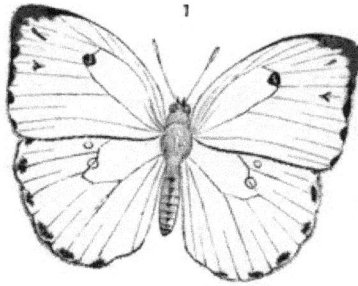

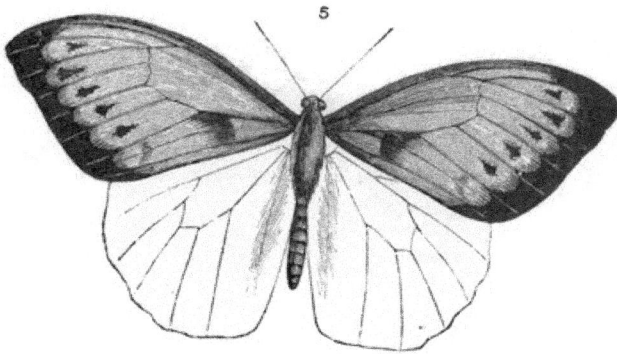

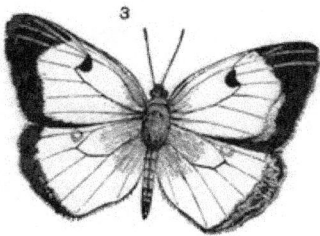

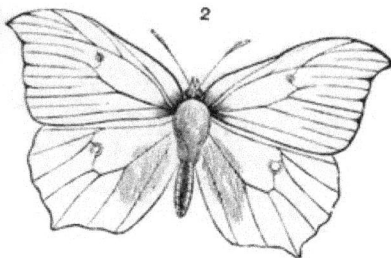

Plate LI.

Plate LII

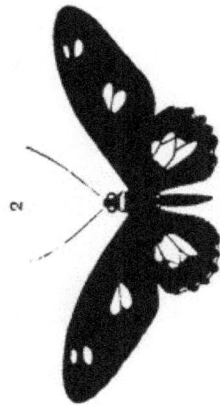

Plate LIII.

PLATE LIV.

LEPIDOPTERA RHOPALOCERA.

Papilionidæ — Papilioninæ.

2

3

Plate LIV.

PLATE LV.

LEPIDOPTERA RHOPALOCERA.

Papilionidæ—Papilioninæ.

Plate LV.

8

PLATE LVI.

LEPIDOPTERA RHOPALOCERA.

Papilionidæ—Papilioninæ.

1

3

5

4

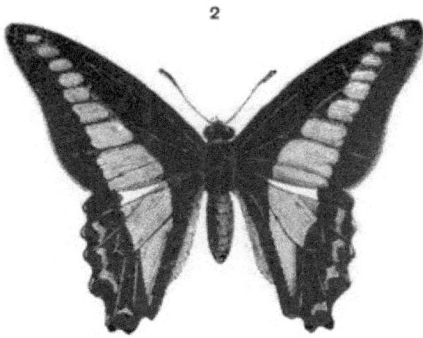

2

Plate LVI.

PLATE LVII.

LEPIDOPTERA RHOPALOCERA.

Plate LVII.

PLATE LVIII.

LEPIDOPTERA HETEROCERA

Sphingidæ.

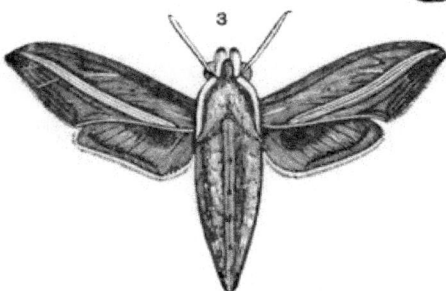

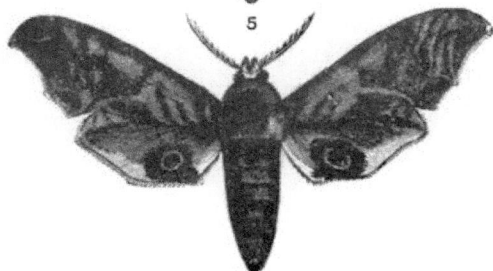

Plate LVIII

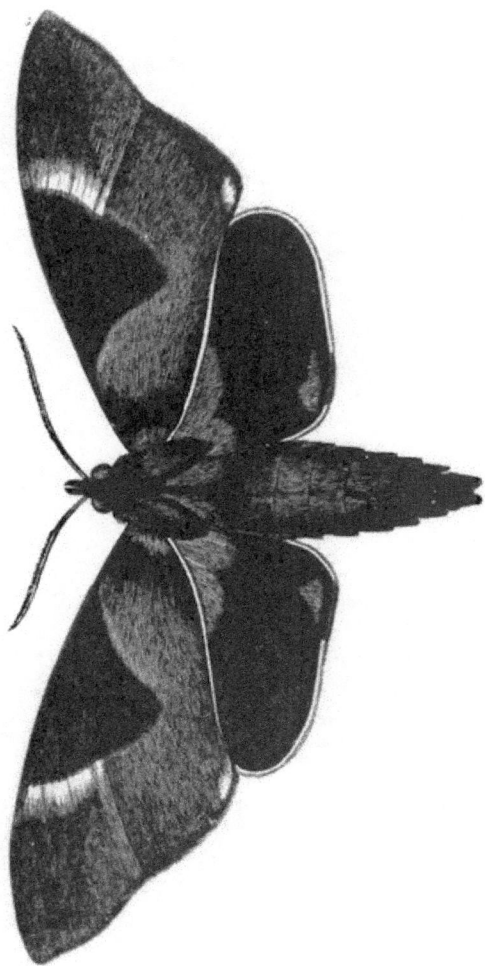

Plate LIX.

PLATE LX.

LEPIDOPTERA HETEROCERA.

Sphingidæ.

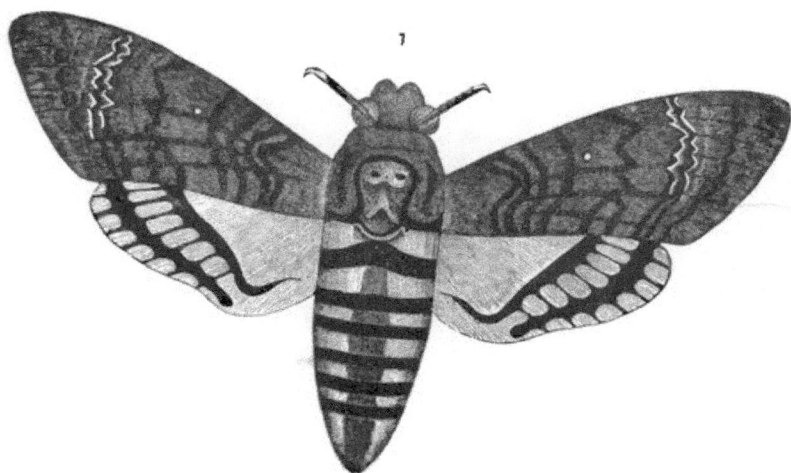

1

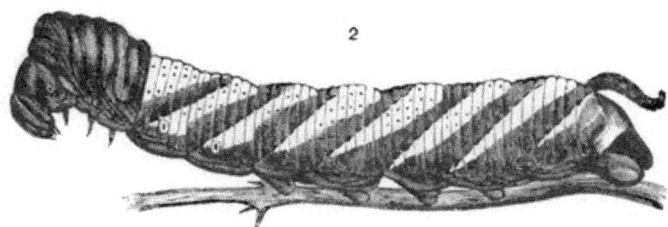

2

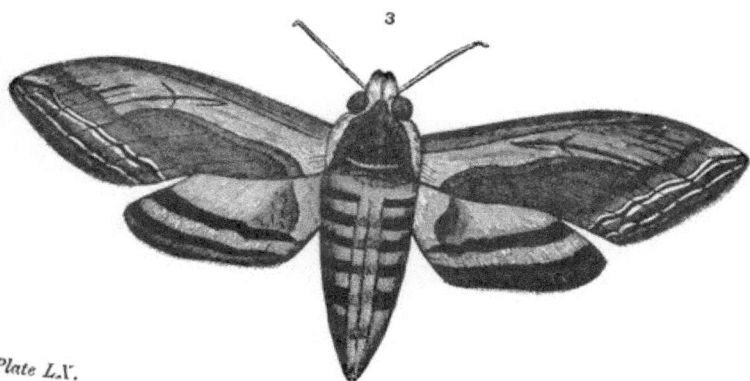

3

Plate LX.

PLATE LXI.

LEPIDOPTERA HETEROCERA.

Egeriidæ.

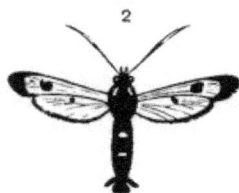

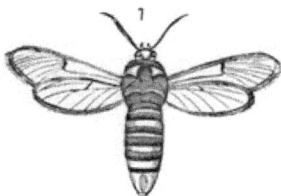

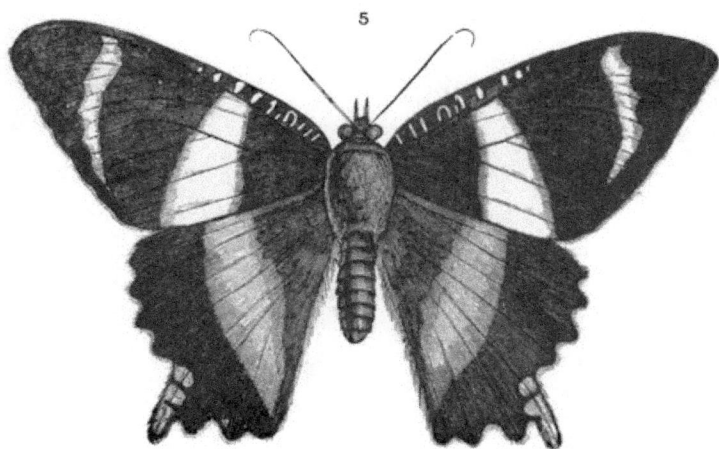

Plate LXI.

PLATE LXII.

LEPIDOPTERA HETEROCERA.

2

3

Plate LXII.

PLATE LXIII.

LEPIDOPTERA HETEROCERA.

Agaristidæ.

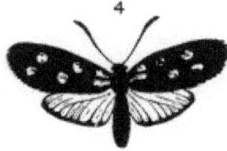

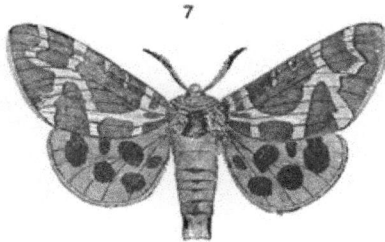

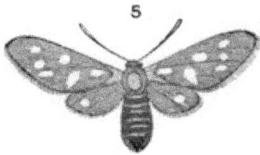

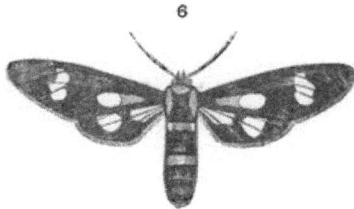

Plate LXIII.

PLATE LXIV.

LEPIDOPTERA HETEROCERA.

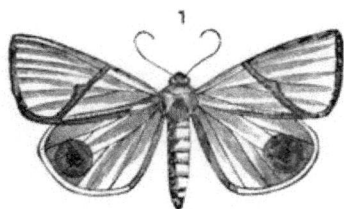

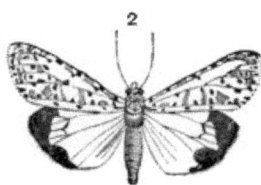

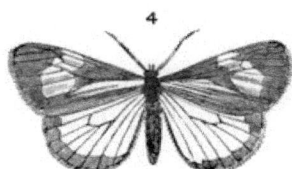

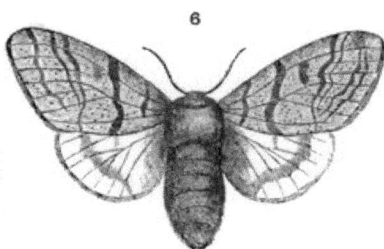

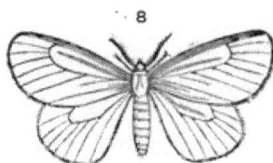

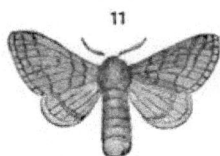

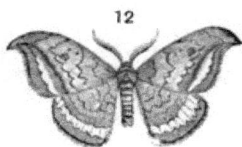

Plate LXIV.

Plate LXV.

PLATE LXVI.

LEPIDOPTERA HETEROCERA.

Saturniidæ.

Plate LXVI.

PLATE LXVII.

LEPIDOPTERA HETEROCERA.

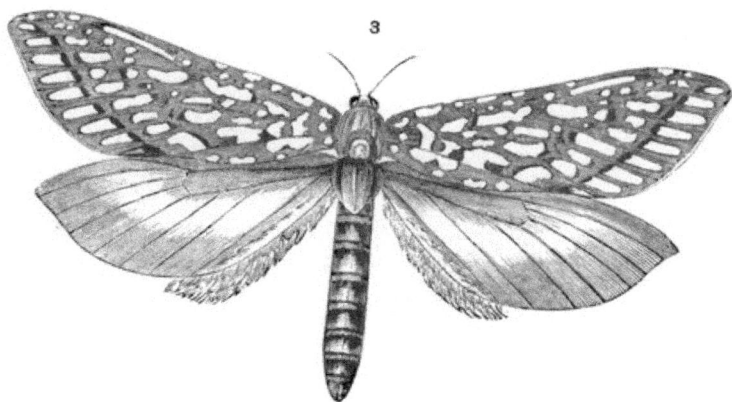

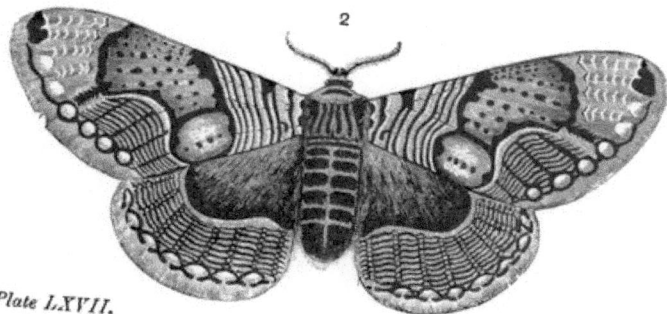

1

3

2

Plate LXVII.

PLATE LXVIII.

LEPIDOPTERA HETEROCERA.

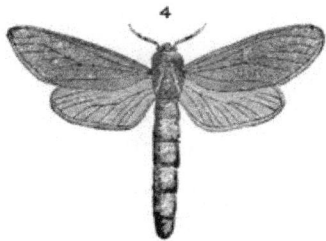

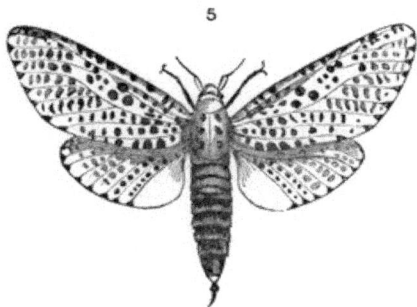

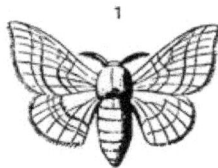

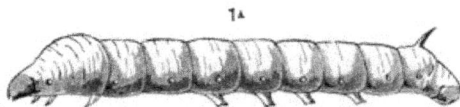

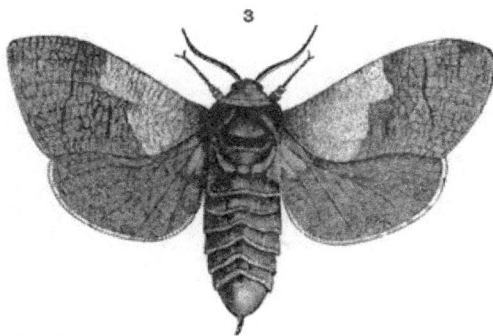

Plate LXVIII.

PLATE LXIX.

LEPIDOPTERA HETEROCERA.

Noctuæ.

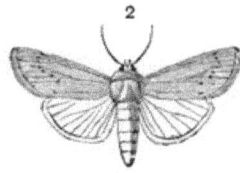

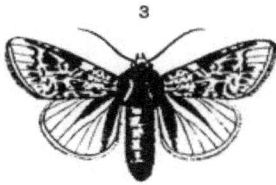

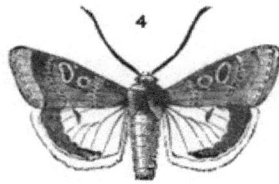

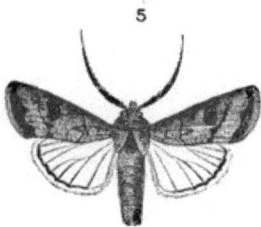

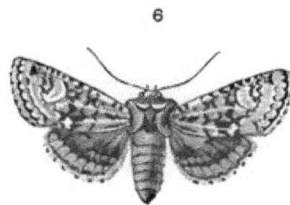

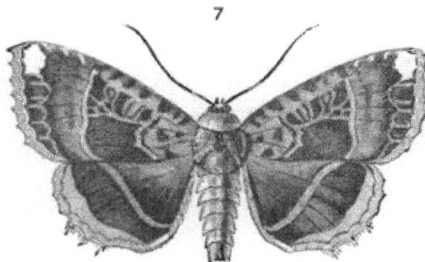

1

2

3

4

5

6

7

Plate LXIX.

PLATE LXX.

LEPIDOPTERA HETEROCERA.

Noctuæ.

Plate LXX.

PLATE LXXI.

LEPIDOPTERA HETEROCERA.

Noctuæ.

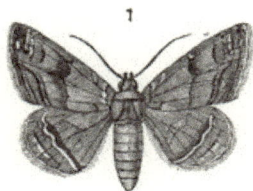

1

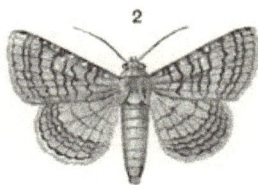

2

3

5

4

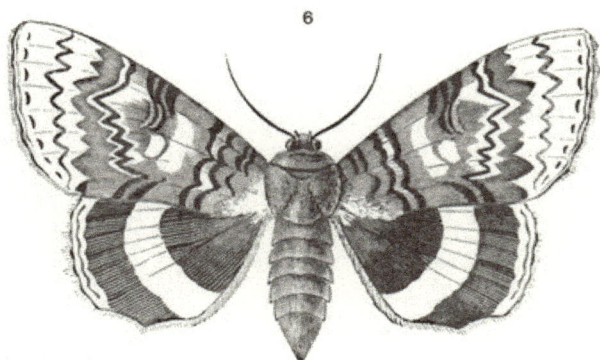

6

Plate LXXI.

10

PLATE LXXII.

LEPIDOPTERA HETEROCERA.

Noctuæ.

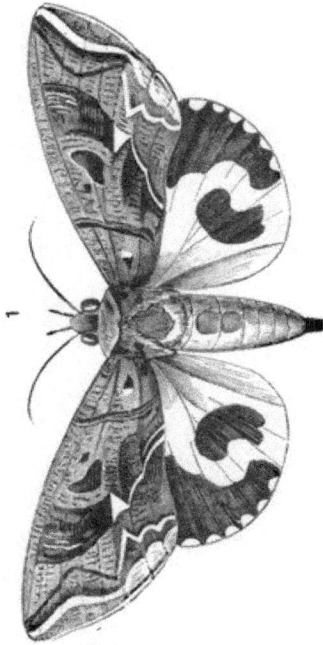

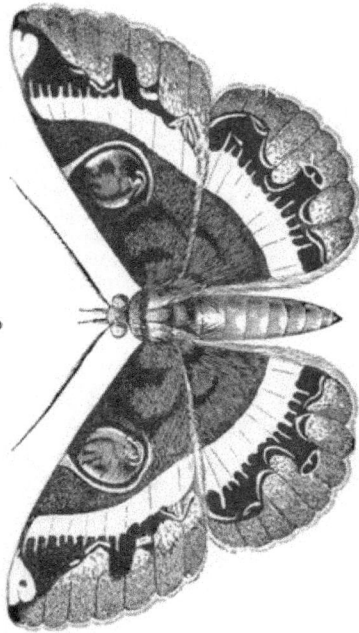

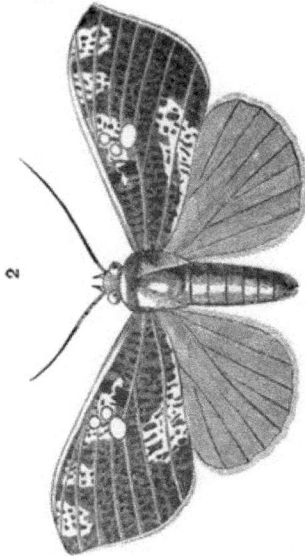

Plate LXXII.

PLATE LXXIII.

LEPIDOPTERA HETEROCERA.

Noctuæ.

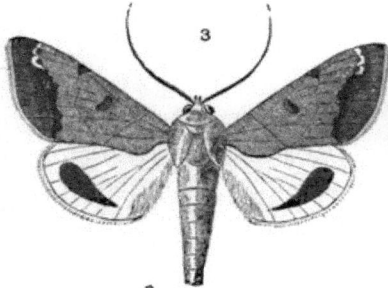

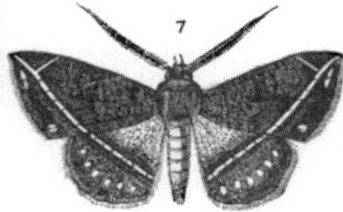

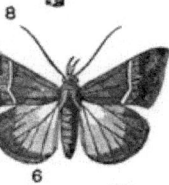

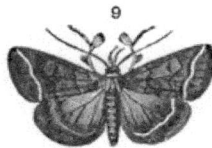

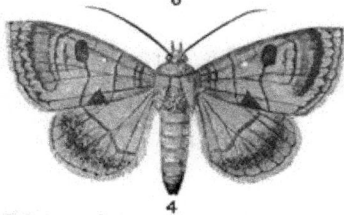

Plate LXXIII.

PLATE LXXIV.

LEPIDOPTERA HETEROCERA.

Geometræ.

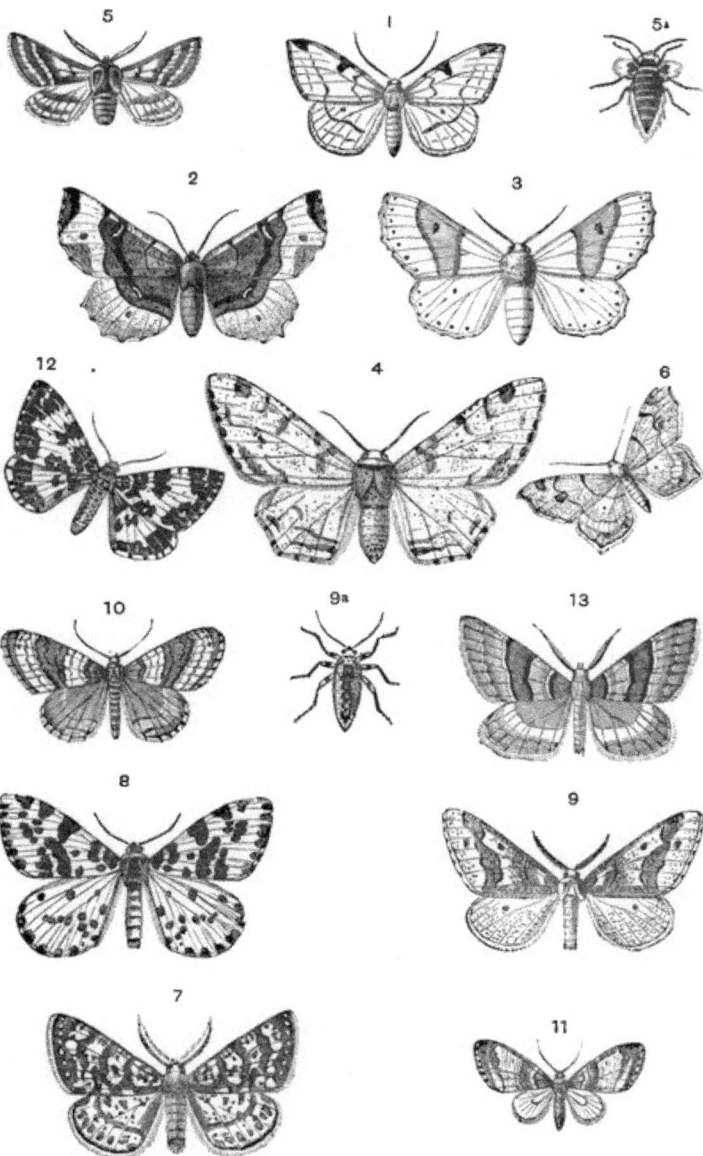

Plate LXXIV.

PLATE LXXV.

LEPIDOPTERA HETEROCERA.

Pyrales.

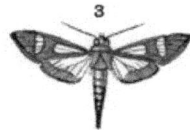

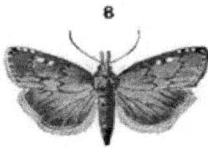

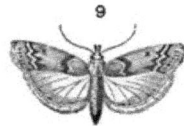

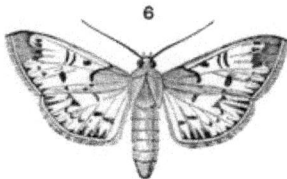

Plate LXXV.

PLATE LXXVI.

LEPIDOPTERA HETEROCERA.

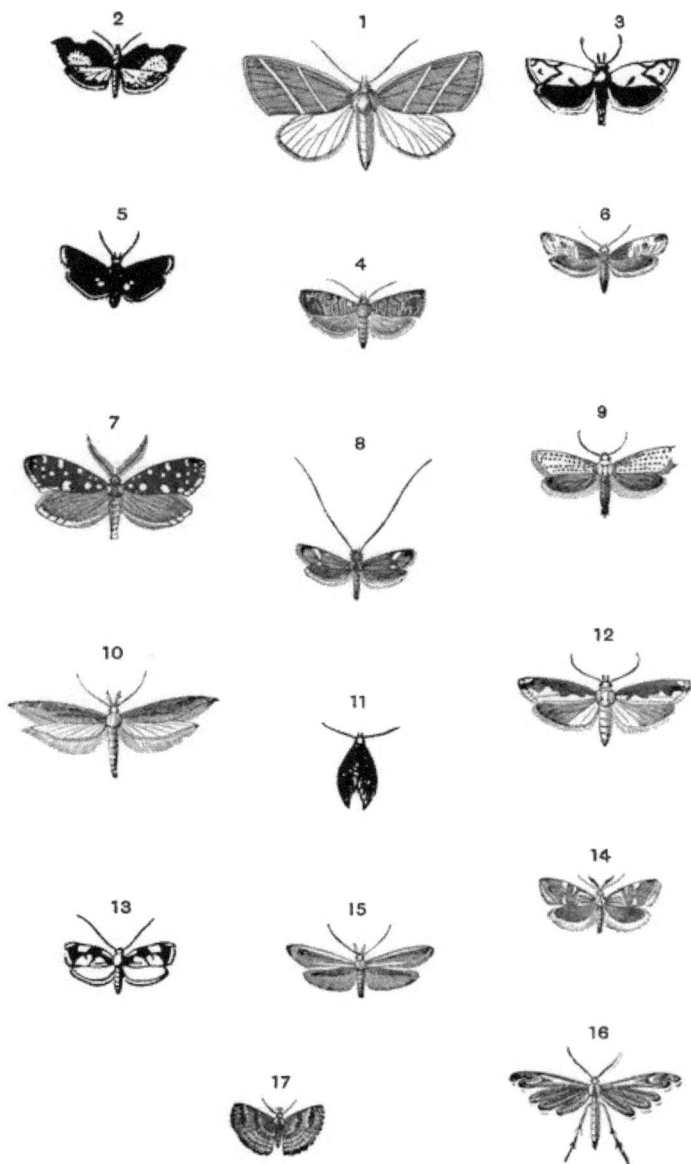

Plate LXXVI.

PLATE LXXVII.

HEMIPTERA HETEROPTERA.

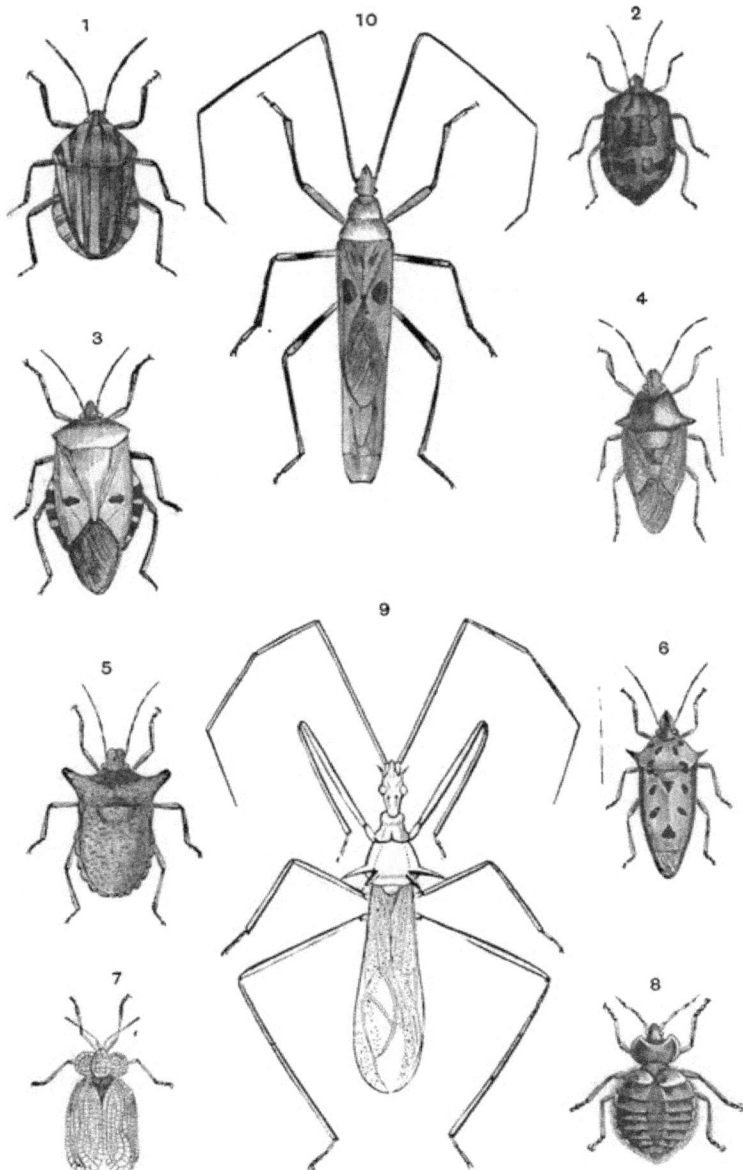

Plate *LXXVII.*

PLATE LXXVIII.

HEMIPTERA HETEROPTERA.

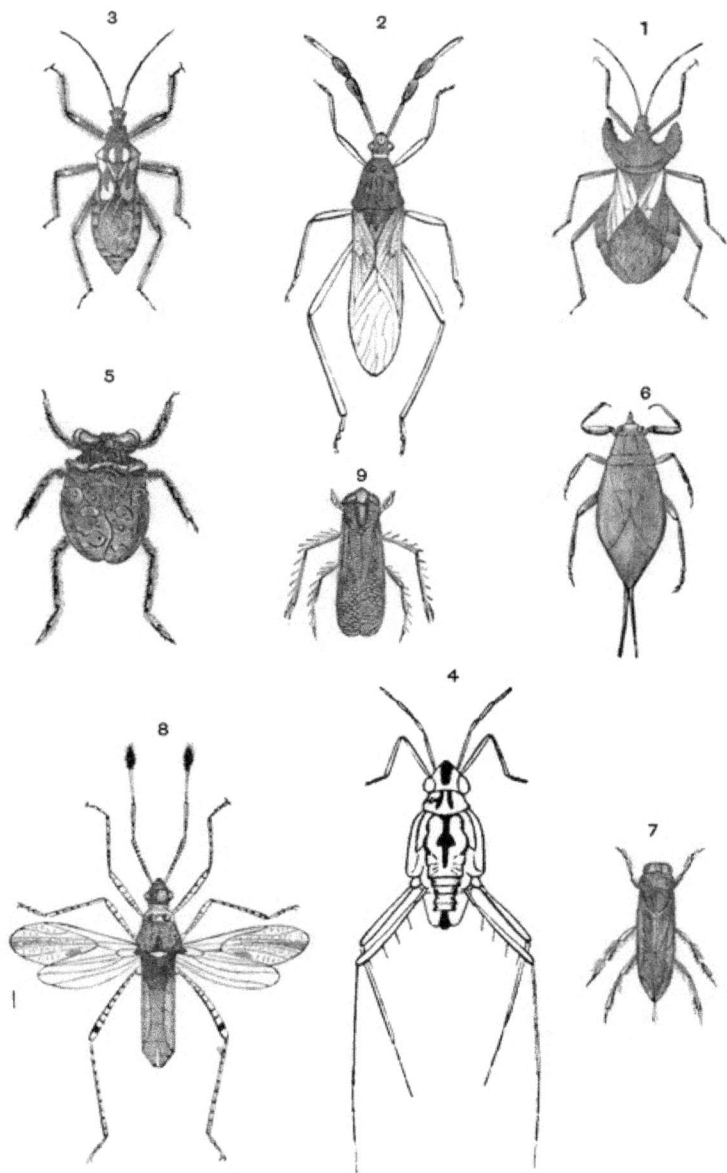

Plate LXXVIII.

PLATE LXXIX.

HEMIPTERA HOMOPTERA.

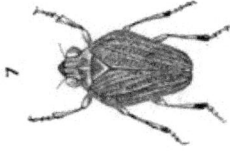

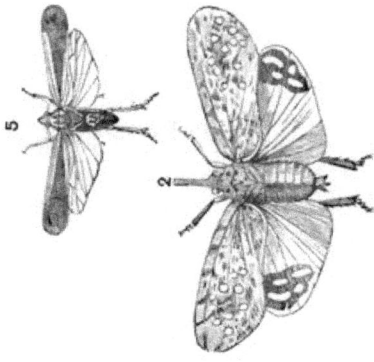

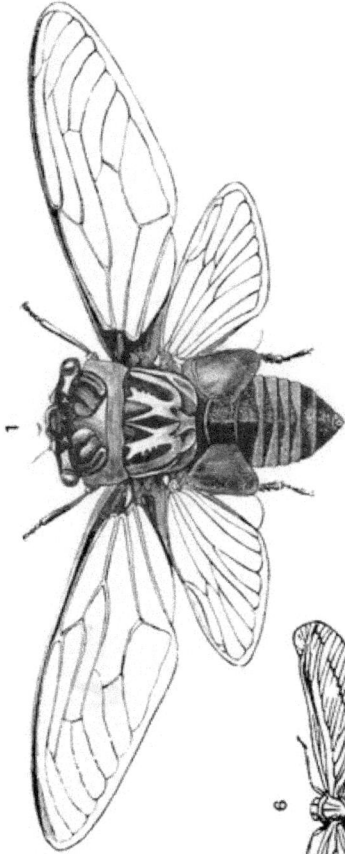

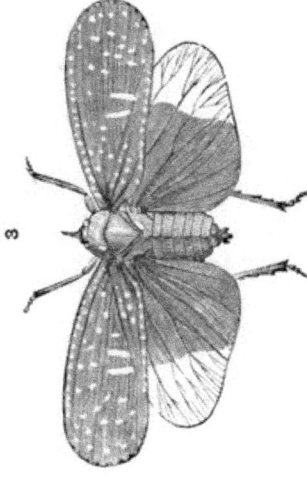

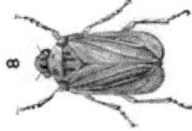

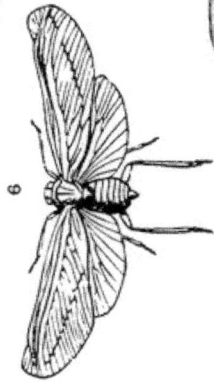

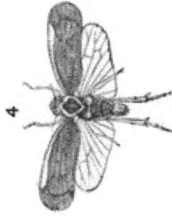

Plate LXXIX

11

PLATE LXXX.

HEMIPTERA HOMOPTERA.

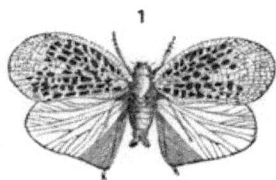

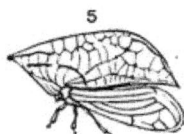

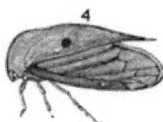

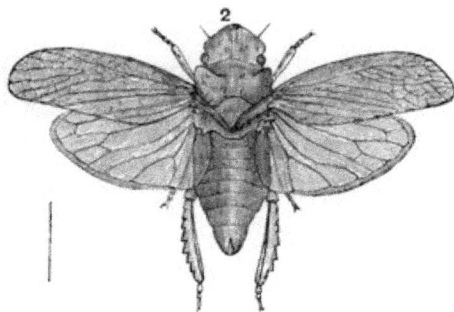

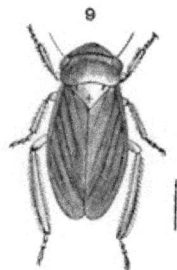

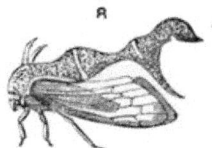

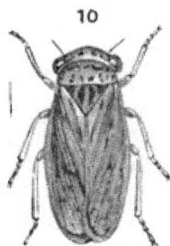

Plate LXXX.

PLATE LXXXI.

HEMIPTERA HOMOPTERA.

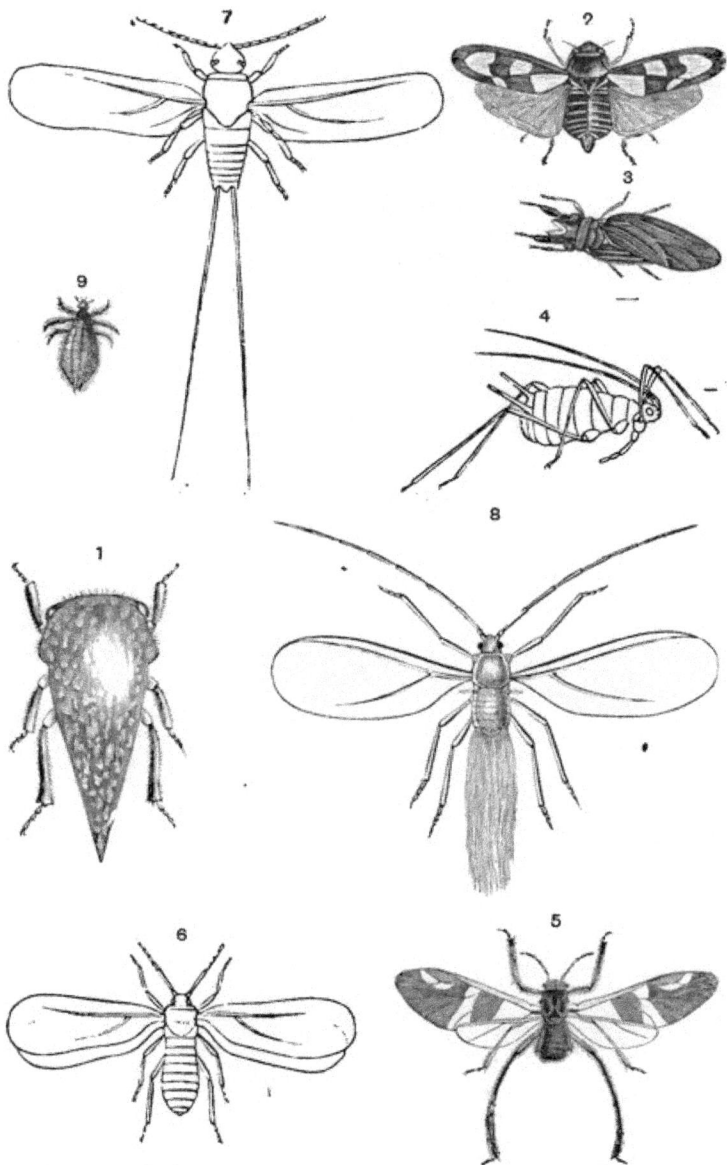

Plate LXXXI.

PLATE LXXXII.

DIPTERA.

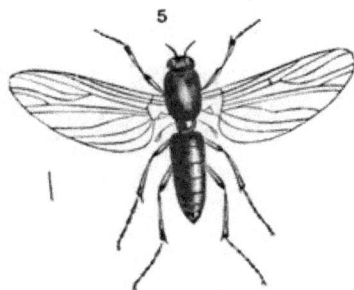

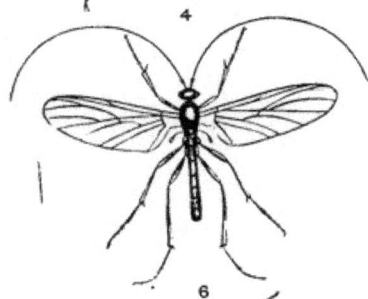

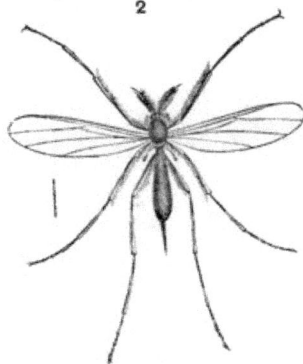

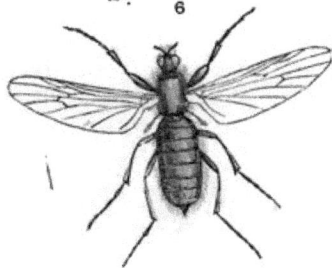

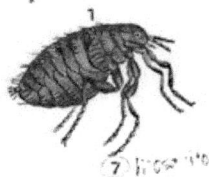

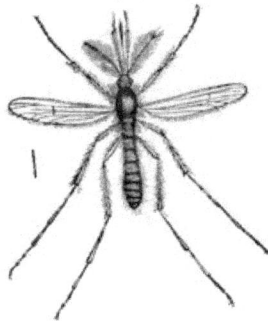

Plate *LXXII.*

PLATE LXXXIII.

DIPTERA.

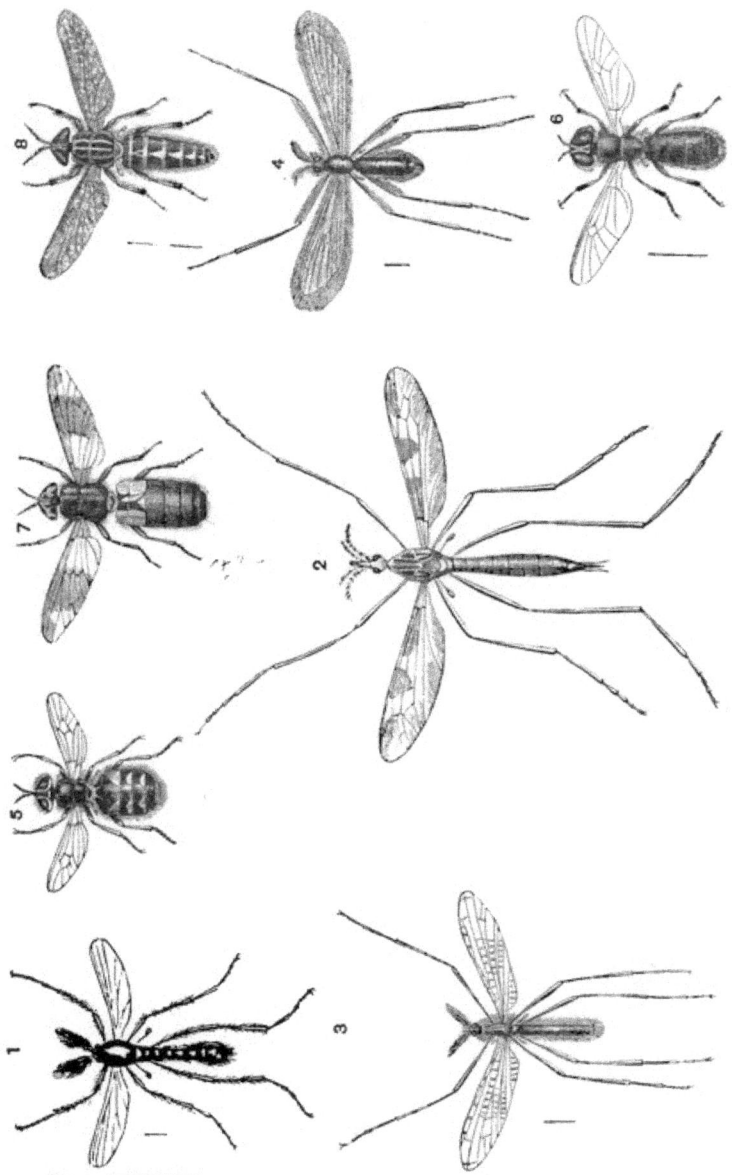

Peate LXXXIII.

PLATE LXXXIV.

DIPTERA.

Brachycera.

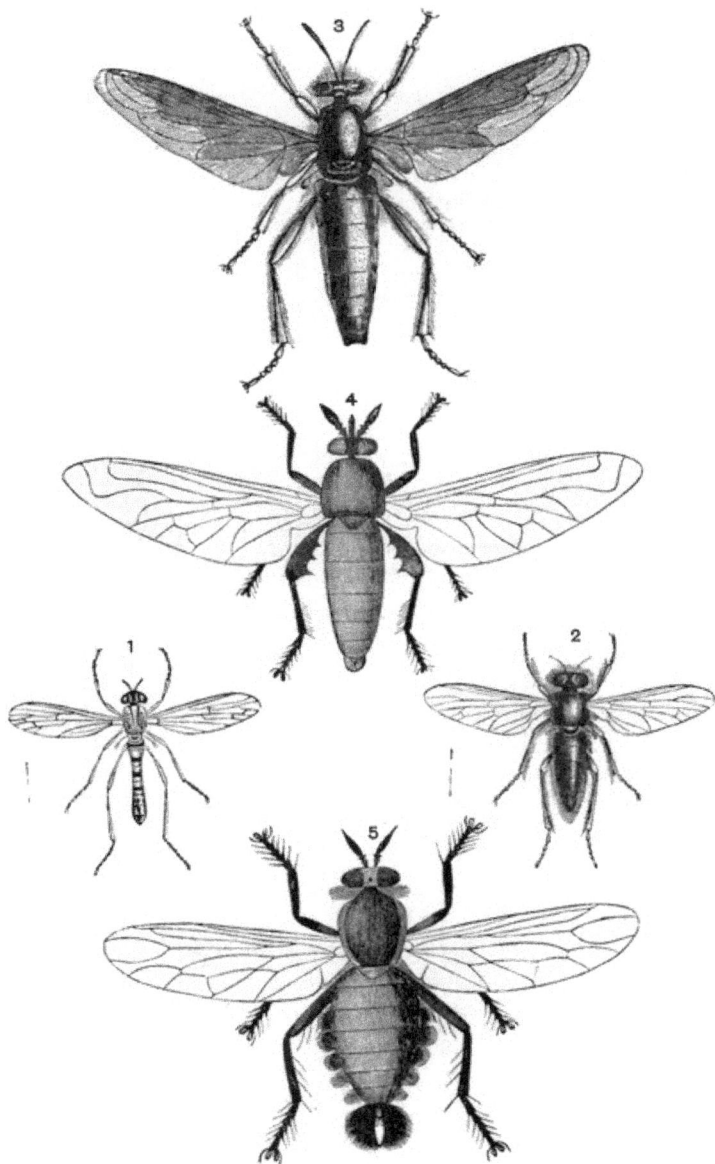

Plate LXXXIV.

PLATE LXXXV.

DIPTERA.

Brachycera.

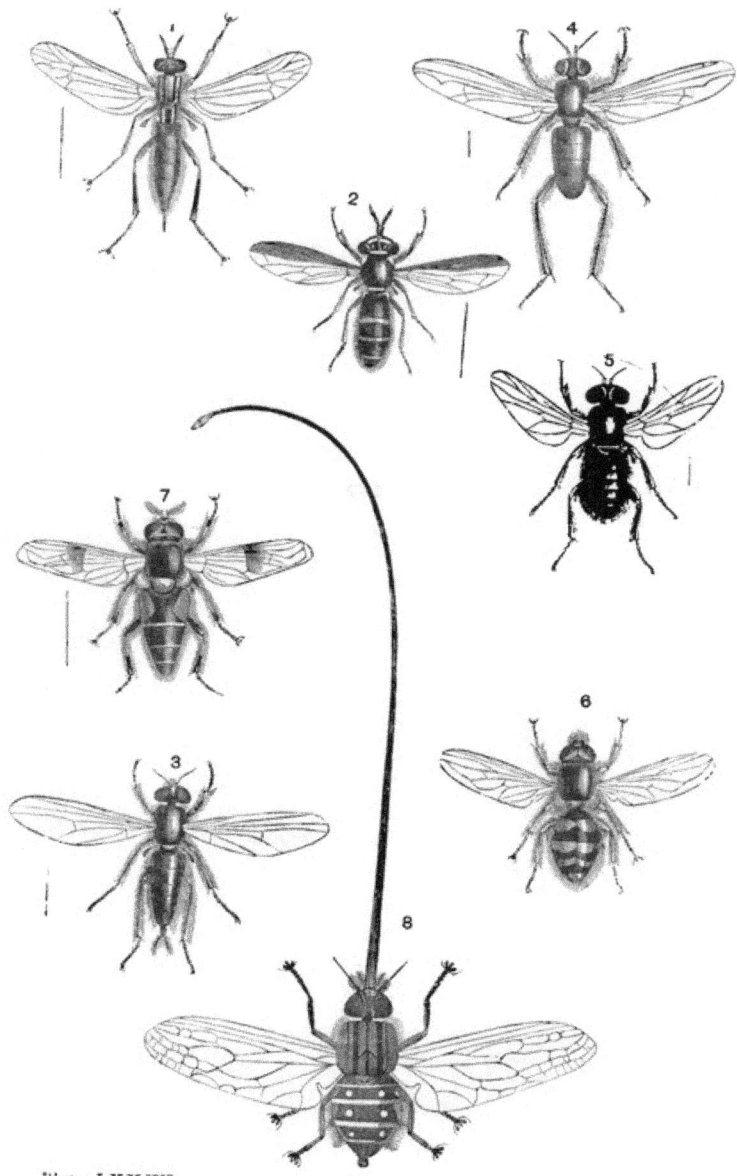

Plate LXXXV.

PLATE LXXXVI.

DIPTERA.

Brachycera.

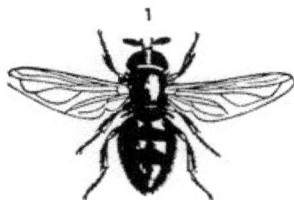

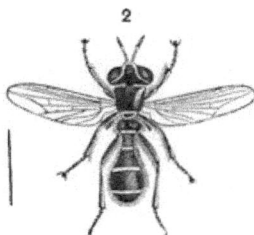

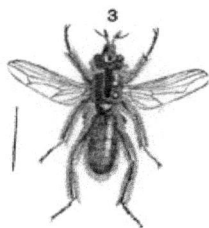

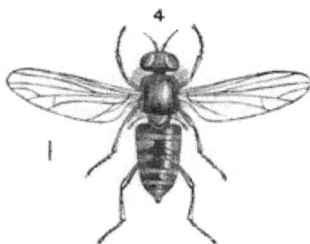

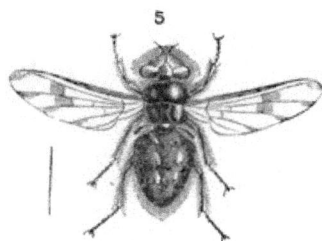

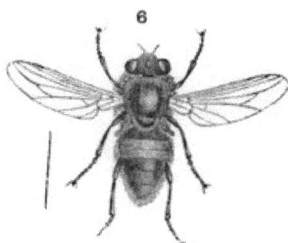

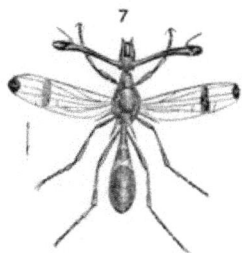

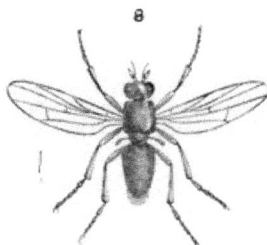

Plate LXXXVI.

www.ingramcontent.com/pod-product-compliance
Lightning Source LLC
Chambersburg PA
CBHW032310280326
41932CB00009B/765